Commemorations

Commemorations

THE POLITICS OF
NATIONAL IDENTITY

Edited by
John R. Gillis

PRINCETON UNIVERSITY PRESS

PRINCETON, NEW JERSEY

Library of Congress Cataloging-in-Publication Data

Commemorations : the politics of national identity /
edited by John R. Gillis.
p.   cm.
Includes bibliographical references and index.
ISBN 0-691-03200-9 (cloth)
1. Nationalism—History.   2. Ethnicity—History.   3. Memory—
Social aspects—History.   4. National characteristics—
History.   I. Gillis, John R.
CB197.C66   1994   305.8'009—dc20   93-15827

This book has been composed in Sabon

Princeton University Press books are printed on
acid-free paper and meet the guidelines for permanence
and durability of the Committee on Production
Guidelines for Book Longevity of the
Council on Library Resources

Printed in the United States of America
1 3 5 7 9 10 8 6 4 2

Dedicated to the memory of
Benjamin Robert Gillis

who died at Masai Mara, Kenya,
December 26, 1991,
doing what he loved so much
and did so well

CONTENTS

ACKNOWLEDGMENTS

THIS VOLUME owes much to the two-year project on "The Historical Construction of Identities" sponsored by the Rutgers Center for Historical Analysis, of which I was project leader from 1989 to 1991, working closely with both Richard L. McCormick and Rudy Bell, the first directors of the center. Memory was an important project theme from the very beginning, but I owe particular thanks to the 1989–1990 center fellows, who included Roger Bartra, Robert and Mary Jo Nye, Tamas Hofer, George Chauncey, Jacqueline Urla, Linda Dowling, Dorothy and Edward Thompson, Barbara Sicherman, Sy Becker, Steve Cagan, Marcia Ian, Neil Smith, Linda Zerilli, Deborah Cornelius, Jerma Jackson, Ron Nieberding, and Pamela Walker. I will always remember that year as one of the most productive and pleasurable I have ever experienced.

All the authors presented here have been patient and supportive throughout the long process that resulted in this volume. It is a particular pleasure to know that many of the contacts made in 1990 have developed into ongoing intellectual exchanges, another example of the way memory shapes identity.

In addition, I would like to thank others who attended the May 1990 conference "Public Memory and Collective Identity," from which this volume was constructed, especially Jonathan Boyarin, Stefan Tanaka, Michael Kammen, David Glassberg, and Bob Scally. Subsequent discussions with Jay Winter, David Thelen, Randy Starn, Emmanuel Sivan, Victoria de Grazia, Eviatar Zerubavel, Victoria Smith, Leonardo Paggi, Scott Sandage, and Gabriel Bar-Haim have further shaped my thinking, convincing me that memory is a topic not just deserving but demanding the attention of historians.

This volume would not have been possible without the encouragement of Ed Tenner, Kathleen Roos, Joanna Hitchcock, and Lauren Osborne of Princeton University Press.

NOTES ON CONTRIBUTORS

John Bodnar teaches American history at Indiana University. His *Remaking America: Public Memory, Commemoration and Patriotism in the Twentieth Century* appeared in 1991.

David Cressy is Professor of History at California State University, Long Beach. A specialist in early modern British history, his most recent book is *Bonfires and Bells: National Memory and the Protestant Calendar in Elizabethan and Stuart England*.

Eric Davis is a member of the Political Science Department at Rutgers University. He is currently working on *Memories of State: Politics, History, and Collective Identity in Modern Iraq*.

John R. Gillis teaches at Rutgers University and was the first Project Leader of the Rutgers Center for Historical Analysis. He is currently working on the role of memory in modern family life.

Richard Handler is Professor of Anthropology at the University of Virginia. He is the author of *Nationalism and the Politics of Culture in Quebec* and is completing an ethnography of tourism in Colonial Williamsburg.

Claudia Koonz is Professor of History at Duke University and the author of *Mothers in the Fatherland: Women, the Family, and Nazi Politics*.

Rudy J. Koshar is teaching at the University of Wisconsin at Madison. His latest book is *Transient Pasts: Post-Modernity and Historic Preservation in Twentieth-Century Germany*.

Thomas W. Laqueur is Director of the Doreen B. Thownsend Center for the Humanities at the University of California, Berkeley. He is the author of *Making Sex: Body and Gender from the Greeks to Freud* and is working on the memorialization of war.

Herman Lebovics teaches modern French history at the State University of New York at Stony Brook. *True France: The Wars over Cultural Identity, 1900–1945* is his most recent publication.

David Lowenthal is Emeritus Professor of Geography at the University of London. He is the author of *The Past Is a Foreign Country* and is currently conducting research on the ideas and practices of heritage.

G. Kurt Piehler is Assistant Editor of the Gallatin Papers at Baruch College of the City University of New York and Adjunct Assistant Professor at Drew University. His book *Remembering War the American Way: 1783 to the Present* will appear shortly.

Kirk Savage is a member of the Art History Department at the University of Pittsburgh and has been a fellow at the Commonwealth Center for the Study of American Culture at the College of William and Mary where he completed *Standing Soldiers, Kneeling Slaves: Race, Art, and the Meaning of Civil War*.

Daniel J. Sherman teaches French history at Rice University and is the author of *Worthy Monuments: Art Museums and the Politics of Culture in Nineteenth-Century France*.

Yael Zerubavel teaches modern Hebrew literature and culture at the University of Pennsylvania and is a member of the graduate faculty of folklore there. She is soon to publish *Recovered Roots: Collective Memory and the Making of Israeli National Tradition.*

Commemorations

MEMORY AND IDENTITY:
THE HISTORY OF A RELATIONSHIP

JOHN R. GILLIS

MEMORY AND IDENTITY are two of the most frequently used terms in contemporary public and private discourse, though their status as key words is relatively recent.[1] Identity, a term first popularized by Erik Erickson in the late 1950s in connection with individual sense of self, subsequently took on such a bewildering variety of meanings that it became, in the words of Robert Coles, "The purest of clichés."[2] Memory also seems to be losing precise meaning in proportion to its growing rhetorical power.[3] Today, both words resonate not just in their original Western contexts, but globally. Yet, in the process, they have lost all historical context. Detached from their original meanings, they have the status of free-floating phenomena, the same anywhere and anytime. Reconnecting memory and identity in time and place is the task that this volume undertakes.

The parallel lives of these two terms alert us to the fact that the notion of identity depends on the idea of memory, and vice versa. The core meaning of any individual or group identity, namely, a sense of sameness over time and space, is sustained by remembering; and what is remembered is defined by the assumed identity. That identities and memories change over time tends to be obscured by the fact that we too often refer to both as if they had the status of material objects—memory as something to be retrieved; identity as something that can be lost as well as found. We need to be reminded that memories and identities are not fixed things, but representations or constructions of reality, subjective rather than objective phenomena. As the contributions to this volume demonstrate, we are constantly revising our memories to suit our current identities. Memories help us make sense of the world we live in; and "memory work" is, like any other kind of physical or mental labor, embedded in complex class, gender and power relations that determine what is remembered (or forgotten), by whom, and for what end.[4]

If memory has its politics, so too does identity. As Richard Handler points out, the Western world has been accustomed for more than two centuries to thinking about identity as an object bounded in time and space, as something with clear beginnings and endings, with its own territoriality. David Lowenthal's essay shows how this way of thinking is now current throughout the world, providing the basis for what has been called "identity politics."[5] Today it seems that everyone claims a right to their own identity. Individuals, subgroups, and nations all demand identity as if it were a necessity of life itself. Identity has taken on the status of a sacred object, an "ultimate concern," worth fighting and even dying for. To those who believe they do not have it, identity appears even more scarce and precious. On the other hand, contemporary society requires that we play so many different roles that at least some of us are afflicted by what Kenneth Gergen has called "multiphrenia," a condition of having too many conflicting selves, too many identities.[6]

I

Ironically, fierce battles over identity and memory are erupting at the very moment when psychologists, anthropologists, and historians are becoming increasingly aware of the subjective nature of both. These struggles make it all the more apparent that identities and memories are highly selective, inscriptive rather than descriptive, serving particular interests and ideological positions. Just as memory and identity support one another, they also sustain certain subjective positions, social boundaries, and, of course, power.

Every identity, notes Eric Leed, implies and at the same time masks a particular relationship.[7] When we speak of *the* Germans, we imagine ourselves to be referring to some objective entity, but in fact we are participating in the process by which certain relationships among people we call Germans and between them and others we call *the* French or *the* Americans are constructed and sustained. We talk as if deprived of their berets the French would cease to be French; and, if they ceased to be punctual, Germans would no longer be German. The fact that only men traditionally wore berets and that punctuality is a class-based Prussian trait should alert us to the fact that in defining Frenchness and Germanness in these ways we are endorsing a certain gender order in one case and a specific political settlement in the other. National identities are, like everything historical, constructed and reconstructed; and it is our responsibility to decode them in order to discover the relationships they create and sustain.[8] Today, the constructed nature of identities is becoming evident, particularly in the Western world, where the old bases of national identities are being rapidly undermined by economic globalization and transnational political integration. By inquiring further into the history of similar historical constructions, we are beginning to learn more about those who deploy them and whose interests they serve.

But recent critiques of national identity have scarcely weakened the rhetorical power of the word itself. From the period of the French and American revolutions through World War II, national identity asserted itself over the claims of both local and international relationships. Now it is these particularistic and cosmopolitan tendencies that challenge nationalism. In Europe we are confronted with quite contradictory tendencies toward unification and disintegration, a pattern that appears to be emerging in virtually every other part of the world as well.[9]

At this particular historical moment, it is all the more apparent that both identity and memory are political and social constructs, and should be treated as such. We can no longer afford to assign either the status of a natural object, treating it as "fact" with an existence outside language. Identities and memories are not things we think *about*, but things we think *with*. As such they have no existence beyond our politics, our social relations, and our histories. We must take responsibility for their uses and abuses, recognizing that every assertion of identity involves a choice that affects not just ourselves but others.

The relationship between memory and identity is historical; and the record of that relationship can be traced through various forms of commemoration discussed in this volume. Commemorative activity is by definition social and political, for it involves the coordination of individual and group memories, whose results may appear consensual when they are in fact the product of processes of intense contest, struggle, and, in some instances, annihilation. In this collection the focus is on public rather than private commemoration, though the parallels between the way identity and memory operate in personal and public life are striking and a reminder that the division between public and private is also historical, appearing natural only in retrospect.[10]

II

These essays were first presented at a conference on Public Memory and Collective Identity sponsored by the Rutgers Center for Historical Analysis in the spring of 1990. They range over a wide time span and equally broad geographical space. While there are many "blanks" still to be filled in, it is nevertheless possible to speculate on the broad outlines of the history of commemoration, which, at least for the Western world, can be divided into roughly three overlapping phases: the pre-national (before the late eighteenth century), the national (from the American and French revolutions to the 1960s), and the present, post-national phase.

We know very little about the early history of memory (or, more properly, memories), but what is certain is that its practice(s) was either highly localized or relatively cosmopolitan.[11] Pierre Nora argues that prior to the nineteenth century memory was such a pervasive part of life—the "milieu of memory" is what he calls it—that people were hardly aware of its existence. Only the aristocracy, the church, and the monarchical state had need of institutionalized memory. Outside the elite classes, archives, genealogies, family portraits, and biographies were extremely rare; and there was no vast bureaucracy of memory as there is today. Ordinary people felt the past to be so much a part of their present that they perceived no urgent need to record, objectify, and preserve it.[12]

Popular memory appears to have differed from elite memory in important ways. While the latter attempted to create a consecutive account of all that had happened from a particular point in the past, popular memory made no effort to fill in all the blanks. If elite time marched in a more or less linear manner, popular time danced and leaped. Elite time colonized and helped construct the boundaries of territories that we have come to call nations. But popular time was more local as well as episodic, consolidating, as in rural Ulster today, certain "Great Days which rise out of time like hills off the land, signaling centers, letting boundaries drift from attention."[13] This was not a time that could be contained within fixed boundaries. It was measured not from beginnings but from centers: "From the Great Days, time spreads both ways, backward and forward, to form seasons; seasons become years, years lost to time."[14] Content to live in a present that contained both the past and the future, ordinary people did not feel compelled to invest in archives, monuments, and other permanent sites of memory, but rather they relied on living memory.

Under the old regimes, popular memories were neither very wide territorially nor, in the sense of a consecutive account from some distant past, very deep. When the Englishman Richard Gough constructed his *The History of Myddle* about 1700, he relied mainly on his own recollections and on what he had been "credibly informed by antient persons."[15] Although Gough consulted manor court rolls, deeds, leases, and parish registers, his history was not for the most part something found in the archives. He did not experience the pastness of the past as we do. The parish church was Gough's site of memory, and he used the layout of the pews (which he reproduced in his book) to remind him of the families who occupied them. Because it was property-owning males (or their widows) who owned those pews, his account systematically ignores women, young persons, and propertyless people generally. Gough's narrative barely connects the history of Myddle with those of surrounding communities, much less with English history generally, with the result that those who left the village are permitted an identity only insofar as they are connected to the place itself. There are no English people in Myddle, only Myddle people in England. A specifically English identity, based on a specifically English memory, had little meaning to Gough or his contemporaries.

III

As David Cressy's contribution to this volume suggests, a different kind of memory was already developing in England under the Tudors and the Stuarts. A set of memories that were not purely local or cosmopolitan arose in sixteenth-century England out of the convergence of Protestantism and Tudor dynastic motivations. The self-conceptions of "God's Englishmen," who, like the chosen people of the Old Testament, claimed for themselves a unique future as well as a distinctive past, required an investment in new forms of memory. But this scarcely penetrated the consciousness of more than a small part of the population. Institutionalized forms of memory were too precious to be wasted on the common people. Furthermore, Protestants had no wish to commemorate with Catholics and vice versa. Prior to the era of the French and American revolutions, memory tended to divide rather than unite, just as it continues to do in places like northern Ireland.[16]

This began to change as a result of the simultaneous political and economic revolutions of the late eighteenth century.[17] The demand for commemoration was then taken up by the urban middle and working classes, gradually expanding until, today, everyone is obsessed with recording, preserving, and remembering. According to Nora, "we speak so much of memory because there is so little of it left," referring to the kind of living memory, communicated face to face, that still exists in rural Ireland, but which now has to compete with a multitude of other memories, some official, others commercialized.[18]

National memory is shared by people who have never seen or heard of one another, yet who regard themselves as having a common history. They are bound together as much by forgetting as by remembering, for modern memory was born at a moment when Americans and Europeans launched a massive effort to reject the past and construct a radically new future. The American revolutionaries urged their compatriots to forget everything and start afresh. Jefferson declared that "the dead have no rights. . . . Our Creator made the world for the use of the living and not of the dead." And the French Republic embarked on the extraordinary project of altering the time consciousness of the entire Christian world by declaring 1792 to be Year I, a symbol of their conception of new beginnings.[19]

New memories required concerted forgettings, a process Benedict Anderson describes as collective amnesia. Changes occurring at the economic as well as the political level created such a sense of distance between now and then that people found it impossible to remember what life had been like only a few decades earlier. The past went blank and had to be filled in, a task taken up with great fervor by professional historians from the early nineteenth century onward. Their task, as Jules Michelet conceived it, was to speak for past generations, to bestow on them a national history regardless of whether they were aware of themselves as French, German, or English at the time they were alive.[20]

In the case of both the French and American revolutions, the need to commemorate arose directly out of an ideologically driven desire to break with the past, to construct as great a distance as possible between the new age and the old. It was the French revolutionaries who invented the "Old Regime," exaggerating its backwardness as well as its injustices in order to justify their claim that 1789 represented a remarkable leap forward. Conceiving of themselves as standing at the starting point of a new era, revolutionaries on both sides of the Atlantic created a cult of new beginnings and, with it, a whole set of memory practices and sites that were as controversial then as they are today.[21]

As Mona Ozouf's vivid account of the festive life of the French Revolution suggests, it was the cult of new beginnings that produced the first truly national commemoration in Europe, centering on July 14, the date of the Fall of the Bastille.[22] The Americans, who liked to think of their revolution in terms of continuity rather than total rupture, were slower to create a national holiday. As John Bodnar tells us, July 4 was not celebrated nationally until the 1820s, at a point when Americans had begun to feel that history was accelerating and the heroic past was slipping away from them.[23]

By contrast, the British, who insisted on the continuity of their history, produced no official holidays of a patriotic kind, confirming Nora's point that temporal and topographical memory sites emerge at those times and in those places where there is a perceived or constructed break with the past.[24] But, even though continuity of the state precluded commemorations on a national scale, the British nevertheless produced many new commemorative practices as a result of their experience of the disruptive effects of their industrial revolution. Memory was as central to the making of English working-class identities as it was to the class consciousness of the British bourgeoisie, both of which were constructed in the nineteenth century. Modern memory was born not just from the sense of a break with the past, but from an intense awareness of the conflicting representations of the past and the effort of each group to make its version the basis of national identity.[25]

This is not to say that there is something automatic about commemorative activity. In both Europe and North America, national commemorations were fiercely contested from the very beginning. French conservatives objected to the concept of the nation and refused to participate in its anniversaries, preferring to remember instead the birth and death dates of the Bourbons. The peasantry refused to exchange local for national memory until almost the First World War, and then only when they had been effectively colonized by the state.[26]

But even those who subscribed to the idea of a sovereign people could divide on what should constitute the national identity; and it was not until 1880 that Bastille Day became a permanent part of France's public calendar. In Philadelphia, the place where American independence was declared, there was no consensus on how the anniversary should be honored until the 1850s. Rival elites and working-class groups paraded their differences in the streets, sometimes clashing violently over the interpretation of the revolutionary heritage. It was only when this struggle abated that Americans began to celebrate July 4 in a consensual manner.[27]

The fact that both new nations were initially so fragile only seems to have intensified the commemorative efforts. If the conflicts of the present seemed intractable, the past offered a screen on which desires for unity and continuity, that is, identity, could be projected. In both France and the United States, the foundational moment took on mythic proportions in the eyes of succeeding generations.[28] For the left, it was a time of heroes, pure idealism, and perfect consensus. For the right, it remained a moment of villainy, degradation, and disintegration. What they had in common, however, was their belief in a national memory as well as a national identity, something that, as Herman Lebovics's essay on the fierce debates in France in the 1930s and 1940s demonstrates, was evident in all subsequent political struggles.

New nations as well as old states require ancient pasts. As soon as Germany unified, its elites also felt a desperate need to commemorate. In a relatively brief time they too constructed what they regarded as a truly Germanic heritage, but, as Rudy Koshar observes, "concepts of identity and memory are subverted by being posited," and the Germans soon found themselves as divided as the French concerning their newfound legacy. Koshar's essay shows how the historic preservation movement floundered from the very beginning, while Yael Zerubavel's study of the Israeli legend of settler heroism at Tel Hai shows how it has been contested and revised right from its beginnings in the 1920s to the present day.

IV

Nineteenth-century commemorations were largely for, but not of, the people. Fallen kings and martyred revolutionary leaders were remembered, generals had their memorials, but ordinary participants in war and revolution were consigned to oblivion. Plans drawn up in France as early as 1792 to give fallen citizen soldiers of the new Republic a place of burial in the very center of Paris never materialized.[29] Throughout the nineteenth century only officers had their graves marked and their names inscribed on

European war memorials. The first military cemeteries were created during the American Civil War, but Europeans did not take up the idea that men who fought together should be buried together.

Yet American memory was selective in other ways. As Kirk Savage shows us in his fascinating account of post–Civil War monument building in the American North and South, these memories in stone provided a basis for consensus between old enemies. However, they were the icons of whites only. Post–Civil War American identity was forged by forgetting the contributions of African Americans to the military effort, forgetting even what the struggle had been about. Faced with oblivion as the quintessential American "other," ex-slaves invented their own commemoration of the Emancipation Proclamation, known to them (and largely only to them) as "Juneteenth."[30]

On both sides of the Atlantic, national commemorations were largely the preserve of elite males, the designated carriers of progress, who, as a consequence of newly defined gender divisions, felt the past to be slipping away from them much faster than did women. The new imperatives of individualism set men on a fast track, producing among them a profound sense of losing touch with the past. Thought of as belonging more to the past, women came to serve in various (and usually unpaid) ways as the keepers and embodiments of memory. They provided consolation to men terrified that they had become rootless as a result of their own upward and outward mobility.[31]

The role of women in national commemoration was largely allegorical, however. The figure of Liberty came to stand in both France and the United States as a symbol of national identity, but the history of real women was systematically forgotten.[32] In the old regimes, famous queens were remembered, but in the new democracies even so important a figure as Victoria was commemorated mainly as a wife and mother, not as a political figure.[33] The creation of national mother's days in America and Europe on the eve of the First World War simply underlined the gendered nature of national commemorative practice, for it was not for their deeds but for their being that women were remembered.[34]

Workers, racial minorities, young people, and women gained admission to national memories at an even slower pace than they were admitted to national representative and educational institutions. Ironically, it was the dominant male elites, who imagined themselves at the cutting edge of progress, who, feeling the loss of the past most acutely, were most insistent that it be restored and preserved. Until very recently they were also the only ones to be commemorated. Women and minorities often serve as symbols of a "lost" past, nostalgically perceived and romantically constructed, but their actual lives are most readily forgotten. Americans now celebrate Martin Luther King, Jr., with a national holiday, but they have yet to memorialize a woman. Apart from Queen Victoria, virtually all the women to whom monuments are erected in France and England are figures of premodern times.[35]

V

It is also one of the peculiarities of the national phase of commemoration that it consistently preferred the dead to the living. The old regimes felt more comfortable with honoring both because before the Enlightenment had thoroughly disenchanted the world, the dead and the living were perceived as inhabiting the same space and time. In an era when there was less finality about death, the dead haunted the living, who seem to have felt a greater need to forget than to remember.

By the end of the eighteenth century, however, the living had begun to haunt the dead, interring them in elaborately maintained cemeteries, visiting their graves, even attempting to communicate with them through spiritualist mediums.[36] Middle-class Victorians were the first generation to deny death and have trouble letting go of the dead. But by the end of the nineteenth century the cult of the dead had become democratized, and in the course of the First World War resort to spiritualist mediums became a mass phenomenon.[37] Europeans adopted the American notion of military cemeteries, where officers and men would finally lie side by side. Post–World War I memorials were qualitatively as well as quantitatively different from anything that had gone before. As Thomas Laqueur's essay demonstrates, nations now felt the need to leave a tangible trace of all their dead either through graves or inscriptions.[38] The effort to preserve a trace of every fallen soldier reached its limits in the interwar period with the monument building in France during the 1920s described here by Daniel Sherman. The scale of death was so massive and so many mortal remains were missing that all the major combatant nations eventually resorted to erecting the so-called tombs of unknown soldiers, thereby remembering everyone by remembering no one in particular. This was the only way that memory of this terrible period of time could be materialized in a single place.

Yet, as national memory practices became more democratic, they also became more impersonal. Kurt Piehler describes how American families refused to surrender their sons' bodies to foreign soil. In Europe, where the state was stronger, even death did not release a man from national service. In the interwar period the spirit and image of the fallen were repeatedly mobilized on film as well as in political rhetoric to serve a variety of causes, left as well as right. They had become the very embodiment of national identities in virtually every place but the new Soviet Union, where the war was seen as a wasted imperialist venture. The industrialization of modern warfare had consigned individual heroism to oblivion. Even the victors commemorated sacrifice rather than triumph; and, in Germany, where defeat and revolution were perceived as a total breach with the past, the dead came to stand for all that was worthy in the German past and redeeming in its future.[39] No wonder that men who survived the war often identified with the dead, for there were few tributes, material or symbolic, for World War I veterans, few lands fit for heroes, much less for heroines.

As for the women who had contributed so much to the world's first total war effort, there would be no monuments. Their assigned role was still, as it was in the private cults of the dead in the nineteenth century, that of chief mourners and mediums. The organized cemetery pilgrimages popular during the interwar years were largely women's affairs.[40] In the era of Nazism and Fascism, when nations tried to suppress class if not ethnic differences, the gender division of memory became even more pronounced. Women remembered the men, while their own contributions were represented largely in terms of sacrifice, a traditional female role that only reinforced gender stereotypes.

VI

It was not until after the Second World War that national commemoration began to alter. Of the great powers, only the Soviet Union, which had not been able to honor its dead of the first war because of that conflict's association with the czarist regime, encouraged the cult of the dead on a mass scale. The Germans were forbidden to build military cemeteries until the 1950s; and many of their old memorials were pulled down by the occupying allies, who preferred that Germans forget the Prussian tradition.[41] The Japanese were similarly encouraged to forget their militaristic past, something that they were quite willing to do. Japan proved particularly adept at constructing a cult of new beginnings, treating the war as an aberration and reading its history as if it had begun in 1945.[42]

Constructing a new Japan and two new Germanies demanded forgetting rather than remembering. Even Jews focused more on the present than the past in the first years of the new state of Israel. The memories of individual survivors were vivid enough, but it was not until the late 1950s that they found expression in a collective memory of "Holocaust," a concept that came into popular circulation in Israel only after the new state was firmly established and Jews could begin to reflect on the pastness of the European past. When the memory of those terrible events could no longer be taken for granted, there was suddenly a powerful reason to commemorate, to save both individual and collective recollections from oblivion.

But even among the victorious nations memory took a different shape after World War II. This second round of total war had resulted in more civilian than military deaths, and it was no longer possible to ignore the contributions made at the home front. Military cemeteries were constructed, but so too were so-called living memorials—churches, sports stadiums, parks, and hospitals—which had begun to be erected in America in the 1920s and 1930s and now began to fill the bombed-out spaces of Europe as well. The cult of the fallen soldier was replaced by a new emphasis on veterans, who were immensely better treated than any of their predecessors. This time around the promise of a land fit for heroes would not go unfulfilled. The fact that the returning soldiers could actually find a place in the present reduced considerably the pressure to memorialize them. Parades replaced cemetery pilgrimages as the typical memorial day activity. Now it became possible for women, even those who had not been mobilized, to feel that they too had been a part of history, not just as widows and war mothers, making sacrifices through husbands and sons, but in their own right. While the memory of women war workers was not to gain public recognition until the 1970s, the door to national memory was now ajar, not only for them but for racial and sexual minorities.[43]

The Cold War contributed in its own way to shifts in the forms and location of memory. The blurring of the old distinction between war and peace meant that it was very difficult to define the beginnings or endings that had previously been the focus of memory. The Korean, Algerian, and Vietnam conflicts proved extremely difficult to commemorate, except on a private basis. The Korean conflict has yet to receive a national monument; and the Vietnam Memorial, with its wall of names, is generally agreed to represent a turning point in the history of public memory, a decisive departure from the anonymity of the Tomb of the Unknown Soldier and a growing acknowledgment that everyone now deserves equal recognition at all times in wholly accessible places.[44]

In contrast to the highly institutionalized rites of memory carried out at set times across the river at the Tomb of the Unknown Soldier in Arlington National Cemetery, the memorial on the Mall stimulates an anarchy of memory. At Arlington it is the honor guard that performs the rites of remembering, limiting the spectators largely to the role of audience. Most visitors confine their activity to picture taking, thus further distancing themselves from the event itself. By contrast, the monument on the Mall is an event, demanding that everyone who passes by do his or her duty to memory in one way or another. To visit both places is to move not just in space, but in time. Arlington and the Mall belong not just to two different sides of the Potomac, but two different eras in the history of commemoration, the national and the post-national.

VII

By the late 1960s the era of national commemoration was clearly drawing to a close, but not before bequeathing to later generations a plethora of monuments, holidays, cemeteries, museums, and archives that still continue to function today. These remain very effective in concentrating time in space, in providing many people with a sense of common identity no matter how dispersed they may be by class, region, gender, religion, or race. Millions still make their secular pilgrimages to places like Gettysburg, Auschwitz, and Hiroshima, but no longer in quite the same compulsory, ritualized manner.

We are more likely to do our "memory work" at times and places of our own choosing. Whereas there was once "a time and a place for everything," the distinctions between different kinds of times and places seem to be collapsing. As global markets work around the clock and the speed of communications shrinks our sense of distance, there is both more memory work to do and less time and space to do it in. As the world implodes upon us, we feel an even greater pressure as individuals to record, preserve, and collect. Again, Pierre Nora: "When memory is no longer everywhere, it will not be anywhere unless one takes the responsibility to recapture it through individual means."[45]

In the past two decades memory has simultaneously become more global and more local. Events and places with international meaning such as Hiroshima, Chernobyl, Auschwitz, and Nanjing capture the world's attention even when the nations responsible may wish to forget them.[46] At the same time, people now prefer to devote more time to local, ethnic, and family memory, often using the old national calendars and spaces for these new purposes. As John Bodnar notes, the experience of the American bicentennial celebrations suggests that people now find much more meaning in local than in national commemorations, forcing the latter to acquiesce to a new pluralism of celebrations. The fact that family genealogists now outnumber professional historians in the archives of France and elsewhere is yet further evidence of the same tendency toward the personalization of memory.[47]

Yet the recent proliferation of anniversaries, memorial services, and ethnic celebrations suggests that, while memory has become more democratic, it has also become more burdensome.[48] Today, time takes no prisoners. Pockets of pastness—ethnic neighborhoods, rural backwaters, the intact family—are fast disappearing. Those who were once perceived as our connection to the past—old people, women, immigrants, minorities—are now swimming in the same flood of change that previously created such a profound sense of loss among elite males. Grandparents are no longer doing the memory work they once performed. In particular families, it is wives and mothers who pick up the slack. Every attic is an archive, every living room a museum. Never before has so much been recorded, collected; and never before has remembering been so compulsive, even as rote memorization ceases to be central to the educational process. What we can no longer keep in our heads is now kept in storage.

It seems that as collective forms of memory decline an increasing burden is placed on the individual. One is reminded of one of Jorge Luis Borges's characters, Funes, the Memorious, who, having fallen off his horse at age nineteen, finds he can forget nothing. Funes laments that he has "more memories in myself alone than all men have had since the world was a world. . . . My memory, sir, is like a garbage disposal."[49] Today, it is as if we have all suffered Funes's fall, for we are under obligation to remember more and more, due in large part to the fact that in modern society everyone belongs simultaneously to several different groups, each with its own collective memory. Finding ourselves in this demanding situation, we rely on a multitude of devices—calendars, Filofaxes, computerized memory banks—to remind ourselves of that which we as individuals cannot master. Our problem stems not from the brain's inability to remember, but rather from the fact that, as individuals, we cannot rely on the support of collective memory in the same way people in earlier periods could. Dependent on several collective memories, but masters of none, we are only too aware of the gap between the enormous obligation to remember and the individual's incapacity to do so without the assistance of mechanical reminders, souvenirs, and memory sites.

"Modern memory," Nora observes, "is, above all, archival. It relies entirely on the materiality of the trace, the immediacy of the recording, the visibility of the image."[50] On one hand, the past has become so distant and the future so uncertain that we can no longer be sure what to save, so we save everything. It seems that every historic dwelling, every species, every landscape is destined to have its own preservation order because "no one knows what the past will be made of next."[51] On the other hand, never has the past been so accessible on film, on tape, and in mass-produced images. Virtually all the songs, television programs, fads and fashions of our childhood and youth are now as close as the library, video store, or flea market. The scale of collecting increases in inverse proportion to our depth perception. Now that old is equated with yesterday, we allow nothing to disappear. And surrounded by a forest of monuments and souvenirs so dense that it makes it virtually impossible to decipher their historical references, so burdened by current compulsion to remember the birthdays and anniversaries of family, schoolmates, and fellow workers that "birthday books have become a standard household item: one's memory is inadequate to record the festivities for which one is responsible."[52]

Not surprisingly, individual identities are proliferating at precisely the same rate as memories. In contemporary society each of us enters daily into a multitude of situations—home, work, leisure, peer groups—each of which is a world of its own with a distinctive history. Life can no longer be lived sequentially along a single time line; and even elite males can no longer expect the kind of continuity that we used to call a career. As a result of the global economic restructuring that has taken place since the 1960s, millions of workers have found themselves "recycled," forced to change jobs and locations.[53] This, combined with the unprecedentedly high divorce rates since 1970, means that everyone has now as many pasts as he or she has different jobs, spouses, parents, children, or residences.

"In effect, as we move through life, the cast of relevant characters is ever expanding," writes Kenneth Gergen.[54] Today it is not only rare, but actually frowned upon, to have only one identity. "One of the worst mistakes in middle age is to confine oneself—and to continue to define oneself—by a single source of identity," writes Gail Sheehy.[55] And this applies on the political as well as on the personal level, as the good fortunes of Kuwaitis with dual citizenship who were able to flee to Cairo or Miami when their country was invaded can testify. Of course, there are those, like the Palestinians, for whom several identities are a tragic burden. But there is no question but that in the transnational world of late twentieth-century capitalism increasing numbers of persons are forced to contend with multiple identities and multiple memories, as they are moved from place to place, time after time.[56]

VIII

It is no wonder that these new conditions have produced a new self-consciousness about identity and memory. Since the 1960s, not only particular memories but memory itself has become the subject of intense public as well as scholarly debate. The study of collective memory, initiated by Halbwachs in the 1930s, has been given new life. Simultaneously, identity has undergone a denaturalization process, with scholars from a wide variety of fields agreeing that it is subjective and constructed.[57] Yoked together by their common past, memory and identity now undergo the same scrutiny.

It is not surprising that much of the rethinking has taken place in Germany, where the issue of memory has such huge significance and where, as Claudia Koonz's discussion of the current debate about the concentration camps demonstrates, the struggle intensifies rather than diminishes. Since the 1970s, a radical critique of older institutionalized memory practice has developed. Monuments have been subject to particular attention by critics who argue that the traditional memory sites actually discourage engagement with the past and induce forgetting rather than remembering. The leaders of recent avant-garde counter monument movements, many of whom are politically active artists, would have citizens do more rather than less memory work. They advocate radical designs that, like the monument on the Mall, not only invite more interaction, but challenge the status of memory as a knowable object. In 1986 the first of the counter monuments was erected in Harburg, a lead-sheathed obelisk dedicated to the victims of

Nazism that invited the public to inscribe their names and messages on its surfaces. As these were filled, the obelisk was lowered gradually into the ground, where it eventually disappeared, leaving as its only trace the living memories of those who visited the site previously.[58]

The anti-monument movement represents a radical turn not only aesthetically but epistemologically. Its advocates reject the notion of memory sites and want to deritualize and dematerialize remembering so that it becomes more a part of everyday life, thus closing the gap between the past and the present, between memory and history. By dematerializing memory they also wish to strip it of all appearances of objectivity, thereby forcing everyone to confront her or his own subjectivity, while at the same time acknowledging a civic responsibility not to let the past repeat itself.

Whether these aims are achieved is an open question. It would appear that most people find it difficult to remember without having access to mementos, images, and physical sites to objectify their memory.[59] Yet the controversy over the counter monuments is symptomatic of the rethinking of memory practice going on in the United States, Europe, and many other parts of the world. Museum reformers have also begun to search for new ways to engage visitors. Movements to liberate history from its association with particular times and places—the classroom, library, and archive— have been active since the 1960s.[60] These efforts coincide with a remarkable surge in the popular historical practice. The "roots" phenomenon has inspired mass interest in genealogy, producing in the case of the Mormons what Alex Shoumatoff aptly describes as a "mountain of names."[61] Virtually every community, religion, business, and voluntary association must now have its own history, just as it must have its own identity.

Today everyone is her or his own historian, and this democratization of the past causes some anxiety among professionals, most of whom still write in the nationalist tradition, and who still retain a near monopoly over professorships and curatorships, even as they lose touch with the general public. Most people have long since turned to more heterogeneous representations of the past. And while conservatives decry Americans' lack of factual knowledge about their national history, fearing the loss of a common heritage will lead to a loss of national identity, the reality is that the nation is no longer the site or frame of memory for most people and therefore national history is no longer a proper measure of what people really know about their pasts.[62] In fact, there is good evidence to show that ordinary people are more interested in and know more about their pasts than ever before, though their knowledge is no longer confined to compulsory time frames and spaces of the old national historiography. Both Americans and Europeans have become compulsive consumers of the past, shopping for that which best suits their particular sense of self at the moment, constructing out of a bewildering variety of materials, times, and

places the multiple identities that are demanded of them in the post-
national era.[63]

Eric Davis's contribution on the politics of museum building in Iraq
suggests that the old compulsory forms of commemoration survive, but
only where states are still in the process of constructing a singular national
identity. Yet even in dictatorships it is not clear how long this monopoly
will last. Identity politics are becoming as divisive in the former Soviet
Union and former Yugoslavia as they are in Western Europe and North
America. Everywhere the ability to cope with a plurality of pasts is being
severely tested, and only time will tell whether societies will be able to
tolerate the diversity with which they are now confronted.

IX

It seems clear that we are experiencing not just another intellectual fad but
a deep cultural shift, whose dynamics remind us of the struggles at the time
of the Reformation that pitted anti-ritualistic, iconoclastic Protestants
against the older Catholic practices of locating the sacred only in certain
times and places. Radical Protestants demanded that the sacred be brought
into everyday life, into history itself; and to do so they abolished the
separation of holy from secular days, insisting that the divine leave its old
haunts—churches and pilgrimage sites—to become a part of the work-
place, the household, to be identified with the history of peoples (at first
reforming sects, later with whole nations) chosen by God to carry out his
divine purpose in secular time and space.

At its most extreme the goal was nothing short of the deinstitutionaliza-
tion of religion and its internalization in the hearts and minds of all believers. At first, this required the separation of the chosen people, a journey,
as in the case of the Puritans who migrated to America, into the "wilderness" where a New Jerusalem beckoned. In time, the Protestant notion of
the chosen few would expand to include all who were willing to pledge
their allegiance to God's chosen nation. The homeland became the New
Jerusalem.

In the end, the Reformation contributed not to the sacralization of the
world, but to its secularization. Protestants displaced the cosmopolitanism
of Catholicism with territorially based churches, more closely aligned with
nation-states. Their territories became the secular equivalent of the old
holy places, soil sanctified by the blood of heroic ancestors. To defend its
position, the once universal Catholic church was forced to make alliance
with its ancient rival, the monarchical state. By the end of the eighteenth
century, the relationship between the two was so close that revolutionary
movements saw no alternative but to separate church and state, replacing
God with History, saints with secular martyrs. In revolutionary France the

great events of the nation's history took on the sacred significance once reserved only for holy days.[64]

In the course of the nineteenth century nations came to worship themselves through their pasts, ritualizing and commemorating to the point that their sacred sites and times became the secular equivalent of shrines and holy days. There was always a certain amount of ambivalence about memory among those nations born of revolution. Although the Americans were relatively quick to designate certain men as Founding Fathers, they wished to keep the revolution alive in each new generation. "Democracy has no monuments. It strikes no medals. It bears the head of no man on a coin," declared John Quincy Adams.[65] Initially, the French revolutionaries did everything possible to forget their ancestry. As Balzac put it, "by cutting off the head of Louis XVI, the Republic cut off the heads of all fathers of families."[66] Too much remembering was initially regarded as counterrevolutionary, though, in time, the French, like the Americans, would strike their medals and erect their monuments.

From the mid-nineteenth century onward history became the modern world's oracle. The terrible consequences of collective self-worship eventually became evident in the course of two world wars, but it took until the 1960s for a new iconoclasm to develop. This time the attack was directed not against the churches but against the schools, the universities, and the shrines and holidays of the nation-state, whose representations of itself had become too impersonal, totalizing, and alienating. The task then became one of finding usable pasts capable of serving the heterogeneity of new groups that had become active on the national and international stage: racial and sexual minorities, women, youth, and dozens of new nations and ethnic groups aspiring to sovereign status.

In many respects this secular reformation has been remarkably successful in desacralizing the nation-state, but the struggle is not yet over and its most intense period may be ahead of us. For those who regard the national "heritage" as a sacred text, the democratization of memory is equivalent to profanation, or, what is worse, cultural suicide. Just as some accuse the anti-monument movement of "manufacturing oblivion," there are those who regard any revision of the traditional curriculum as threatening national security. Reformers reply that all literary canons, standardized texts, and preferred lists of names and dates are themselves deadly, cutting off the present from the past, discouraging rather than enhancing active citizenship.

Of course, taking memory out of the hands of specialists, diffusing its practices over time and space, runs the risk of merely privatizing rather than really democratizing it. Today packaged forms of both memory and history have proved so profitable that we must be wary of the results of commodification and commercialization as much as the consequences of

political manipulation. Yet there are also examples of collective memorialization that owe little or nothing to either the market or to church and
state. In the wake of the 1948 Arab-Israeli war, there was a spontaneous,
uncoordinated proliferation of "booklets of commemoration" honoring
the memory of Israeli soldiers killed in combat. Often consisting of only a
few mimeographed pages, and mainly secular in character, they were entirely the work of friends, family, and colleagues, a testament to the vitality
of collective memory in modern society.[67] One could easily add many other
more recent examples.

X

There is a chance that, like Funes, the Memorious, we may drown in floods
of memories, just as we may be torn apart by the multitude of identities.
The future is unpredictable, and not a little frightening, but there is no
turning back. We have no alternative but to construct new memories as well
as new identities better suited to the complexities of a post-national era.
The old holidays and monuments have lost much of their power to commemorate, to forge and sustain a single vision of the past, but they remain
useful as times and places where groups with very different memories of the
same events can communicate, appreciate, and negotiate their respective
differences. In this difficult and conflicted period of transition, democratic
societies need to publicize rather than privatize the memories and identities
of all groups, so that each may know and respect the other's versions of the
past, thereby understanding better what divides as well as unites us.[68] In
this era of plural identities, we need civil times and civil spaces more than
ever, for these are essential to the democratic processes by which individuals and groups come together to discuss, debate, and negotiate the past
and, through this process, define the future.

NOTES

1. They do not appear in the 1976 or 1983 editions of Raymond Williams,
Keywords: A Vocabulary of Culture and Society, rev. ed. (New York: Oxford
University Press, 1983).

2. Philip Gleason, "Identifying Identity: A Semantic History," *Journal of American History,* vol. 69, no. 4 (March 1983), p. 913.

3. For a review of recent approaches, see Barry Schwartz, "The Social Control of
Commemoration: A Study in Collective Memory," *Social Forces,* vol. 61, no. 2
(December 1982). Among the classic studies of memory are F.C. Bartlett, *Remembering: A Study in Experimental and Social Psychology* (Cambridge: Cambridge
University Press, 1932); Maurice Halbwachs, *The Collective Memory,* trans. F.J.
Ditter (New York: Harper & Row, 1980). Much of the new work on memory is
psychological, but there is now a growing interest in the social and political dimen-

sions. See Paul Connerton, *How Societies Remember* (Cambridge: Cambridge University Press, 1989); Thomas Butler, ed., *Memory: History, Culture and the Mind* (Oxford: Basil Blackwell, 1989).

4. See Jacques Le Goff, *History and Memory*, trans. Steven Rendall and Elizabeth Clamon (New York: Columbia University Press, 1992), pp. 98–99; and Natalie Zemon Davis and Randolph Starn, "Introduction to Special Issue on Memory and Counter Memory," *Representations*, no. 25 (Spring 1989), p. 2.

5. Valentine Moghadam, "Introduction," *Women and Identity Politics in Theoretical and Comparative Perspective*, forthcoming.

6. Kenneth J. Gergen, *The Saturated Self: Dilemmas of Identity in Contemporary Life* (New York: Basic Books, 1991), chap. 3.

7. Eric Leed, remarks made at Rutgers Center for Historical Analysis, April 1991. Also see his *Mind of the Traveller: From Gilgamesh to Global Tourism* (New York: Basic Books, 1991).

8. Eric Hobsbawm and Terrence Ranger, eds., *The Invention of Tradition* (Cambridge: Cambridge University Press, 1983).

9. Eric Hobsbawm, *Nations and Nationalism since 1780* (Cambridge: Cambridge University Press, 1990), chap. 6.

10. For new work on private memory, see Raphael Samuel and Paul Thompson, eds., *Myths We Live By* (New York: Routledge, 1990). On the need to work out the history of memory (or, more properly, memories), see Davis and Starn, "Introduction," p. 2.

11. What is known about ancient and medieval forms of memory is summarized by Le Goff, *History and Memory*, pp. 51–81.

12. Georges Duby, "Solitude: Eleventh to Thirteenth Century," *A History of Private Life*, ed. Georges Duby (Cambridge: Harvard University Press, 1988), vol. 2, pp. 619–20.

13. Henry Glassie, *Passing the Time in Ballymenone: Culture and History of an Ulster Community* (Philadelphia: University of Pennsylvania Press, 1982), p. 353.

14. Ibid., p. 354.

15. Richard Gough, *The History of Myddle*, ed. David Hey (Harmondsworth: Penguin, 1981), p. 96; on the role of older males as "memory-men," see Le Goff, *History and Memory*, pp. 73–74.

16. Glassie, *Passing the Time in Ballymenone*, pp. 352–53.

17. Le Goff, *History and Memory*, pp. 81–90.

18. Pierre Nora, "Between Memory and History: Les Lieux de Memoire," *Representations*, no. 26 (Spring 1989), p. 7; the fate of living memory in a French village has been carefully studied by Francoise Zonabend, *The Enduring Memory: Time and History in a French Village*, trans. Anthony Forster (Manchester: University of Manchester Press, 1984).

19. On America, see David Lowenthal, *The Past Is a Foreign Country* (Cambridge: Cambridge University Press, 1985), pp. 105–13; on the French Revolutionary calendar, see Eviatar Zerubavel, *Hidden Rhythms: Schedules and Calendars in Social Life* (Chicago: University of Chicago Press, 1981), pp. 82–96.

20. Benedict Anderson, *Imagined Communities: Reflections on the Origin and Spread of Nationalism*, rev. ed. (New York: Verso, 1991), chap. 11.

21. On the invention of the "Old Regime" see Pierre Goubert, *L'ancien regime*

(Paris: Colin, 1969); also Lynn Hunt, *Politics, Culture, and Class in the French Revolution* (Berkeley: University of California Press, 1984), part 1.

22. Mona Ozouf, *Festivals and the French Revolution* (Cambridge: Harvard University Press, 1988).

23. John Bodnar, *Remaking America: Public Memory, Commemoration, and Patriotism in the Twentieth Century* (Princeton: Princeton University Press, 1992), chap. 2; also Barry Schwartz, *George Washington: The Making of an American Symbol* (New York: Free Press, 1987).

24. Nora, "Between Memory and History," p. 7.

25. Edward Thompson, *The Making of the English Working Class* (New York: Vintage, 1966), especially pp. 418–29; on the uses of memory by the middle classes, see Patrick Joyce, *Work, Society, and Politics: The Culture of the Factory in Later Victorian England* (New Brunswick: Rutgers University Press, 1980), chap. 4. The effort to shape a national past through the creation of certain national traditions is explored in Eric Hobsbawm, "Mass Producing Traditions: Europe, 1870–1914," in *The Invention of Tradition*, pp. 263–307.

26. Eugen Weber, *Peasants into Frenchmen: The Modernization of Rural France, 1870–1914* (Stanford: Stanford University Press, 1976).

27. Susan G. Davis, *Parades and Power: Street Theatre in Nineteenth-Century Philadelphia* (Berkeley: University of California Press, 1988), pp. 166–73; also Mary Ryan, *Women in Public: Between Banners and Ballots, 1825–1880* (Baltimore: Johns Hopkins University Press, 1991). I thank Professor Philip Nord for the information on Bastille Day.

28. Schwartz, *George Washington*, pp. 376–77; Hunt, *Politics, Culture, and Class*, pp. 70–71.

29. George Mosse, *Fallen Soldiers: Reshaping the Memory of the World Wars* (New York: Oxford University Press, 1990), p. 19.

30. Michael Kammen, *Mystic Chords of Memory: The Transformation of Tradition in American Culture* (New York: Knopf, 1991), p. 120. On the efforts by W.E.B. Du Bois to construct a viable memory for African Americans left out of historical pageantry, see David Glassberg, *American Historical Pageantry: The Use of Tradition in the Early Twentieth Century* (Chapel Hill: University of North Carolina Press, 1990), p. 132.

31. These are some of the themes explored in John Gillis, *Our Imagined Families: The Origins of the Myths and Rituals We Live By* (New York: Basic Books, forthcoming).

32. Hunt, *Politics, Culture, and Class*, pp. 60–66; further, Maurice Agulhon, *Marianne into Battle: Republican Imagery and Symbolism in France, 1789–1880* (Cambridge: Cambridge University Press, 1981); Marina Warner, *Monuments and Maidens: The Allegory of Female Forms* (New York: Atheneum, 1985).

33. I owe this insight to Victoria Smith, who is currently completing her dissertation on memorial statues of Queen Victoria in Britain, Canada, and India.

34. See Thomas Richards, "The Image of Victoria in the Year of Jubilee," in his *Commodity Culture of Victorian England: Advertising and Spectacle, 1851–1914* (Stanford: Stanford University Press, 1990), chap. 2. On Mother's Day, see Karin Hausen, "Mothers, Sons, and the Sale of Symbols and Goods: German Mother's Days, 1923–1933," in H. Medick and D. Sabean, eds., *Interest and Emotion*

(Cambridge: Cambridge University Press, 1984), pp. 371–413; and J. Gillis, *For Better for Worse: British Marriages 1600 to the Present* (New York: Oxford University Press, 1985), pp. 253–54.

35. Notable American women have received recognition only through stamps and local monuments. A statue of Susan B. Anthony exists in the Capitol building in Washington, D.C., but it is in an obscure corner of the lower floor. On the struggle of African Americans to claim a national memory site, see Scott Sandage, "A Marble House Divided: The Lincoln Memorial, the Civil Rights Movement and the Politics of Memory, 1939–1963," *Journal of American History*, vol. 8, no. 1 (June 1993), pp. 135–167.

36. Philippe Ariès, *The Hour of Our Death* (New York: Vintage, 1982), chap. 11; Mosse, *Fallen Soldiers*, pp. 39ff.

37. I owe the information on spiritualism to J.M. Winter, who is currently writing *The Persistence of Tradition: The Cultural History of Bereavement in the Period of the Great War*.

38. Mosse, *Fallen Soldiers*, chap. 5.

39. Ibid., pp. 102ff.

40. Ibid., pp. 152–54.

41. Ibid., chap. 10. On the most recent phase of the German politics of memory: Charles Maier, "Remembering and Forgetting: The Third Reich and the G.D.R.," lecture at Rutgers University, April 18, 1991.

42. Carol Gluck, "The Disappearing Past: Public Memory in Contemporary Japan," lecture at Rutgers University, April 18, 1991.

43. Allan Berube, *Coming Out Under Fire: The History of Gay Men and Women in World War Two* (New York: Free Press, 1990).

44. Mosse, *Fallen Soldiers*, pp. 221–25.

45. Nora, "Between Memory and History," p. 16.

46. Steven Weisman, "Pearl Harbor in the Mind of Japan," *New York Times Magazine*, Nov. 3, 1991, pp. 30–33, 42, 47, 68. On the struggle for German memory, see Charles S. Maier, *The Unmasterable Past: History, Holocaust, and German National Identity* (Cambridge: Harvard University Press, 1988).

47. Nora, "Between Memory and History," p. 15; similar trends are documented by David Lowenthal, *The Past Is a Foreign Country*, chap. 7.

48. On the proliferation of official anniversaries, see William M. Johnston, *Celebrations: The Cult of Anniversaries in Europe and the United States* (New Brunswick: Transaction Publishers, 1991).

49. Jorge Luis Borges, *Ficciones*, trans. Anthony Kerrigan (New York: Grove Press, 1962), p. 112. The Borges story was called to my attention by Yosef Haym Yerushalmi, *Zakhor: Jewish History and Jewish Memory* (Seattle: University of Washington Press, 1982), p. 102.

50. Nora, "Between Memory and History," p. 13.

51. Ibid., p. 17.

52. Gergen, *The Saturated Self*, p. 62; also John Gillis, "Remembering Memory: A Challenge for Public Historians in a Post-National Era," *The Public Historian*, vol. 14, no. 4 (Fall 1992), pp. 83–93; on the growth of birthday celebrations, see Howard P. Chudacoff, *How Old Are You? Age Consciousness in American Culture* (Princeton: Princeton University Press, 1989), chap. 6.

24 JOHN R. GILLIS

53. David Harvey, *The Condition of Postmodernity* (Oxford: Basil Blackwell, 1989), parts 3 & 4; also John Gillis, "The Case against Chronologization: Changes in the Anglo-American Life Cycle, 1600 to the Present," *Ethnologia Europea*, vol. 17, no. 2 (1988), pp. 97–106.

54. Gergen, *The Saturated Self*, p. 62.

55. Gail Sheehy, *Pathfinders* (New York: Morrow, 1981), p. 294.

56. Harvey, *The Condition of Postmodernity*, passim; "A New Divide for Kuwaitis: Who Stayed and Who Fled," *New York Times*, Oct. 12, 1991.

57. The new interest in memory is documented by Schwartz, "The Social Control of Commemoration"; Davis and Starn, "Introduction"; Kammen, *Mystic Chords;* Connerton, *How Societies Remember;* and the special issue of the *Journal of American History* on memory in March 1989.

58. James Young, "The Counter Monument: Memory Against Itself in Germany Today," *Critical Inquiry*, vol. 18, no. 2 (Winter 1992), pp. 267–96; also his *The Texture of Memory: Holocaust Memorials and Meaning* (New Haven and London: Yale University Press, 1993).

59. On the objectification of memory in family settings, see Asa Boholm, *Swedish Kinship: An Exploration into Cultural Processes of Belonging and Continuity* (Goteborg: Acta Universitatis Gothoburgensis, 1983), chap. 4; on the issue of objectification generally, see Eviatar Zerubavel, *The Fine Line: Making Distinctions in Everyday Life* (New York: Free Press, 1991), passim.

60. A useful survey of these trends is provided by David Thelen, "History-Making in America: A Populist Perspective" (Laramie: Wyoming Council on the Humanities, 1991); revised and reprinted in *The Historian*, vol. 53, no. 4 (Summer 1991), pp. 633–48.

61. Alex Shoumatoff is referring not only to the current fascination with family history, but to the Utah range where the Mormons secure the computer tapes of their massive collection of the names of those they expect to sponsor to eternal life. Shoumatoff, *The Mountain of Names: A History of the Human Family* (New York: Simon & Schuster, 1985).

62. See Michael Frisch, "American History and the Structures of Collective Memory: A Modern Exercise in Empirical Iconography," *Journal of American History*, vol. 75, no. 4 (March 1989), pp. 1130–55.

63. Gergen, *The Saturated Self*, pp. 75–77.

64. Zerubavel, *Hidden Rhythms*, pp. 82–100.

65. Kammen, *Mystic Chords*, p. 19.

66. Quoted in Lynn Hunt, *The Family Romance of the French Revolution* (Berkeley: University of California Press, 1992), pp. 72–73.

67. The creation of thousands of "books of commemoration" is described by Emmanuel Sivan in *The 1948 War* [Hebrew], Tel Aviv, 1991. I am indebted to Professor Sivan for sharing his ideas with me. An English translation of his book is forthcoming.

68. This point is made eloquently by Le Goff, *History and Memory*, p. 99.

PART ONE

The Problem of Identity and Memory

Chapter I

IS "IDENTITY" A USEFUL CROSS-CULTURAL CONCEPT?

Richard Handler

DURING THE past twenty years, social scientists have devoted much attention to the "invention" of cultures and traditions, particularly as this process is associated with nationalist and ethnic politics. One result of this scholarship is that analysts are increasingly wary of employing reifying conceptions of nation, ethnic group, culture, and tradition. It is no longer thought useful to treat such phenomena as though they existed as bounded and unchanging entities. Rather, cultures and social groups—taken at any level of analysis (local, regional, national, transnational)—are now conceptualized in terms of ongoing processes of "construction" and "negotiation."

Yet, reification is an epistemological problem not easily vanquished, for it pervades the rhetorical and conceptual apparatus of our scientific worldview. Thus we may succeed in discarding one set of reifying concepts from our scholarly tool kit, only to find ourselves employing others in their stead. Such is the case with "identity." Much new writing on cultural processes, while suspicious of terms like "tradition" and "ethnic group," falls comfortably back upon "identity." Cultures, it seems, get constructed, deconstructed, and reconstructed as people pursue their identities. Yet the idea of "identity," as it is used in the new literature on nationalism and ethnicity, has not been much examined—despite the fact that the epistemological presuppositions that the concept carries are similar, if not identical, to those that have made other terms suspect.

The present paper argues that we should be as suspicious of "identity" as we have learned to be of "culture," "tradition," "nation," and "ethnic group." Identity has become a salient scholarly and cultural construct in the mid-twentieth century, particularly in social-scientific scholarship in the United States. Its prominence in that context, however, does not mean that the concept can be applied unthinkingly to other places and times. To the contrary, its use as a cross-culturally neutral conceptual tool should be avoided, for, as historical analysis and ethnographic data suggest, the concept of "identity" is peculiar to the modern Western world.

I

In the human sciences (and, more generally, in everyday discourse) "identity" is used in reference to three aspects of human experience: first, to individual human persons; second, to collectivities or groups of human beings that are imagined to be individuated somewhat as human persons are imagined to be discrete one from another; and third, to the relationship between these two—in particular, to the ways in which human persons are imagined to assimilate elements of collective identities into their unique personal identities. Moreover, most scholarly usage of the term reflects our commonsense notion of identity, which I would gloss, colloquially, in this way: "the identity of a person or group is what it really is, uniquely, in and of itself, in its inner being and without reference to externals." If we turn to the *Oxford English Dictionary*, we find similar, though more elegant, glosses:

1. The quality or condition of being the same in substance, composition, nature, properties, or in particular qualities under consideration; absolute or essential sameness; oneness. . . .
2. The sameness of a person or thing at all times or in all circumstances; the condition or fact that a person or thing is itself and not something else; individuality, personality.[1]

Instances of " identity" used in approximately these senses recur routinely both in social-scientific literature and the discourse of cultural politics. Consider, as a first example, some remarks from an archaeological conference on heritage management: "[A]rchaeology is no longer used solely in a search for historical roots and identity. In many regions it has become part of a struggle to recapture a cultural identity that was lost during colonization."[2] "Identity" figures similarly in a recent volume on "historical literacy" written by the Bradley Commission on History in Schools: "For the first aim, personal growth, history is the central humanistic discipline. It can satisfy young people's longing for a sense of identity and of their time and place in the human story. . . . American history [is needed] to tell us who we are and who we are becoming."[3] As a final example, consider the claims of a Palestinian student at the University of Virginia, writing in a university-wide "multicultural journal": "Did the Palestinians cease to exist because their homeland was taken from them? No, they most certainly did not. They refused to give up their identity and assimilate themselves into oblivion—they continued to struggle to maintain their Palestinian identity, culture, and values. It is this struggle for identity that confronts me now."[4]

These usages are consistent with a widespread theory of culture and society that underpins a globally hegemonic nationalist ideology. In this perspective, nations are imagined as natural objects or things in the real world. As such, that is, as natural things, they have a unique identity, and that identity can be defined by reference to precise spatial, temporal, and cultural boundaries. Nations are thought to begin or to be bounded in time—they are said to have definite historical origins or at least historical roots that can be traced back to an indefinite past. Nations may also be said to end in time, though most nationalist ideologies see the death of a nation as an unnatural disaster and most do not admit to their own deaths (though they constantly predict national demise unless restorative political and cultural action is taken). Nations are also said to be bounded in space, as indicated on current maps of the world that separate nations by un-broken dark lines. Finally, nations are imagined to be internally homoge-neous in terms of what is taken to be shared cultural content—the very stuff, as it were, of identity. Internal diversity of region, gender, ethnicity, and class may be recognized—even celebrated as indicative of the nation's complexity and rich heritage. However, in nationalist ideology internal diversity is always encompassed by national homogeneity. Whatever differ-ences there may be among nationals, their common nationality is thought both to unite them and to distinguish them from all other nationalities. Thus on "political" (as opposed, say, to "physical") maps of the world, each nation, enclosed by an unbroken dark line, is uniformly colored, and the colors of adjoining nations are always different.[5]

In current scholarly analyses of collective identities, there is a tension between the notion that identity is essential, fundamental, unitary, and unchanging, and the notion that identities are constructed and recon-structed through historical action. Indeed, the most significant develop-ment in culture theory of the past twenty years has been the attack on reifying and essentialist models of culture, as summarized in the titles of two widely cited books: *The Invention of Culture* and *The Invention of Tradition*.[6] Many scholars now agree that there is no unchanging "es-sence" or "character" to particular cultures; indeed, that cultures are not individuated entities existing as natural objects with neat temporal and spatial boundaries. James Clifford has summarized these new theoretical trends as "the predicament of culture," as the title of his 1988 book puts it. "Culture," Clifford says, "is a deeply compromised idea I cannot yet do without."[7]

Current insights about the "construction" of culture present a predica-ment because the very idea of culture has been elaborated in terms of boundedness, homogeneity, and the idea of immutable natural essence. We speak more readily of culture as a noun—"a" culture, "this" culture, "our" culture—than as a verb indicating process, intercommunication, and the ongoing construction and reconstruction of boundaries that are symbolic and not naturally given. Furthermore, this tension in culture theory is found in commonsense and nationalist discourse as well as in the work of scholars. Nationalists believe profoundly in the uniqueness of their cultural identity. They also believe that the boundaries they construct to define that identity are naturally given and *not* a symbolic construction of their own devising. Thus the Palestinian student quoted above speaks of the maintenance of a cultural identity conceived, apparently, to be unchanging even in changing cultural contexts. However, imbued with modern notions of progress and linear temporality, nationalists also see the nation as a project of becoming. They speak, as did the Bradley Commission historians, both of "who we are"—as if that could be defined—and of "who we are becoming." Or they speak, as the archaeologist quoted above, about restoring or recapturing a lost identity, as if a definitive collective identity existed in the past and can be recovered through correct historical scholarship and political action.

In contrast to this sort of culture theory, I would avoid—or, at least, refuse to privilege—the discourse of "who we are," that is, of identity. Groups are not bounded objects in the natural world. Rather, "they" are symbolic processes that emerge and dissolve in particular contexts of action. Groups do not have essential identities; indeed, they ought not to be defined as things at all. For any imaginable social group—defined in terms of nationality, class, locality, or gender—there is no definitive way to specify "who we are," for "who we are" is a communicative process that includes many voices and varying degrees of understanding and, importantly, misunderstanding. Moreover, there is an infinite regress or a reflexivity built into human communication: the uttering of every statement about "who we are" changes, if only slightly, our relationship to who we are. Thus to talk about identity is to change or construct it, despite the dominant epistemology of identity, which specifies immutability.

That nationalist ideologues and the scholars who write about them are wedded to a discourse of identity is a sociocultural fact of no small importance; but as analysts, we need a language other than the discourse of identity in order to be able to comment creatively upon that discourse.

II

There is a growing literature on cross-cultural conceptions of "the self" and of "the person."[8] For the most part, this literature concludes that there are significant differences in the ways in which "person" and "self" are conceived by people in different parts of the world. However, the concept of identity seems to have escaped such scrutiny. Even discussions of the construction of identity tend to presuppose that identity, though continually changing, is nonetheless relevant to people everywhere. However, if identity implies the notions of boundedness and homogeneity that I have sketched, it would follow that people who do not routinely imagine human activities in terms of such bounded, unique agents would have less interest in the notion of identity (whether personal or collective) than we often ascribe to them.

The question, then, is this: Are there worldviews in which human personhood, human agency, and human collectivity are imagined in terms that do not presuppose identity, that is, do not presuppose the oneness, continuity, and boundedness of the person, agent, or group? According to the ethnographic record, the answer to this question is clearly yes. But before turning to that record, it is well to set before ourselves, once again, the Western conception of personal identity, which I want to suggest is absent in many other cultural contexts. This time, consider as a definition seminal for modern individualism that of John Locke, from the *Essay Concerning Human Understanding:* "The identity of the same *man* consists . . . in nothing but a participation of the same continued life, by constantly fleeting particles of matter, in succession vitally united to the same organized body."[9] Note that this definition includes the elements already discussed: a continuity over time that encompasses any change or variation thought to occur *within* the self-identical unit, which is itself packaged in a bounded physical body. Or, as Erving Goffman puts it, "the first point to note about biographies [or, for our purposes, personal identities] is that we assume that an individual can really have only one of them, this being guaranteed by the laws of physics rather than those of society."[10]

In consulting the ethnographic record, note, first, that Western notions of the boundedness of the human person, and of the dualisms used to express that boundedness—in other words, dualities of mind and body, mind and matter, person and world, natural reality and the supernatural— are frequently absent elsewhere. For example, Benjamin Lee Whorf notes that unlike Westerners, who imagine their thoughts to be enclosed in an inner space contained within their skulls, the Hopi (southwestern United States) consider that human thought acts routinely as a force in the outer world: "The Hopi thought-world has no imaginary space. The corollary to this is that it may not locate thought dealing with real space anywhere but in real space, nor insulate real space from the effects of thought. A Hopi would naturally suppose that his thought (or he himself) traffics with the . . . corn plant . . . that he is thinking about."[11]

To cite another North American example, Irving Hallowell reports that the category of the person among the Ojibwa of central Canada includes beings that Westerners would consider to be either supernatural, such as thunderbirds, or inanimate, such as stones. "I once asked an old man," Hallowell reports, "Are *all* the stones we see about us here alive? He reflected a long while and then replied, 'No! But *some* are.'" Hallowell goes on to describe how Ojibwa interact with beings whom we would consider to be supernatural, but whom Ojibwa see as part of their daily world. Like human individuals, thunderbirds, bears, and many other beings are imagined as persons, but personhood is not defined in terms of physical boundedness: "So far as appearance is concerned, there is no hard and fast line that can be drawn between an animal form and a human form because metamorphosis is possible."[12]

Despite their violation of Western conceptions of physical boundedness, these examples might be construed in such a way as to leave the notion of a unique inner person, or soul, intact. However, if we turn to various Eastern traditions, it is not difficult to find examples in which the soul itself has no unchanging identity. Writing on Hindu exchanges of goods and services, McKim Marriott argues that "Indian thought about transactions differs from much of Western . . . thought in not presuming the separability of actors from actions." Persons and other beings have "composite natures and power" that are constantly changing. Some beings, in some contexts, seek to maintain an achieved equilibrium, and monitor their ceremonial, culinary, and economic transactions with others accordingly. In other cases, people seek to transform themselves or are transformed against their wishes. Thus, Marriott notes,

> persons—single actors—are not thought in South Asia to be "individual," that is, indivisible, bounded units. . . . Instead, it appears that persons are generally thought by South Asians to be "dividual" or divisible. To exist, dividual persons absorb heterogeneous material influences. . . . Dividual persons, who must exchange in such ways, are therefore always composites of the substance-codes that they take in.[13]

As a final example, recall Clifford Geertz's classic essay on Balinese conceptions of personhood. Balinese personhood is "depersonalizing."[14] Geertz argues for this interpretation by examining Balinese systems of naming, kinship terminology, and status titles. For our purposes, we can review two of these systems, which will give us a sense of the ways in which Balinese blur boundaries that we consider to be natural and normal for human thought. Personal names, to take the first of these, are "arbitrarily coined nonsense syllables" that are rarely used and almost completely forgotten by the end of a person's life.[15] Thus the type of personal identification that is so crucial to us and which we find symbolized first of all in our personal names is lacking in Bali.

But lacking personal names, Balinese children are given birth order names. There are four such names, which indicate the first-, second-, third-, and fourth-born children. After the birth of a couple's fourth child, the cycle of terms repeats itself, so that a fifth-born child will be called, in effect, "first-born." Moreover, given high birthrates and high rates of infant mortality, a fourth-born child may be the oldest in a family of several children. And, given the lack of knowledge about personal names, all the children of Balinese villages are routinely addressed by the same four birth order names. This system of naming suggests, as Geertz interprets it,

> that for all procreating couples, births form a circular succession . . . , an endless four-stage replication of an imperishable form. Physically men come and go as the ephemerae they are, but socially the *dramatis personae* remain eternally the same as new [children] . . . emerge from the timeless world of the gods . . . to replace those who dissolve once more into it.[16]

Thus, as Geertz suggests, Balinese conceptions of the person work to mute or minimize the "idiosyncratic" details of personal biography that Westerners consider essential. There is no sense of an essential human personality that is continuous from birth to death. Rather, persons orient themselves to a divine and unchanging cosmic realm in which the details of an individual's unique personality have no importance.

It might perhaps be thought that these ethnographic examples of non-Western conceptions of personhood are irrelevant to the question of those *collective* identities that figure so prominently in nationalist ideologies and in social science. However, they are centrally relevant because, as I have argued elsewhere, following the work of Louis Dumont, Western notions of collectivity are grounded in individualist metaphors.[17] That is, collectivities in Western social theory are imagined as though they are human individuals writ large. The attributes of boundedness, continuity, uniqueness, and homogeneity that are ascribed to human persons are ascribed as well to social groups. Thus, it seems to me that if other cultures imagine personhood and human activity in terms other than those that we use, we should not expect them to rely on Western individualistic assumptions in describing social collectivities.

And, of course, they don't. Again we can turn to the ethnographic record to find worldviews in which social life is not conceptualized in terms of bounded social groups. Consider examples bearing on just one feature of social groups, their boundaries. We find, then, that boundedness, while by no means peculiar to the modern West, is often not a salient feature of social arenas in other cultural contexts. When, for example, Val Daniel asked Tamils to draw maps of their villages, he found that "the drawing began not with the periphery of the village but at its center." From the villagers' perspective, villages were not surrounded by a boundary line but by "shrines and intersecting roads that mark the vulnerable points along the village frontier."[18] And Geertz notes that in the classical Balinese negara, or state, rulers competed for the allegiance of men, not for territory. Indeed, any village was made up of neighbors whose allegiances were divided among many competing overlords. Linear boundaries were simply not relevant, a point which Geertz illustrates with the following anecdote:

The Dutch, who wanted . . . to get the boundary between two petty prince-doms straight once and for all, called in the princes concerned and asked them where indeed the borders lay. Both agreed that the border of princedom A lay at the farthest point from which a man could still see the swamps, and the border of princedom B lay at the point from which a man could still see the sea. Had they, then, never fought over the land between, from which one could see neither swamp nor sea? "Mijnheer," one of the old princes replied, "we had much better reasons to fight with one another than these shabby hills."[19]

III

I mentioned before that "identity" as a scholarly concept has escaped critical scrutiny. What is needed, it seems to me, is an account of the intellectual history of this term, a project well begun by the historian Philip Gleason. Gleason notes that identity "came into use as a popular social-science term only in the 1950s" and quotes the immigrant psychoanalyst Erik Erikson, who explained that his development of the term grew out of "the experience of emigration, immigration, and Americanization." How-ever, in writing his essay on "American Identity and Americanization" for the *Harvard Encyclopedia of American Ethnic Groups,* Gleason saw fit to use identity "interchangeably with 'American nationality' and 'American character.'" Moreover, Gleason employs all three terms in reference to two hundred years of American history. He thereby presupposes that our cur-rent understanding of boundedness and individuality is unproblematically relevant to earlier phases of modern Western history.[20]

Yet it is just this presupposition that I question. Moreover, it seems to me that historically oriented ethnographers and ethnographically informed historians are in a position to explore, first, the utility of the term "iden-tity" for the analysis of various contexts within the history of the modern world and, second, the precise notions of boundedness, continuity, and agency that people of varying eras and social positions attached to their understanding of human activity. To suggest what I have in mind, let me develop an example based on an anthropological analysis of Jane Austen's novels that Daniel Segal and I have completed.[21] Writing at the turn of the nineteenth century, Austen depicted a world that is closely related to our own, yet also, in certain respects, less "individualistic." To explore how "identity" and related concepts figure in that world will sensitize us to the peculiarities of our own discourse about identity.

The first thing to note about identity in Jane Austen's novels is that, to the best of my knowledge, the word is never used. When Austen's narrators or characters talk about what we would today call identity, they use such words as family, friends, connections, and relations. Consider the follow-ing two examples. In the first, the heroine, Anne Elliott, insists on visiting

Mrs. Smith, an old school friend who has fallen on hard times. She does so despite the objections of her sister, Elizabeth, and her father, Sir Walter, both of whom are depicted throughout the novel as being foolishly obsessed with matters of social rank:

> [T]here were questions enough asked, to make it understood what this old schoolfellow was; and Elizabeth was disdainful, and Sir Walter severe.
>
> "Westgate-Buildings!" said he; "and who is Miss Anne Elliott to be visiting in Westgate-Buildings?—A Mrs. Smith. A widow Mrs. Smith,—and who was her husband? One of the five thousand Mr. Smiths whose names are to be met with every where. And what is her attraction? That she is old and sickly.— Upon my word, Miss Anne Elliott, you have the most extraordinary taste!"[22]

In the second example, the snobbish heroine, Emma, reflects on a woman about to be married into the local community. Emma has reason in advance to dislike the woman, for her husband-to-be, Mr. Elton, had snubbed Emma's protégé, Harriet Smith, whom he considered to be beneath himself in social worth:

> Of the lady, individually, Emma thought very little. . . . *What* she was, must be uncertain; but *who* she was, might be found out; and setting aside the 10,000 pounds it did not appear that she was at all Harriet's superior. She brought no name, no blood, no alliance. Miss Hawkins was the youngest of the two daughters of a Bristol—merchant, of course, he must be called. . . . [And] though the father and mother had died some years ago, an uncle remained—in the law line—nothing more distinctly honourable was hazarded of him, than that he was in the law line; and with him the daughter had lived. Emma guessed him to be the drudge of some attorney, and too stupid to rise. And all the grandeur of the connection seemed dependent on the elder sister, who was *very well married*, to a gentleman in a *great way*, near Bristol, who kept two carriages! That was the wind-up of the history; that was the glory of Miss Hawkins.[23]

In both these passages, an explicit distinction is drawn between "what" and "who" a person is. The "what" of a person seems to refer to characteristics of appearance, manner, mind, and situation that have been ascertained from personal experience of the person in question. Emma muses that she cannot *yet* know what Miss Hawkins is, for she has neither met her nor heard a reliable report about her from someone who knows her. Sir Walter and Elizabeth learn enough about Mrs. Smith from questioning Anne about the details of her situation to claim to be able to know what Mrs. Smith is.

By contrast, the "who" of a person clearly refers to a web of social relations that places the individual in question with respect to family, connections, and social rank. Note that "who" a person is can be narrated in terms of what today would be considered a rather lengthy list of relations and connections. We are told not merely of Miss Hawkins's mother and father, but of her uncle, her uncle's employer, her sister, and her brother-in-law.

This sort of extended narration of family connections is used in the opening paragraphs of all six of Austen's novels. Moreover, only one of her six novels is named for its central character (*Emma*). Two of the six are named after family estates (*Mansfield Park, Northanger Abbey*), and the titles of the remaining three name moral qualities or actions (*Sense and Sensibility, Pride and Prejudice,* and *Persuasion*). It is true that, like most novels, Austen's profoundly explore the character and consciousness of individual protagonists; as Ian Watt has remarked, the novel as a literary form is historically linked to the emergence of bourgeois individualism and self-consciousness.[24] Nonetheless, there are varieties and degrees of individualism, and Austen's novels are interesting with respect to the question of identity precisely because they inscribe a world in which individuality is complexly balanced with the nonindividualistic social forms of rank and the patriarchal family.

This balance between individualism and social ties can be illustrated with a brief discussion of rank. Social hierarchy in Austen's world is conceptualized in terms of "independence" and "dependence." To be independent is to be governed only by one's own will—in other words, to have the power as an individual to make choices and to be governed by those choices alone. By contrast, to be dependent is to be governed by the will of others—to have others either choose for one, or to be oneself the choice of others. These two possibilities are ranked: it is better to be independent than dependent, "better to chuse than to be chosen"—for it is better to be an individual who can, to borrow Louis Dumont's term, "encompass" others than to be an incomplete person who depends upon superiors.[25] Indeed, in the Austen texts, a person dependent upon another is included within the latter's social identity and is, thus, not fully a person in his or her own right. As C. B. Macpherson has argued in his analysis of English political theory, to be dependent upon another is to be incomplete as a human being.[26] By contrast, to be independent of others is to achieve the apex of civil society and to have the greatest power to order society hierarchically.

The cultural distinction between independent and dependent persons is most unambiguously expressed in the relationship between masters and servants. The latter are often discussed as objects of property rather than as persons. For instance, in a conversation about the relative merits of indoor and outdoor parties, Mr. Knightley of *Emma* argues: "The nature and the simplicity of gentlemen and ladies, with their servants and furniture, I think is best observed by meals within doors."[27]

Of course, hierarchy in Austen's social world is too complex to be re-duced to a binary opposition between masters and servants. Most individ-uals find themselves independent in relation to some—that is, above them—and dependent upon, or beneath, some others. But the categorical superiority of independence over dependence is stated unequivocally by most of the characters, even in cases where the independence is relative. As Mr. Knightley says: "when it comes to the question of dependence or independence . . . it must be better to have only one to please, than two."[28] The distinction between masters and servants powerfully, but crudely, il-lustrates what is more subtly articulated in such diverse social features as age and generation, sex and marital status, and relations to property and production—all of which are commonly structured by, and understood in terms of, the recurring cultural distinction between independence and dependence.

Finally, we must recognize a fundamental irony, if not tension, within the ideology of independence: to attain independence is not to isolate oneself from others (that is, to be truly independent and separate), but to create particular relationships in which one's choices dominate or override those of others. Independence, then, is a relationship between two or more, and not—contrary to the professed cultural model—a property or essence within a person or even a patriline.[29]

IV

What is the significance of this excursion into the novels of Jane Austen and the ethnographic record for our understanding of the term "identity"? First, the absence of the twentieth-century notion of identity from the worlds surveyed in these literatures is a crucial fact. We cannot simply appropriate from our own, mid-twentieth-century discourse the term "identity" to use as a cross-cultural analytic operator. People in Austen's world, and many other people from even more distant times and places, do *not* use the concept of identity as we do, or at all; nor do they understand human personhood and social collectivities in terms of what identity im-plies. Our examination of these other worldviews should give us occasion to recognize what is peculiar in our own discourse rather than to discover elsewhere what we imagine to be the universality of our own ways of thinking.

Second, the use of the concept of identity is particularly unhelpful, it seems to me, in scholarly analyses of ethnic or nationalist activism, his-torical preservation, and the creation of tradition. Ethnic leaders and ministries of culture around the globe speak in terms of protecting and en-hancing national identities by way of heritage preservation, language legis-lation, cultural festivals, and many other actions and policies.[30] This discourse on identity, though global, is recent. It testifies more to the rapid spread of hegemonic ideas about modernity and ethnicity than it does to the universality of collective concerns about identity. Yet, as I have suggested above, we as scholarly analysts cannot effectively scrutinize public discourses (such as those on the politics of identity) without separating ourselves, as much as is consciously possible, from their implicit premises. To do otherwise is to risk merely reproducing—or, worse yet, celebrating in a scientistic jargon that too frequently legitimizes what it names—an ideology of identity from which we should, I believe, distance ourselves.[31]

Yet, to distance ourselves epistemologically from ideologies of identity is a politically delicate task, for many of the claimants to collective identity whose cultural philosophy we may dispute are nonetheless peoples whose struggles for social justice we support. Indeed, it is no wonder that political and cultural leaders everywhere have learned to phrase claims for international recognition in the language of identity: that is a language the empowered understand. Whether claimants believe their rhetoric is perhaps beside the point. But we cannot ignore the potential political consequences of our attempts to deconstruct identity claims.

On the one hand, to deconstruct notions of cultural identity at precisely the moment when the disempowered turn to them may aid the reactionary social forces who seek to reassert the validity of homogeneous "mainstream" collective identities against proponents of "multicultural" diversity.[32] On the other hand, to support without criticism identity claims is to aid in the reproduction of an ideology that is both hegemonic and, I believe, oppressive.

There is no easy resolution to this dilemma, but two tactics can help. First, we can make sure that our critiques of identity focus on those mainstream claims that too often go unchallenged. In other words, rather than writing exclusively of the "invention" of minority identities, traditions, and cultures, we can turn our attention to the ways in which the majority or mainstream is itself continually reconstructed and reimagined as a homogeneous cultural entity. But, second, we must learn to argue civilly about identity and culture with "minorities" whose oppression we deplore. Such discussions are crucial, for a renewed politics of cultural diversity cannot be built on the old epistemology of identity, no matter whose homogeneous cultural identity is successfully asserted in the end.

NOTES

1. 1971 ed., p. 1368.
2. Kristian Kristiansen, "Perspectives on the Archaeological Heritage: History and Future," in *Archaeological Heritage Management in the Modern World*, ed. Henry F. Cleere (London, 1989), 24.

3. Paul Gagnon, ed., *Historical Literacy: The Case for History in American Education* (New York, 1989), 22, 24.

4. Mazen Saah, "Denied Identity," *Seasons* (University of Virginia Multicultural Journal) 4 [1] (1990), 28.

5. Richard Handler, *Nationalism and the Politics of Culture in Quebec* (Madison, 1988); Daniel Segal, "Nationalism, Comparatively Speaking," *Journal of Historical Sociology* 1 [3] (1988), 300–321.

6. Roy Wagner, *The Invention of Culture* (Englewood Cliffs, NJ, 1975); Eric Hobsbawm and Terence Ranger, eds., *The Invention of Tradition* (Cambridge, 1983).

7. James Clifford, *The Predicament of Culture* (Cambridge, 1988), 10. For a report in the popular press on anthropology's new wisdom, see John Noble Wilford, "Anthropology Seen as Father of Maori Lore," *New York Times*, February 20, 1990, B1, B8.

8. Paul Heelas and Andrew Lock, eds., *Indigenous Psychologies: The Anthropology of the Self* (London, 1981); E. Valentine Daniel, *Fluid Signs: Being a Person the Tamil Way* (Berkeley, 1984); Richard Shweder and Edmund Bourne, "Does the Concept of the Person Vary Cross-Culturally?" in *Culture Theory: Essays on Mind, Self, and Emotion*, ed. Shweder and R. A. LeVine (Cambridge, 1984), 158–199; Michael Carrithers, Steven Collins, and Steven Lukes, eds., *The Category of the Person* (Cambridge, 1985); Alan Roland, *In Search of Self in India and Japan* (Princeton, 1988); Katherine P. Ewing, "The Illusion of Wholeness: Culture, Self, and the Experience of Inconsistency," *Ethnos* 18 (September 1990), 251–278.

9. John Locke, *An Essay Concerning Human Understanding*, ed. A. D. Woozley (Cleveland, 1964 [1690]), 210.

10. Erving Goffman, *Stigma* (Englewood Cliffs, NJ, 1963), 62.

11. Benjamin Lee Whorf, "The Relation of Habitual Thought and Behavior to Language," in *Language, Thought, and Reality* (Cambridge, 1956), 150.

12. A. Irving Hallowell, "Ojibwa Ontology, Behavior, and World View," in *Contributions to Anthropology: Selected Papers of A. Irving Hallowell* (Chicago, 1976), 362, 376.

13. McKim Marriott, "Hindu Transactions: Diversity without Dualism," in *Transaction and Meaning*, ed. Bruce Kapferer (Philadelphia, 1976), 109–111.

14. Clifford Geertz, "Person, Time, and Conduct in Bali," in *The Interpretation of Cultures* (New York, 1973), 390.

15. Ibid., 369–370.

16. Ibid., 371–372.

17. Handler, *Nationalism and the Politics of Culture*, 32–47; Louis Dumont, "Religion, Politics, and Society in the Individualistic Universe," *Proceedings of the Royal Anthropological Institute* (1970), 31–45.

18. Daniel, *Fluid Signs*, 74–78.

19. Clifford Geertz, *Negara: The Theatre State in Nineteenth-Century Bali* (Princeton, 1980), 24–25.

20. Philip Gleason, "Identifying Identity: A Semantic History," *Journal of American History* 69 (March 1983), 910; "American Identity and Americanization," in *Harvard Encyclopedia of American Ethnic Groups* (Cambridge, 1980), 31.

21. Richard Handler and Daniel Segal, *The Fiction of Culture: Jane Austen and the Narration of Social Realities* (Tucson, 1990).

22. Jane Austen, *Persuasion,* vol. 5, *The Novels of Jane Austen,* 3rd ed., ed. R. W. Chapman (Oxford, 1933), 157.

23. Jane Austen, *Emma,* vol. 4, *The Novels of Jane Austen,* 3rd ed., ed. R. W. Chapman (Oxford, 1933), 183.

24. Ian Watt, *The Rise of the Novel* (Berkeley, 1957).

25. Austen, *Emma,* 17; Louis Dumont, *Homo Hierarchicus* (Chicago, 1970), xii.

26. C. B. Macpherson, *The Political Theory of Possessive Individualism: Hobbes to Locke* (Oxford, 1962).

27. Austen, *Emma,* 355.

28. Ibid., 10.

29. The last three paragraphs are drawn from Richard Handler and Daniel Segal, "Hierarchies of Choice: The Social Construction of Rank in Jane Austen," *American Ethnologist* 12 (November 1985), 692–693.

30. For representative writing in this mode, see Henry F. Cleere, ed., *Archaeological Heritage Management in the Modern World* (London, 1989); Yudhishthir Raj Isar, ed., *The Challenge to Our Cultural Heritage* (Washington, DC, 1986).

31. Handler, *Nationalism and the Politics of Culture,* 6–9.

32. Eric Gable, Richard Handler, and Anna Lawson, "On the Uses of Relativism: Fact, Conjecture, and Black and White Histories at Colonial Williamsburg," *American Ethnologist* 19 (November 1992), 791–805.

Chapter II

IDENTITY, HERITAGE, AND HISTORY

David Lowenthal

THE CONCEPTS of identity and heritage long antedate the conjoined usage of these terms today. In the past, identity referred not to self-consciousness but to likeness, and heritage was mainly a matter of family legacies. In the present, these terms swim in a self-congratulatory swamp of collective memory. Heritage now is that with which we all individually or collectively identify. It is considered the rightful (though sometimes unwelcome) legacy of every distinct people.

How these identities resemble or differ from one another is, however, poorly and, in the main, only anecdotally known. The global amalgamation of identity and heritage does not facilitate cross-cultural comparisons. Indeed, modes of national-cum-individual identity tend to be incommensurable even *within* traditional Western communities, because the essential mystique of heritage renders each group's separate identity by definition incomparable.

Heritage addresses common needs and embodies common traits the world over. But the needs are defined and the traits cherished by chauvinist jealousy. We confront one another armored in identities whose likenesses we ignore or disown and whose differences we distort or invent to emphasize our own superior worth. Lauding our own legacies and excluding or discrediting those of others, we commit ourselves to endemic rivalry and conflict.

I

The psychic and social implications of identity in earlier epochs are largely a matter of conjecture. Evidence from memoirs and from wills suggests that pre-Enlightenment folk were generally enjoined to submerge personal in favor of collective consciousness, both of the social hierarchy and of the chain of progenitors and descendants to which they belonged. An account of William Marshal, seneschal to Plantagenet kings, underscores the primacy of family identity in thirteenth-century feudal England, with clan fealty almost wholly submerging individuality.[1]

Residues of such relational emphases echo in Virginia Woolf's account of her half brothers' upbringing at the turn of this century. Stamped and molded by patriarchal expectations, men were fated to assume generically ascribed roles in school, at university, and in their careers. "Every one of our male relations was shot into that machine and came out at the other end, at the age of sixty or so, a Headmaster, an Admiral, a Cabinet Minister, a Judge." No trace of individuality or private will was permitted to interfere with this lockstep march to a preordained destiny.[2]

Well into the 1930s the same prototype still dominated elite Westminster School, as "a system in which boys were educated for the express purpose of belonging to a career such as politics or the law."[3] An analogous eclipse of individual identity features a prize-winning novel's postwar protagonist butler; so effaced by his sense of duty is his personal identity that the unpropitious hour of his father's demise keeps him from the deathbed.[4]

Explicit assertions of selfhood—Saint Augustine's is paradigmatic—are rare until Rousseau. And not until the latter half of the nineteenth century did the individualism associated with bourgeois *mentalité* bring the rewards of Franklinesque self-fashioning to substantial numbers.[5] Yet we should be wary of assuming, simply from the absence of explicit avowals, that individual identity was unknown or inconsequential. In the small, relatively self-contained communities that housed most preindustrial peoples, individual self-consciousness may simply have gone unrecorded.

Alternatively, their voices may have been stilled as antipathetic to group solidarity, as still happens in many peripheral and isolated societies.[6] Only for strangers do we need to produce individual life stories, in order to justify our presence or our participation. In communities where individuals largely remember in common and gaps in shared memory are few, mutual lifelong familiarities and daily gossip leave little space for the presentation of self in everyday life.[7]

II

Like identity, heritage is today a realm of well-nigh universal concern. It betokens interest in manifold pasts—family history, buildings and landmarks, prehistory and antiques, music and paintings, plants and animals, language and folklore—ranging from remote to recent times. So widespread and fast growing is such interest that heritage defies definition. Indeed, the term celebrates every conceivable thing and theme: anchorites and anoraks, Berlin and Bengal, conkers and castles, dog breeds and dental fillings, finials and fax machines, gorgonzola and goalposts are topics typical of a thousand recent books entitled *Heritage of* _____. Pervading life and thought as never before, heritage suffuses attitudes toward everything.

A term vested with so much virtue, and often peddled as such, inevitably attracts odium. All the rage, heritage likewise enrages critics who deplore its overuse, ready perversion, arrant chauvinism, or bland emptiness. They assail the "heritage industry" for turning history into escapist nostalgia.[8]

These charges have some force. Yet heritage is still the term that best denotes our inescapable dependence on the past. What we inherit is integral to our being. Without memory and tradition we could neither function now nor plan ahead. For all but amnesiacs, heritage distills the past into icons of identity, bonding us with precursors and progenitors, with our own earlier selves, and with our promised successors.

III

Heritage has always obsessed those fortunate enough to have it. But very few in most past societies could hope to be so rich or powerful. The properties and positions these few inherited and bequeathed symbolized their elevated social place. To be sure, others too were left or acquired chattels, skills, attachments to kinfolk and masters, codes of behavior and morality. But this was not seen as "heritage"; heritage was exclusive to princes and prelates, magnates and merchants.

Heritage thus circumscribed differed in makeup and meaning from what it now is. It then explicitly endowed its possessors with sovereignty over others' lands and lives, and lent permanence to power and privilege. The spiritual realm echoed the secular: relics and regalia played a like emblematic role. Heritage was not only what rulers were entitled to; it defined them and assured their rule. And its loss spelled impotence.

Echoes of these older modes of heritage can yet be heard. Possession of the Stone of Scone still validates British sovereignty and accounts for its episodic kidnapping by Scottish Nationalists. English manorial lordships now devoid of tangible perquisites nonetheless remain prestigious, as their lucrative sale attests. But such functions of heritage are mainly obsolete; others now supersede them.

The reason is patent. Heritage is no longer confined to the rich and the powerful; it now belongs to everyone. To be sure, populism has not made us all equal: some inherit much, others little or nothing; some rule, others submit. But more *do* inherit. And heritage also now embraces things and ideas that give us *collective* identity.

Inclusive notions of heritage prevail even where disparities of wealth and power are extreme. Few individuals expect sizable material or even spiritual legacies. But most now are normally conceded a full share of the communal heritage. Heritage in this sense has become a defining trait of ethnic and territorial groups, above all of national states.

Formerly elite, heritage is now popular. But populism alters both its makeup and its meaning. Norms and forms that once entailed family property and power through the generations have weakened: three centuries ago four-fifths of English realty was so constrained; today less than one-fifth is, and land is a diminishing fraction of inherited wealth.

Heritage remains metaphorically ancestral. But the main function of blood ties today is to confirm the identity and boost the solidarity of nations and self-assured ethnic groups.[9] Stigmatized minorities find their racially ascribed identity little bettered by modern ethnic chic. Approaching the Mexican-American writer Richard Rodriguez "cautiously, as if I were a stone totem," a Berkeley student said "with no discernable trace of irony, 'God, it must be cool to be related to Aztecs.'"[10] Aztec or African, such ancestors nonetheless carry weight. Alex Haley's *Roots* and the ensuing black American ancestral quest are the *fons et origo* of the current cult of ethnic heritage.

IV

Needed by and thought the rightful legacy of everyone, heritage displays increasingly universal traits and trends. Its ideals and aims converge from culture to culture, country to country, class to class. People the world over refer to aspects of their heritage in the same way. Although they stress quite distinctive histories and traditions, these evince similar concerns with precedence, antiquity, continuity, coherence, heroism, sacrifice. Even when exalting unique heroes and virtues, different peoples celebrate success, stability, progress in much the same way.

Heritage categories—legend and language, landscape and history, archaeology and architecture, art and antiquities—are likewise homogenized. If exotic dragonflies and endangered dialects have yet to join Derain and Degas in Sotheby sales books, their collectors and would-be saviors talk the same heritage lingo. The worth of unique relics of nature and culture is similarly gauged in Australia and Amazonia, New Mexico and New Guinea. And intangible no less than material aspects of heritage have become international commodities.

Global interdependence likewise makes heritage universal. The legacy of nature—ecosystems and gene pools, fresh water and fossil fuels—is common to all, and requires the care of all. Exploitative technology diminishes and noxious residues despoil a natural legacy whose stewardship requires worldwide action.

The world's cultural legacies also belong in some measure to all its inhabitants jointly. The heritage of myriad culture hearths enriches not only those realms' genetic descendants and political heirs; it enhances lives wherever those discoveries and creations are disseminated and emulated. Classical Greek architectural and poetic heritages, biblical and Confucian precepts, suffuse the consciousness of every continent.

Unique national features are likewise valued as universal heritage. Convinced that the loss of Kathmandu or Karnak, Avebury or the Acropolis, would impoverish not just their parent lands but all of us, member states of the World Heritage Organization collectively designate outstanding heritage sites. Global citation attests their universal fame and secures international safeguards.

The growth of concern about identity, and the concomitant pursuit of "heritage" now felt required to sustain it, are ingrained into individual and collective awareness the world over. Self-identification in such terms is now as commonplace outside as within Euro-America. The Westernized identities deployed by non-Western collectivities are perhaps more crucial to their self-images than are attempts to resuscitate pride in their antecedent "native" cultures. The erosion of viable alternative modes of self-construction may seem regrettable, but it cannot be denied that a personalized Western sense of identity is now adopted and internalized right around the world.

Three examples illustrate how Western concepts of identity and heritage are superseding other cultural values. One is the saga of the Ekpu, wooden figurines that the Oron people of southeast Nigeria erected outside their dwellings. Once venerated ancestor carvings, these pieces were later taken into a local museum, became trophies and victims of conflict during the Nigerian Civil War, were clandestinely exported to Western collectors, and have at length emerged as symbols of Nigerian national identity. The Ekpu became valuable at the national level in Nigeria largely because these vicissitudes had drawn global attention to them. But their transition from local ritual use to global art objects and icons of national pride is typical of how items of symbolic value become globally commodified and reified in Western terms.[11]

The international campaign for cultural restitution provides a second illustration. Attachments to national heritage have everywhere intensified efforts to keep it in place or to secure its return. Originally a focus of nineteenth-century European nationalism, antiquities are now prime symbols of collective identity all over the world. Architectural and other material manifestations of heritage augment identity and community self-esteem in every state. A rich and representative patrimony is held to promote citizenship, to catalyze creativity, to attract foreign sympathy, and to enhance all aspects of national life.[12]

Sovereignty modeled on European and American nationalisms leads Third and Fourth World states to emphasize material relics as icons of group identity. To validate ancestral antecedents, former colonies grub for tangible roots among relics still held in Western collections. The Algerian chairman of the UNESCO committee charged with this mission saw "the restitution and return of cultural property [as] one of the key problems of the Third World."[13]

46   DAVID LOWENTHAL

The ex-colonial rhetoric of this crusade is implicitly anti-European: "The vicissitudes of history have . . . robbed many peoples of a priceless portion of [their] inheritance in which their enduring identity finds its embodiment." Former imperial states should relinquish these cultural treasures to "enable a people to recover part of its memory and identity."[14] However, the underlying rationale is wholly Western; European notions of national identity and heritage are always deployed. "Despite often bitter disagreements," notes Handler, "the disputants in contemporary 'culture wars' share an understanding of what cultural property is; . . . current, would-be, and former imperialists, as well as oppressed minorities, ex-colonies, and aspiring new nations—have agreed to a world view in which culture has come to be represented as and by 'things'."[15]

My third illustration shows how minorities adopt the dominant Western paradigm even in asserting the distinctive virtues of their own racial and ethnic identities. Arguing that others besides WASP Founding Fathers contributed significantly to the making of America, minority students at Stanford University campaigned successfully to restructure the compulsory "Western Culture" course (now "Cultures, Ideas, and Values") to include exemplary figures from their own backgrounds.

This shift of emphasis did add to the canon heretofore neglected works by women, blacks, and other "minorities." But it also reinforced the Western individualistic tradition. Saul Bellow's taunt at effort to raise minority self-esteem—"Who is the Tolstoy of the Zulus, the Proust of the Papuans?"—cannot be countered by searching for such heroes, but only by rejecting the enterprise itself as part and parcel of the Western perspective. Idealizing individual creativity and innovation is only Western culture's normative tradition, not a universal value. But it is a perspective more and more internalized among cultures and minorities the world over.

V

Heritage thus reflects ever more widely shared values. But it is at the same time invincibly unique. To forge identity and buttress self-esteem, each people vaunts or invents a distinctive legacy. Many assert their heritage's moral or military, mental or material superiority; many others claim exclusive rights to heritage traits and emblems they consider crucial to their identity. Both types of claim mirror stereotypes that arrogate virtue to us and deny it to others: *we* are civilized and steadfast; *they* are barbarian and fanatical, or primitive and blind.

Most heritage reflects personal or communal self-interest. Things are valued as *my* heritage or *our* heritage; we may be modest about what we *are*, but rarely about what we *were*. Even a shameful past may earn self-admiration for facing up to it. In celebrating symbols of their histories, societies in fact worship themselves.[16]

Exclusive to us, *our* past is unlike anyone else's. Its uniqueness vaunts our own superiority. Admirers may fruitfully adopt our legacy, but priority gives us prime rights in it; English remains for the English *their* language, a bit tarnished by dissemination abroad. Heritage *distinguishes* us from others; it gets passed on only to descendants, to our own flesh and blood; newcomers, outsiders, foreigners all erode or debase it.[17]

This collective heritage functions much like that of hereditary elites, who first delineated and often still monopolize it. "Objects attesting to nobility . . . cannot be acquired either by proxy or in haste." Treasured antiques, fine wines, hunting skills—"these competences are ancient, they can be learned only slowly, they can be enjoyed only by those who take their time, they manifest a concern for things that last." As Paul Connerton concludes, such "ceremonial avocations affirm the principle of hereditary transmission."[18]

Thus the English National Trust's impeccably run country houses highlight continuity by encouraging aristocratic former owners to stay on as chatelains. Only the old elite can be trusted to cherish beauty as social stability. When hard-up aristocrats were advised to give way to the new rich, Lord Saye and Sele of Broughton Castle characteristically responded: "Do you think that by removing us from here, and installing a *nouveau riche* family, the heritage would be maintained in the way that *we* maintain it? Do you think they would want to open their Peter Jones–furnished houses to the Public?"[19] Genealogical snobbery sustains both the heritage and the tourist industry.

Each group's heritage is by definition incomparable. The past we prize is domestic; those of foreign lands are alien and incompatible with ours. National identity requires both having a heritage and thinking it unique. It is heritage that *differentiates* us; we treasure most what sets us apart.

The rationale of their heritage supremacy was exemplified for the English by the historian Herbert Butterfield. In 1931 he had demolished Whig history, the habit of viewing modern England as the culmination of centuries of progress;[20] thirteen years later, in the dark days of the Second World War, Butterfield recanted to extol traditionalism:

> English institutions have century upon century of the past, lying fold upon fold within them. . . . Because we English have maintained the threads between past and present we do not, like some younger states, have to go hunting for our own personalities. We do not have to set about the deliberate manufacture of a national consciousness, or to strain ourselves, like the Irish, . . . to create a "nationalism" out of the broken fragments of tradition, out of the ruins of a tragic past. . . . Our history is here and active, giving meaning to the present.[21]

Heritage uniqueness is daily celebrated by every great power (as I wrote this Britain was lauded for having "enjoyed sovereignty on as absolute a scale as it has ever existed"[22]). Steeped in eccentricities that make their heritage incomprehensible to the rest of the world, the French likewise assume France is a font of universal emulation.[23]

Britons convinced that their heritage is utterly unique take special pride in knowing and caring so little about others. Tracing English separatism to thirteenth-century efforts to purge England of foreign influences and a "stubborn desire to manage its own affairs in its own way," a historian a century ago applauded the "long-standing . . . air of condescension towards foreigners." Brits opposing Napoleon were said to share the "happy privileges and advantage" of a common birthright that distinguished them "from every other people upon the earth." Uniquely content with his own ways and "not particularly sensitive to the opinion of others," the Englishman "labours under a defective sympathy with other institutions than his own."[24] Emerson found the English so sure of their preeminence as to be "provokingly incurious about other nations."[25]

Willful ignorance of others extends to the heritage of recent British immigrants. Britons of Indian and West Indian descent seek in vain to add their own backgrounds to school curricula. As one Brit responds to such multicultural pleas, "if people feel proud of their identity and rich in their cultural inheritance, why should they . . . want to spend time learning about those of others?"[26]

To be sure, no heritage is wholly immune to outside judgment. German national identity today is being reforged under the scrutiny of a world still traumatized by the uniquely unspeakable Nazi past. Germans' sense of heritage reflects these memories along with their own half-century of efforts to overcome oblivion and disbelief. A heritage ignored or mocked by outsiders—Basque, Breton, Cornish, Occitan—may lose credibility at home. But most group heritage pays little heed to outsiders' views and indeed asserts pride in being inscrutable.

Other collectivities each have their own special identities, valued for their unique attributes; but they are all similarly deficient in being unlike us. Our identity and its expression in our heritage are real, authentic, unselfconscious; those of others—to the extent we know them at all—strike us as partial, pastiche, contrived.

The mystique of superior uniqueness is not, however, exclusive to great nation-states or even to lesser sovereignties. Populist and underdog legacies are no less incomparable. The deprived, like the privileged, care most for what they think unique in *their* heritage, special to them, unknowable by outsiders. Bereft of place and power, land and language, they may doubly cherish a glorified past as all they have left. Hence the claims that only blacks can do black history, only Scots understand Scottish life, only women should write about women. Whatever feels distinctive to any group becomes a jealously *un*shared possession. Were it open to others it would forfeit its value as an emblem of solidarity. By extension, the heritage of others is little known. We are necessarily as ignorant of other peoples' heritage as they of ours.

This is the crux of what distinguishes heritage from history. To serve as a collective symbol heritage must be widely accepted by insiders, yet inaccessible to outsiders. Its data are social, not scientific. Socially binding traditions must be accepted on faith, not by reasoning. Heritage thus defies empirical analysis; it features fantasy, invention, mystery, error.

The quintessential avowal of English uniqueness comes from a former Conservative Party chairman:

> As different as our Continental neighbours are from each other, we are even more different from each of them. . . . These fundamental differences have developed from, and in turn fostered, a sense of nationality and social cohesion that has saved us not only from foreign conquest but violent revolution and civil strife too. Our nationalism is of a different kind to much of that on the Continent.[27]

Britain may not be uniquely unique. But a French observer finds "no country more consistently *bent upon* differing from others."[28]

German heritage is unique for other reasons, as noted above. Since the Third Reich Germans have taken less pride in national heritage than most,[29] but German self-doubt is also historically rooted. Nineteenth-century nationalists seeking a German identity seized on sundry models, in turn cosmopolitan France (through immigrant Huguenots), universal classical Greece, and imperial Britain, even adopting others' heroes (Washington, Napoleon, Gustavus Adolphus).

"The German nation has no national character in the way that other nations have," claimed the philosopher Bogumib Goltz in 1860; instead it "unites all the characteristic properties, talents and virtues of all countries." Hence Germans claimed to have made themselves as hardworking as the Chinese, as thorough as the English, as skilled and elegant as the French, better musicians than the Italians, avid nature lovers like Poles and Hungarians. Such borrowings persisted down to the 1936 Olympics, where officials exhorted Germans to "be more charming than Parisians, more vital than Russians, more practical than New Yorkers."[30]

Not until the late nineteenth century did the German national heritage, termed by Nietzsche "more intangible, incalculable and undefinable than any other,"[31] emphasize the mystique of racial purity that resonated from Wagner through Hitler. Unable to revivify Germany, Wagner fantasized transplanting the Teutonic heritage overseas: "Like Wotan to Alberich, the Old World can say to America: 'Take my heritage!'"[32] That obsessive borrowing and neurotic insecurity themselves endangered German nationality, Treitschke a century ago made Germans agonizingly aware. Post-

Holocaust identity doubts and heritage qualms are symptomatic of post-modern Western heritage crises in general, yet again they also constitute uniquely German dilemmas.[33]

Thus while "some nations are prouder and more jealously attached to their past grandeur than others, [each one] is persuaded it has contributed in a decisive manner to Europe (and the world's) civilization." Hence, adds Luigi Barzini, "each of them clings to the memory of its glorious past, and mounts guard, jealously and suspiciously, over its unique heritage."[34]

Nations are unique not only in what they choose to remember but in what they feel forced to forget. The heritage of tragedy may well be more effective than that of triumph: "suffering in common unifies more than joy does," wrote Renan over a century ago. "Where national memories are concerned, griefs are of more value than triumphs, for they impose duties, and require a common effort." Yet Renan also believed that communal identity required forgetting many shameful episodes, disabling tragedies, conflicting loyalties; "every French citizen has to have forgotten the massacre of St Bartholemew, or the massacres that took place in the Midi in the 13th century."[35]

Like modes of memorialization, forms of amnesia differ from state to state. "Every nation edits its own past," explains a Portuguese historian:

> But we're not skilled with cosmetics like the Americans, nor in self-censorship like the Russians. The aggressive amnesia of the Germans doesn't appeal to us either. Our specialty is the invocation of shadows . . . the same old film playing THE LOST EMPIRE . . . We have never recovered and are unable to forget it. Only somehow we can't quite remember the massacres we carried out . . . If you switch off the light in a room, you see . . . its afterimage on the retina. That is our situation with the lost colonial empire.[36]

So demanding are national attachments to identity that they often leave little room for individual, local, or regional heritage. Emphasis on Polish national identity is so intense that many Poles feel deprived of psychic attachments at any other level; some young people have gone so far as to seek out Buddhism as an acceptable refuge from all-engulfing national patriotism.[37]

Among my academic colleagues in the early 1960s most had no notion who their great-grandparents were; many did not even know the names of grandparents. Told that most Americans had a pretty good idea of all their forebears back to their arrival in the New World, they responded, "Well, we don't need genealogical fetishes; we have a secure *national* identity." Subsequently diminished pride in nationhood may partly explain why so many British now emulate Americans in searching out forebears.

Today's plethora of nationalist claims blinds us to historical circumstances in which national origins were not always a matter for congratulation. For example, ancient Greeks sometimes denied their own heritage. In exposing the inventions of Eurocentric scholars for whom Greece *had* to be Aryan, not Oriental or African, Martin Bernal underscores numerous classical North African and Asian affinities; he reminds us that Herodotus himself ascribed Egyptian origins to many things Greek.[38]

Would proud and xenophobic Greeks have falsely credited despised foreigners with their own inventions? Well, in fact yes, retorts a classical scholar. They strove to outshine and do down their immediate *Greek* predecessors. The Egyptians served as a stick with which Greeks beat other Greeks; rather than give any credit to his forerunner Hecataeus, Herodotus ascribed to Egyptians ideas familiar in Greece but quite alien to Egypt. So with other great Greek figures: "Pythagoras an original thinker? He picked up his ideas in Egypt! So did Plato! And Homer too!" Thus "the Egyptians came to be credited with . . . views, not in accord with their actual accomplishments, but in line with Greek polemics against other Greeks."[39]

As aspects of heritage come into or go out of favor, they are seen anew as domestic or as foreign. English antiquaries once derogated Stonehenge and Avebury as pagan sites, and so thought their origins Mediterranean; like the Druids they became British only when scholars began to praise them. Some German historians today strenuously seek to link the Holocaust with forces of evil not solely Nazi, but Stalinoid or even global. Only when the Holocaust gets objectified as a part of world "history" can Germans shrug off their national burden of inherited blame.[40]

For the most part, however, obsessive emphasis on exclusive, unique, and fiercely acquisitive national identities suffuses the debate over heritage with tension and conflict. There are two major arenas of conflict: boasts of precedence and preeminence that deny and clash with others'; and rival claims to the same valued heritage icons. In both cases, possessive jealousies embitter national as they do personal legatees.

International heritage disputes are private feuds writ large. Rivals contesting sovereign icons resemble siblings squabbling over parental bequests. Europe asperses Africa as incapable of husbanding the treasures it lost to imperial conquest; Third World states outlaw Western heritage holdings as illegal or ill-gotten. Greece is denied the Elgin Marbles on the ground (among others) that Slav ancestry discredits the kinship of modern Greeks with classical Athens. Maoris are denied ancestral relics lest they confine display to a male elite, aborigines lest they purify them by ritual destruction. And because each of us has multiple identities and allegiances, overlapping loyalties breed further strife.

Such disputes pervade politics and public consciousness. States quarrel incessantly over icons of identity. And heritage crusades are intensely righteous. Unless it is justified by claims of previous possession, to seize or demand land or resources is reprehended;[41] to seize or demand icons of identity may be condoned, even when it infringes others' integrity. Despite French remonstrances, the theft by a Mexican of a pre-Columbian codex from the Louvre was widely lauded as a patriotic act of restitution.

Rhetorical bombast marks heritage brawls. And communal identity is often secured, honor satisfied, simply by fervent reiteration of a claim. It may better serve Greek pride to go on demanding the Elgin Marbles' return than actually to get them back. Nothing rouses popular feeling more than a grievance unrectified. To gain Québecois sovereignty or Scottish home rule would at once deprive separatists of their prime weapon. Identity is more zealously husbanded by the quest for a lost heritage than by its nurture when regained. Basque extremism dwindled to aimless anger once they gained autonomy. "Before, we had answers to our problems," says a Basque spokesman. "They were self-government, *conciertos económicos,* the restoration of Basque culture. All that has been achieved. Now our problems seem to have no answers at all and what we have won doesn't seem that important."[42]

Many conflicts fester unresolved because bereaved claimants are poor and weak. No wonder ex-colonial Asian and African nations spearhead UNESCO's heritage restitution drive. Though now sovereign, these states often seek in vain to regain purloined icons of identity. Lacking armed clout, they rely on moral entreaty, with predictably few victories.

Nonetheless, minority causes now increasingly converge. This reflects both the global spread of communications and the universalizing rhetoric of heritage debate. Skilled in survival strategies featuring adaptive social manipulations, minorities deploy ethnic identity as a battering ram. And their crusades globally interlink: separatist movements in Canada are inflamed by those in Africa, those in Yugoslavia by pressures from the Baltic. Aboriginal Australians, Maori New Zealanders, native Hawaiians and Americans borrow each other's strategies and legal expertise at recurrent international gatherings.[43]

Different realms of heritage generate special conflicts. Endemic to archaeology are disputes over national or ethnic primacy, the validity of famed relics, the favoring of some epochs over others, the repatriation of autochthonous skeletal remains, the primacy of scholarly or sacred-site values. Lands that restrict access to nationals are at loggerheads with archaeologists worldwide. National, regional, local, and in situ interests contest finds allocated for display. Impassioned disputes attest the close tie of heritage with habitat, the felt fusion of identity with locale. Where access rights embroil rival claimants, as at Stonehenge, custodial fears lead to draconian protection that vitiates most heritage use.

Architectural heritage breeds other rivalries. Nations vaunt built legacies as the finest survivals of this or that generic tradition; thus British Norman abbeys are acclaimed for unique Romanesque purity, Germans praise Gothic genius as wholly Teutonic, and so forth. Antiquarian purists inveigh against restorers, devotees of original use against adaptation, adherents of continuity against reversion to any epoch, strict preservers against tourism. Bitterly contested are the merits of public or private stewardship, of ruins or reroofed buildings, of museums or living pasts.

Building legacies depend on place and locale. But the environmental heritage calls up other issues. Where wilderness is the prized milieu, custodians debate how to protect remnants of nature and whether to restore or memorialize what has been lost. Where the landscape legacy is domestic, as in Britain, some extol traditional set scenes, others a dynamic compage; whether farmers and landowners, the countryside's customary stewards, should still be trusted as its best guardians, is hotly argued. In many lands a tradition of public access is set against ecological sanctuary, cherished rural anachronisms against agricultural efficiency, the survival of native species against the introduction of alien exotics.

Historical texts embellish all heritage. And histories do not merely illustrate or eulogize but *explain* a people's special genius. Early chroniclers openly lauded their patrons; later historians promoted communal and then national patriotism; national and ethnic chauvinism fuels history texts to this day. Textual heritage comprises not only tragic and triumphal tales but uniquely national modes of explanation—the Whig interpretation of English history, the American mystique of Manifest Destiny, the grandeur of an eternal France, one and indivisible. As the recent British school history debate shows, when national identity seems at stake heritage supersedes history. The special national mission—or affliction—supplants comparative insight.

History co-opted by heritage exaggerates or denies accepted fact to assert a primacy, an ancestry, a continuity. It underwrites a founding myth meant to exclude others. Whatever their specific focus—archaeology or architecture, landscape or history, language or religion—such avowals embroil heritage claimants. Since neither ideas nor artifacts heed territorial bounds, icons of group identity require a privatizing mystique others will then contest.

Myopia as well as conflict plagues us. Besotted with our own heritage and ignorant of others', we forgo useful comparisons. As each heritage seems unique, so do its vexed management problems. Guardians of heritage suppose their own dilemmas singular. Self-destructive mocking of tradition is thought peculiar to Australians; remnants of ancient history supposedly snarl only Italian city centers; Greeks feel uniquely deprived by the classical legacy's global dispersal; Poles alone mistrust all their official history; none but Israelis suffer a suicidal Masada complex; Egyptians singularly lack empathy with their ancient (because non-Islamic) roots. Only proprietary Brits insist that "what's ours is ours, and however we got it, what's yours is ours, too," even as the heritage drains away to Japan or the Getty. Only Americans smother the past in patriotic hype, degrade it with Disney, and feel guilty on both counts. These and other quandaries are wrongly thought to be solitary defects.

To be sure, heritage issues must be seen in national and social context. But comparisons reveal, parallels instruct. It helps caretakers to realize their problems are *not* exclusive but bedevil others too. Israelis distressed by moral decay since the heroic Zionist founders learn from the filial stress that perplexed sons of American Founding Fathers. Poles embarrassed by an officially imposed homogeneity see from French amnesia over Alsace and the Albigensians, Greek oblivion of Ottoman roots and ancient Slavonic admixture, that the denial of minority existence is not uniquely Polish. Swedish and Danish museum curators toured the 1987 Smithsonian exhibition on Nisei internment camps; stunned by American infamy thus self-revealed, they were moved to review what hidden and shameful aspects of their *own* histories they might fruitfully display.

Nations, like individuals, can come to accept that their heritage stems not simply from one taproot, but from a congeries of pasts. For example, the classical legacy Greece and Britain both claim owes its very existence to a motley history. British classicism reflects a long-drawn-out sequence of Roman invaders, Byzantine Christianity, Renaissance notions of Greece via Rome, eighteenth-century Palladianism, and nineteenth-century love of all things Greek. And the Greeks gained much from Britain, along with other countries. European Romantics fired Greek classical zeal: pan-Hellenists from *other* lands sired the modern Greek state with its proud and crippling archaisms.

Similarly, Greece today is a richer land for legacies that transcend classical Athens. Archaizing folklorists all too successfully purified rural folklore of "Turkish" and "Balkan" elements, while a compulsory Hellenism insisted that Greek buildings reflect classical tenets alone. But as the anthropologist Michael Herzfeld shows, Greek houses are two-faced: without, columns and orders, arches and architraves are ubiquitous. Within they remain what they were through the Ottoman centuries— essentially Turkish. Like Greek cuisine, interiors are Levantine; like Greek folklore, exteriors are purified to reflect "ancient" ideals. But what is indigenous is often Slavonic or Turkish; the Hellenic is official, imposed, recent.[44]

We validate public and private memories and construct self-identities not just through single-minded obsession with one thread of our past but through catholic awareness of the whole patchwork quilt. National heritage emerges from linkages (and rivalries) among all the identities that inhabit us.

NOTES

1. Georges Duby, *William Marshal, the Flower of Chivalry* (New York: Pantheon, 1985).

2. Virginia Woolf, *Moments of Being* (Sussex: The University Press, 1976), p. 132.

3. Peter Ustinov, "My School Days: Sporting Trial of a Weighty Free Thinker," *Sunday Times* (London), 6 May 1990, p. C11.

4. Kazuo Ishiguro, *The Remains of the Day* (London: Faber and Faber, 1989).

5. Jonas Frykman and Orvar Löfgren, *Culture Builders: A Historical Anthropology of Middle-Class Life* (New Brunswick, N.J.: Rutgers University Press, 1987).

6. Anthony P. Cohen, ed., *Belonging: Identity and Social Organisation in British Rural Cultures* (Manchester: Manchester University Press, 1982); Murray Chapman, "Pacific Island Movement and Socioeconomic Change: Metaphors of Misunderstanding," *Population and Development Review* 17 (1991): 263–92.

7. Paul Connerton, *How Societies Remember* (Cambridge: Cambridge University Press, 1980), p. 17. The development of a continuous sense of self is complex and little understood. See my *Past Is a Foreign Country* (Cambridge: Cambridge University Press, 1985), pp. 198–99; and Jeremy Campbell, *Winston Churchill's Afternoon Nap* (London: Paladin, 1988), pp. 355–69.

8. Robert Hewison, *The Heritage Industry: Britain in a Climate of Decline* (London: Methuen, 1987).

9. Mary C. Waters, *Ethnic Options: Choosing Identities in America* (Berkeley: University of California Press, 1990), shows how white Americans today extend immigrant forebears' family and kinship into a purely voluntaristic, undemanding ethnicity.

10. Richard Rodriguez, "An American Writer," in Werner Sollors, ed., *The Invention of Ethnicity* (New York: Oxford University Press, 1989), p. 10.

11. Keith Nicklin, "The Epic of the *Ekpu:* Ancestor Figures of Oron, South-east Nigeria," in Peter Gathercole and David Lowenthal, eds., *The Politics of the Past* (London: Unwin Hyman, 1989), pp. 291–301.

12. Paul M. Bator, *The International Trade in Art* (Chicago: University of Chicago Press, 1983); David Lowenthal, "Where Does Our Architectural Heritage Belong?" in *Old Cultures in New Worlds,* Proc. ICOMOS 8th General Assembly (Washington, D.C.: 1987), 2:685–92; Jeanette Greenfield, *The Return of Cultural Treasures* (Cambridge: Cambridge University Press, 1989).

13. Salah Stétié, "The Intergovernmental Committee: Mechanisms for a New Dialogue," *Museum* 33:1 (1981): 116–17.

14. Amadou-Mahtar M'Bow, "A Plea for the Return of an Irreplaceable Cultural Heritage to Those Who Created It," *Museum* 31:1 (1979): 58.

15. Richard Handler, *Nationalism and the Politics of Culture in Quebec* (Madison: University of Wisconsin Press, 1988), pp. 157–58.

16. Émile Durkheim, *The Elementary Forms of the Religious Life: A Study in Religious Sociology* (London, 1915), pp. 206–14, 230–32.

17. Robert Bridges, "The Society's Work" (Tract 21, 1925), in W. F. Bolton and

56 DAVID LOWENTHAL

D. Crystal, eds., *The English Language: Essays by Linguists and Men of Letters* (Cambridge: Cambridge University Press, 1969), 2:86–99.

18. Connerton, *How Societies Remember*, p. 87.

19. Martin Fletcher, "Sell Stately Homes to Nouveaux Riches, Says Ridley," *The Times* (London), 23 November 1988; Lord Saye and Sele, quoted in Sally Brompton, "Family Castle Not for Sale," *The Times* (London), 17 December 1988. I discuss this issue more fully in "British National Identity and the English Landscape," *Rural History* 2 (1991): 205–30.

20. Herbert Butterfield, *The Whig Interpretation of History* (London: G. Bell, 1931).

21. Herbert Butterfield, *The Englishman and His History* (Cambridge: The University Press, 1945), pp. 114, 6–7, 11, 72.

22. Sir Geoffrey Howe, quoted in Jonathan Clark, "England's Very Peculiar State," *The Times* (London), 19 June 1991, p. 14.

23. Richard Bernstein, *Fragile Glory: A Portrait of France and the French* (London: Bodley Head, 1991), pp. 105–6.

24. Mandell Creighton, *The English National Character* (The Romanes Lecture; London: Henry Frowde, 1896), pp. 23, 11, 16, 17; for the Napoleonic boast, Stella Cottrell, "The Devil on Two Sticks: Franco-phobia in 1803," and Linda Colley, "Radical Patriotism in Eighteenth-century England," both in Raphael Samuel, ed., *Patriotism: The Making and Unmaking of British National Identity,* vol. 1, *History and Identity* (London: Routledge, 1989), pp. 263 and 169–87.

25. Ralph Waldo Emerson, "English Traits" (1856), in *The Portable Emerson* (New York: Viking, 1946), pp. 353–488, ref. p. 425.

26. Jim Murphy, Henley Centre for Forecasting, quoted in *Observer* (London), 10 December 1989, p. 16. See Douglas Broom, "Call to Abandon a Sterile Debate," *The Times* (London), 11 August 1989, p. 5; Satie Stethi, "New Heritages We Should Welcome," *The Times* (London), 23 October 1989, p. 35.

27. Norman Tebbit, "Being British, What It Means to Me: Time We Learned to Be Insular," *The Field* 272 (May 1990): 76–78.

28. Jacques Darras, "Should We Go on Growing Roses in Picardy? The Future for Our Cultural Heritage in Europe," *Royal Society of Arts Journal* 138 (1990): 524–30, ref. p. 526.

29. A 1991 Gallup poll found 52 percent of Britons "very proud" to be British, 18 percent of Germans "very proud" to be German, at the European extremes (*The Times* [London], 22 November 1991, p. 24).

30. Harold James, *A German Identity 1770–1990* (London: Weidenfeld & Nicolson, 1989), pp. 6–30, 46.

31. Perry Anderson, "Nation-states and National Identity," *London Review of Books,* 9 May 1991, pp. 3–8.

32. James, *German Identity,* p. 96.

33. Christian Meier and Michael Stürmer emphasize both German uniqueness and universality (Ralf Dahrendorf, ed., *The Unresolved Past: A Debate in German History* [London: Weidenfeld & Nicolson, 1990], pp. 10, 15).

34. Luigi Barzini, *The Europeans* (Harmondsworth: Penguin, 1984), pp. 258–59.

35. Ernest Renan, "What Is a Nation?" (1882), in Homi K. Bhabha, ed., *Nation and Narration* (London: Routledge & Kegan Paul, 1990), pp. 8–22, quotations on pp. 19, 11; Martin Thom, "Tribes within Nations: The Ancient Germans and the History of Modern France," in idem, pp. 23–43.

36. Xavier Pitafo, quoted in Hans Magnus Enzensberger, *Europe, Europe: Forays into a Continent* (London: Picador, 1990), pp. 159–60.

37. Norman Davies, "Poland's Dreams of Past Glories," *History Today* 32 (November 1982): 23–30.

38. Martin Bernal, *Black Athena: The Afroasiatic Roots of Classical Civilization*, vol. 1, *The Fabrication of Ancient Greece, 1785–1985* (London: Free Association Books, 1987), pp. 98–101.

39. Jasper Griffin, "Who Are These Coming to the Sacrifice?" *New York Review of Books*, 15 June 1989, pp. 25–27.

40. German historical guilt is explored in Richard J. Evans, *In Hitler's Shadow: West German Historians and the Attempt to Escape from the Nazi Past* (London: I. B. Tauris & Co., 1989); Charles S. Maier, *The Unmasterable Past: History, Holocaust, and German National Identity* (Cambridge: Harvard University Press, 1988); Per Ohrgaard, "Nazism and National Identity: A Current Issue in West Germany," *Culture & History* 4 (Copenhagen: Museum Tusculanum Press, 1989): 65–90.

41. Alexander B. Murphy, "Historical Justifications for Territorial Claims," *Annals of the Association of American Geographers* 80 (1990): 531–48.

42. Marianne Heiberg, *The Making of the Basque Nation* (Cambridge: Cambridge University Press, 1989), p. 230.

43. Anya Peterson Royce, *Ethnic Identity: Strategies of Diversity* (Bloomington: Indiana University Press, 1982); Henry Reynolds and Richard Nile, eds., *Indigenous Rights in the Pacific and North America: Race and Nation in the Late Twentieth Century* (London: Sir Robert Menzies Centre for Australian Studies, Institute of Commonwealth Studies, University of London, 1992).

44. Michael Herzfeld, *Ours Once More: Folklore, Ideology, and the Making of Modern Greece* (Austin: University of Texas Press, 1982); idem, "'Law' and 'Custom': Ethnography in Greek National Identity," *Journal of Modern Greek Studies* 3 (1985): 167–85. Modes of mediating these oppositions are explored in Herzfeld's *A Place in History: Social and Monumental Time in a Cretan Town* (Princeton: Princeton University Press, 1991).

PART TWO

Memory in the Construction of National Identities

Chapter III

NATIONAL MEMORY IN
EARLY MODERN ENGLAND

David Cressy

Long before the modern period, as early as the sixteenth century, English governments made calculated use of national memory for dynastic, political, religious, and cultural purposes. And by the seventeenth century, when politics and religion became dangerously fraught and fractured, much of England's political discourse, including the discourse of opposition and contest, revolved around the interpretation, celebration, and control of remembered historical events. England's past became an issue in England's present to a degree unknown elsewhere in early modern Christendom. A deliberately cultivated vision of the past was incorporated into the English calendar, reiterated in sermons, reviewed in almanacs, and given physical form by memorials and monuments. At first this project was driven by the ruling regime, the court, and its religious supporters; but soon there developed competing strands of memory and rival patterns of memorialization, with their own providences, heroes, martyrs, and shrines. Public commemoration in early modern England, as in other, later societies, served both as a unifying and as a divisive force.

As early as the 1530s, after Henry VIII's break with Rome, the propagandist Sir Richard Moryson tried to persuade the king to adopt "an annual triumph, with bonfires, feasts and prayers, to act as a perpetual memorial to the good fortune of the English people in their deliverance from the bondage of the papacy."[1] Moryson's idea was not immediately taken up, but the Tudor regime adopted other measures to project and solidify its position as the divinely ordained guardian of the nation. Graphic reminders of the royal sovereignty—the secular foundation of the English Reformation—decorated the frontispiece to the new English Bible, and the royal coat of arms erected in most parish churches served similarly to combine the aura and authority of church and state. Following the reestablishment of Protestantism under Queen Elizabeth, John Foxe's "Book of Martyrs" was ordered for every parish, in order to memorialize the origins and sufferings of the Church of England. Significantly, the formal title of this widely read work was *Actes and Monuments of Matters Most Speciall and Memorable.*[2]

The Protestant leaders of early modern England developed a distinctive view of English history, and buttressed their position by the invocation and manipulation of memory. They saw themselves as the heirs of ancient Israel, bound by a covenant with a demanding but Anglophile divinity. Historic episodes from the middle of the sixteenth century to the end of the seventeenth were carefully memorialized and commemorated as signs of God's special interest in his Protestant nation. The accession of Queen Elizabeth, the victory over the Spanish Armada, deliverance from the Gunpowder Plot, and the fortunes of the Stuart kings became landmarks in the development of an English identity, and cumulative elements of the national memory. They formed a repertory of remarkable occurrences that continued to reverberate through time, requiring instruction across the generations and solemnity or festivity on their anniversaries. Prayers and sermons, statutes and proclamations, almanacs and chronicles, set forth a pattern of providences that served as a reminder of the nation's distinctiveness, of God's mercies, and of England's particular religious and dynastic good fortune. Taken together, they set forth a view of English identity, with historical, religious, and dynastic dimensions, that transcended regional and local loyalties. This was not nationhood or nationalism in the nineteenth-century sense, but it did instill a precocious sense of purpose and heritage that was unmatched in continental Europe. Only the seventeenth-century Dutch came close.[3]

Leading propagandists held that 17 November—the anniversary of Queen Elizabeth's accession in 1558—represented the turning point in England's religious history. They construed this date as a providential divide between the nightmare of popery and the promise of the development of God's true church. John Foxe set the tone when he dedicated *Actes and Monuments* to Queen Elizabeth: "What bitter blasts, what smarting storms have been felt in England during the space of certain years, till at last God's pitiful grace sent us your majesty to quench firebrands, to assuage rage, to relieve innocents."[4]

Preachers throughout the kingdom elaborated this message in their annual Accession Day sermons. Though crafted by the clerical elite, these works reached a broad popular audience. Thomas Holland of Oxford recalled 17 November as "a day registered in all our chronicles to all happy remembrance . . . a day wherein our nation received a new light after a fearful and bloody eclipse." The London preacher Thomas White urged, "every twelve month, let us in thanksgiving remember her, to whom, under God, we owe all our service upon earth." "The queen's holy day," as some called it, was royal and dynastic, religious and patriotic, and it stirred common action in support of a national ideological position.[5]

From its tentative beginning around 1569, the accession anniversary custom had become firmly established by the 1580s. One Elizabethan described 17 November as "a holiday which passed all the pope's holidays," and this competitive element was clearly part of its didactic message.[6] The day was marked by prayers and sermons, tournaments and pageants, cannonades, music, drinking, feasting, and, throughout the kingdom, by joyful ringing of bells. The prompts and instructions clearly came from above, descending through the matrix of command, but the festivities served to fix the date in the local calendar, to root it in popular memory, and to lend unity to an emergent political culture. Hearing the same prayers, listening to similar sermons, and engaging in comparable festivities, celebrants throughout the nation danced briefly to the same tune. Not only while the queen lived but also for several generations after, 17 November was an occasion to recall past providences and to check that England still followed God's course. Such anniversaries served as bridges between elite and popular culture, as well as between the present and the past.

I

The events of 1588 confirmed the promise, the implied covenant, of Elizabeth's accession. This was the year when King Philip II of Spain set out to invade England and to remove its heretic bastard usurper queen. But, as the Protestant commemorative motto boasted, "God breathed, and they were scattered."[7] Elizabeth's triumph over the Spanish Armada was quickly memorialized as a signal historic event. Invested with mythic properties, the events of 1588 were taken as confirmation of the special destiny reserved for God's Englishmen. They were commemorated in medals and tapestries, paintings and poems, sermons and prayers. The Elizabethan diarist Richard Rogers called this deliverance "as memorable a work of God as ever was in any my remembrance."[8] Remembering it became an integral part of its meaning.

The official "prayer of thanksgiving" for 1588—sent forth from London for use in parish churches everywhere—promised everlasting gratitude, "we never forgetting, but bearing in perpetual memory this thy merciful protection and deliverance of us." Citing the Psalms, the English promised to "offer unto [God] the sacrifice of thanksgiving and tell out his works with gladness." "The works of the Lord are great, and ought to be had in remembrance of them that fear him . . . for one generation shall praise thy works to another generation, and declare thy power."[9] One remarkable publication of 1588 was a reordering of the Psalms, substituting "England" for "Israel" and "our queen" for King David, self-consciously associating the biblical past with the Elizabethan present. Drawing on history and scripture, text and memory, Protestant theorists made England's role as God's "elect nation" a standard feature of post-Armada sermons. Preachers promised that "continually we may . . . speak of [the deliverance] to our children, and they to their children's children, that so the memory of this thy glorious fact may be continued from generation to generation on even for ever."[10]

Elizabethan England created no "Armada day," no national calendrical occasion to commemorate the deliverance from the Spanish invasion. Yet the queen's anniversary each November became a time for retelling the story and for castigating the Catholics. Seventeenth-century memorialists cherished the deliverance of 1588 as one of the principal icons in the shrine of national memory. Preaching on 17 November 1601, already a dozen years after the failed invasion, William Leigh promised, "that *mirabilis annus* of '88 will never be forgotten, so long as the sun and moon en- dureth."[11] The story was kept alive by the repeated need for reassurance about England's special mission, and by the recurrence of danger from Spain and from Rome.

Memories of the Armada fed into the renewed wave of anti-Spanish hysteria that swept through early-Stuart England. In 1624, amidst calls for renewed war with Spain, Bishop George Carleton recalled the *mirabilis annus* of 1588 in his *Thankfull Remembrance of Gods Mercy.* "We are now come to that fateful year" of the cruel Armada, he wrote, designed "utterly to overthrow the church of England and state." Carleton concluded, "if a man with an unpartial eye look upon these, though he be an enemy, though he be a Jesuit, he must needs confess that God was on our side."[12] Recollec- tions of this deliverance provided comfort, instruction, and inspiration, and 1588 was invoked in succeeding generations at times of international crisis. As a set piece of English history the mythologized Armada was still serviceable in the 1940s when England again faced invasion, and in the 1980s at the time of the Falklands-Malvinas war. It became an indispens- able ingredient of "our island story." The celebrations in 1988 of the four- hundredth anniversary of the Spanish Armada, at a time when Britain's economic and political future was pledged to Europe, showed once more the continuing sensitivity and ambivalence of the past.

II

In the Stuart era the deliverance of 1588 was confirmed and compounded by the even more remarkable deliverance from the Gunpowder Plot. This was 5 November 1605, when Guy Fawkes and a group of Catholic conspir- ators attempted to kill the king and most of the government of James I by blowing up the Houses of Parliament. Events acquired coherence by seeing them in patterns, and historically minded preachers immediately and con- sistently linked 1588 and 1605. Once again, God had given providential protection to his Protestant Englishmen. Once again, divine intervention in

English history would never be forgotten. Histories, laws, litanies, and sermons helped imprint the memory of the Gunpowder Plot on the English popular consciousness. Almanacs marked the Powder Treason day among the few enduringly important anniversaries, distinguished by red letters and crude verse. Several generations later, in 1695, "Poor Robin's" almanac observed, "What ere's forgot, the memory o' the Powder Plot will hardly die."[13]

In addition to highlighting its calendar, the almanac perpetuated the memory of important events by listing them in a "compendious chronology" or "chronological description of many things worthy of memory." This was not simply padding, nor was it intended for idle amusement; the chronology served a solemn didactic function, reminding the reader of the passage of time, of the purposeful working out of providence over the years and centuries. It allowed English readers to place their country's recent political and religious history in a scheme of events stretching back to the creation of the world and, by implication, looking forward to its end. Richard Allestree's almanac for 1628, for example, noted the years "since the creation of the world 5598 . . . since the destruction of Sodom with fire and brimstone, 3543 . . . since the beginning of Blessed Queen Elizabeth's Reign, 70 . . . since the [Spanish Armada], 39," and "since the Damnable Powder Treason, November 5, 23" years.[14]

Understanding one's place in time required periodically recalling these crucial events to memory. From the viewpoint of the 1620s the previous hundred years contained a compacted history of combat between the forces of God and the forces of the devil, between Christ and Antichrist, between light and dark. English history since the Reformation had become foreshortened and crowded with significant moments, as time accelerated toward the present. Events like the Armada and the Gunpowder Plot could be seen as hinge-points in time, the resolution of critically dangerous uncertainty, and moments when English history was fatefully determined.

James I's government responded to the Gunpowder Plot by legislating an annual commemoration with both secular and religious observances. The statute was titled "An Act for Public Thanksgiving to Almighty God Every Year on the Fifth Day of November . . . to the End this Unfained Thankfulness May Never be Forgotten, but be had in Perpetual Remembrance." Providing a model for subsequent attempts at legislated memory and official commemoration, this law of 1606 remained in force until 1859.[15] Approved publications invoked yet again the importance of memory and invited the populace to join in commemoration. "The Powder-treason, that monstrous birth of the Romish harlot, cannot be forgotten without great impiety and injury to ourselves. . . . We shall be guilty of horrible ingratitude, the foulest of all vices, if we do not embrace all means of perpetuating the memory of so great, so gracious, and wonderful a preservation."[16]

Even more than the Armada, the Gunpowder Plot became a cultural landmark, its meaning bound up with its memory. Commemorative interpretations, though mediated by the elite at the center, were embraced and modified by the populace at the periphery. Parish after parish adopted the anniversary for an annual festivity, involving drinking and noise-making, bonfires and bells, as well as sermons and prayers. Local traditions of pageant and procession were grafted onto this new national celebration. And even today this anniversary is kept in England with bonfires and fireworks, as part of an evolving if degenerated tradition. Every English child knows the rhyme

> Remember, remember, the fifth of November,
> The Gunpowder Treason and Plot.
> I see no reason why Gunpowder Treason
> Should ever be forgot.[17]

The deliverance of 1605, thundered the Jacobean Puritan Samuel Garey, cannot be "buried in oblivion." It was, rather, to be kept as "a holy feast unto the Lord throughout the generations." Memory and commemoration were vital instruments for godliness, so keeping the holy day of 5 November became part of the covenant between God and his Englishmen. "How unworthy shall we be of future favors, if so unthankful for past blessings?" We were duty-bound, argued Garey, "to imprint an eternal memento in the calendar of our hearts forever, of the marvellous mercy of God in keeping us from that intended destruction."[18] Telling the story, alongside ringing the bells, became part of the ritual of commemoration, a layering and reinforcing of memory by words and action.

Later in the seventeenth century the conduct and resonance of the Gunpowder anniversary shifted with the national political and religious agenda. Once again the present made urgent demands on the past. Renewed anxieties about international Catholicism in the 1620s refocused interest in the discovery of the Guy Fawkes plot and in the covenant myth that it represented. Preacher after preacher dwelt on "that matchless villainy and that unconceivable treachery which the papists had contrived" back in 1605. Conservatives and radicals agreed that the plot had threatened the entire social and religious order, and that every English subject had a stake in its outcome, and an obligation to its memory. But by this time the tone of the anniversary was shifting from joy at deliverance to apprehension of a continuing menace. Memory became a call to action. And during the 1630s the anniversary changed again in response to domestic politics, and came to symbolize the cleavage between Laudians and Puritans as well as the larger struggle of Protestants against Catholics. The government lost exclusive control of the cultivation of memory, so that English history became contested among competing religious and political groups.

Though still a day of public commemoration, enjoined by statute, the fifth of November under Charles I took on an increasingly embattled tone. The unifying festivity of the early seventeenth century was overlaid by criticism and recrimination, as Puritan preachers used Gunpowder Treason Day to emphasize the dangers of creeping popery, and the Caroline regime sought to muffle the commemoration. Government sponsorship of anti-Catholic memorials was now muted in deference to Charles I's Catholic wife, and the most militant memory of 1605 belonged to the king's critics. The culture of memory fragmented into partisan and competitive strands as rival factions sought control of the past. Parish bells still rang loud on 5 November, and again on the 17th, but often without official prompting or permission. Ostensibly they celebrated the deliverance of the crown and the established Church of England, but they also signaled, for some, that the covenant with God was in danger.

Thrown onto the defensive by the rise of Archbishop Laud and the Arminians, Puritans clung to the calendrical occasion of the Gunpowder anniversary, and indeed developed it as an occasion for indirect criticism. Some godly ministers of the 1630s took the opportunity of 5 November to preach against the resurgence of popish superstition, pollutions, and persecutions, while others took comfort in the underlying message of deliverance. The London minister Henry Burton told his congregation on 5 November 1636, "This is a time of sorrow and humiliation, but this day a day of joy and festivity." It was time, guided by the anniversary, to recall the true meaning of the Gunpowder deliverance, "a deliverance never to be cancelled out of the calendar, but to be written in men's hearts forever." The treason of 1605 had threatened explosive change, but now, Burton argued, England faced a subtler enemy, "popery, like a thief, stolen upon us step by step."[19] Hot Protestants deployed the Armada and Gunpowder Plot as battle ensigns in the war against Antichrist; but dynastic loyalists interpreted the same events as providential endorsements of the crown. England's special anniversaries acquired ambivalent mnemonic power, allowing activists of varying persuasions to rally support through ritual commemoration of the past.

III

The reluctant revolutionaries of the 1640s and 1650s repeatedly justified their actions in terms of remembered history. Increasingly, as the revolution unfolded, they turned commemoration of England's significant anniversaries into calls for immediate political action. Memory concerned the present and future as well as the past; it was a stimulus to godliness, as well as a matter of thanksgiving. Commemoration of previous mercies was not only a way to praise God and acknowledge his divine power, but also a pressing civic activity and an essential part of the task of building a godly society.

Preaching before Parliament on 5 November 1641, Cornelius Burgess reminded the members that the Gunpowder anniversary was no mere antiquarian commemoration, but rather belonged to a significant and unfolding present. "That great deliverance we now celebrate was not as a dead bush to stop a present gap only, nor a mercy expiring with that hour and occasion; but intended for a living, lasting, breeding mercy, that hath been very fertile ever since." The lesson of the Gunpowder Plot, forcefully reiterated, was *never* to trust or accommodate the Catholics, who even now were "walking too openly, and boldly . . . pressing too near." Preaching the anniversary sermon the following year, Matthew Newcomen charged that memory alone was not enough. "Arise, arise . . . ye members of the honorable houses of parliament, act something this day . . . worthy of this day."[20]

During the interregnum in 1654 the lord mayor and aldermen of London assembled to hear a Gunpowder sermon by Thomas Horton, professor at Gresham College. The preacher stressed that the deliverance of 1605 was "a monument of God's goodness to the nation . . . a deliverance and pre-servation which is never to be forgotten by us, nor our posterity after us, so long as the sun and moon shall endure in heaven." Without perpetual attention to past mercies, Horton warned, England could not expect fur-ther dispensations of God's goodness in the future—a pertinent message in the confusions of the protectorate. "Memory is a slippery thing," noted another preacher of the 1650s, but the Gunpowder Treason should be firmly recalled in our "catalogues of mercies" and ledgers of debts.[21] This was by now a traditional message on the importance of memory, commem-oration, and civic obligations, but the bookkeeping image was especially appropriate for a congregation of merchants and shopkeepers.

As the revolution disintegrated it became even more urgent to cling to the shining past. Writing late in 1657, Samuel Clarke set down "a true and full narrative of those two never to be forgotten deliverances, the one from the Spanish invasion in eighty-eight, the other from the hellish powder plot." Clarke's intention was to show, as had been shown often before, "the wonderful power and mercy of God to us in this poor nation." His larger purpose, however, was to ensure attentiveness to the past as the foundation for godliness in the present and future. Remembering and commemorating England's significant history was a matter of keeping the faith, as well as signaling gratitude for past favors. "If there be not such a recognition of former deliverances, we that should be as temples of [God's] praise shall be as graves of his benefits. Our souls indeed are too like filthy ponds, wherein fish die soon and frogs live long. Rotten stuff is remembered, memorable mercies are forgotten; whereas the soul should be an holy Ark, the memory the pot of Manna, preserving holy truths and special mercies."[22] Forgetfulness implied ingratitude, denial of the covenant, and descent into foul bestiality.

IV

The second half of the seventeenth century saw a broader and more insistent focus on public memory, not only because there was more to remember, but because the arenas for religious and political activity had broadened, and so many fundamental issues were in dispute. Ideological and partisan issues spilled over from the court and the council to the tavern and the street. Debates about policy and preferment, the succession, and religion all became infused with memory and commemoration. Invariably, the discovery of new popish plotting recalled previous outrages and deliverances. By the late 1670s there was a memorial calendar for the Tories and a competing regime for the Whigs, each with its high-cultural and popular dimensions. At the same time there were counter-memories, suppressed memories, even legislated Acts of Oblivion, to extinguish the deeds of the revolution.

The Restoration added two more special days to the calendar, commemorating the sufferings and successes of the Stuart dynasty and the Anglican church. The first was 30 January, the anniversary of the execution of King Charles, the royal martyr, which was to be observed with solemn fasts and sermons; the second was 29 May, Royal Oak Day, King Charles II's birthday and the anniversary of his restoration, to be observed with prayer and frolic. These days joined 5 November, a venerable anniversary that could be observed with enthusiasm (though differently interpreted) by both supporters and critics of the Stuart crown. Gunpowder Treason had long been an anniversary of sensitivity and ambivalence, and was to provide a fresh focus for dissent in the later seventeenth century. The new anniversaries, too, were susceptible of different interpretations, ranging from dynastic legitimacy and Anglican conservatism to militant anti-Catholicism and the radicalism of the "good old cause."

The Elizabethan anniversary of 17 November was also revived in the 1670s. "Queen Elizabeth of famous memory" (significantly, her standard epithet) was harnessed to the cause of Whig politics, and the November Pope-burning processions reached their climax beneath an oversized statue of the virgin queen carrying a representation of Magna Carta. Elizabeth was now remembered, or remade, as the protectress of English liberties as well as the guardian of English Protestantism. Displayed in effigy and constructed in memory, she was, of course, a reproach to her more compromised Stuart successors.[23]

Gunpowder Treason Day under Charles II remained a statutary occasion recognized by state and church, as well as an enduring popular custom. This day saw polite and pious observances at court, as well as rowdy outbursts with bonfires and fireworks in the streets and villages. Inflammatory activities on 5 November always had the potential for trouble, so the establishment sought to contain them by restricting the vocabulary of celebration. The trick was to maintain a solemn Protestant commemoration without inspiring too much anti-Catholic enthusiasm, to keep the national memory alive without its being used as a divisive political weapon. From the point of view of the court, it was enough that the anniversary should be marked by the decorum of sermons and bells.

England's historic deliverances of the Elizabethan and Jacobean period lay, by this time, beyond the reach of most living memory, yet they continued to influence religious consciousness and political behavior. Rather than fading with time, such "mercies" as the triumphs of Queen Elizabeth and the discovery of the Gunpowder Plot remained in view as highly charged points of reference and commentary. Any danger that they might lapse into oblivion was overcome by their continuing utility for religious polemic and political mobilization. Instead of being drained of meaning they were reinfused with significance in the face of recurrent popish threats. The recollection of historic threats and deliverances served to warn against the ceaseless machinations of popery, and to reassure believers that God would again rescue his Protestant Englishmen from danger. As Thomas Wilson observed in a sermon on 5 November 1679, in the past "God had delivered us, so he will deliver us still, if we hold his truth without corruption."[24] The renewed fear of Catholics in the 1670s, and the volatile religious politics of the period that followed, brought the memory of past providences to the fore and shaped them to the fears and pressures of the moment. Sermons and pamphlets, as well as the annual reminder of the calendar, kept these memories alive.

So too did sculpted monuments and inscriptions. After the Great Fire of London in 1666, Parliament commissioned a monument, "the better to preserve the memory of this direful visitation." This Doric column—202 feet high, designed by Sir Christopher Wren—was a monument to the disaster and to the confident rebuilding of the city. But it soon took on other meanings. Rumor persisted that the fire was no accident, but rather had been the work of papist incendiaries. Their alleged attempt to destroy London became linked to traditions of Catholic conspiracy going back to the Gunpowder Plot and Elizabethan times. Wren's monument became a venue for anti-Catholic demonstrations, especially on 5 November, a new contribution to the symbolic geography of the city. The structure itself became an architectural prompt for the same anti-Catholic memories that were stimulated by the calendar. In 1681, fifteen years after the fire but at the height of the exclusion crisis, Whig politicians added a new masonry inscription, a further appeal to memory: "This pillar was set up in perpetual remembrance of the most dreadful burning of this Protestant city, begun and carried on by the treachery and malice of the popish faction . . . in order to the carrying on their horrid plot for extirpating the Protestant religion and old English liberty, and introducing popery and slavery."[25] The inscription condensed the teaching of traditional memorial sermons and provided the text for new ones, and the site took on more of the features of an anti-Catholic shrine. Not surprisingly James II had the inscription removed, but it was restored after the Protestant triumph at the Glorious Revolution. Only in 1830, after Catholic emancipation, was the memorial inscription permanently removed.

V

The kind of public memory that operated in early modern England was clearly a political construction, derived from the needs of dynastic or religious authorities. Its primary features were imposed from above and mediated through magistrates and ministers, before being adopted and internalized by the people at large. Reiterated in every town and parish, and reinforced by annual ritual commemoration, the story of English Protestant deliverances provided one of the distinctive ligaments of national political culture. This is not to say that popular culture was passive or uncreative in this regard, but rather to point to a valence of interaction that calls for further research. Nor does it assume that Elizabethan or Stuart England displayed the kind of national identity that would characterize the Georgian or Victorian periods. The political culture of Tudor and Stuart England was shaped by those leaders and preachers who invested particular parts of their history with special meaning—religious, political, and patriotic. But their manipulation of memory would have been more difficult without a receptive environment, and without the use of traditional forms of communication. Eventually, it escaped from official control. By the end of the seventeenth century a canon of memories that once bound the nation to its crown and its church had become the contested ground of rival ideologies and faiths. Then as now, national memory was selective, subjective, and inscriptive, and responsive to a changing present. Then as now, the question of who owned memory was contested and open-ended. The myriad local modifications of the common national commemorations point to a restless popular creativity operating in counterpoint with a divided political elite.

NOTES

1. Sydney Anglo, "An Early Tudor Programme for Plays and Other Demonstrations against the Pope," *Journal of the Warburg and Courtauld Institute*, 20 (1957), pp. 176–9.

2. John Foxe, *Actes and Monuments of These Latter and Perillous Days* (London, 1563), became *Actes and Monuments of Matters Most Speciall and Memorable* in later editions. The 1533 Act of Appeals declared that "this realm of England is an empire," sovereign within its territorial limits.

3. This argument is developed in David Cressy, *Bonfires and Bells: National Memory and the Protestant Calendar in Elizabethan and Stuart England* (Berkeley and Los Angeles, 1990). For Dutch identification with God's chosen people, see Simon Schama, *The Embarrassment of Riches: An Interpretation of Dutch Culture in the Golden Age* (Berkeley and Los Angeles, 1988).

4. Foxe, *Actes and Monuments*, dedication. See also William Haller, *Foxe's Book of Martyrs and the Elect Nation* (London, 1963).

5. Thomas Holland, *Panegyris D. Elizabethae . . . A sermon preached at Pauls in London the 17 of November Ann. Do, 1599* (Oxford, 1601); Thomas White, *A Sermon Preached at Paules Crosse the 17 of November* (London, 1589).

6. Roy Strong, "The Popular Celebration of the Accession Day of Queen Elizabeth I," *Journal of the Warburg and Courtauld Institute*, 21 (1959), p. 87.

7. M. J. Rodriguez-Salgado, *Armada: 1588–1988* (London, 1988), p. 276; Colin Martin and Geoffrey Parker, *The Spanish Armada* (London, 1988), p. 14.

8. "The Diary of Richard Rogers," in M. M. Knappen (ed.), *Two Elizabethan Puritan Diaries* (Chicago, 1933), p. 81.

9. John Strype, *Annals of the Reformation* (Oxford, 1824), vol. 3, part 2, pp. 28–9.

10. *A Psalme and Collect of Thankesgiving, not Unmeet for this Present Time: to be Said or Sung in Churches* (London, 1588); Oliver Pigge, *Meditations Concerning Praiers to Almightie God* (London, 1589), p. 36.

11. William Leigh, *Queen Elizabeth Paraleld in her Princely Vertues, with David, Iosua, and Hezekia* (London, 1612), p. 93.

12. George Carleton, *A Thankfull Remembrance of Gods Mercy* (London, 1624), pp. 119–47.

13. "Poor Robin," *An Almanac After the Old and New Fashion* (London, 1695); David Cressy, "The Fifth of November Remembered," in Roy Porter (ed.), *Myths of the English* (Oxford, 1992).

14. Richard Allestree, *A New Almanacke and Prognostication* (London, 1628).

15. 3 Jac. I c. 1 (1606); Cressy, "The Fifth of November Remembered."

16. Francis Herring, *Popish Pietie, or the First Part of the Historie of that Horrible and Barbarous Conspiracie, Called the Powder-Treason* (London, 1610), sigs. A3v–A4.

17. Cressy, "The Fifth of November Remembered."

18. Samuel Garey, *Amphitheatrum Scelerum: or the Transcendent of Treason* (London, 1618), pp. 184–5. See also John Vicars, *Mischeefs Mysterie: or, Treasons Master-Peece* (London, 1617).

19. Henry Burton, *For God and the King. The Summe of Two sermons Preached on the Fifth of November Last* (London, 1636).

20. Cornelius Burgess, *Another Sermon Preached to the Honorable House of Commons* (London, 1641), pp. 19, 54, 60; Matthew Newcomen, *The Craft and Cruelty of the Churches Adversaries* (London, 1642), pp. 20, 31, 33.

21. Thomas Horton, *The Pillar and Pattern of England's Deliverances* (London,

1655), pp. 2, 40; Ralph Venning, *Mercies Memorial: or, Israel's Thankful Remembrance of God* (London, 1657), p. 23.

22. Samuel Clarke, *England's Remembrancer* (London, 1657; 1671 ed.), title page, sigs. A3v–A4.

23. Cressy, *Bonfires and Bells*, pp. 171–89; Tim Harris, *London Crowds in the Reign of Charles II* (Cambridge, 1987).

24. Thomas Wilson, *A Sermon on the Gunpowder Treason with Reflections on the Late Plot* (London, 1679), pp. 1, 10, 11, 18.

25. Walter George Bell, *The Great Fire of London* (London, 1920), p. 208; James Leasor, *The Plague and the Fire* (London, 1962), p. 258; Harris, *London Crowds,* p. 111.

Chapter IV

PUBLIC MEMORY IN AN AMERICAN CITY: COMMEMORATION IN CLEVELAND

John Bodnar

THE DEBATE that took place in the 1980s over the design for a national memorial to Vietnam veterans served as a startling reminder that memory is a subject of public concern. When the final design for the memorial—a chevron of black granite rising from the earth and inscribed with the names of the war dead—was unveiled in 1981, a storm of controversy erupted. Citizens divided over the symbolic import of the plan. One side argued that the design lacked a sense of patriotism and glory. These critics felt that the memorial emphasized death and mourning to a disproportionate extent and was nothing but a "black gash of shame" to the nation. Defenders of the design, however, thought the memorial met their powerful need to express sympathy for fallen soldiers, often comrades they had known, and to recognize all who suffered. Their commemorative impulse did not originate in any drive to honor the nation-state.[1]

The argument over the memorial design underscored a fundamental point. The shaping of a past worthy of public commemoration in the present was contested, involving a considerable degree of public discourse, emotional energy, and political debate. If the Vietnam Veterans Memorial is any guide, it is logical to expect that these issues always involve such considerations. And, by implication, some commemorative interests certainly predominate over others. It is the intent of this essay to explore the subject of publicly constructed memory in modern America, something that historians have seldom examined, and suggest some of the fundamental issues and debates that it entails.

The debate over the Vietnam memorial involved interests that can be called vernacular and official. The dominant interest expressed in the memorial originated in the consciousness of those ordinary people most directly involved in the war: the veterans who fought there and the people who cared about them. In the context of American society they represented a vernacular culture that formulated specialized concerns for the warriors who fought and died. They manifested these concerns in the memorial itself. Standing opposed to their concerns and ultimately accommodating them were the defenders of the nation-state. The structure of national power was safeguarded by national political leaders who saw in the monument a device to foster national unity and patriotism and by other citizens who celebrated the ideal of patriotic duty. These guardians of the nation were representatives of an overarching or official culture that resisted cultural expressions that minimized the degree to which service in Vietnam may have been valorous.

Public memory emerges from the intersection of official and vernacular cultural expressions. Official views originate in the concerns of cultural leaders or authorities at all levels of society. Whether in positions of prominence in small towns, in ethnic communities, or in educational, governmental, or military bureaucracies, these leaders share a common interest in social unity, the continuity of existing institutions, and loyalty to the status quo. They attempt to advance these concerns by promoting interpretations of past and present reality that reduce the power of competing interests that appear to threaten the attainment of their goals. Official culture relies on "dogmatic formalism" and the restatement of reality in ideal rather than complex or ambiguous terms. It desires to present the past on an abstract basis of timelessness and sacredness. Thus officials and their followers preferred to commemorate the Vietnam War in the ideal language of patriotism rather than in the real language of grief and sorrow. Normally, official culture promotes a nationalistic, patriotic culture of the whole that mediates an assortment of vernacular interests. But seldom has it sought mediation at the expense of ascendancy.[2]

Vernacular culture, on the other hand, represents an array of specialized interests that are grounded in parts of the whole. These interests are diverse and changing and can be reformulated from time to time by the creation of new social units, such as soldiers and their friends who share an experience in war or immigrants who settle a particular place. Defenders of such cultures are numerous and intent on protecting values and restating views of reality derived from firsthand experience in small-scale communities rather than the "imagined communities" of a large nation. Both cultures are championed by leaders and gain adherents from throughout the population, and individuals can support aspects of both cultures at once. But, normally, vernacular expressions convey what social reality feels like rather than what it should be like. Its very existence threatens the dogmatic and timeless nature of official expressions.

Public memory is a system of beliefs and views that is produced from a political discussion that involves the fundamental issues relating to the entire existence of a society: its organization, structure of power, and the very meaning of its past and present. Rooted in the quest to interpret reality and connect the past with the present, the ideas and symbols of public memory attempt to mediate the contradictions of a social system: ethnic and national, men and women, young and old, professionals and clients, leaders and followers, soldiers and their commanders. The competing restatements of reality expressed by these antinomies drive the need for reconciliation and the use of symbols, beliefs, and stories that people can use to understand and to dominate others. Thus, the symbolic language of patriotism is central to public memory discussions in nations like the United States because such language has the capacity to mediate both vernacular loyalties to local and familiar places and official loyalties to national and imagined structures.[3]

Public memory is a body of beliefs and ideas about the past that help a public or society understand both its past and its present, and, by implication, its future. It is fashioned ideally in a public sphere in which various parts of the social structure exchange views. The major focus of this communicative and cognitive process is not the past, however, but serious matters in the present such as the nature of power and the question of loyalty to both official and vernacular cultures. Public memory speaks primarily about the structure of power in society because that power is always in question in a world of polarities and contradictions and because cultural understanding is always grounded in the material structure of society itself. Memory adds perspective and authenticity to the views articulated in this exchange; defenders of official and vernacular interests are selectively retrieved from the past to perform similar functions in the present.

Adherents of official and vernacular interests demonstrate conflicting obsessions. Cultural leaders orchestrate commemorative events to calm anxiety about change or political events, eliminate citizen indifference toward official concerns, promote exemplary patterns of citizen behavior, and stress citizen duties over rights. They feel the need to do this because of the existence of social contradictions, alternative views, and indifference that perpetuates fears of societal dissolution and unregulated political behavior.

Ordinary citizens, on the other hand, react to the actions of leaders in a variety of ways. At times they accept official interpretations of reality, as when an individual declares that a son died in defense of his country or an immigrant ancestor emigrated to build a new nation. Sometimes individuals express alternative renditions of reality, as they do when they feel a war death was needless or an immigrant ancestor moved simply to support his family. Frequently people put official agendas to unintended uses, as they almost always do when they use commemorative time for recreational purposes or patriotic symbols to demand political rights.[4]

The debate over public memory in modern America has taken place not only on a national scale but in cities and towns in every region of the country. Local variations in the social and political structure could distort the terms of the discussion, but nearly always defenders of official and vernacular cultures pleaded their cases. The point is revealed clearly in an examination of public commemoration in a large urban area—Cleveland, Ohio—during the course of this century.

The public discussion over commemorating the past in Cleveland moved through three distinct stages. Prior to World War I, civic leaders and citizens with memories of the Civil War desired to commemorate both their own role in preserving the nation and the sacrifices local citizens made in the conflict. They were, above all, patriots, whose memories and interpretations of reality were grounded in a heroic ideal—the struggle for national unity. Their major commemorative achievement was the erection of a monument to their deeds on the city's public square.

Two factors altered the political framework that had supported the first state of commemoration: World War I and massive immigration to the city. The war certainly reinforced the drive to link citizens to the nation-state. Immigration, however, meant that a narrow focus on the Civil War would not meet the vernacular interests of thousands who had only recently arrived in the Ohio city. By 1920 some 30 percent of Cleveland's population consisted of foreign-born residents, many of whom insisted on commemorating homelands and ethnic cultures. Between World War I and World War II, during a second stage of commemoration in the city, this immigrant population and their children acquired political power. The official promotion of the heritage of the Civil War and patriotism in general gave way to memories of a different nature at the Cleveland Cultural Gardens.

The patriotic mobilization of World War II diminished the power of ethnic interests in public commemoration. During the war and in its aftermath, patriotism reasserted itself. But this revival proved to be short-lived, and in a third stage, after the 1940s, neither dogmatic patriotism nor variations of ethnic heritage held the power they once did. In the postwar era public commemoration was more diffuse; leisure and recreation commanded more attention on civic holidays, for instance, than did expressions of loyalty to nation or subgroup.

The dominance of patriotism was unmistakable in Cleveland's commemorative activity, however, before 1918. It was aggressively promoted by veterans and by local feelings of pride and sorrow for the sacrifices of friends and ancestors. To be sure, other interests existed in the city. During the celebration of Cleveland's centennial in 1896, which was organized by prominent entrepreneurs and the local Chamber of Commerce, the symbolic emphasis was predictably on material progress. A log cabin was built on the public square to honor the pioneers, but it was strategically placed across the street from a modern bank building in order to emphasize the progress the city had made from "poverty to wealth." A marching pageant viewed by thousands of citizens began with a scene of "Cleveland of 1796," showing Indians and pioneers, and ended with depictions of the com-

merce, art, and industry of the city in 1896.[5] But no commemorative event
was a more important expression of the interests that dominated memory
in the city at the turn of the century than the construction of a monument to
honor the soldiers and sailors from the Cleveland area who had fought in
the Civil War.

Despite the obvious support that existed for the idea to memorialize
local citizens who had helped save the nation, the effort to build the monument, which was led by a delegation of veterans who were also prominent
citizens, encountered difficulties. Some of the problems, such as the matter
of raising funds, were normal for such efforts. Others were unique. Overall
the project dramatically revealed not only what was important to the city's
public memory but how serious matters of commemoration could become.

Few people dissented from the idea of honoring individuals from
Cuyahoga County who had served the Union when the monument was
first proposed by William Gleason, a leader among local veterans, in 1879.
The state legislature readily approved a temporary tax to help fund the
endeavor. Legislators were apparently moved by arguments that the monument would be placed in the center of the city, where people would pass it
every day and be reminded of "love of country" and their duty to their
"native land."[6]

This official promotion of patriotism, however, did not move forward
without some resistance from people tied to a different set of memories.
Civil War veterans had got the city to form a monument commission to
administer their project. Inevitably the commission not only desired to
place the memorial on the city's public square, but wanted no other structure to overshadow it. Few citizens took issue with the idea that the new
memorial should stand in the square. But a great many Clevelanders were
unprepared to accept the commission's proposal to replace the most important monument in the city—the memorial erected in 1860 to Oliver Haz-
ard Perry and his victory over the British in the Battle of Lake Erie in
1812—with the new one.[7]

The plan to replace the Perry memorial provoked genuine opposition
when it was formulated in the early 1890s. The new monument commission rejected suggestions by the city park commission that they select a site
other than where the Perry memorial stood. The Civil War group became
militant and "took possession" of the ground they wanted by erecting a
fence around it. Defenders of the Perry monument, which by now had
become a vernacular symbol of local memory and part of the existing
environment, angrily retaliated by tearing down the fence in 1890 and
making speeches against the planned structure. It took an Ohio Supreme
Court ruling in favor of the monument commission for the Perry memorial
to be removed on September 12, 1892, the anniversary date of the first
news of Perry's battle. When a crowd gathered on the square that day, the

Cleveland Plain Dealer astutely observed that they came not only to honor Perry but to protest the removal of a memorial that had been part of their memories for more than three decades.[8]

The dedication of the Soldiers and Sailors Monument on July 4, 1894, represented the major commemorative event in the city between 1865 and 1918. The monument itself effectively integrated the sense of pride and loss that the community itself felt over its veterans, along with a strong declaration for the continuing need for patriotism and civic duty traditionally stressed by political, business, and veteran leaders. The sense of personal loss and pride was conveyed by carving into the interior walls of the monument the names of the nine thousand Cuyahoga County residents who had served in the Civil War. This listing was the result of a tremendous effort by local volunteers, who distributed more than ten thousand copies of a list of veterans for revisions and additions and handled more than five thousand pieces of correspondence with area families. But the nation and prominent people had to be acknowledged as well. Images of Ohio war governors and generals were cast in bronze and installed inside the monument. On top of the shaft a statue of the Goddess of Liberty was placed as an emblem of loyalty to the nation.[9]

The elaborate dedication ceremonies included the expression of numerous interests: patriotism, entertainment, civic order, antiradicalism, and local pride. Lanterns were strung across downtown streets, and the square was decorated to look like "a magnificent temple." The railroads sold special excursion tickets to the city, and "thousands upon thousands" of citizens came to see displays of Civil War battle flags, parades, speeches, and the monument itself. Governor William McKinley, who personally recalled hearing the historian George Bancroft speak at the dedication of the Perry memorial and viewing the body of Lincoln on the square, told the assemblage that the monument represented the notion of national unity. The governor felt that the republic was secure as long as "we continue to honor the memory of the men who died by the tens of thousands to preserve it."[10]

The power of the Civil War as a patriotic symbol declined significantly in Cleveland's commemorations after 1918. The presence of increasing numbers of immigrants in the city caused officials both to intensify their efforts at spreading patriotic messages and to alter their memory symbols. Newcomers did not share memories of the Civil War and were more interested in a past that included messages about their homelands. The heightened desire to Americanize the immigrant during the world war, and during the radical political turmoil after the war, meant that civic leaders and immigrants would have to reach some agreement on just exactly what public memory in Cleveland would be.

The period from 1918 to 1921 provided ample evidence that forces

existed in the city that could threaten not only civic order but the traditional political and economic power of business and civic leaders who
usually orchestrated commemoration. Ethnic power was manifested in
events such as the Americanization parade of the Fourth of July, 1918,
when some seventy-five thousand immigrants and their children marched
through the downtown streets. Obviously the ethnic communities made a
point of demonstrating their loyalty to America in a parade organized by
the mayor's Americanization committee, a group of prominent, native-
born civic leaders. The marchers carried American flags and mounted
floats that expressed patriotic messages. Immigrants from Germany and
Hungary, always suspect during 1918, wore red, white, and blue sashes in
the parade that carried the inscription "America First."

But the foreign-born were also insistent on proclaiming pride in their
memories of homelands and backgrounds, and this is what made them
appear threatening to the proponents of official culture. Numerous groups
marched in native costumes or built floats that depicted a past dominated
by memories of European villages. Lithuanians, for instance, presented a
"crude cart constructed of rough boughs and branches of trees" and drawn
by a horse, thus evoking images of their peasant past.[11]

The specter of radical socialism also manifested itself in the city and
reinforced civic leaders' desire to accommodate newcomers. In the minds
of many officials most immigrants were radicals. This point was made in
dramatic fashion in the commemoration of May Day in Cleveland in 1919.
In a graphic reversal of the orderly marches of immigrants the year before, a
parade of Socialists in the city turned into a full-scale riot. The Socialists
were led by Charles Ruthenberg, a Cleveland native who was preparing a
run for the mayor's office, and a number of veterans; participants included
"Ukrainian Socialists," who carried a large red flag. Marchers waved banners that did not proclaim loyalty but, instead, demanded rights: the release of Eugene Debs from jail and help for the unemployed. Family and
friends of the marchers stood on the sidewalks, wore red ribbons, and
applauded, but many other citizens jeered. The jeers soon turned to beat-
ings and assaults when scattered groups of veterans, youths, and apparently some police attacked marchers and destroyed Socialist headquarters.
The ensuing riot, which resulted in one death and scores of injuries, necessitated the use of "war tanks" and "army tanks" to "crash through the
maddening crowds."

In the aftermath of the riot Ruthenberg was arrested, outdoor meetings
of Socialists were banned, the red flag was prohibited from parades, and
Cleveland police placed an order for several more tanks. Some evidence
exists to suggest that the local business community, which had usually
celebrated progress and patriotism in public commemoration, actually had
armed citizens with clubs in anticipation of the Socialist march. Most of

the restrictions implemented after the riot were directed against the victims and not the alleged perpetrators. The events of the war era, however, had certainly reinforced the notion that future discussion over the interpretation of past and present events would be contested.[12]

The newfound diversity of power in Cleveland was evident in the city's major commemorative activity between World War I and World War II: the Cleveland Cultural Gardens. The commemoration of the war dead and patriotism was never forgotten in this era. Veterans were honored in a War Memorial Day parade in 1921 and every year on Armistice Day and Memorial Day. But it was the cultural gardens that occupied the attention of both civic and immigrant leaders in their attempt to accommodate each other's interests.[13] Today visitors to the monuments and gardens that stretch for more than a mile on the east side of the city find busts, statues, and ornate columns in a park-like setting defaced with graffiti. But for the generation that lived in the city after World War I, the gardens offered a place for the symbolic expression and exchange of ideals and viewpoints that were of the utmost importance.

The cultural gardens were created by members of the professional classes inside and outside ethnic communities in Cleveland who favored notions of pluralism and tolerance over the aggressive Americanism that proved powerful in the 1920s. These leaders were not in the least opposed to Americanization; they generally saw it as inevitable and were themselves models of upwardly mobile professionals who had thrived in new urban structures. But many were also dependent upon urban ethnic communities for their status, for their clientele, and sometimes for their votes. Those from ethnic backgrounds also shared many memories with others of similar origins. Furthermore, the ethnic leaders prominent in the effort to build the cultural gardens easily found common ground with the native-born middle class in the city, which had long sought to foster Americanization more directly through calls for patriotism, dutiful citizenship, and even the celebration of ethnic cultures cleansed of any ideals that could in the least way be construed as politically oppositional.

Leo Weidenthal, the editor of a Jewish-American newspaper in the city, first conceived the idea of the cultural gardens to commemorate what he felt was the "earliest memory" of mankind. This idealist felt that at some point in the past, before the onset of mass warfare, racial feuds, and rampant individualism ruled by the "jungle law of the survival of the fittest," all men shared a "common cultural memory" of peace, harmony, and cultural expression in the arts. By celebrating various ethnic groups' attainment of high culture in the past, Weidenthal and those who shared his dream hoped not only to encourage ethnic harmony and, therefore, civic order in Cleveland but also to promote efforts toward international peace and brotherhood.[14]

By 1926 civic reformers, political officials, and representatives of the city's major ethnic groups had formed the Cleveland Cultural Gardens Federation, with Charles Wolfram, a leader in the city's German-American community, as president. The goals of this organization were not as lofty as Weidenthal's. They simply wished to deal with the pluralistic structure of power in Cleveland, encourage friendly intercourse, and "inculcate appreciation of our cultures." The emphasis upon culture was not accidental. It represented part of Weidenthal's original vision, but also represented an attempt to transcend the political conflict that had emerged in the wake of Cleveland's growing diversity and industrialization. Cultural symbols rather than political ones were to be memorialized in the gardens. When ethnic organizations proposed to honor local political leaders on several occasions, they were turned down: the attempt here would be to reconstruct a public memory devoid of controversial statements. The cultural gardens board claimed that it zealously guarded against placing anything of a political or military nature in the gardens in order to avoid any "controversy of feelings."[15]

The responsibility for selecting commemorative symbols for the gardens was centralized from the very beginning. In the early 1930s the Cultural Gardens Federation organized a group of ethnic representatives who were to convey plans and suggestions from their respective groups to the federation's board of trustees. These representatives were all prominent members of their ethnic communities. Louis Petrash, for instance, was a Hungarian-American lawyer; Dr. Ignatius Jarzynski was a Polish-American physician; Anton Grdina, a Slovene-American, and Philip Garbo, an Italian-American, were businessmen. Andrew Bilinski of the Ukrainian-American community was a lawyer, and Joseph Mancovic, a Russian-American, was a physician. Once the board had approved an ethnic community's plan, it was the responsibility of the ethnic group to raise the necessary funds, usually through community dances, dinners, and other social activities. Contributions of labor were also made to the projects by the city and, during the 1930s, by the Work Projects Administration.[16]

A survey of the "cultural heroes" eventually commemorated in the various gardens reveals that the attempt to commemorate individuals who were culturally but not politically significant was only partially successful. In reality a number of political messages and heroes were given prominent places within these gardens. Moreover, the tolerance that Cleveland officials showed for ethnic distinctiveness resulted in a celebration of individuals who, while not always American heroes, were often patriots in their own right—a symbol that had always appealed to the middle class. Indeed, it was neither ethnic diversity nor American heroes that were missing in the gardens but ordinary people—immigrant pioneers—who had created the great migration streams to America in the first place and who had lived and toiled in Cleveland's ethnic neighborhoods.

Before World War II ethnic communities raised funds largely to commemorate heroes who defended the ideal of an ethnic homeland. These individuals were appropriate symbols to trustees because they tended to be cultural figures such as poets, composers, and writers; their cultural attainments helped to mute the legacy of political rebellion they also represented. Ethnic leaders, in other words, did not inevitably move toward the celebration of American patriots or founding fathers when given the freedom of choice to commemorate ordinary people from their own ranks. Rather, they moved toward a cultural and political middle ground that used the homeland symbol to please both their peers in the larger American society who were interested in the ideals of patriotism and national loyalty and their cohabitants in ethnic enclaves who still felt the emotional pull of images from their homeland. This was an attempt to reconcile official and vernacular cultures.

Ethnic groups commemorated a long list of cultural heroes who served both the cause of ethnic pride and the ideal of patriotism. Germans erected statues to two poet-philosophers: Johann Wolfgang von Goethe and Friedrich von Schiller, both of whom represented nationalistic as well as cultural themes.[17] In a similar way Poles commemorated Frédéric Chopin and Ignacy Jan Paderewski.[18] Slovaks unveiled two busts in the gardens in 1934. From their past they selected religious leaders—an indication of the power of such figures in their communities—who were also advocates of ethnic culture and homeland nationalism. The fact that one came from Cleveland's Slovak Lutherans and the other from the Catholics probably represented something of a political compromise within the group. The Reverend Stefan Furdek, who had emigrated to the United States in 1882, served as a Slovak and Catholic leader in Cleveland for more than thirty years, founded a number of Slovak fraternal unions, and published a series of books for immigrant schoolchildren on subjects that included the homeland and Slovak language instruction. Jan Kollár, the Lutheran minister who was also honored, had fought "fearlessly" for educational and language rights for all Slovaks, regardless of religion, in the homeland under Hungarian rule. Furdek was an especially important historical symbol for the larger Catholic majority, who continued to celebrate him for years afterward as an "outstanding man among American Slovaks" and as someone who stood for "God and Nation." He embodied what most ethnic symbols did: loyalty to religious and political structures.[19] At the same time, his memory sustained an interest in ethnic identity in a form that was not threatening to the host society.

Activities at the gardens turned decidedly patriotic, however, during World War II. As in 1918, ethnic communities were encouraged directly to demonstrate their loyalty to the United States. In 1942 a series of festivals was held at the gardens to commemorate the principles enunciated in the Atlantic Charter, such as the right of a people to resist territorial aggrandizement by outsiders, a point that reinforced both American and ethnic interests during the war. These festivals usually consisted of dramatic presentations at various gardens that spoke of ethnic contributions to the building of America rather than of heroes who had contributed to the maintenance of the ethnic group or the homeland. Thus, Italians presented a play on the discovery of America by Columbus. Unlike prewar gatherings, which were orchestrated by the ethnic groups themselves, these depictions of history were based on professionally written scripts that were given to the respective groups. One Cleveland newspaper even called upon ethnic groups to use their traditional folk stories to assist the cause of American patriotism. Slovaks were told, for instance, to use their folk hero Janosik and tell their children that he was the "Ethan Allen of the Slovaks" and that they should serve their new nation as well as he had served his.[20]

Cleveland's ethnic communities quickly fell into this patriotic march. In the Hungarian gardens a forty-foot steel flagpole with an American flag was erected next to the bust of Franz Liszt. The Slovak Cultural Gardens Association transferred all of its activity to war-bond solicitation and to "patriotic unity programs."[21]

Ethnic harmony rather than homeland heroes dominated the message in the city's commemoration of its sesquicentennial in 1946. A seven-mile parade from the city's downtown eastward to the cultural gardens was a highlight of the event and celebrated the theme of "One World" both at home and on the international level. This time ethnic interests, while not abandoned, were presented more forcefully within the larger structure of the city's history; ethnic contributions to America formed a more important theme than the cause of independent homelands. The parade was led by political officials and members of the Early Settlers Association, "who were cheered all along the line" for their depiction of the city's founding in 1796. Pioneer symbols followed with a Conestoga wagon. The ethnic groups came next, with themes that were aimed at pleasing the host society. Greek-Americans featured a float with a replica of the Parthenon, which symbolized the idea of democracy. Hungarian-Americans presented several floats. One did depict a homeland scene, but the audience was told that it was meant to show the "transplanting" of Hungarian culture and vitality to America. Other Hungarian representations told of Hungarian-American industrial workers and professionals who had been assimilated into this country and had contributed to its rise and war success.[22]

By the 1950s the assertion of ethnic interests in the homeland or ethnic heroes was less frequent than it had been before World War II. More common in events at the Cultural Gardens were the themes of "One World," in which harmony between ethnic groups was stressed over distinctive ethnic cultures, or "Contributions," in which groups recalled a past that spoke of their participation in building the American nation. The only homelands that were recalled were those under Communist domination. Interest in captive homelands usually served to reinforce the ideology of the American nation and its Cold War interests rather than ethnic pride in a land left behind. Thus, during the 1953 Ohio sesquicentennial celebration, One World Day, which was celebrated every year after 1946, involved speeches and a pageant at the gardens. Curtis Lee Smith, president of the Cleveland Chamber of Commerce, told the audience that Cleveland's creation of its own "One World" of nationality groups should serve as an ideal of unity and cooperation. The pageant that year commemorated immigrants as patriots who contributed to the building of the city, the state, and the nation. The arrival of the first settlers to Cleveland was depicted, as were the comings of the Irish, Germans, Jews, Hungarians, Poles, Slovaks, Italians, Slovenes, and others. At the conclusion of the pageant a young woman dressed as the Statue of Liberty emerged to demonstrate symbolically that all groups now merged under the dominance of American ideals.[23]

As the expression of patriotism became more dogmatic and less multivocal in the 1950s, the intensity of patriotic commemorations declined. Patriotism had dominated commemorations during World War II, especially the huge Festival of Freedom at Cleveland Stadium, held every Fourth of July and usually celebrating military heroes like Douglas MacArthur. By the 1950s, however, the traditional commemorative days such as Memorial Day, the Fourth of July, and Armistice Day were invested with less emotional energy. On these days and others the expression of sorrow for the dead, patriotism, and even ethnic sentiments gave way to rather bland pursuits of leisure and recreation. Ordinary citizens had always enjoyed these interests, but now their pursuit was not challenged as much by the aggressive mobilizations of various leaders with distinct commemorative agendas.[24]

If there was a revival of assertive interests in commemorative events in Cleveland, it was during the late 1960s. Disorder in the form of a race riot in 1968 and reactions to the Vietnam War prompted calls for patriotism and unity as well as public expressions of grief and sorrow. Memorial and Veterans Day celebrations downtown in 1968 and 1969 were larger than they had been for a while. Speakers at these events, always from the military, told crowds of about ten thousand on the public square that they must defeat "subversion" and "aggression" wherever they existed. On Memorial Day in 1969 local high-school students formed a human cross to commemorate the deaths of Cleveland-area residents who had died in Vietnam, and the local press printed a list of the dead. In fact, the vernacular dimension of patriotism, in this case sorrow for the dead rather than calls for loyalty to authority, was dominant in 1969, as local newspapers printed hundreds of expressions of grief and sorrow for loved ones who had died for whatever reason. The decline in the power of official patriotism over public discourse was evident as the Vietnam and other dead were recalled with "loving memory." The deceased were remembered not only as patriots but as brothers, sisters, and parents.[25]

During the 1970s, entertainment and leisure pursuits dominated commemorative events more than ever before. The program for the celebration of the city's 175th anniversary in 1971 revolved around performances by celebrities and a modest reenactment of the city's founding. Pioneers, immigrant heritages, and even patriots were hardly mentioned at all. For the bicentennial celebration of July 4, 1976, a religious-oriented service called "One Nation Under God" was held on the square, and baseball, picnics, and fireworks predominated. Public expressions of official culture were much weaker than earlier in the century, although they certainly were presented. But official activities did not draw as much attention as ethnic festivals and programs on black history. The *Plain Dealer* presented a feature on the history of the local black community and black political leaders and described in detail the city's role in the operation of the Underground Railroad. The newspaper claimed that Cleveland's neighborhoods no longer had an "ethnic purity" about them, but "that does not mean heritages and identities are lost."[26]

Impulses to commemorate a black past existed in the city's black community before the 1970s, but were usually not implemented in public space due to the lack of black political power. A prime example was the work of Icabod Flewellen, a black war veteran, who opened an African-American museum in his own home in 1953. It was not until 1984 that Flewellen's project received public support from the city and the Cleveland Public Library and moved into a vacant public building. The influence of African Americans in local politics increased after the election of a black mayor in 1967. In 1988 Liberty Boulevard, which runs in the vicinity of the Cultural Gardens, was renamed Martin Luther King, Jr., Boulevard. The next year blacks asked for the establishment of the Afro-American gardens. Thus far, a stone map of Africa has been erected, and plans exist for a statue of King. A monument to Booker T. Washington was erected in the cultural gardens during World War II, but according to a past president of the Cultural Gardens Federation the push for this memorial came from whites interested in nurturing black patriotism.[27]

Patriotism has dominated public commemoration in Cleveland throughout much of the twentieth century. Civic leaders were eager to promote symbols and actions from the past that honored service to the nation and, by implication, to all forms of authority. It was somewhat easier to do this in the era prior to World War I, because the social structure of the city was not nearly as diverse as it would become. After 1918, however, class discord and, especially, ethnic pluralism sharpened the exchange of cultural expressions over public memory and necessitated greater efforts at accommodation between native-born and foreign-born interests. The result was the creation of the Cleveland Cultural Gardens, a cultural hybrid that attempted to serve the interests of both American patriotism and ethnic nationalists.

The patriotic mobilizations of World War II and the early Cold War added political weight to the official dimensions of commemoration and severely weakened vernacular ones during the 1940s and 1950s. By the late 1960s, however, the contest between official and vernacular memory was weakened by a decline in political exchanges overall. In fact, the assertion of patriotic and ethnic memory appeared only episodically. The assortment of commemorative programs in 1976 suggested that official interpretations of the past could compete with but not dominate vernacular interests such as celebrations of ethnic or racial pride. It was this overall decline in the cultural power of official symbols after the 1960s that would help to explain the powerful emergence of vernacular interests in the Vietnam Veterans Memorial itself.

NOTES

1. See Jan C. Scruggs and Joel Swerdlow, *To Heal a Nation: The Vietnam Veterans Memorial* (New York: Harper and Row, 1985), 16; Rick Atkinson, *The Long Gray Line* (Boston: Houghton Mifflin, 1989), 463–80; Tom Carhart, "Statement to the U.S. Fine Arts Commission, Oct., 1981," container 76, Records of the Vietnam Veterans Memorial Foundation, Library of Congress.

2. For a fuller discussion of the debate over the Vietnam memorial and official and vernacular cultures, see John Bodnar, *Remaking America: Public Memory, Commemoration, and Patriotism in the Twentieth Century* (Princeton: Princeton University Press, 1992), 3–20. I have borrowed the terms *vernacular culture* and *official culture* from Susan G. Davis, *Parades and Power: Street Theatre in Nineteenth-Century Philadelphia* (Philadelphia: Temple University Press, 1986), 16–18; Terence Ranger and Eric Hobsbawm, eds., *The Invention of Tradition* (Cambridge: Cambridge University Press, 1983), 1–13; David Lowenthal, *The Past Is a Foreign Country* (Cambridge: Cambridge University Press, 1985), 7–15; Maurice Godelier, "The Ideal in the Real," in *Culture, Ideology, and Politics*, ed. R. Samuel and G.S. Jones (London: Routledge, 1982), 16–34. For a discussion of the dogmatic quality of some cultural forms and their ability to privilege abstraction over experience, see George Lipsitz, *Time Passages: Collective Memory and American Popular Culture* (Minneapolis: University of Minnesota Press, 1990), 14.

3. On "contradictions" in the social system, see Mark Poster, *Foucault, Marxism, and History: Mode of Production Versus Mode of Information* (Cambridge, Engl.: Polity Press, 1984), 48, 60, 84–85. On patriotism see Hans Kohn, *The Idea of Nationalism in the Twentieth Century* (London and New York: Basil Blackwell, 1979), 8, 87–88, 205–6; Raphael Samuel, "Introduction: Exciting to Be English,"

in *Patriotism: The Making and Unmaking of British National Identity,* ed. Raphael Samuel (London: Routledge, 1989), 1:xvii–lx.

4. Anthony D. Smith, *The Ethnic Origins of Nations* (New York: Basil Blackwell, 1986), 156, 201.

5. James H. Kennedy, *A History of the City of Cleveland* (Cleveland: Imperial Press, 1896), 520–53.

6. *Cleveland Plain Dealer,* July 4, 1894, II, 1–2; George E. Condon, *Cleveland: The Best Kept Secret* (Garden City, N.Y.: Doubleday, 1967), 79.

7. *Cleveland Plain Dealer,* July 4, 1894, 1–2.

8. Ibid. The Early Settlers Association has now taken the monument from storage, refurbished it, and placed it for public view in a small park in the downtown area.

9. Ibid.; Condon, *Cleveland,* 79–80.

10. *Cleveland Plain Dealer,* July 5, 1894, pp. 1, 3, 5, 8.

11. Ibid., July 4, 1918, pp. 1, 12; July 5, 1918, pp. 1, 4. On the widespread Americanization programs in Cleveland during the entire era, see "Report of the Work of the Cleveland Americanization Committee" (Cleveland: Cleveland Americanization Committee, 1918); Edward M. Miggins, "Becoming American: Americanization and the Reform of the Cleveland Public Schools," in *The Birth of Modern Cleveland, 1865–1930,* ed. Thomas F. Campbell and Edward M. Miggins (Cleveland: Western Reserve Historical Society, 1988), 345–73. Miggins makes a good point when he suggests that Americanization efforts in the city changed in 1918 from a focus on "social uplift" to one that attempted to secure social unity to win the war. Although it could be argued that the goal of social unity and civic order was always part of the Americanization effort.

12. The charge that the riot may have been fomented by business interests in the city is found in Oakley C. Johnson, *The Day Is Coming: Life and Work of Charles E. Ruthenberg, 1882–1927* (New York: International Publishers, 1957), 144. On the riot itself see the *Cleveland Plain Dealer,* May 2, 1919, pp. 1–2; May 3, 1919, p. 1. Another account describing police brutality in the Cleveland riot can be found in Frank Marquart, *An Auto Worker's Journal: The UAW from Crusade to One-Party Union* (University Park: Penn State University Press, 1975), 22–23.

13. *Cleveland Plain Dealer,* Nov. 12, 1919, p. 1; "Official Program of 125th Anniversary Celebration of Cleveland" (Cleveland, 1921).

14. Clara Lederer, *Their Paths Are Peace: The Story of the Cleveland Cultural Gardens* (Cleveland: Cleveland Cultural Gardens Federation, 1954), 9–19.

15. "Cleveland Cultural Gardens Federation Minutes," Jan. 31, 1941, Cleveland Cultural Gardens Federation Records (CCGFR), box 1, Western Reserve Historical Society; Lederer, *Their Paths Are Peace,* 19.

16. "Cleveland Cultural Gardens Federation Minutes," Jan. 13, 1933; Jan. 27, 1933; Apr. 28, 1933; CCGFR, box 1. The occupations of ethnic representatives were obtained from the *Cleveland City Directory* (1932).

17. Lederer, *Their Paths Are Peace,* 47–49; *Cleveland News,* Oct. 14, 1935, clipping in CCGFR, box 5.

18. *Cleveland News,* May 30, 1937; *Catholic Universe Bulletin,* June 27, 1947; *Cleveland Plain Dealer,* Oct. 28, 1934, clippings in CCGFR, box 5.

19. Lederer, *Their Paths Are Peace,* 91–92; *Jednota,* Sept. 24, 1952, p. 7.

20. *Cleveland News,* July 25, 1942, and *Cleveland Plain Dealer,* Sept. 27, 1942, clippings in CCGFR, box 2.

21. Lederer, *Their Paths Are Peace,* 61–63, 92.

22. *Cleveland Plain Dealer,* July 22, 1946, pp. 1, 7.

23. Lederer, *Their Paths Are Peace,* 26–27; *Cleveland Plain Dealer,* Sept. 15, 1952, clipping in CCGFR, box 5.

24. *Cleveland Plain Dealer,* July 5, 1942, p. 1.

25. Ibid., May 30, 1969, sect. AA, pp. 4–5; May 31, 1968, p. 12.

26. Ibid., July 4, 1976, pp. 3, 21; sect. AA, p. 4. American Revolution Bicentennial Administration, *The Bicentennial of the United States of America* (Washington, D.C.: Government Printing Office, 1977), 5:14–16. On changes in Cleveland's political structure in the 1960s and 1970s, see Todd Swanstrom, *The Crisis of Growth Politics: Cleveland, Kucinich, and the Challenge of Urban Populism* (Philadelphia: Temple University Press, 1985).

27. Interview with Clay Herrick by John Bodnar, June 17, 1992. Mr. Herrick was a president of the Cultural Gardens and an officer of the Early Settlers Association. On the Afro-American museum see *Northern Ohio Live* (August 1988), pp. 11–13, and the various brochures supplied by the museum itself at 1765 Crawford Road, Cleveland.

Chapter V

THE MUSEUM AND THE POLITICS
OF SOCIAL CONTROL IN
MODERN IRAQ

Eric Davis

WHAT IS the relationship between the museum and the state? More precisely, in what ways does the publicly sponsored museum reflect efforts by the state to expand its power in society at large? This question has only recently begun to be raised within the Western context and, to my knowledge, has not been raised at all in the Middle East. In Iraq, as in most countries, the museum is not just a neutral public space where citizens come to view painting, sculpture, or artifacts of the past. As with other aspects of Iraqi cultural life, the museum has become highly politicized. Both in their conceptual foundations and contents, the museums established by the Iraqi state during the twentieth century reflect very specific ends.

This is especially true of museums established by the Ba'thist regime under Saddam Husayn that came to power in July 1968. The state's attempt to use the museum as a symbolic tool to enhance its power and authority points to the shortcomings of the discourse of violence and coercion that has been the dominant conceptual prism through which most Third World regimes have been viewed. Even the most repressive regimes, of which the Iraqi Ba'th is an exemplar, seek to develop ideologies that generate "self-discipline" among the populace at large. In this context, a study of the museum becomes not only an end in itself but also a corrective to social control understood only through violence and coercion.

Does this approach mean that all cultural representation in Iraqi museums can be reduced to some instrumentalist logic? Such an argument would be far too simplistic. Power, as Foucault argues, is not a static element waiting to be appropriated by a Great Leader or a ruling group. Rather power must be understood as an ever-changing set of relationships between dominator and dominated. Power becomes effective only if a social and cultural grid within which it can be exercised already exists. Thus, it does not inhere in the state but rather requires the complicity of subaltern groups.[1] This argumentation necessitates first and foremost a historical analysis not only of the growth of the museum as a form of social control, but also of the social, cultural, and political environment—the "fertile soil" as it were—that has allowed it to assume this quality. Put differently, how did the museum become part of national political discourse, and how did social conditions propitious for the use of the museum to advance state power develop in Iraq?

It might be useful to begin this historical analysis by contrasting the museum in Iraq with the growth of its counterpart in the United States. The development of the museum in Iraq, as opposed to its development in the West, occurred under direct state tutelage. In the United States, the Massachusetts Historical Society, the Pennsylvania Academy of Fine Arts, the New York Historical Society, and grander museums such as the Metropolitan Museum of Art and the Boston Museum of Fine Arts were the creation of an emerging bourgeoisie rather than the state. As has been persuasively argued, the American museum, especially following the Civil War, served an important role in consolidating the status and power of many nouveau riche families. During the late nineteenth century, the museum served a nationalist function as well, as the United States began to expand into the world market and sought to assume a position equal to that of its European competitors.[2] In more recent times, as the works of Tompkins, Silverman, Rosler, Haacke, and Schiller indicate, the museum has increasingly assumed marketing and consumerist functions.[3]

The museum's development in Iraq followed a very different historical trajectory. Rather than being the creation of a powerful Iraqi bourgeoisie, the first museums were established by a relatively weak state. The first major museum to be founded by the state was the Iraqi Museum, in 1923, which contained exhibits drawn almost exclusively from Iraq's pre-Islamic and pre-Arab past. The 1930s witnessed the opening of the Museum of National Costumes and the Museum of Arab Antiquities.[4] During the 1930s, the state began to send Iraqi artists and archaeologists to study in Europe. As a result, archaeological excavations and restorations of antiquities increased dramatically during the 1930s. State funds were used to publish numerous directories of excavated sites.[5] In 1943 the Iraqi state opened the first gallery of modern art in the country.[6]

Although, on the face of it, none of these developments was particularly unusual, they did reflect a number of underlying social tensions and power struggles. First, the Iraqi state's renewed interest during the 1930s in the country's Mesopotamian heritage, and its history and artistic creativity more broadly defined, reflected the intensification of the nationalist struggle that emerged following Great Britain's conquest of Ottoman forces and its occupation of Iraq in 1917. The mass-based Iraqi Revolution of 1920 and the League of Nations' subsequent designation of Britain as a mandatory power in 1921 were two critical events that further agitated nationalist feelings. As in other countries under colonial domination, the increasing polarization between nationalists and their foreign overlords served to intensify the dichotomy between self and other.

Questions were raised as to what gave a country its distinctive sense of national identity. What did Great Britain possess that was lacking in Iraq and that enabled it to assume the role of imperialist power? The sharpening of the boundaries between "we" and "they" and the spread of concern with questions of self-identity began to make explicit the political issues that had heretofore been much more implicit and diffuse in national discourse. Specifically, a large debate began to develop around the question of Iraqi heritage.[7] Should Iraq define itself in terms of its Arab heritage, should it look to ancient Mesopotamia or Islam, or should it forge a new identity from a populist heritage such as that proffered by the nascent Iraqi Communist party?

It is within this context that the question of the nation's antiquities became a political issue. During the early part of this century, many Iraqi nationalists were angered that foreign nationals were depleting Iraq of thousands of ancient artifacts over which the state exercised little control. Despite an Iraqi law stipulating that archaeological finds be divided in half between the state and foreign excavation teams, in reality foreigners were taking far more than half, and the most important discoveries at that. Thus, qualitatively and quantitatively, Iraq was losing much of its national heritage.

The excavation movement in Iraq, undertaken by French, British, and German scholars during the first half of the nineteenth century and joined by American scholars by the end of the century, led to numerous discoveries. Under the Ottoman Empire's antiquities law, all archaeological finds became the property of the Sublime Porte.[8] However, thousands of items found their way into European and later American museums as well as into the private collections of wealthy collectors of art. In addition to the loss of much of their ancient heritage, what Iraqi nationalists found particularly galling was the complete lack of interest among Western researchers in the country's "living heritage," namely, its Arab and Islamic past. It was almost as if foreigners saw the country's Arab and Muslim inhabitants as interlopers who might threaten what they considered their legitimate efforts to appropriate knowledge and representations of the "cradle of (Western) civilization." The Iraqi often felt "invisible" in the eyes of the Westerner, who, in preferring the necropolises and monuments of ancient Mesopotamia to all other aspects of the country's heritage, would just as soon have seen the land devoid of its modern inhabitants.

With the rise of nationalism during the First World War, Iraqis, as well as other Arabs, refused to remain invisible. Mass-based uprisings broke out in Egypt and Iraq in 1919 and 1920 respectively, as well as in other parts of the Arab world such as Palestine, Greater Syria, and North Africa. Following the 1920 Revolution, British colonial officials developed a system of indirect rule in Iraq.[9] Under this system, a British adviser was attached to each Iraqi ministry and became the effective decision-making force, since all decisions required his or her approval.

Attached to the Ministry of Education, the Iraqi Museum came under the tutelage of Gertrude Bell, the Oriental secretary of the British high commissioner and honorary advisor to the ministry.[10] Efforts by Iraqi nationalists within the ministry to revise the antiquities laws Iraq inherited from the Ottomans ran up against Bell's opposition. She argued that if Iraq's laws were changed to give more favorable terms to the state the number of foreign teams coming to Iraq would sharply decline. When Sati‛ al-Husari, a ministry official who later became director general of antiquities, pointed out that in Crete all items discovered during excavations were given to the national museum, Bell simply replied that "Iraq is one thing and Crete is another thing altogether."[11] Using the argument that the Iraqi Museum concerned itself primarily with stone objects and architecture, elements associated with engineering, Bell advocated removing it from the Ministry of Education and attaching it to the Ministry of Public Works and Transportation, as had been done with its counterpart in Egypt. Since the latter ministry did not contain a large contingent of nationalists who would fight to protect the museum's interests, Bell was effectively able to remove control over the disposition of newly discovered antiquities from any Iraqi authority.[12]

This particular incident underlines not only the extent to which the emergence of the museum as a domain of struggle was tied to the rise of the Iraqi nationalist movement but also the need to situate the museum historically in order to understand its political and social meaning. A historical approach indicates that the state's efforts to use the museum to strengthen its power and authority did not begin with the rise to power of the current Ba‛thist regime and the dramatic influx of oil wealth during the 1970s. The complex network of social, cultural, and political relationships upon which the contemporary state could build in expanding its base of power was set in place well before it came to power in 1968. How was this foundation established?

In Iraq, as in other societies, the museum is situated within a multi-faceted network of oppositional relationships. In the writings of Arab nationalist, such as the *Memoirs* of Sati‛ al-Husari, the museum becomes a metaphor for a nation's ability to assert control over its cultural heritage. When al-Husari first entered the Iraqi Museum during the early 1920s, his shock at the lack of exhibits from Iraq's Arab or Islamic past was less a parochial reaction than a realization that this past represented a heritage to which the British accorded little or no relevance.[13] For Iraqi nationalists, the museum thus became a contested domain in two senses. One part of the

struggle was to force the British to accept Iraqi control over the disposition
of excavated artifacts. The other entailed forcing the museum to open its
purview to cultural heritages other than those of the Sumerian, Akkadian,
and Assyrian civilizations of ancient Mesopotamia. What Iraqi nationalists were in effect trying to accomplish was to force Western colonialists to
confront Iraq as a living and not a dead culture. Of course, it was much
easier for the British state to legitimate the subjugation of another people if
indeed they had no valid "living" culture.

   During the 1920s, the modern Iraqi state was in its formative stages. In
one of the more bizarre incidents in the annals of colonial history, the
British imposed a monarchy upon Iraq that was drawn from the Hashimite
family, who were the guardians of Makka (Mecca) and al-Madina, the two
most holy cities in Islam. Recruiting Iraq's new monarch from the Hijaz
(presently part of the Kingdom of Saudi Arabia), as well as establishing
another Hashimite dynasty in the newly created and neighboring Kingdom
of Transjordan, represented an attempt to appease Arab nationalists who
had risen up against Ottoman forces in the Hijaz during the First World
War. These nationalists expected the British to follow through on their
promise to found an independent Arab state that would include all of the
Hijaz, Palestine, and the Levant following the war's end. Offering the
monarchy to Faysal was also part of the British strategy to maintain a
trustworthy ruler in Iraq, which was considered a vital link to India. The
Balfour Declaration issued to the Zionist movement in Britain in 1917 and
the secret Sykes-Picot Treaty dividing up the former Ottoman colonies
between the British and the French signed the previous year indicated that
the MacMahon-Husayn correspondence promising the Arabs political independence was never seriously considered by the British. After the French
crushed, in 1920, the short-lived Arab republic in Syria that had been
founded in 1918 and headed by Sharif Husayn's son, Prince Faysal, the
British offered Faysal rule of Iraq.

   The new Iraqi monarchy found itself ruling over a country where effective power was in the hands of the British, where urban nationalists re-
sented what they considered to be an alien ruler imposed from outside, and
where the refusal of tribal shaykhs in the Tigris-Euphrates Delta to cede
authority to the central government in Baghdad was only encouraged by
favorable tax policies enacted by the British. With few resources, either
political or financial, at its disposal, it is understandable why the monarchy should have become interested in promoting Iraqi culture and heritage as one means whereby it could forge an alliance with elements of the
growing nationalist movement. In Gramscian terms, the newly formed
state was promoting the development of a rudimentary "historical bloc."[14]
Since the Hashimite family could trace its lineage to the family of the
Prophet Muhammad in Makka, it did possess some legitimacy among the
Iraqi populace due to its links to an Arabo-Islamic heritage.[15]

Despite its inherently elitist and exclusionary character, there was no contradiction in the monarchy's promotion of Arabism in the form of the Museum of Arab Antiquities, opened in 1937 in a famous Baghdadi covered market, the Khan Murjan, and the Museum of National Costumes. The fact that the Hashimite family traced much of its own heritage to the beduin tradition of the Arabian Peninsula led it to promote what later came to be known as folklore or popular heritage (al-turath al-sha'bi). The "costumes" worn by many Iraqis, whether from the Tigris-Euphrates Delta or from the desert, were similar to the traditional or ceremonial garb of the Hashimites. With the growth of urban areas as a result of the decline of Iraqi agriculture following World War I and the migration of large numbers of peasants to major cities such as Baghdad, Basra, and Musul, a yearning for the simpler past of rural life began to be articulated in Iraqi literature and newspaper articles.[16] The state was thus able to conflate efforts to promote its own legitimacy with urban nationalists' concern for Iraq's Arab and Islamic past and folklore, given their desire to gain a better sense of their historical roots and rural heritage. While this pattern whereby the state sought to appropriate an oppositional space for its own ends was only crudely developed under the monarchy, it has been much more skillfully pursued by the current regime under Saddam Husayn and the Ba'th party.

In addition to the Iraqi Museum, which was meant to preserve artifacts from Iraq's Mesopotamian past, and the Museum of Arab Antiquities and the Museum of National Costumes—which reflected a rudimentary attempt to integrate Iraq's diverse ethnolinguistic and confessional groups through representing the country's Arabo-Islamic and folkloric heritage as a unified past—the state sponsored a third type of cultural institution, intended to promote the development of Western fine arts. The Institute of Music, established in 1937, the Iraq School of Fine Arts, opened in 1939, and the state-sponsored Museum of Modern Art, established in 1943, were prominent examples of this type of cultural orientation.[17]

Cultural institutions intended to promote Western fine arts highlight yet another arena of struggle. In this instance, an effort was being expended to "prove" to the West that Iraqis were "civilized." Thus the Museum of Modern Art (later the Museum of Iraqi Art Pioneers), established to enshrine the realist school of Iraqi painters that developed during the 1940s, represented an attempt to erode the Orientalist perspective of Iraq as a "backward," "uncivilized," and parochial society unable to come to terms with Western artistic currents.[18]

Thus it is possible to speak of four types of representation in Iraqi museums that had developed prior to the 1958 revolution that overthrew the monarchy. One was concerned with Iraq's ancient Mesopotamian past, one with Iraq's Arabo-Islamic past, especially that linked to the 'Abbasid Empire, which was centered in Baghdad between A.D. 750 and 1258, another with folklore broadly defined, and one with Western artistic traditions. In arguing that the state promoted these types of representations in museums and affiliated institutions, it is important that we not treat the state as a monolith. While the monarchy supported the establishment of museums and other cultural institutions, it was within the ministries, especially in the nationalistically oriented Ministry of Education, and in the Iraqi parliament, that the impetus for their development really began. Ultimately, it was within the higher echelons of the state that decisions were finalized as to which projects would be given an official imprimatur. Political factors, I would argue, were uppermost in all these decisions. Again, the need for a historical dimension is apparent. Many of the ideas that would later become influential in the writings of the architects of current Ba'thist efforts to rewrite history and reinterpret popular culture were being formulated by lower-level officials within the Iraqi state during the prerevolutionary period. Many of these lesser bureaucrats would assume much more prominent positions in the postrevolution regimes.

The 1958 Revolution brought with it a tremendous expansion of state activity in the cultural sphere. Given the constant political turmoil that plagued Iraqi society from the end of the Second World War until 1958, under the monarchy, the state's support for archaeological research and the arts had declined as it became preoccupied with domestic security and the increasingly troubled international politics of the Middle East. One of the first tasks of the new military regime of ʿAbd al-Karim Qasim was to establish a Ministry of Guidance. As outlined in *The Iraqi Revolution in Its Fourth Year,* "The Ministry of Guidance is shouldered with two main tasks, first, to orientate [*sic*] Iraqi individuals according to sound national principles, and second, to introduce the Republic of Iraq to the outside world."[19] The period between 1958 and the overthrow of the Qasim regime in 1963 saw the establishment of guidance centers throughout the major regions of the country, where the populace was exposed to lectures, films, publications, photography exhibits, and speeches by Qasim himself. For the first time, the state pursued a comprehensive study of folklore. Research teams were sent to the northern and southern portions of the country to document, photograph, and collect as many aspects of Iraqi folk culture as possible.[20] The regime stated that one of its primary objectives was to revive handicraft production and an interest in folklore.

Since many of the museums owned by the state had fallen into disrepair prior to the 1958 Revolution, one of the first activities of the Ministry of Guidance was to transfer operation of museums to its own control. The Museum of National Costumes was transferred from the Directorate of Antiquities to the ministry's Directorate of Popular Arts and Culture, as was the Museum of Modern Art, later the Museum of Iraqi Art Pioneers.[21] The state's active role in promoting culture, especially popular culture, was at one level a reflection of its mass base. It also reflected the presence within the state bureaucracy of many members and sympathizers of the Iraqi Communist party (ICP). Iraqi leftists saw the 1958 Revolution as a golden opportunity to enact the type of people's democracy that the ICP had been advocating since its founding in 1934. In this sense, the museum as it developed under Qasim's republican regime reflected pressures from below in the form of the ICP and Iraq's powerful and radical trade-union movement, which was closely linked to the party.[22]

In its cultural orientation, the Qasim regime did not place a strong emphasis upon Arab nationalism. Its retreat from Arab nationalism was a result of several factors. First, many members of the regime, especially leftists and Communists, felt that culture should reflect the ethnolinguistic and confessional diversity of the country. Second, a competition existed between Iraq and the Arab nationalist regime in Egypt under Jamal ʿAbd al-Nasir, which was striving to achieve a dominant leadership role within the Arab world. Symbols drawn from Iraq's Mesopotamian heritage were incorporated into the new flag and the emblem of the revolution. Communists and shiʿis who supported the regime were especially hostile to the corporatist Arab nationalism advocated by Iraqi Nasirists and Baʿthists, since their ideologies denied the primacy of class conflict in social change and privileged sunni Islam to the detriment of shiʿi Islam. In other words, many Iraqi Nasirists and Baʿthists were unwilling to accept the reality of Iraq as a class-based and multiethnic and multiconfessional society.

The period between 1958 and 1963 thus represented a critical period in the struggle over the official definition of Iraq's national identity. Would modern Iraq choose a narrow Arab Nationalist interpretation of Iraqi national character, or would it opt for a broader interpretation that would allow for expression of sociocultural difference? It also represented a struggle over whether political participation and a fairer distribution of economic wealth would be made available to a broader sector of Iraqi society. In short, would Iraq become a society in which equity and tolerance of sociocultural difference were promoted by the state?

The coup d'état of February 1963, which brought a coalition of Baʿthists and Nasirists to power, answered this question in the negative, as thousands of Communist party members, workers, and leftist intellectuals were killed or imprisoned. While there was little significant cultural development between 1963 and 1968, when the current regime under Saddam Husayn was able to come to power by capitalizing on the continuing political instability that beset the country, the post-1968 period saw a tremendous outpouring of state-sponsored cultural production. Part of this process entailed a greatly expanded political role for the museum that was intended to promote nationalist feelings among Iraqis.

At least nine new museums were founded between the 1968 coup d'état and 1977. One of these, the Museum of the Arab Baʿth Socialist Party, was

established in the residency of Ahmad Hasan al-Bakr, a respected general
and party member who became president in 1968 and was removed by
Saddam Husayn in 1979.[23] The museum was designed to document the
underground struggle of the Ba'th party against the monarchy, the Qasim
regime, and the rival wing of the party, which was eliminated during the
July 1968 "revolution."[24] Arabo-Islamic and children's museums were
also built, as well as numerous museums in the provinces in order to spread
cultural activity outside Baghdad, which had been its main venue to date.
Older museums, such as the Iraqi Museum and the Museum of National
Costumes—now broadened in scope and renamed the Costume and Folklore Museum—were greatly expanded and given the responsibility of developing traveling exhibits throughout the provinces. The budget of the
Directorate of Antiquities was also increased, with the expectation that the
expanded number of excavations it would undertake would produce artifacts to fill the newly created museums.[25]

What did all this activity reflect? In the most immediate sense, the expanded cultural activity of the state was intended to bolster the legitimacy
of the Bakr-Husayn regime. Despite the state's designation of the events
between July 17 and 30, 1968, as a revolution, most Iraqis saw this period
as only another in a long line of factional struggles. The one weapon that
the new regime soon came to possess that had not been available to its
predecessors was a tremendous increase in revenues due to a dramatic rise
in oil prices during the early 1970s.

For the new regime, the museum was first and foremost part of a larger
strategy designed to demonstrate the Ba'th party's populist character. Despite having lost a substantial portion of its cadres in 1963, the ICP had
been able to reorganize by the end of the 1960s. The fact that the party had
become so powerful under the Qasim regime and that it continued to be
popular among the working class and intelligentsia and among segments
of the peasantry worried the regime.

One way to compete with the ICP for the loyalties of the masses was
through emphasizing folklore. Not only did the regime expand the Costume and Folklore Museum, but it also established an institution known as
Dar al-Turath al-Sha'bi (the House of Popular Culture) in 1972. The purpose of this latter institution was to revive the production of traditional
crafts. The state argued that the revival of folklore was key to progressive
national development, since one of the aims of imperialism was to sever the
Iraqi populace's links to its past. As the monarchy had attempted much less
effectively earlier in the century, the Ba'thist state co-opted the desire of
large segments of the populace, especially the upwardly mobile middle
class, to understand better their history and national heritage. This and
other social strata faced rapid change that included the breakdown of the
traditional extended family and the rapid expansion of urban areas, char-

acterized by an erosion of traditional values governing child-rearing practices and gender and business relations, as well as the spread of materialism
and a consumerist mentality promoted by the influx of oil wealth. As a
consequence many Iraqis felt more and more isolated and alienated. Increasingly these feelings were manifested in literature, films, and programs
in the mass media.[26] The massive migration to urban areas that characterized Iraqi society between the 1930s and the 1970s provided fertile
ground for the state's attempts to restructure the society's understanding of
its national heritage.

The emphasis on popular culture, which was a key component in this
process, became a way of ameliorating feelings of social disorientation by
giving the public an ersatz version of Iraqi history and folklore. It is important to recognize that the Dar al-Turath al-Sha'bi was entrusted not only
with preserving Iraq's folkloric heritage but also with reviving it. It is in this
latter sphere that political ends could best be pursued, since it was here that
the state maintained the best opportunities to "invent tradition."[27] Arguing that prior regimes collaborated with imperialism to deprive Iraqis of
their heritage through neglecting their history and folklore, the official task
of the House of Popular Culture and its companion institute, the Institute
of Arts and Craft Industries, was to create a new generation of nationalistically oriented artists.[28] Many of the activities of the Dar al-Turath
al-Sha'bi point to their underlying political ends. One example is the manu-
facture of traditional rugs containing the Ba'th party emblem and slogans
by students in the Section for Weaving and Handmade Rugs.[29] Another is
the incorporation in works produced in the Section for Painting and
Sketching of imagery from the Battle of Qadisiya, where, in A.D. 637, Arab
forces in Iraq were able to defeat the Persian Sassanians.[30] Appropriated to
become "Qadisiyat Saddam," or Saddam's Qadisiya, after the outbreak of
the Iraq-Iran War in 1980, folkloric production centered around this historic battle was used to mobilize the populace against the Iranian enemy.[31]
Similar examples can also be found in the production of traditional
clothing and ceramics. Although at the time of this writing the Iraqi Ba'th
faces an uncertain future given continued uprisings by Kurds in the north
and dissident shi'is in the south, undoubtedly the Dar al-Turath al-Sha'bi
will work to develop an officially sanctioned iconography surrounding the
1991 Gulf War that supports the regime's current campaign to turn defeat
into "victory."

The state's effort to penetrate "low culture" initially represented an
attempt to enhance its legitimacy and outflank a possible resurgence of
strength by the ICP. It was later expanded to incorporate efforts to combat
a rise of radical Islam among sections of Iraq's shi'i population following
the successful Islamic revolution in neighboring Iran. Given the historic
economic and cultural ties between Iraqi and Iranian shi'is, the Ba'thist

regime distrusted the loyalty of the shiʿa, who comprise 60 percent of the populace. The new type of museum, in the form of a combined craft center and exhibit space, was also used further to deny social difference. Folklore could become the common denominator of all Iraqis—sunni Muslims, shiʿi Muslims, and Kurds alike—who shared more or less the same type of food, clothing, rituals, games, music, and family structure. In other words, as constructed by the state, folklore not only proved that Iraqis represented a unified national culture and political community but also provided a link to Iraq's Mesopotamian heritage, since many cultural patterns practiced by the ancient inhabitants of the region were said to parallel those of modern Iraqis.[32]

Prior to the debacle in Kuwait, the regime of Saddam Husayn had been successful in either co-opting or physically eliminating opponents during its first decade in power and, during its second decade, defeating or at least fighting to a stalemate a much larger Iranian army. The false sense of security that the regime had built up before August 1990 was reflected in the development of the museum. While the museum and visual representation in general continued to be manipulated by the state, wall posters and official photographs being two prominent examples, more recent efforts were directed at the commodification of culture. This reflected the continuing move to the right and the gradual dispensing of the radical anti-imperialist and socialist rhetoric that had characterized the early years of the Baʿthist regime. Using the argument that prices of traditional handicraft production had declined through neglect, the regime began to emphasize marketing both within Iraq and abroad the production of craft centers such as the House of Popular Culture.[33] During the late 1970s, a Dar al-Azya' (House of Fashion) was established to revive ancient Mesopotamian dress.[34] Attempts at marketing fashionable dresses that mix Western and Mesopotamian styles were also initiated.

These efforts reflected not only the greater political security that the state felt during the 1980s but also the dramatic growth of a new Iraqi bourgeoisie tied to oil wealth. Perhaps an argument could be made for a parallel between the relationship of the museum and the bourgeoisie in the United States and the museum and the bourgeoisie tied to the state in Iraq. In each case, the historical pattern indicates that, in its earlier stages, the museum was used to promote nationalism and enhance the bourgeoisie's social status. As the bourgeoisie came to feel more established both politically and culturally, the museum assumed an additional function in augmenting the bourgeoisie's financial interests. Just as artistic production has become a big business in the West, so the 1980s witnessed the beginnings of a similar process, albeit much more limited and tied primarily to "primitive" folkloric art, in Iraq.

The weakened Iraqi state that emerged from the massive defeat of its armed forces in Kuwait can no longer afford, either in financial or human resources, to continue the intensity of its campaign to reinterpret the country's national heritage. Thus we can expect that the pace of establishing new museums will slacken. However, the ability of Saddam Husayn to exploit the Gulf Crisis should not be underestimated. "Museums" may assume more unorthodox forms, as with the so-called Victory Arch monument (qaws al-nasr) constructed by Saddam to celebrate and personalize his supposed vanquishing of the Iranian enemy.[35] Certainly the regime will continue its efforts to exploit the suffering that the populace endured during the Gulf War to direct hostility against its two main enemies, the United States and Israel. Material manifestations of that suffering will undoubtedly become the exhibits of new museums, designed to glorify the regime's "courage" in standing up to foreign aggression, especially the massive military might of the United States.

Under the Iraqi Ba'th, the museum remains, at its most basic level, a form of social control. Whether relating to "high culture" in the form of the Iraqi Museum or the 'Abbasid Museum, or "low culture" in the form of the Costume and Folklore Museum or the House of Popular Culture, the regime has used the representation of the past to diffuse very well-defined ideological messages to the populace at large. These messages are that Iraqis are hewn from a similar cast and that any expression of cultural difference that challenges the regime's power in any way will not be tolerated. While the past is glorified, it is simultaneously denigrated. Aspects of Iraqi culture contained in museums are to be praised and perhaps even trotted out for certain rituals and national holidays. However, by being placed in the museum, they are deemed no longer appropriate for everyday life. Those who persist in adhering to culture as represented in the museum, especially elements of tribal or religious culture that can be mobilized symbolically by oppositional groups, oppose the progress of the nation toward greater technological development and modernity. They are thus enemies of the state. In this manner, traditional sectors of the shi'i, Kurdish, and even sunni communities, as well as other minorities, the left, and the poor, find themselves marginalized and outside the economic and political mainstream unless they submit to the culturally hegemonic dictates of the state.

NOTES

1. Michel Foucault, "Two Lectures," in Power/Knowledge: Selected Interviews and Writings, 1972–1977, ed. Colin Gordon (New York: Pantheon, 1980), p. 98.

2. Karl E. Meyer, The Art Museum: Power, Money, Ethics (New York: William Morrow, 1979), pp. 23–25.

3. See Calvin Tompkins, Merchants and Masterpieces: The Story of the Metro-

politan Museum of Art (New York: E.P. Dutton & Co., 1970); Martha Rosler, "Lookers, Buyers, Dealers and Makers: Thoughts on Audience," in *Art After Modernism: Rethinking Representation,* ed. Brian Wallis (New York and Boston: New Museum of Contemporary Art and David R. Godine, 1984), pp. 311–340; Debora Silverman, *Selling Culture* (New York: Pantheon Books, 1986); Brian Wallis, ed., *Hans Haacke: Unfinished Business* (New York and Cambridge, MA: New Museum of Contemporary Art and M.I.T. Press, 1986); and Herbert I. Schiller, *Culture, Inc.: The Corporate Takeover of Public Expression* (New York and Oxford: Oxford University Press, 1989), esp. pp. 91–98.

4. See, for example, Directorate of Antiquities, *dalil mathaf al-athar al-'arabiya* [Guide to the Museum of Arab Antiquities] (Baghdad: Matba'at al-Hukuma, 1938), esp. pp. 17–18.

5. See, for example, Directorate of Antiquities, *jisr harba* (Baghdad: Matba'at al-Hukuma, 1935).

6. Directorate General of Propaganda, *Kingdom of Iraq* (Baltimore: Lord Baltimore Press, n.d.), p. 79.

7. For elements of this debate, see Eric Davis and Nicolas Gavrielides, "Statecraft, Historical Memory and Popular Culture in Iraq and Kuwait," in *Statecraft in the Middle East: Oil, Historical Memory and Popular Culture,* ed. E. Davis and N. Gavrielides (Miami: Florida International University Press, 1991), esp. pp. 123–128 and 132–140.

8. Abu al-Khaldun Sati' al-Husari, *mudhakkarati fi-l-'iraq, 1921–1941* [My Iraqi memoirs, 1921–1941] (Beirut: Dar al-Tali'a, 1967), vol. 1, 1921–1927, p. 178.

9. For an extensive discussion of British colonial policy in Iraq, see Daniel Silverfarb, *Britain's Informal Empire in the Middle East: A Case Study of Iraq, 1929–1941* (New York and Oxford: Oxford University Press, 1986).

10. On her activities in Iraq, see Sarah Graham-Brown's introduction to Bell's *The Desert and the Sown* (Boston: Beacon Press, 1987), pp. xi–xviii; and H.V.F. Winstone, *Gertrude Bell* (London: Quartet Books, 1980). Bell's influence on early British policy in Iraq is underlined by her unofficial title as "the uncrowned queen of Iraq" (Graham-Brown, p. xi).

11. al-Husari, *mudhakkarati: fi-l-'iraq,* vol. 1, p. 180.

12. Ibid., p. 181.

13. Abu al-Khaldun Sati' al-Husari, *mudhakkarati, fi-l-'iraq, 1921–1941* [My Iraqi memoirs, 1921–1941] (Beirut: Dar al-Tali'a, 1968), vol. 2, 1927–1941, p. 409.

14. On the concept of the "historical bloc," see Antonio Gramsci, *Selections from the Prison Notebooks* (London: Lawrence & Wishart, 1971), pp. 157–158, 418.

15. This element was stressed in all official publications that described the royal family. See *Kingdom of Iraq,* pp. 3, 9.

16. See Muhsin Jassim al-Musawi, "The Sociopolitical Context of the Iraqi Short Story, 1908–1968," in Davis and Gavrielides, *Statecraft in the Middle East,* pp. 214–217.

17. *Kingdom of Iraq,* pp. 78–79. At its founding, the museum was simply referred to as a "gallery of fine art."

MUSEUM AND SOCIAL CONTROL IN IRAQ 103

18. Ministry of Culture and Arts, *Culture and Arts in Iraq: Celebrating the Tenth Anniversary of the July 17–30 Revolution* (Baghdad, 1978), p. 25; ʿAdil Kamil, *al-haraka al-tashkiliya al-muʿasira fi-l-ʿiraq: marhalat al-ruwwad* [The contemporary art movement in Iraq: The "pioneer" period] (Baghdad: Ministry of Culture and Information, Dar al-Rashid li-l-Nashr, 1980), pp. 5–18. See also Shawkat al-Rabʿi, *lawhat wa afkar* [Paintings and ideas] (Baghdad: Ministry of Information, Dar al-Hurriya li-l-Tibaʿa, 1976); and ʿAbdallah al-Khatib, *al-funun al-tashkiliya wa-l-thawra* [The plastic arts and revolution] (Baghdad: Ministry of Information, Dar al-Hurriya li-l-Tibaʿa, 1976).

19. Ministry of Guidance, High Committee for the Celebration of the July 14 Revolution, *The Iraqi Revolution in Its Fourth Year* (Baghdad: Times Press, 1962).

20. Ibid., pp. 630–631.

21. Ibid., p. 633.

22. The impact of the Iraqi labor movement on political and cultural representation in Iraq is discussed in my "History for the Many or History for the Few? The Historiography of the Iraqi Working Class," in *Workers and Working Classes in the Middle East: Struggles, Histories and Historiographies*, ed. Zachary Lockman (Albany: State University of New York Press, forthcoming).

23. For photographs of the *mathaf al-hizb* (the Party Museum), see *al-masira:lamahat mudayiʾa min nidal hizb al-baʿth al-ʿarabi al-ishtiraki/ Images of the Struggle of the Arab Baʾath Socialist Party* (Baghdad: n.d.), pp. 86–87, 91, 92, 93–94. This volume contains parallel Arabic, English, and French texts.

24. The group of military officers and civilians that overthrew the regime of ʿAbd al-Rahman ʿArif in July 1968 was in turn beset by internal struggles shortly after coming to power. Between July 17 and 30, Bakr, Husayn, and their supporters were able in two separate coups first to eliminate ʿArif and then to consolidate their control. As Hanna Batatu points out, these events essentially constituted a "palace coup" (*The Old Social Classes and the Revolutionary Movements of Iraq* [Princeton, N.J.: Princeton University Press, 1978], p. 1073). Despite the flagrant distortion of reality, the official designation of this two-week period continues to be the "Revolution of July 17–30, 1968."

25. *Culture and Arts in Iraq*, pp. 74, 91–93.

26. On this point, see al-Musawi, "The Sociopolitical Context of the Iraqi Short Story," pp. 218–225.

27. On this notion, see Eric Hobsbawm and Terence Ranger, eds., *The Invention of Tradition* (Cambridge: Cambridge University Press, 1983).

28. *al-turath al-shaʿbi* [The journal of popular heritage], *mulhaq khass ʿan al-hiraf wa-l-sinaʿat al-shaʿbiya fi-l-ʿiraq* [Special supplement on popular artisan and craft production in Iraq] (Baghdad: Dar al-Hurriya li-l-Nashr, 1984), pp. 6, 8.

29. Ibid., p. 7.

30. Ibid., p. 12.

31. For the Baʿth's efforts to stimulate anti-Iranian feeling, see my "State-Building in Iraq During the Iran-Iraq War and the Gulf Crisis," in *The Internationalization of Communal Strife*, ed. Manus I. Midlarksy (London and New York: Routledge, 1992), esp. pp. 71–72.

32. See, for example, Tariq al-Nasiri, *al-riyada badaʾat fi wadi al-rafidayn* [Sports in the (*sic*) ancient Mesopotamia] (Baghdad: Dar al-Qadisiya li-l-Tibaʿa,

104   ERIC DAVIS

1983); and Subhi Anwar Rashid, *al-musiqa fi-l-'iraq al-qadim* [Music in ancient Iraq] (Baghdad: Ministry of Culture and Information, Dar al-Shu'un al-Thaqafiya al-'Amma, 1988). Texts such as these resonate far more with the literate public than more didactic writings such as those by the prominent historian Anmad al-Susa, e.g., *hidarat al-'arab wa marahil tatawwuruha 'abar al-'usur* [Arab culture and the stages of its development through the ages] (Baghdad: Ministry of Culture and Information, Dar al-Hurriya li-l-Tiba'a, 1979); *hidarat wadi al-rafidayn bayn al-samiyin wa-l-sumariyin* [Mesopotamian culture between the Semites and the Sumerians] (Baghdad: Ministry of Culture and Information, Dar al-Rashid li-l-Nashr, 1980); and *tarikh hidarat wadi al-rafidayn fi daw' mashari' al-rayy al-zira'iya wa-l-muktashafat al-athariya wa-l-masadir al-tarikhiya* [The history of Mesopotamian civilization in light of agricultural irrigation projects, archaeological discoveries and historical sources] (Baghdad: Dar al-Hurriya li-l-Tiba'a, 1983), vol. 1. Susa's works attempt to demonstrate the racial ties between the ancient Sumerians and the Arabs of modern Iraq.

33. *al-turath al-sha'bi, mulhaq khass,* pp. 9–10, 12.

34. *Culture and Arts in Iraq,* pp. 162–164.

35. For a detailed analysis of the meaning of the Victory Arch for Iraqi politics and cultural development, see Samir al-Khalil, *The Monument: Art, Vulgarity and Responsibility in Iraq* (Berkeley and Los Angeles: University of California Press, 1991).

Chapter VI

THE HISTORIC, THE LEGENDARY, AND THE INCREDIBLE: INVENTED TRADITION AND COLLECTIVE MEMORY IN ISRAEL

Yael Zerubavel

IN DAILY as well as scholarly discourse, "history" and "legend" suggest two very different cultural representations of the past. While "history" relates to the record of actual occurrences that took place in the past, "legend" implies a fictitious tale, the product of folk imagination. Even the concept of "historical legend," which attempts to mediate between the two, reveals the tension between them. It indicates that although those who engage in the transmission of the narrative believe it to be a true account of a historical figure or event, others recognize the imaginary elements that have been woven into the past and hence define it as legend.[1] This definition, too, essentially considers the "historical" and the "legendary" aspects of the narrative as mutually exclusive. It is only the acknowledged disparity between the insiders' and the outsiders' perspectives that accounts for the otherwise impossible combination of these two categories. Indeed, once the fabricated elements are identified, the narrative loses its status as a historical account and moves out of the field of history and into the field of folklore.

Yet a close examination of references to narratives about the past may reveal that the line separating "history" from "legend" is neither that clear nor necessarily consistent. This ambiguity does not stem only from the historical dimension of the legend, but may also result from the literary qualities of the historical narrative. When history is rendered in a story form that follows the structure of the legend, the classification of the narrative can easily become open to negotiation. The starting point of the discussion here is the actual use of the terms "history" and "legend" in a certain culture, and not their scholarly definition as analytical categories. By exploring the meaning of these terms in their context of use, this study shows the cultural ambiguity regarding the conception of history and analyzes how it turns the commemoration of the past into a contested area.

When a society undergoes rapid developments that shatter its social and political order, its need to restructure the past is as great as its desire to set its future agenda. As Hobsbawm and Ranger observed, such periods often stimulate the creation of new cultural forms that replace the weakening older traditions.[2] These "invented traditions" are particularly significant for the legitimation of the emergent social and political order, and their success depends, to a large measure, on their ability to reconstruct an acceptable view of the past. These newly constructed commemorations are successful when they manage to project an aura of traditionality that obscures their brief career as cultural representations of the past. But "invented traditions" might succeed only partially or otherwise fail to convince of their traditional status when members of the society become aware of their fabricated character. Such awareness may lead to doubts about the appropriateness and validity of their commemoration of the past.

The analysis of such a cultural dialogue on the credibility of a commemorative narrative allows us to explore the potential fluidity of history and legend as culturally constructed categories. The study of a popular yet conscious attempt to turn history into a legend in order to create a new national tradition of modern Israeli society provides the focus for the present inquiry into these issues.

I

The historical event that originated the "legend" took place in the northern Galilee on March 1, 1920. Several Jewish settlers died in a battle in the settlement of Tel Ḥai, the most famous among them being Yoseph Trumpeldor, an ex-officer and military hero of the czarist army and a known Zionist activist. Tel Ḥai was one of a few small and isolated Jewish settlements in the northern frontier of the Upper Galilee, far from the center of the Jewish population of Palestine. While most Jewish settlers lived under the British mandatory rule, the settlers of the northern Galilee found themselves in an ambiguous political situation as the British army retreated to the south and the French assumed control over this area toward the end of 1919. The growing militancy of the local Muslim population against the French and the lack of clarity regarding the border separating the French and the British mandates threatened the safety of the Jewish settlers there. As hostilities increased, many Jewish settlers left the Upper Galilee. But those who continued there maintained that it was important to hold onto those settlements at all cost. Trumpeldor, who had joined the northern settlers only a couple of months earlier, stayed there to help them organize their defense in the face of the growing danger.[3]

On March 1, 1920, Arab forces assembled near Tel Ḥai.[4] Their representatives insisted on their right to check if French soldiers were hiding in the settlement. Although the settlers allowed them in, shooting exchanges erupted, several men died, and others were wounded. At the end of that day, after the Arabs had retreated, the small group of Jewish settlers that had survived the battle decided to leave Tel Ḥai and join a neighboring settlement. Two days later the Jewish settlers evacuated the Upper Galilee and retreated to a safer area in the south. Eight settlers had died in the defense of Tel Ḥai.

The outpouring of oral and written literature that began soon after the event—speeches, articles, poems, and songs—reveals the frequent use of the Hebrew terms *aggada* (legend) and *aggadati* (legendary). "Days will come and songs will be sung about [the heroes of Tel Ḥai] and legends will be formed about them," pronounced a well-known scholar a year following the historical event.[5] An important Hebrew socialist publication carried the statement that "[Trumpeldor's] legendary, historical figure has already become a model and a flag to many."[6] Even biographical works about Trumpeldor did not shy away from alluding to the "legendary" dimensions of his life. Thus, early biographers stated that "this is the route of the real hero to appear at the right time, as if by miracle, in the place most in need" and that "he ended his legendary life with a legendary death."[7]

The use of the term "legend" in conjunction with Tel Ḥai and Trumpeldor was not meant to challenge the historicity of the narrative. The Zionist pioneers used the term to express their view that Trumpeldor, the historical man, was a larger-than-life figure, a national symbol of extraordinary dimensions. The very act of referring to him as a "legend" was, in itself, a way of singling him out in that historical context. It was designed to articulate and create an attitude of veneration toward Trumpeldor and to establish the story about Tel Ḥai as part of the new national lore of the Jewish society in Palestine.

Like other cases of "invented tradition," this attempt to develop a new historical legend emerged during a period of rapid social, cultural, and political developments, when old traditions no longer seemed to offer a valid answer for members of the society. In this particular case, the founders of Israeli society, who had left behind Jewish life in exile, sought to create a historical rupture with the exilic past of two thousand years that would weaken the ties with the discredited cultural and political heritage of Exile. To achieve this end it was essential to encourage the formation of a new national tradition in Palestine. The roots of this national revival led to an older and more glorified past, to the "golden age" of Antiquity when the Hebrews lived as a nation on their own land, the Land of Israel. The Zionist ideology therefore emphasized the theme of "restoring" the ancient Hebrew national identity and the significance of reviving a genuinely native Hebrew culture.

In these efforts, the Jewish society of Palestine was no different than other groups who select an appropriate past to support their national aspirations: When recent history denies their claim for nationhood, these groups turn to a more remote past to provide evidence of their distinct historical roots.[8] Despite the manifest claim for "restoration,"[9] the portrayal of this remote past is clearly shaped by the need to highlight a symbolic continuity with the present. The formation of the Tel Ḥai commemorative narrative, which emphasizes a new beginning but provides its hero with the aura of antiquity, could similarly combine the benefit of history with the power of tradition.

The historical defense of Tel Ḥai was both different and dramatic enough to emerge as a powerful narrative. It offered the appropriate ingredients for the making of a modern historical legend—a hero, a conflict, a dramatic ending, and a moral lesson. The early Zionist settlers regarded the defense of Tel Ḥai as the first full-scale battle for the Jewish settlement of Palestine.[16] For their contemporaries, the Tel Ḥai settlers' courage in defending their homes demonstrated a fundamental change from Jewish exilic mentality, marked by passivity vis-à-vis persecution.[11] The battle of Tel Ḥai thus symbolized the emergence of a new type of Jew, tough, strong, and resourceful, who stands up to his enemies, a Jew who assumes charge of his own history and fate rather than depends on others' will to provide him with security.[12]

As with other historical heroes, Trumpeldor's life and character lent themselves to the formation of his "legendary" image.[13] It was easy to portray him as the counterimage of the traditional exilic Jew: he grew up outside the traditional Jewish community to assimilated parents, had almost no Jewish education, and did not know Yiddish, the lingua franca of East European Jews at the time. While most Russian Jews tried to evade the military service, he was proud to join the czarist army and excelled as a soldier. He received honorary military citations for his courage and was the first Jew promoted to the rank of an officer.[14] With the amputation of his left arm (due to an injury in the Russian-Japanese war) and his military appearance and mannerisms, Trumpeldor not only looked "non-Jewish" but also offered an image that was antitraditional at its core.[15]

The relatively little information available about his childhood, outsiders' early recognition of his leadership qualities, and his tragic end on the battlefield further fitted the familiar patterns of folk narratives.[16] And like other famous heroes, the dying Trumpeldor provided his legacy for future generations: "never mind, it is good to die for our country."[17] With its powerful ideological message, this statement was soon to emerge as a national slogan of modern Israeli society.

A memorial day for Tel Ḥai on the Eleventh of Adar (the date of the battle according to the Jewish calendar) created a fixed point in time for its commemoration and a base for the development of a new ritual. The media, public institutions, youth movements, and schools marked Tel Ḥai Day, and a new youth tradition of pilgrimage to the famous monument of "the roaring lion," built on the tomb of the fallen heroes, developed within a few years and is continued to this day by schools, youth movements, and the Israel Defense Forces.

The establishing of Tel Ḥai Day was most important for the process of transforming the historical event into a "legend." The educational agents of the pre-state era (mostly schools and youth movements) actively participated in the mission of "turning this story to an enchanted legend which has its foundations in reality yet is wrapped with a glamorous halo."[18] Hebrew writers' active involvement in the pre-state educational system and their ideological commitment to the formation of a new Hebrew culture contributed to this process of legendization.[19] School textbooks and special anthologies for Tel Ḥai Day thus drew upon this new Hebrew literature written for and about the Tel Ḥai heroes.

The legendizing process began soon after the historical event. The oral and written literature about Trumpeldor often created a link between him and the famous Jewish heroes of Antiquity. Trumpeldor was called the "great-grandson of the ancient heroes" and described as "a soldier in Bar Kokhba's army who has come to us from previous generations."[20] The ahistorical dimension of Trumpeldor's legendary image was further enhanced by new legends that depicted him appearing in front of Israeli children or directly intervening in contemporary Israeli matters long after his death.[21]

Trumpeldor's presentation as the modern reincarnation of the ancient heroes elevated him beyond the immediate historical situation and assured him an honorable position in the pantheon of Jewish heroes. The "legendary" framework served to legitimize the chronological incongruity of condensing two periods, historically separated by two thousand years, into a single heroic lore. The popularity of this theme in the discourse about Trumpeldor, especially during the pre-state period,[23] indicates the appeal of the ancient Hebrews as direct inspiration for the Zionist national revival in the first half of the twentieth century. The effectiveness of this symbolic conflation of time was explicitly acknowledged in a discussion about its educational value for young children for whom "there is not much difference between two thousand years ago—Judah and Maccabee and Bar Kokhba, and twenty years ago—Yoseph, the one-armed."[23] That this approach was indeed effective is evident in a piece written by a student in a school newsletter a decade and a half after the historical event: "Only fifteen years passed since the wondrous defense of Tel Ḥai. . . . Within a short period, though, we remember these heroes *as if they lived thousands of years ago*. So wonderful was this legend about the heroes, those spiritual heroes, [that] our hearts continue to tremble as we raise their names on our lips!"[24]

The hero's amputated arm emerged as a major object of glorification in the Trumpeldor "legend." An amputation due to war injury was so un-usual among the Jewish pioneers and so integral to Trumpeldor's heroic image that the epithets "the amputee" (ha-gidem) and "the amputated hero" (ha-gibor ha-gidem) became unique designations for Trumpeldor and were even used in naming streets in his honor. If the accepted image of the Zionist pioneer portrays him as holding a plow with one of his arms and a gun with the other, the Tel Hai lore portrays Trumpeldor as holding both plow and gun with his single arm.[25] Indeed, his sheer ability to perform these tasks with a single arm raised him above and beyond all other settlers and contributed to his "legendary" image.

The strategy of "legendizing" Trumpeldor was designed to turn the hero and the historical battle of Tel Hai into a major cultural text of the New Hebrew nation. Tel Hai Day ("the Eleventh of Adar") is the only distinct national memorial day besides the official Memorial Day for Israeli sol-diers, established after the foundation of the state. Moreover, while the national commemoration of Israeli soldiers refers to them as an anony-mous collectivity, Trumpeldor's central place within the commemoration of Tel Hai reinforces his unique status as the most prominent hero of modern Israeli society.[26] His famous last words, "it is good to die for our country," enhance his role as the forerunner of contemporary Israeli sol-diers and provide an important educational slogan for the indoctrination of the young. To impress students further with its symbolic message, teachers often featured the slogan on classroom walls during the annual commemoration of Tel Hai.

The new "legend" was thus constructed as a paradigmatic text for a new age, creating a countertradition to the Jewish lore of exile. But even though the new narrative developed out of an antitraditional ideology, it adopted some traditional patterns and techniques, even if selectively. The formation of a new aggada about Trumpeldor follows the long tradition of Jewish legends about prominent historical figures. Like the traditional aggada,[27] the Trumpeldor "legend" has largely developed as an educational narrative and it follows common literary strategies of the traditional legend, such as condensing historical periods and linking heroes who were not historically connected in order to highlight the ideological message of the story.[28] But the differences between traditional legends and this modern narrative are also significant. While traditional historical legends focus primarily on prominent religious figures and are imbued with theological significance, the Trumpeldor narrative was constructed within the secular national Hebrew culture and deliberately sought to highlight an image of a secular hero.

Thus, the social construction of a new "legend" reveals a highly selective attitude toward tradition. Although much of the urge to create a new sacred text for a new age stemmed from a conscious reaction against the world of tradition, this overtly antitraditional attitude implied a heightened—even if negative—awareness of tradition. The very use of the traditional concept of *aggada* in reference to the Trumpeldor narrative suggests unacknowledged ambivalence toward the old tradition that the new cultural text was set to replace. The creation of a new "legend" was thus seen as an important step in the formation of a new national tradition, in many ways different yet not detached from the old Jewish tradition. The use of the term "legend" articulated the importance of the particular historical event to which it relates and created the desired "traditional" appearance of this new text.

II

Following the foundation of the State of Israel in 1948, Trumpeldor's stature as a central national Israeli symbol began to decline. School ceremonies, special programs on the government-sponsored networks, and pilgrimages by youth movement members and army units continue to mark Tel Ḥai Day each year, but the Trumpeldor "legend" has gradually lost its prominence as a major sacred text of Israeli national culture. Trumpeldor's symbolic role as the forerunner of the New Hebrews was central to the efforts to create a new type of Jew during the formative years of Israeli society. But his image does not hold the same magic for those younger Israelis who grew up in the Hebrew culture, whose own memories are tied to life in the Jewish state, and whose socialization occurred within its transformed political culture.[29]

But there were other social and political reasons for the decline of Tel Ḥai's importance. A massive wave of traditionally oriented Middle Eastern Jews immigrated to Israel following the foundation of the state and contributed to the growing diversification of Israeli society. This process has also weakened the hegemonic image of the New Hebrew, fashioned by the East European Jewish settlers at the beginning of the century. During the 1950s, Israelis also began to show a greater readiness to deal with the collective Jewish trauma of the Holocaust, which they had repressed during the years of the national struggle to establish a state, the War of Independence, and the first period of transition into statehood. Moreover, during the 1970s and the 1980s Israelis became more interested in learning about their personal and collective roots in the Diaspora past and the traditions that the new Hebrew culture of the pre-state period attempted to suppress. The opening of a Diaspora museum in Tel Aviv, a growing trend among Israelis to return to visit their countries of origin, and the recent outpouring of autobiographical works relating to the pre-Israeli past articulate this cultural trend. From this perspective, the anti-Diaspora and antitraditional dimensions of Trumpeldor's heroic image lost much of their appeal for contemporary Israeli society.

The recurrent wars and military operations in which Israelis have been involved during the years following the foundation of the state have a direct bearing on the decline of Tel Ḥai. The frequent military confrontations that Israelis experience clearly diminish the memory of Trumpeldor's heroism: the sheer act of dying in combat while defending a settlement does not inspire today the same attitude of awe and admiration if evoked during the pre-state and early state periods. Trumpeldor has, therefore, lost much of his unique status as hero. As the following quotations from my informants indicate,[30] the once legendary hero can be perceived as a common, and rather outdated, example: "In those days, [Trumpeldor] was really a hero. But today, there have been so many wars. . . . Then, this was heroism; today, it would have been considered like a child's play." "Trumpeldor as a symbol was justified in the 1930s. Today, there are thousands of Trumpeldors."

This attitude does not imply the devaluation of Trumpeldor's heroism in itself. Trumpeldor's courage and commitment are appreciated within the immediate historical context of the early pioneering past. The new skepticism challenges the validity of the "legendary image" of the historical man as an immortal symbol and a role model for contemporary Israelis. As Klapp observes, the excessive "editing" of the hero's image can result in his "loss of character."[31] Ironically, the founding generation's desire to portray Trumpeldor as the prototypical representation of the New Hebrew has eventually undermined the reliability of his public image and has created a lifeless, two-dimensional figure. As an Israeli journalist complained, "it is difficult to identify with a 'monument' whose only attributes are a few loaded, patriotic statements [and] whose actions are so purely heroic."[32]

During the 1970s and the 1980s, the skepticism toward what was now seen as an excessive glorification of the pioneering past became even more pronounced. Trumpeldor's "legend," which had occupied a central position within Israeli national heroic lore, became an obvious target. Aharon Megged's novel *Living on the Dead,* published in Israel in 1965, provided an early literary expression of the new critical attitude toward the "hero cult" of the pre-state and early state periods. The protagonist, who is commissioned to write a biography of Davidov (a fictitious pioneer), cannot produce the expected volume once he unfolds the history behind the legend and discovers that Davidov was "just an ordinary man." The following reference to Trumpeldor reveals the extent of this generation's disillusionment with the heroic "legends" of the past:

> Every year on the Eleventh of Adar according to the Jewish calendar they wring tears from the school-children and sing with great feeling: "Once there was this wondrous hero, one arm alone he had." *Who was this wondrous hero, after all?* An ex-officer called Trumpeldor, not a bad soldier, who defended his home against robbers. *So what?* There are any number of them like

that all over the world, but nobody remembers their names. Here for almost forty years we've been standing at attention in his memory, singing the anthem, waving the flag, sending the kids home at eleven and letting the teachers lie down to rest. . . . *What do we need heroes for in this country?*[33]

But perhaps the most central reason for the decline of the "legend" is a growing skepticism about the message of his famous last words, "it is good to die for our country." The continuing Israeli-Palestinian conflict and the intense divisions within Israeli society with regard to its resolution have shaken the national consensus about the Lebanon War and the policy toward the occupied territories. Within the context of the post-1967 political reality, it is no longer possible to accept as given the message that Trumpeldor's statement conveys. It is not surprising, therefore, that this statement became the major target of doubts about the authenticity of his "legend."

The discrediting of Trumpeldor's famous words spread quickly during the 1970s.[34] The authenticity of Trumpeldor's last words was challenged on two accounts. First, Trumpeldor's knowledge of Hebrew was limited, and he could not possibly have uttered those Hebrew words that the "legend" attributes to him. Second, it is inconceivable that any person would say that "it is good to die," especially while actually dying. As one of my informants emphatically stated: "It has been proven that he did not say 'It is good to die for our country'. . . . It is unnatural for a person to say such a thing, and Trumpeldor was not superhuman!"

This modified perception of Trumpeldor's saying as "legend" is even more fascinating if we consider that historical evidence suggests that Trumpeldor in fact articulated the idea that it was good to die for the country before he passed away.[35] The early "legend" text, then, appears to be historically sound. But Isrealis' awareness of the "invented" character of Trumpeldor's "legend" has contributed to the growing skepticism about the validity of this narrative, regardless of available historical information. This may explain in part why the historical evidence in support of the authenticity of his saying does not change the popular view that it is a fictitious construct. The assumption that the famous last words were fabricated has thus become part and parcel of contemporary Israeli folklore. One of the parents I interviewed expressed her resentment of this unnecessary "addition" to Trumpeldor's public image: "It is typical of the Jews that if they finally have a hero, his own heroism is not sufficient. They have to 'decorate' it further. . . . Not enough that his arm was amputated and that he organized the people around him so well when he was wounded. All this was not enough!? They didn't have to add 'It is good to die for our country.' And now, as it has turned out, this isn't true."

The changing attitude toward the Trumpeldor narrative thus reveals a

new conception of the relationship between the historical and the legendary. The legend is no longer seen as a support of history. Rather, the two
appear as mutually exclusive representations of the past: the "legendary"
has become the incredible, those "false elements" of the Trumpeldor narrative, while the "historical" refers to the credible aspects of the story.
Whereas earlier generations believed that the "legendary Trumpeldor"
further elevated the historical man, the new voices of skepticism express
the view that the legendary ultimately detracts from the historical.

The publicity around the publication in 1972 of Laskov's biography of
Trumpeldor provides another ironical twist to the changing relations between "history" and "legend." While the legendary hero appears to be
declining as an overly used, worn-out symbol, the historical Yoseph Trumpeldor suddenly becomes a novelty and a newsworthy topic. An advertisement for the book uses this tension to provoke the reader's curiosity: "The
first authoritative biography of a wonder-man: a soldier and an officer, an
agricultural worker and a leader (and by training, a dentist and a lawyer).
This is the story of the loves and the separations, the achievements and the
failures of *a historical leader who became a legend.*"[36] Laskov's biography
received the Yitzhak Sade Award for Military History upon its publication.
In its statement, the selecting committee explicitly referred to the book's
contribution to the declining legend:

> With Trumpeldor's death . . . *the man became a legend.* His grave in the
> Galilee attracted thousands of pilgrims and his name was used in many books
> and folksongs. As time went by, Trumpeldor's real image seemed to have
> become blurred and has gradually faded into the past. New fateful wars have
> given rise to new heroes.
>
> Shulamit Laskov's book which was written 52 years after [Trumpeldor's]
> death brings back to us a forgotten hero. It provides his life with a realistic
> quality, a quality by which one can educate no less than by the halo of a
> legend. . . .
>
> . . . *Shulamit Laskov's biography does not abuse the Trumpeldor legend.* It
> illuminates it, explains it, and it becomes better clarified and understood and
> more humane.[37]

While the founders of Israeli society believed that the legendary halo
would enhance the historical figure, the renewed focus on the historical
person is now hailed as a means of supporting the ailing legend. In a
personal letter to Laskov, later published in a daily Hebrew newspaper, a
well-known public figure expressed his sheer surprise at discovering the
individual human being behind the platitudes of the legend.[38] But Laskov's
book has not reversed the cultural trend of decline as far as the "legend" is
concerned. Although educational literature and official publications continue to offer the early "legend" text, the doubts about the historical valid-

ity of Trumpeldor's last words persist. Moreover, a competing version of what Trumpeldor actually said before he died has become increasingly popular and has further contributed to the pervasive confusion between "history" and "legend" in relation to the Trumpeldor narrative.

The new version of Trumpeldor's last words offers an alternative ending to the Tel Ḥai narrative. According to this version, when Trumpeldor realized that he was about to die, he uttered a strong and juicy curse in Russian, most often identified as *iob tvoiu mat* (i.e., fuck your mother). While the sound of these Russian words is close to the opening words of the "legendary" Hebrew saying—*tov lamut* (i.e., it is good to die)—they radically transform the meaning of his message.[39]

The contrast between the old and the new versions is, indeed, dramatic. The substitution of a patriotic Hebrew statement with a Russian curse suggests a complete inversion of the hero's legacy and public image. While the earlier text portrayed Trumpeldor as glorifying death for his country, the new version claims that he, in fact, cursed his misfortune when he was about to die. The revised text thus transforms Trumpeldor from the prototype of "the New Hebrew" to a "Russian immigrant," from a prominent Zionist figure who provided the nation with an educational slogan to a soldier who broke into profanities, from a self-sacrificing hero to a reluctant victim.

While the solemn text of the "legend" was constructed to evoke deep awe and veneration, the shocking ending of the new, subversive text produces a deliberate comic effect. In other circumstances, a story about a severely wounded man cursing his fate as he is about to die would hardly be considered funny. But when the man is identified as the famous, self-sacrificing hero and his famous last words are turned into a curse in Russian, the humor inevitably asserts itself through this morbid framework. Although this is by far the most popular inversion of the "legend" text, I have also collected other crude jokes and cynical references to Trumpeldor that likewise target his "legendary" image and defy his patriotic legend.[40]

Although official publications and educational agencies continue to present the "legend" as constructed in the pre-state era and use the "traditional" rhetoric referring to the story of Tel Ḥai as a "folk legend,"[41] the original "legend" is not maintained only by official support. Several informants who were aware of the challenge of Trumpeldor's famous last words argued that the significance of the educational message supersedes any question about their historical validity.[42] Even though only one version of Tel Ḥai enjoys official support as "history," we cannot reduce this dialogue to an "official versus popular" stance.

Nonetheless, the new version of the Trumpeldor narrative has gained so much popularity in Israel that Trumpeldor's biographer found it necessary to address this issue directly:

The view regarding the Russian curse is not supported by people who had been around him before he died. . . . Dr. Gary [to whom Trumpeldor reportedly said his famous words] did not know Russian and the language in which he communicated with Trumpeldor was Hebrew. As for the view that he could not have been thinking about anything except for his enormous physical pain, the fact is that in spite of his suffering he frequently inquired about what was happening [in the battle] and expressed his wish that the comrades would continue to offer an honorable resistance. Finally, one should note that he often communicated statements in the same spirit of "it was good to die."[43]

Thus, while the new popular version discredits the Tel Hai commemorative narrative as "legend," the historical evidence suggests that the older version actually provides a more accurate representation of the past. This support for the older commemorative narrative implies that the more recent version of "history" is, in fact, a "legend."

That the subtext of the dialogue on the authenticity of the Tel Hai commemorative narrative is not its historical validity is quite clear. After all, the new scholarly support for Trumpeldor's famous last words has not altered or weakened the spreading of the notion that they are fabricated, nor did it diminish the belief that before he died he uttered a curse in Russian. It appears that the Tel Hai commemorative narrative could serve as the hegemonic, authoritative text about the historical event only as long as its symbolic message fitted the dominant ideology and nationalist sentiments of the young Israeli society. Tel Hai's central legacy, expressed in Trumpeldor's famous last words, was the importance of self-defense and self-sacrifice for the process of the Zionist revival of Jewish national life in Palestine. This was the prevalent ideological climate in Israel prior to the establishment of the state and during the first decades of its existence, when this call for sacrifice was associated with what was believed to be a transitory stage. But the routinization of sacrifice by repeated wars and military confrontations has evoked a new anxiety about a situation that puts a constant demand on human life and to which there is no apparent solution in the future. In this context, Trumpeldor's excited embracement of death appears incongruent with contemporary Israelis' growing frustration at being faced with a repeated call for patriotic sacrifice. In contrast, the new version's portrayal of Trumpeldor cursing his misfortune at having to die in a war is seen as persuasively authentic.

In fact, with its use of profanity and crude humor, the alternative version deliberately transgresses the sacredness of the Tel Hai commemorative narrative and ridicules its ideological message.[44] This transformation is part of a broader cultural trend in contemporary Israel in which subversive humor functions as a channel for political protest and the demythologization of the pioneering past has become the topic of public and scholarly discourse.[45]

Indeed, it should not come as a surprise that a society torn by political controversies over its conflict with Arab countries and its handling of the Palestinian issue, strained by economic hardships and by considerable ethnic and religious tensions, has generated more than one version of the past. Although many Israelis are aware of two opposing versions of the "history" of Tel Ḥai, I have not detected a similar awareness of the coexistence of two opposing usages of the term "legend." A statement by one of the survivors of Tel Ḥai, who attempted to defend the original text against the new version, illustrates this point. In one and the same breath he used both meanings of "legend," arguing that "rivals who were interested in diminishing Trumpeldor's *legendary* image . . . spread the notion that the saying was a *legend*."[46]

III

The examination of the popular meaning of "history" and "legend" in reference to the commemoration of a single historical event reveals how the meaning of these categories is socially constructed and subject to change. This study shows that "history" and "legend" are not always considered mutually exclusive categories and that the relation between them shifts in line with other social and political changes that the society undergoes.

The Israeli discourse on Tel Ḥai shows that at times the historical and the legendary aspects of the commemorative narrative can be seen as essentially complementary. The attribution of the term "legend" to the narrative can articulate a belief in its great historical value. In this case, then, the legendizing process becomes the means of guaranteeing the place of this event in the collective memory of the society. In a different sociopolitical context, however, the application of the same term, "legend," to the same commemorative narrative is accusatory in nature and assumes an adversarial relation to history. In this case, the framing of the text as "legendary" implies its dismissal as a "historical" narrative.

The analysis of the popular discourse about Tel Ḥai also suggests that although the classification of a commemorative narrative as legend or history appears to focus on the issue of *historical validity*, it in fact revolves around the issue of *credibility*. As long as members of the society accept the commemorative text as credible, questions about historical validity do not enter into the discourse. But when the symbolic message loses its credibility, even the historian's findings cannot effectively dispel pervasive doubts about its historical foundation. By popular vote, the historical narrative is then redefined as a "legend." Because credibility is not an inherent quality of the commemorative narrative but rather reflects the social attitude toward this narrative, "history" and "legend" constitute fluid cultural categories.

That a commemorative narrative invokes ambiguity regarding its classification confirms an important aspect of both history and legend: both represent the past through the act of creating narratives. Although the historical narrative and the historical legend differ in the kinds of materials upon which they draw—the former is based on historical records, while the latter mixes facts with fiction—both need to organize information in a story form, which requires the selection of an appropriate plot structure and literary style. While we are used to exploring the ways in which legend develops out of history, little attention has been paid until quite recently to the impact of fiction upon the construction of history.[47] When history provides the stuff from which legends are made, the historical narrative can adopt the familiar structure of legendary tales and use it for enhancing its rhetorical impact. But as the case of Tel Ḥai demonstrates, structural affinity with the legend can also render the narrative vulnerable to questions concerning its validity as a historical account. Whether this affinity leads to a public debate or not ultimately rests on the credibility of the past as shaped by the narrative. The study of the cultural interplay of "history" and "legend" reveals the transformative character of collective memory and its susceptibility to conflicting views that turn the past into a contested arena.

NOTES

I would like to thank Dan Ben-Amos, John Gillis, Elliott Oring, Barry Schwartz, Janet Theophano, and Eviatar Zerubavel for their comments on an earlier draft of this article.

1. Following the Grimm brothers' approach, Bascom defines legends as "prose narratives which, like myths, are regarded as true by the narrator and his audience, but they are set in a period considered less remote, when the world was much as it is today. Legends are more often secular than sacred and their principal characters are human" (William Bascom, "The Forms of Folklore: Prose Narratives," *Journal of American Folklore* 78 [1965]: 4). More recent studies of the element of belief in legend have qualified this definition, suggesting that not all those who participate in the legend transmission process believe in its truth, but someone, at some point, must have believed in it. See Linda Dégh and A. Vázsonyi, "Legend and Belief," *Genre* 4 (September 1971): 281–304, reprinted in *Folklore Genres*, ed. by Dan Ben-Amos (Austin: University of Texas Press, 1976), pp. 93–123; Heda Jason, "Concerning the 'Historical' and the 'Local' Legends and Their Relatives," in *Toward New Perspectives in Folklore*, ed. by A. Paredes and R. Bauman (Austin: University of Texas Press, 1972), pp. 134–44; and Elliott Oring, "Legend, Truth, and News," *Southern Folklore* 47 (1990): 163–77.

2. Eric Hobsbawm and T. Ranger, eds., *The Invention of Tradition* (Cambridge: Cambridge University Press, 1983).

3. Several biographies of Trumpeldor have been published since his death. The biographical references in this work are based on the most recent and best-documented work by Shulamit Laskov, *Yoseph Trumpeldor: Sipur Ḥayay* [Yoseph

Trumpeldor: A biography] (Haifa: Shikmona, 1972), and on a critical study of the Tel Ḥai battle and the events leading up to it by Nakdimon Rogel, *Tel Ḥai: Ḥazit lelo Oref* [Tel Ḥai: A front without rear] (Tel Aviv: Yariv-Hadar, 1979).

4. It is interesting to note that the earlier reports on the Tel Ḥai battle refer to the attackers as "robbers," "Bedouins," and "Arabs" interchangeably. Later, the texts identify the enemy as "Arabs." This change may be the result of the later establishment of the Arabs as the archenemy of Israelis. See also the discussion of this issue in Charles Liebman and Eliezer Don-Yeḥiya, *Civil Religion in Israel* (Berkeley: University of California Press, 1983), p. 46.

5. Yosef Klausner, "Al Kedushat ha-Aretz" [On the sanctification of the country], *ha-Aretz* (March 21, 1921): 2.

6. Snir, "Trumpeldor," *Kuntres* no. 208 (10 Adar 1925): 5–6.

7. Y. Ya'ari-Polskin, *Ḥolmim ve-Loḥamim* [Dreamers and fighters] (Jaffa: Gissin, 1922), p. 296; and David Tidhar, ed., *Entsiklopedia le-Ḥalustsei ha-Yishuv u-Vonav* [The encyclopedia of Israeli pioneers], (Tel Aviv: Sifriyat Rishonim, 1950), vol. 4, p. 1591.

8. Compare with the similar searches for an appropriate national past by the Finn nationalists, who supported their goal to dissociate from Russia by claiming continuity with the ancient Finns through the collection and construction of the Kalevala; the Greek nationalist movement, which based its claim for independence from the Ottoman Empire on enhancing the direct continuity with the ancient Greeks and Hellenic culture; and the Bulgarians, who reached back to a pre-Ottoman past to present their distinct national roots. For respective studies of these cases, see William A. Wilson, *Folklore and Nationalism in Modern Finland* (Bloomington: Indiana University Press, 1976); Michael Herzfeld, *Ours Once More: Folklore, Ideology, and the Making of Modern Greece* (New York: Pella, 1986); and Carol Silverman, "Reconstructing Folklore: Media and Cultural Policy in Eastern Europe," *Communication* 11 (1989): 141–60.

9. For further discussion on "restoring" the past, see David Lowenthal, *The Past Is a Foreign Country* (Cambridge: Cambridge University Press, 1985), p. 40; and Edward Shils, *Tradition* (Chicago: University of Chicago Press, 1981), p. 206. See also Michael Kammen's extensive study of "restoration" in American culture in *Mystic Chords of Memory: The Transformation of Tradition in American Culture* (New York: Alfred A. Knopf, 1991), pp. 299–374, 407–43, 537–70. Any such "restoration" entails a selective attitude toward the past and its re-creation in folklore, often designed to fit the nationalist agenda.

10. Incidents between Jews and Arabs also occurred prior to Tel Ḥai, but the commemoration of those earlier encounters focused on dead individuals and not on the specific events that led to their deaths. Yisrael Heilprin, *Sefer ha-Gevura: Antologia Historit Sifrutit* [The book of heroism: A historical literary anthology] (Tel Aviv: Am Oved [1950–51], 1977), vol. 3, pp. 276–97; and Jonathan Frankel, "The 'Yizkor' Book of 1911—A Note on National Myths in the Second Aliya," in *Religion, Ideology and Nationalism in Europe and America: Essays Presented in Honor of Yehoshua Arieli* (Jerusalem: The Historical Society of Israel and the Zahman Shazar Center for Jewish History, 1986), pp. 355–84.

11. Yosef Klausner, "Hem Naflu Ḥalalim" [They died], *ha-Aretz* (March 9, 1920): 2; Ze'ev Jabotinsky, "Kaddish," orig. 1928, reprinted in his *Ketavim:*

Zikhoronot Ben Dori [Collected works: Memoirs of my generation] (Tel Aviv: Ari Jabotinsky, 1947), p. 105; and David Ben-Gurion, "Tsav Tel Hai" [The legacy of Tel Hai], *Kuntres* 1, no. 381 (1944): 3.

12. For further analysis of the social construction of the image of the "New Hebrew" see Samuel Klausner, "ha-Ivri he-Hadash" [The new Hebrew], *Zemanim* nos. 323, 325, 329, 330 (September–October 1954); Ammon Rubinstein, *Liheyot Am Hofshi* [To be a free people] (Tel Aviv: Schocken, 1977), pp. 101–39; and Yael Zerubavel, "The Last Stand: On the Transformation of Symbols in Modern Israeli Culture" (Ph.D. dissertation, University of Pennsylvania, 1980), pp. 301–49.

13. Orrin E. Klapp, *Symbolic Leaders: Public Dramas and Public Men* (Chicago: Aldine, 1964), pp. 32–42, 60; Kent L. Steckmesser, *The Western Hero in History and Legend* (Norman: University of Oklahoma Press, 1965), p. 53; Michael Owens Jones, "(PC + CB) × SD (R + I + E) = Hero," *New York Folklore Quarterly* 28 (1971): 245.

14. Laskov, *Yoseph Trumpeldor*, pp. 14–20, 28.

15. See also Liebman and Don-Yehiya, *Civil Religion in Israel*, p. 45.

16. The hero is often raised outside his immediate family and community and rises to prominence there (Lord Raglan, *The Hero: A Study in Tradition, Myth, and Drama* [New York: Meridian Books, 1979], pp. 174–75). On the cross-cultural pattern of "the last stand," see Bruce Rosenberg, *Custer and the Epic of Defeat* (University Park: Pennsylvania State University Press, 1974).

17. The hero's expression of a total commitment to a transcendent ideal is found cross-culturally. A famous American example of a similar patriotic saying is Nathan Hale's "I regret that I have but one life to lose for my country." Trumpeldor's own last words echo the well-known Roman saying *dulce et decorum est pro patria mori*. See also Horace P. Beck, "The Making of the Popular Legendary Hero," in *American Folk Legend*, ed. Wayland D. Hand (Berkeley: University of California Press, 1971), p. 132; and Rosenberg, *Custer and the Epic of Defeat*, p. 240.

18. *le-Yom Tel Hai: Hoveret Ezer la-Ganenet* [For the Day of Tel Hai: A reader for the nursery school teacher] (Tel Aviv: Histadrut, 1943), p. 10. This brochure is particularly useful because it explicitly addresses the need to create a legend for educational purposes. For further discussion of the role of schools and youth movements in the construction of a new national heroic lore, see Yonathan Shapiro, *Ilit lelo Mamshikhim* [An elite without successors] (Tel Aviv: Sifriyat Poalim, 1984); and Ruth Firer, *Sokhnim shel ha-Hinukh ha-Tsiyoni* [The agents of Zionist education] (Haifa: Haifa University and Tel Aviv: Sifriyat Poalim, 1985).

19. To mention only a few examples, Lamdan, in his famous epic poem "Masada," describes the appearance of "Yoseph the Galilena" as a turning point in the experience of the Jewish settlers (orig. 1927; English translation by Leon I. Yudkin, *Isaac Lamdan: A Study in Twentieth Century Hebrew Poetry* [Ithaca: Cornell University Press, 1971], pp. 199–234). Poets such as Ze'ev Jabotinsky, Yitzhak Shimoni, Avraham Breudes, and Shimshon Meltser wrote poems on Trumpeldor and Tel Hai. For further analysis of these works, see my article "New Beginning, Old Past: The Collective Memory of Pioneering in Israeli Culture," in *New Perspectives on Israeli History: The Early Years of the State* (New York: New York University Press, 1991), pp. 193–215.

20. *ha-Aretz* (March 5, 1920): 1; S. An-Ski, "Trumpeldor," *ha-Aretz* (March 21, 1921): 2. A popular song relating the legends of the Galilee went as far as referring to an "ancient hero" who has a single arm only, an obvious allusion to Trumpeldor (Avraham Breudes, "ba-Galil" [In the Galilee], orig. 1932, reprinted in *Mikraot Yisrael le-Khita Bet* [Textbook for the second grade], ed. by Z. Ariel, M. Blich, and N. Persky [Jerusalem: Massada, 1965]. Similarly, the Greek nationalists described their freedom fighters as the direct descendants of the ancient Greek heroes (Herzfeld, *Ours Once More*, p. 60).

21. H. Tehar-Lev, *Kol mihe-Harim: Maḥaze li-Yeladim* [A voice from the mountains: A children's play] (Jerusalem: Sifriyat Adama, 1959); Levin Kipnis, "ha-Yad ha-Ḥazaka" [The strong arm], in *Sefer ha-Kita Zain* [Textbook for the seventh grade], ed. by A. Buchner, Y. Levinton, and L. Kipnis (Tel Aviv: Dvir, 1965), pp. 362–64.

22. The analogy to the ancient heroes featured often in the pre-state era both in speeches and literary works. See, for example, Max Nordau, "ha-Kapitan Trumpeldor: Divrei Hesped" [Captain Trumpeldor: An obituary], orig. 1920, reprinted in *Yoseph Trumpeldor: Ḥai Shanim le-Moto* [Yoseph Trumpeldor: Eighteenth anniversary of his death] (Tel Aviv: Keren Tel Ḥai, 1938), p. 50; Snir, "Trumpeldor," pp. 5–6; S. Shalom, "Aḥ Bne ha-Galil" [Brother, build the Galilee], in *Moadim le-Simḥa* [Festivals and holidays], ed. by H. Harrari (Tel Aviv: Omanut, 1941), p. 284; and David Shimoni, "le-Trumpeldor" [To Trumpeldor], orig. 1929, reprinted in his *Shirim* [Poems] (Tel Aviv: Massada, 1954), vol. 2, pp. 226–27.

23. *le-Yom Tel Ḥai*, p. 11.

24. *Dror*, a newsletter of ha-Gymnasia ha-Realit Balfour, no. 5 (11 Adar 1935): 11 (The Aviezer Yellin Archives for Jewish Education in Israel and the Diaspora, file 3.147/2). Emphasis added. I would like to thank Nili Arie for bringing this text to my attention.

25. This image of the pioneer, based on the biblical verse Neḥemiah 4:11, was perpetuated by the educational literature until the 1970s (Firer, *Sokhnim shel ha-Ḥinukh ha-Tsiyoni*, pp. 152–63). I have analyzed elsewhere how the elements of the "guard" and the "worker" became the subject of fierce political controversy during the Socialist-Revisionist conflict ("Politics of Interpretation: Tel Ḥai in Israeli Collective Memory," *AJS Review* 16 [1991]: 34–46). The two elements were nonetheless peacefully integrated into the Tel Ḥai commemorative narrative after the foundation of the State of Israel and are still represented in the educational materials for Tel Ḥai. See also Rivka Bakalash, "Mitos Trumpeldor 'Adam, Dam, Adama' be-Vet ha-Sefer ha-Yesodi" [The Trumpeldor myth 'man, blood, earth' in the elementary school] (Masters thesis, Ben-Gurion University of the Negev, 1988).

26. For a more general discussion of the modern phenomenon of anonymous commemoration of fallen soldiers, see George L. Mosse, *Fallen Soldiers: Reshaping the Memory of the World Wars* (New York and Oxford: Oxford University Press, 1990), pp. 37, 94–106. The Tel Ḥai heroes' unique position in Israeli commemoration of its heroic past is visually marked in the cemetery, where the monument of the roaring lion stands high and apart from the uniform rows of graves of the members of the prestigious defense organization ha-Shomer, which was active in those early years of the pioneering period.

27. Within Jewish tradition, the Hebrew term *aggada* was first used in reference

to the nonlegalistic texts in the Talmudic-Midrashic literature that served primarily for teaching ethical and moral principles. Later, *aggada* referred also to historical-biographical texts about postbiblical rabbis. Although these tales are not historically accurate, they are presented as true accounts. See *Encyclopaedia Judaica* 2:354–55; Joseph Heinemann, *Aggadot ve-Toldoteihen* [Aggadah and its development] (Jerusalem: Keter, 1974), pp. 11–12; Dan Ben-Amos, "Generic Distinctions in the Aggada," in *Studies in Jewish Folklore,* ed. F. Talmage (Association for Jewish Studies, 1980), p. 52; and Emanuel Bin-Gorion, *Shevilei ha-Aggada* [The paths of the legend] (Jerusalem: Bialik Institute, 1970), pp. 33–35, 40–44.

28. Joseph Dan, *ha-Sipur ha-Ivri bi-Yemei ha-Beinaim* [The Hebrew story in the Middle Ages] (Jerusalem: Keter, 1974), p. 25.

29. Liebman and Don-Yehiya, *Civil Religion in Israel,* pp. 81–122.

30. I conducted these interviews in Israel in the late 1970s. My informants were students of both the "general" (i.e., nonreligious) and the religious public schools and their parents, a total of 120 people. The students were between the ages of twelve and fourteen.

31. Klapp, *Symbolic Leaders,* p. 215.

32. Ram Evron, "Tov Lamut be'ad Artsenu?" [Is it good to die for our country?], *Davar,* Weekend Magazine (March 24, 1972): 22.

33. Aharon Megged, *ha-Hai al ha-Met* (Tel Aviv: Am Oved, 1965); English translation by Misha Louvish, *Living on the Dead* (McCall, 1970), pp. 67–68; emphasis added.

34. See, for example, Tamar Meroz, "Trumpeldor Basar va-Dam" [Trumpeldor of flesh and blood], *ha-Aretz,* Weekend Magazine (March 20, 1970): 12; Laskov, *Yoseph Trumpeldor,* p. 248; and Evron, "Tov Lamut be'ad Artsenu?" p. 22. Dan Almagor's broadcasting of these speculations on the air was followed by two articles in a daily newspaper: "Ma Be'emet Amar Trumpeldor?" [What did Trumpeldor really say?], *Yediot Ahronot,* Weekend Magazine (March 16, 1979), and "Milim Ahronot al Trumpeldor" [Last words about Trumpeldor], *Yediot Ahronot* (April 13, 1979). About half of the adults and a quarter of the children I interviewed volunteered their opinion that the saying is historically unfounded, although I deliberately avoided asking a direct question about it. Typically, the informants who denied the authenticity of Trumpeldor's last words were adults educated in Israel (as opposed to new immigrants who knew little or nothing of the Trumpeldor narrative). Most children accepted the textbook version they had learned at school.

35. References to the hero's last words appeared in several Hebrew newspapers, including *Doar ha-Yom* (March 8, 1920), *ha-Aretz* (March 8, 1920), *ha-Poel ha-Tsair* (March 12, 1920), and *Kuntres* no. 29 (March 12, 1920), and in private communications following the event (see Rogel, *Tel Hai: Hazit lelo Oref,* pp. 190, 195 n. 45; Laskov, *Yoseph Trumpeldor,* p. 248). Trumpeldor's wording may have been slightly different: "never mind, it is worth dying for the homeland."

36. *Ma'ariv* (Feb. 25, 1972); emphasis added.

37. From Laskov's personal files; emphasis added. See also Evron, "Tov Lamut be'ad Artsenu?" and Meroz, "Trumpeldor Basar va-Dam," on the need to discover the real man behind the legend.

38. A letter from General Meir Zore'a ("Zaro") to Shulamit Laskov (March 28, 1972), from Laskov's personal files; later published in the daily newspaper *Yediot Ahronot* (May 10, 1972.

39. I would like to thank Jonathan Boyarin for first calling my attention to the "sound effect" of the Russian words and its resemblance to the sound of Trumpeldor's famous last words in Hebrew.

40. For further discussion of the humorous lore relating to Trumpeldor, see Zerubavel, "New Beginning, Old Past," pp. 202–7.

41. See, for example, the announcement for Tel Hai Day of 1980 made by the Zionist Council in Israel: "The Defense of Tel Hai turned into a folk legend that served as inspiration for the love of the country and the people" (ha-Aretz [Feb. 27, 1980]: 4). See also Bakalash, "Mitos Trumpeldor."

42. A typical response was that "we need legends by which to educate the young, even if they are not accurate." A teacher in a public junior-high school told me that it is not important if Trumpeldor pronounced his famous last words or not, because "people need legends." And a former general accounted for his decision not to publicize his personal view that Trumpeldor was a disgraceful military model by explaining to me that "the nation needs heroes."

43. Laskov further supports her argument by examples from Trumpeldor's correspondence, in which he similarly asserts his readiness to die for the national cause (Yoseph Trumpeldor, pp. 248–49).

44. On the symbolism of transgression, see also M. M. Bakhtin, Rabelais and His World (Bloomington: Indiana University Press, 1984); Barbara Babcock, The Reversible World: Symbolic Inversion in Art and Society (Ithaca: Cornell University Press, 1978); and Peter Stallybrass and Allon White, The Politics and Poetics of Transgression (Ithaca: Cornell University Press, 1986).

45. For further discussion of Israel subversive humor as protest, see my article "New Beginning, Old Past" and Aliza Shenhar on the emergence of subversive songs during the Lebanon War ("Liheyot Sham: Shirei Meha'a shel Hayalim bi'Levanon" [To be there: Protest songs by soldiers during the Lebanon War], Hetz 1 [April 1989]: 34–43). Current historical interest in the Israeli pioneering period can be seen as stemming from this cultural trend to demythologize the past. As Pierre Nora remarked, the study of tradition implies that "we no longer unquestionably identify with its heritage" ("Between Memory and History: Les Lieux de Mémoire," Representations 26 [1989]: 10). For the controversy on the historiography of Tel Hai as a successful model of settlement and defense following Rogel's study, see Zerubavel, "Politics of Interpretation."

46. Yehuda Kastan, "Ed Shemi'a le-Imrat Trumpeldor" [A witness to Trumpeldor's saying], ha-Aretz (Feb. 28, 1977).

47. The discussion of narrativity in relation to history and the impact of the literary form on the historical representation of the past was stimulated by Hayden White's work. See Tropics of Discourse: Essays in Cultural Criticism (Baltimore: Johns Hopkins University Press, 1978) and The Content of the Form: Narrative Discourse and Historical Representation (Baltimore: Johns Hopkins University Press, 1987). See also Robert H. Canary and Henry Kozicki, eds., The Writing of History: Literary Form and Historical Understanding (Madison: University of Wisconsin Press, 1978).

PART THREE

Memories of War and Wars over Memory

Chapter VII

THE POLITICS OF MEMORY:
BLACK EMANCIPATION AND THE
CIVIL WAR MONUMENT

KIRK SAVAGE

IN MAY 1866 William Dean Howells, back in America after his Civil War exile in Venice, surveyed the vast possibilities for commemorating the late war in an essay entitled "Question of Monuments," and there issued a challenge to the "plastic arts" to prove that "they have suffered the change which has come upon races, ethics, and ideas in this new world."[1] Like many other Americans Howells felt that his nation was at a turning point, propelled almost despite itself by the trauma of the war and the war's most unexpected result: the emancipation of four million slaves of African descent. The question of chattel slavery, which had precipitated the war, was in turn settled by it, but the question of what this nation had become without slavery remained, and still remains, unsettled.

Even as Howells's essay appeared, Northern politicians were embracing an increasingly rigorous program of political equality and civil rights, a movement that soon resulted in the two great legal monuments of Reconstruction, the Fourteenth and Fifteenth amendments to the Constitution.[2] These astonishing initiatives, which would have been inconceivable even two or three years earlier, make sense only when understood as a project of commemoration, an effort to fix the meaning and purpose of the war in an enduring form. The conquering nation sought in the means of law to construct some tangible proofs that the war had achieved a moral reformation justifying its cataclysmic violence.

Howells in his essay attempted to bring this commemorative project to bear on the more familiar monuments of plastic art. For him the "question" was not which heroes or which victories ought to be celebrated, but what *ideas* deserved representation. Ideas of warfare itself—organized violence and destruction—were unfit for representation; Howells was not proposing to close the conventional distance between those subjects considered suitable for bronze and stone and those considered suitable for battle painting or, for that matter, photographs. It was the idea of the cause that interested Howells, the end that justified and thus buried the means. But simply raising an occasional allegorical figure of the cause—a figure standing for liberty or emancipation—was not the answer he had in mind, because he found this formal language dry and effete. So impoverished were the traditional types of sculpture that he could point to only one possible monument that seemed to communicate an important idea: the sculptor John Quincy Adams Ward's statue *The Freedman* (1863) (fig. 1). This superb male nude—his torso pressed forward like the ancient and ennobling prototype the *Torso Belvedere,* his arms and legs locked in one easy circuit of force as they push down against the stump which has meta-phorically held him—Ward executed in the form of a small bronze statuette. Howells saw in this figure "the full expression of one idea that should be commemorated," and he believed that it would "better celebrate the great deeds of our soldiers" than either military representations or suggestively undressed allegories.[3]

Yet Howells's idea remained merely an idea. Although it received critical praise, *The Freedman* was never commissioned at full scale and nothing like it was ever erected in public, the one possible exception being Thomas Ball's freed slave crouching like Mary Magdalene at the feet of the American Christ, Abraham Lincoln (fig. 2)—a work that will be discussed later.

Fig. 1. John Quincy Adams Ward, *The Freedman.* 1863. Bronze. (Photo: The Metropolitan Museum of Art, Gift of Charles Anthony Lamb, 1979)

Fig. 2. Thomas Ball, *Freedman's Memorial* (Washington, D.C.). 1876. Bronze and granite. (Photo: Library of Congress)

Civil War monuments did proliferate in the American landscape, but they were precisely the kind of military monument Howells despised. At the local level, a sort of vernacular monument type emerged—the stone or metal soldier standing intact and ready on a simple pedestal or column (fig. 3)—which foundries and cemetery-monument companies could supply cheaply by catalog to towns in both the North and the South. So far were the two sides from representing the ideas of their cause in plastic form that their monuments became indistinguishable, except in their inscriptions and (if they could afford it) in the arcane details of the uniform.[4]

One basic commemorative impulse unites the local monuments of the North and the South. This impulse, according to local sponsors, was to "perpetuate" the memory of the men who had fought and died. Precisely what perpetuation meant is less clear. The rhetoric used to justify erecting monuments offered various answers, occasionally advancing the argument that people are forgetful and need their social memory bolstered by power-ful mnemonic aids; sometimes arguing instead that memory is safe in the present but monuments are needed to transmit it across generations; yet frequently invoking a startling counterargument—that the memory of

Fig. 3. Samuel E. White, *Confederate Monument* (Fort Mill, S.C.). 1891. Granite. (Photo: author)

heroism is undying and will outlast even monuments, which are therefore built simply as proof of memory's reality and strength.[5] Whether anxious or celebratory, all the rhetoric sprang from a common assumption that shared memory, inhering within "the people," was vital to that people's strength and independence. Nevertheless, the fact remains that public monuments perpetuated memory in *external* deposits, located not within the people but within its shared public space. The increasing tendency in the nineteenth century to construct memory in physical monuments—to inscribe it on the landscape itself—seems symptomatic of an increasing anxiety about memory left to its own unseen devices. Monuments served to anchor collective remembering, a process dispersed, ever changing, and ultimately intangible, in highly condensed, fixed, and tangible sites. Monuments embodied and legitimated the very notion of a common memory, and by extension the notion of the people who possessed and rallied around such a memory.[6] In the case of local Civil War memorials, this embodiment manifests itself in a literal sense in the figure of the common soldier, who is always erect and unwounded—an image of bodily continuity that seeks to displace or overcome the memory of bodies violated and destroyed, even though such violence to the body is the defining premise of warfare. That the common soldier is also always white and Anglo-Saxon in physiognomy suggests that the memorials offer up not a neutral individual body but a collective body conceived with certain boundaries and allegiances.

The rise of a more or less uniform vernacular monument at the local level indicates that towns wanted to participate in a shared and standardized program of memory; while each town fixed and deposited a permanent record of its own involvement in the war, the commemorative grammar imposed such a strong linkage between memorials that they constituted a kind of coordinated front. As local soldiers were loyal to national armies, so local memory earned credibility by its assimilation to a visible national memory. While some localities—particularly big cities—did try consciously to depart from the standard, most were content not to push the frontiers of cultural interpretation and to avoid all but the least controversial views of the war's cause and significance. Thus inscriptions that specify a "cause" generally do so in the most acceptable shorthand form: "the Union" for Northern monuments, "state sovereignty" for Southern monuments.[7] Even the definition of the cause speaks not to moral principles contested but to the local allegiance to higher authority, be it the union or the state. Issues such as slavery were at best subsidiary in the program of local commemoration, lumped in with the stories of Christian bravery and other deeds of heroism invoked by speakers and inscriptions to give the appearance of moral logic to an otherwise unexplained loyalty.[8]

Insofar as a Southern view and a Northern view can be read in these local monuments, the two self-descriptions turn out to be quite compatible. For "union" and "state sovereignty" are not intrinsically incompatible, and after the demise of Reconstruction they were not incompatible even in practice. Slavery was the single issue that had made two distinct sectional identities seem both real and irreconcilable. But once slavery had ended and the nation decided to ignore slavery's legacy—that is, when the federal government stopped trying to enforce the Fourteenth and Fifteenth amendments—a consensus could be reached. This is the tragic irony of the war: the North, which did not go to war to abolish slavery, ended up using abolition to disguise its own racial contradictions and ornament its self-image; while the South, which did go to war to preserve slavery, renounced its proslavery ideology without tearing down the fundamental structure of white supremacy. With the issue of slavery displaced from the ideological center, and the war recast as a struggle between two ultimately compatible "principles" of union and state sovereignty, the four years of the worst bloodshed in American history seem to be an inexplicable, Job-like test. And the local monuments that help recast the war in this light tell us in effect that neither side lost.[9]

For weren't the Confederates loyal and dutiful in their own way? Isn't this all the Southern monuments were trying to say? White America grappled with this question once it had abandoned the Reconstruction agenda of racial justice. While some Northerners were still offended by the Southern commemoration of its former rebels, they could no longer pinpoint a credible reason why. The Southern monuments did not defend slavery or question the blessings of abolition; instead they represented their struggle in a language and form that mimicked the North's own. Northerners looking at Southern monuments could just as easily see reconciliation as treason, and many did. As time wore on, more and more Americans perceived this kind of monument building as part of a healthy process of sectional reconciliation—a process that everyone knew but no one said was for and between whites. Commemoration and reconciliation, two social processes that were diametrically opposed in the aftermath of the Civil War, eventually converged upon a shared, if disguised, racial politics.[10]

Nowhere is this more apparent than in the campaign to memorialize Robert E. Lee. Lee was an ideal figure for postwar Southern commemoration. He fought for the Confederacy not out of any special interest in the system of slavery (his own views on the subject were ambivalent), but out of a sense of loyalty to his home state. In some ways he fit the classical mold of the reluctant leader, as George Washington had, and like Washington he was thought to be above politics; by representing the Confederacy, therefore, he helped dissociate the cause from the politics of slavery, in particular, and redefine it instead in terms of personal qualities like honor and Christian virtue that the white culture at large could embrace. Even his Anglo-Saxon good looks offered material for a moral lesson: Southern whites read the signs of Lee's virtue in his physical appearance. His status as exemplar of "true manhood"—combining physical beauty and moral truth—rested on a thinly disguised racism that placed the nonwhite outside the sphere of both beauty and truth.[11]

The campaign to erect a major monument to Lee in the old Confederate capital, Richmond, Virginia, was a milestone in this cultural effort to remold Lee's image and thereby reconfigure the memory of the Confederacy. The campaign was long and divisive, beginning chaotically in 1870 with rival groups struggling for authority and ending twenty years later as a quasi-official project of Virginia's governor, backed by Richmond's business elite. Far from signifying a quaint or neurotic fixation with the past, as many have assumed, the monument ultimately became a powerful representation of the elite culture of the New South, linking art, business, and white-defined "truth." On a literal level the monument was planned as the centerpiece of a brilliant real-estate speculation, an expensive residential subdivision laid out along a wide boulevard named Monument Avenue. Crowning this grand boulevard, and giving it an aura of gentility, was the equestrian statue of Lee himself, the moral and physical exemplar for the men who would build the mansions clustered beneath his effigy (fig. 4).[12]

The monument committee eschewed popular local sculptors and chose instead a fashionable French sculptor, Antonin Mercie, who could give immediate artistic credibility to the image of Lee supreme. Mercie delivered the goods, distilling the equestrian format to its classic basis as an allegory of power, a study in human mastery over the subservient animal (fig. 5). The monument committee insisted to Mercie that the horse be shown calm, with all four feet on the ground; the idea was to avoid an overt show of Lee's force and to suggest instead his latent power—power so complete and so benign that it required only the slightest tug on the reins. It seems hardly coincidental that this representation parallels literary representations of the good master–faithful slave relationship.[13] In any event Mercie's sculpture succeeds as an image of pregnant repose: seen from any side, its lines form a stable pyramid that culminates in the commander's head and slopes down through the legs of the horse to the edges of the

Fig. 4. Monument Avenue at Lee Circle, Richmond, Va., ca. 1907. (Photo: Cook Collection, Valentine Museum)

Fig. 5. Antonin Mercie and Paul Pujol, *Lee
Monument* (Richmond, Va.). 1890. Bronze
and granite. (Photo: Eleanor S.
Brockenbrough Library, The Museum of the
Confederacy)

pedestal, which in turn spreads gracefully to the ground below. The implicit claims this image made for the prerogative of Southern white manhood were not lost on many people, least of all on the local black population. "The Southern white folks is on top," an elderly black man said when
the statue was dedicated in 1890, "the Southern white folks is on top!"[14]
Black laborers unpacked and hoisted the statue (we see them in figure 6
keeping a respectful distance), prompting John Mitchell, editor of the local
black newspaper, to write defiantly, "The Negro put up the Lee Monument, and should the time come, will be there to take it down."[15]
   The reaction of the Northern press was much less defiant and in fact
largely favorable; many people accepted the Southern argument that Lee
was now an American hero.[16] The legitimation of Lee in national memory
helped erase his status as traitor, as "other," leaving otherness to reside in
the emancipated slaves and their descendants, who could not possibly
accept Lee as their hero. The commemoration of Lee rested on a suppres-

Fig. 6. Hoisting of the Lee statue, 1890. (Photo: Virginia State Library)

sion of black memory, black truth. Thus when Charles Francis Adams argued in 1902 for a statue of Lee in Washington, he ended his speech with precisely the claim that Virginia's business leaders had made for their statue—that it would symbolize the South's postwar progress, its "patient upbuilding of a people under new conditions by constitutional means"— this at the very time the Southern states were completing, by constitutional means, the wholesale disfranchisement of black voters. While the point of his talk ostensibly was to depoliticize Lee and the Confederacy, in the end Adams could not justify a monument to Lee without denying the postwar reality of racial injustice and its congruence with the Confederate cause. "Sectional reconciliation" of this kind was founded on the nonconciliation of African-Americans, and on their exclusion from the legitimate arenas of cultural representation.[17]

Black Americans did not have their own monuments, despite the critical role they had played in swinging the balance of power—both moral and military—to the North. This fact is rarely if ever mentioned in discussions of Civil War monuments. Public monuments do not arise as if by natural law to celebrate the deserving; they are built by people with sufficient power to marshal (or impose) public consent for their erection. In this respect, as I have suggested with Lee's memorial, the public monument represents a kind of collective recognition—in short, legitimacy—for the memory deposited there. Although they proposed monuments to black soldiers from time to time, blacks simply did not have the cultural privilege to seek this form of legitimacy, and whites did not care to give it to them.[18] The standing soldier of Anglo-Saxon feature that appeared on local monuments throughout the North and South did not represent the black soldier and was not meant to. When the black scholar Freeman Murray surveyed American monuments in his unique and unjustly neglected study of 1916, *Emancipation and the Freed in American Sculpture,* he counted a total of three Civil War monuments that represented black soldiers.[19] Two of them show a single black participant in multifigure combat groups. The third and most celebrated, the so-called Shaw memorial in Boston by Augustus Saint-Gaudens and Charles McKim (1897), carries the heaviest representational burden: this monument to a local white hero is the closest the country came to erecting a national tribute to the black soldier and the black cause.[20]

The ambiguity of this burden is immediately apparent in the inscriptions. Is the work a monument to Robert Gould Shaw, the white commander, or to his regiment, the first black troops mustered in the North? The answer is Shaw if we read the front of the monument, the regiment if we read the back of the monument. It was the task of Saint-Gaudens's sculpture to synthesize these competing descriptions and distribute the commemorative focus in one coherent image (fig. 7). Originally the sculptor wanted a more conventional, hierarchical treatment like Mercie's Lee—a freestanding equestrian statue of Shaw raised on a pedestal that could be decorated with low-relief panels of soldiers. Shaw's family vetoed this idea. Eventually Saint-Gaudens devised an ingenious synthesis of statue and pedestal in one huge panel in high relief showing the commander on horseback marching next to his troops on foot, all arranged rigorously parallel to the relief plane and therefore seen in profile. The figure of Shaw retains the formal preeminence Saint-Gaudens wanted, positioned at the center and in highest relief, without leading the march or guiding the narrative. The exceptional and much-observed rhythm of the march—created formally by organizing a jumble of overlapping packs, canteens, guns, legs, and faces into legible repeating patterns that nevertheless defy geometric regularity—manages to control the scene to such an extent that it begins to overcome the formal interruption of the horse and rider. The equestrian neither overpowers nor collapses into the file of troops behind. There is a tension between the foreground and the background that is never quite resolved, a tension that inevitably takes on a racial charge because it springs from the competing claims to memory of the officer and the troops.[21]

Thus the monument facilitates opposing readings of its commemorative

Fig. 7. Augustus Saint-Gaudens and Charles McKim, *Shaw Memorial*
(Boston, Mass.). 1897. Bronze and granite. (Photo: Library of Congress)

intent. Freeman Murray, whose father served in Shaw's regiment, looked at
the compelling portrayal of the black "rank and file" and felt a sense of
validation made all the more powerful because it was otherwise missing in
monumental sculpture. "It seems strangely providential," he wrote, "that
this greatest of American military memorials should have been inspired
primarily by the valor and devotion of Negro-American soldiery."[22] But
this same soldiery could easily be demoted by means of a countercriticism:
the art critic Charles Caffin, for instance, saw in the sculpture a parable of
racial difference, in which the "doglike trustfulness" of the black troops
"contrasted with the serene elevation of their white leader." While this
contrast is hardly apparent in the faces, the literal elevation of Shaw's figure
may be enough to trigger the reading; certainly the undisguised racism of
the reading tallies with Saint-Gaudens's own written descriptions of his
"darkey" models with their "imaginative, though simple, minds."[23] One
cannot forget that the monument was sponsored and designed by the white
elite, and—Murray notwithstanding—without Shaw the monument would
have been unthinkable.

Given that white society fashioned the nation's monuments, there was
still one commemorative subject that seemed bound to engage more di-

rectly the issues raised by emancipation, namely, the subject of Abraham Lincoln. In the first years after Lincoln's death the ramifications of slavery and freedom did indeed loom large as several different groups, all going by the name of the National Lincoln Monument Association, competed to stake their claim on the national memory.[24] One of the groups was a black organization that planned to make its monument an educational institute open to all: "a Monument not of marble or brass merely, but a Monument of Education." The association was proposing not just to lend Lincoln's name to a project sorely needed in the black community but to appropriate Lincoln's memory as well, to align the memory of his achievement and ambition with the fate of the slaves; our dreams are his dreams, the project in effect claimed. But after a well-publicized start, the organization soon disappeared.[25] The most elaborate proposal for a monument came from a semiofficial group of nationally prominent white Republicans, who received a congressional charter for their project in March 1867. Conceived at the height of Reconstruction, their monument was intended to be "an eternal Sentinel, guarding the *era* of emancipation—an immortal Herald proclaiming to all races of men, the nation's great civil and moral *reforms*—slavery blotted out from all her codes, and *equal civil rights* imbedded in her Constitution."[26]

The aim of the monument was nothing less than to reconstruct Lincoln himself, to establish him in official memory as the founder of a new era in American history dedicated to the specific principle of racial equality. The design the sponsors adopted, a mammoth proposal by Clark Mills (fig. 8) modeled loosely on Christian Rauch's monument to Frederick the Great in Berlin, featured a colossal seated Lincoln in the act of signing the Emancipation Proclamation, surmounting what was essentially a vast sculptural scaffold that held six equestrians of Union generals at the base, twenty-one pedestrian portraits of Lincoln's colleagues in the top story, three bas-reliefs, and two allegorical groupings including in the middle a three-part cycle showing the progress of the slave from abject confinement to liberation. While the stated program of the monument was sharply focused, driven by Reconstruction policy, the design was from the start characterized by multiplicity and fragmentation which lent itself to never-ending revision, as the sponsors added and subtracted elements in hopes of finding the right mix of "representative" figures who could attract donations from different constituencies. Most significantly, the sponsors eventually ordered the three-part allegory of the slave's progress to be abandoned and replaced by three separate figures—one of Frederick Douglass, one of a white soldier, one of a woman nurse—hoping thereby to get contributions from three constituencies where previously only one had been represented.[27] While one could argue that the substitution of Douglass enhanced the dignity of the African-American representation even as it re-

Fig. 8. Clark Mills, plaster model of National
Lincoln Monument, ca. 1867 (now lost). (Photo:
Library of Congress)

duced its presence, nevertheless the elimination of the racial allegory
effectively undid any substantial representation of a common moral purpose unifying the vast cross-section of heroes Mills had assembled. The
pedestal, which was already almost unreadable, thus collapsed into a representational hodgepodge of disparate and dispensable elements, which
not even the figure of Lincoln on top, quill in hand, could rescue. This most
ambitious proposal for a monument to Lincoln was dedicated to a new
order that it did not understand and it could not visualize; ultimately the
vast sums needed never materialized, and the project succumbed to its own
contradictions.

Meanwhile the issue of emancipation was "ghettoized" in a small monument located away from the Capitol, the aforementioned Freedman's Memorial to Lincoln of 1876—so-called because the money came from the
contributions of ex-slaves, although, predictably, it was spent by white
sponsors.[28] I use the word "ghettoized" because the monument implicitly

assigns the subject to black memory instead of national memory; the whole project is supposed to record black gratitude to the white benefactor rather than white society's sense of its own transformation. Thomas Ball's well-intentioned but rather servile figure of the slave receiving his savior's blessing (fig. 2) has annoyed blacks from its inception; at the unveiling Frederick Douglass took the extraordinary step of departing from his prepared text to criticize the statue he was ostensibly dedicating.[29]

The national memorial to Lincoln that was finally finished in 1922 bears no relation to any of these early projects. While the Reconstruction proposal would have Lincoln stand for a specific and indeed controversial principle, the twentieth-century project was carefully structured to sidestep the question of what he stood for. A Republican elite promoted the memorial as part of the vast City Beautiful scheme for Washington known as the McMillan Plan of 1901.[30] Under this rubric the memorial was to be above all a grand work of civic beautification, and its site and form were to be determined by art experts rather than untrained laypeople. Thus the Lincoln Memorial Commission deferred to the Fine Arts Commission, which in turn deferred all questions of meaning and sentiment because they were outside its purview. The so-called laypeople who *were* posing these questions in editorials and letters—wondering for example whether the architecture of a slave-owning society like Greece was really appropriate for Lincoln—found their concerns completely excluded from the evasive circuit of decision-making.[31]

Like the campaign for Robert E. Lee, this memorial undertaking pretended to dissociate itself from ideology. But of course the aesthetic assumptions guiding the art experts were not ideologically empty. Their call for a "universal" work of art that would harmonize with its formal surroundings encoded a specific commemorative intent: to remove Lincoln from the trappings of historical and political time and deposit him in the timeless perfection of a classical structure, itself inscribed within the purified, anticommercial order of central Washington. Henry Bacon's superb Doric quasi temple, housing Daniel Chester French's colossal effigy (fig. 9), does the job perfectly. Here was the "real" Lincoln, stripped of his rough, misleading exterior, ex-President Taft argued; just as the monument and its surroundings argue that a real America of stability and unity lies beneath the apparent facts of racial and political strife.[32] But no amount of formal rigor could suppress the contradictions that threatened this white dream of America. They surface even in the monument's official text: the main inscription (fig. 9) deliberately avoids the word "slavery" in the interest of sectional harmony, even though Lincoln's own speech carved on the right describes the war as divine retribution for slavery's offense.[33] Similarly, in the so-called emancipation mural located inside (fig. 10), the painter Jules

Fig. 9. Henry Bacon and Daniel Chester French,
central hall, Lincoln Memorial. 1922. Marble.
(Photo: Library of Congress)

Guerin included dark-skinned models but consciously chose not to portray
American blacks because he considered them undecorative.[34] And perhaps
most blatantly, in the dedication ceremony, Robert Moton, the president of
Tuskegee, was invited to speak for his race, but the black citizens officially
invited to hear him were forced to sit in a rear section separated by a
roadway from the white audience. Here was the culminating spectacle of
the long campaign to build a national Lincoln monument: a mass of white
bodies occupying the approach to the sacred structure (fig. 11), at the head
of which stood the lone black man allowed near his "emancipator's" effigy,
there to speak "for" but not with "the Negro race" on the fruits of his
supposed emancipation.[35] It is not too great a leap from this incongruous
image to the intentionally comic racism of a *National Geographic* photo of
1947 in which black cleaners pose as lilliputian shoeshine boys to scrub the
emancipator's feet (fig. 12).

Fig. 10. Jules Guerin, *Emancipation Mural*. 1919. (Photo: Edward F. Concklin, *The Lincoln Memorial* [Washington: Government Printing Office, 1927])

Fig. 11. Aerial view of Lincoln Memorial dedication, 1922. (Photo: Concklin, *The Lincoln Memorial*)

• • •

The commemoration of the Civil War in physical memorials is ultimately a story of systematic cultural repression, carried out in the guise of reconciliation and harmony. Mundane as they appear to be, at once ubiquitous and hardly noticed, these collective possessions constituted serious, sometimes crucial, tests of cultural authority. Public monuments are important precisely because they do in some measure work to impose a permanent memory on the very landscape within which we order our lives. Inasmuch as the monuments make credible particular collectivities, they must erase others; or more precisely, they erase the very possibility of rival collectivities. But the cultural contest that monuments seem to settle need not end once they are built and dedicated. Monuments can be reappropriated, combatted with countermonuments, or even—as Richmond's John Mitchell envisaged—taken back down. As appalling as the Lincoln Memorial's dedication proved to be, Martin Luther King, Jr., could make that same edifice the dramatic stage for his most celebrated speech, one of the seminal events of the Civil Rights movement. Recently the statues on Monument Avenue, as well as other Confederate monuments in black communities, have begun to provoke public debate over the content and implications of Southern heritage.[36] Perhaps in a distant future, as Eugene Genovese has suggested, the Confederate soldier standing on his pedestal

Fig. 12. "Seated in His Memorial, Abraham
Lincoln Gets White Marble Shoes Shined." (Photo:
National Geographic 91 [June 1947]: 703)

may come to face a statue of Nat Turner. The cultural negotiation this
would require, while barely imaginable, is surely welcome.

NOTES

1. William Dean Howells, "Question of Monuments," *Atlantic Monthly* 18
(May 1866): 646–649.

2. For the best and most recent account of this movement see Eric Foner, *Reconstruction: America's Unfinished Revolution 1863–1877* (New York: Harper &
Row, 1988).

3. Howells, "Question of Monuments," pp. 646–648. On Ward's *Freedman* see
Lewis I. Sharp, *John Quincy Adams Ward: Dean of American Sculpture* (Newark:
University of Delaware Press, 1985), pp. 153–156.

4. Evidence for this claim is necessarily anecdotal, since no full scholarly inventories of local Civil War monuments have been produced. The standing-soldier
monument appeared as early as 1863 but did not become common until the 1880s

and the following several decades. Before the 1880s local war memorials were erected less frequently, often in town cemeteries rather than in public squares, and more often than not, it seems, in the form of obelisks or other nonfigurative shafts. Gaines Foster has charted this iconographic evolution on the Confederate side in his fine book *Ghosts of the Confederacy: Defeat, the Lost Cause, and the Emergence of the New South* (New York: Oxford University Press, 1987). For more information on the origins of the standing-soldier monument and on the monument industry in general, see Michael Panhorst, "Lest We Forget: Monuments and Memorial Sculpture in National Military Parks on Civil War Battlefields, 1861– 1917" (Ph.D. diss., University of Delaware, 1988), chap. 3. (Battlefield monuments constitute another zone of Civil War commemoration deliberately distinct from the local monuments erected in town squares or town cemeteries.)

The two most complete pictorial catalogs of local Confederate and Union monuments are Ralph W. Widener, Jr., *Confederate Monuments: Enduring Symbols of the South and the War Between the States* (Washington, D.C.: Andromeda, 1982); and Mildred C. Baruch and Ellen J. Beckman, *Civil War Union Monuments: A List of Union Monuments, Markers, and Memorials of the American Civil War, 1861– 1865* (Washington, D.C.: Daughters of Union Veterans of the Civil War, 1978). Two earlier compilations of Confederate monuments with interesting commentary are Confederated Southern Memorial Association, *History of the Confederated Memorial Associations of the South* (New Orleans: Graham Press, 1904); and Bettie A. C. Emerson, *Historic Southern Monuments, Representing Memorials of the Heroic Dead of the Southern Confederacy* (New York: Neale Publishing, 1911). To my knowledge there are no such glosses on Union monuments.

Generally, Confederate monuments have received more scholarly attention and cultural analysis. Interpretive overviews include Stephen Davis, "Empty Eyes, Marble Hand: The Confederate Monument and the South," *Journal of Popular Culture* 16 (Winter 1982): 2–21; John J. Winberry, "Symbols in the Landscape: The Confederate Memorial," *Pioneer America Society Transactions* 5 (1982): 9–15. The fact that there are no such overviews of Union monuments is in itself revealing; the linkages between the two traditions have not yet been explored because the ruling assumption has been that the Confederate monuments forge a unique, distinct identity. Foster's book *Ghosts of the Confederacy* offers the beginnings of a corrective view, by examining the ways in which Confederate commemoration helped facilitate the South's reentry into the national mainstream.

5. Published accounts of monument dedication ceremonies are plentiful and constitute a good source for these rhetorical arguments. See, for example, *Dedication of the Soldiers' Monument at Dorchester, September 17, 1867* (Boston: Thomas Groom, 1868); *Dedication of the Soldiers' Monument at Worcester, Massachusetts* (Worcester, 1875); John Esten Cooke, *Stonewall Jackson: A Military Biography, with an appendix containing personal reminiscences, and a full account of the ceremonies attending the unveiling of Foley's statue* (New York: D. Appleton, 1876); Thomas Astley Atkins and John Wise Oliver, *Yonkers in the Rebellion of 1861–1865* (Yonkers, N.Y.: Yonkers Soldiers' and Sailors' Monument Association, 1892); *Addresses Delivered at the Unveiling of the Monument to Confederate Soldiers at Charles City County, Virginia* (Richmond: Whittet & Shepperson, Printers, 1901), pp. 9, 22.

6. Pierre Nora argues that the modern tendency to deposit collective memory in external "traces"—archives, monuments, and so forth—has displaced and depleted "real" memory, which he conceives as an inner, unmediated phenomenon: "The less memory is experienced from the inside the more it exists only through its exterior scaffolding and outward signs" (Nora, "Between Memory and History: *Les Lieux de Memoire,*" *Representations,* no. 26 [Spring 1989]: 7–25, quote on p. 13). There are at least two objections to his argument. First of all, Nora's dichotomy of external and internal memory is misleading: all shared memory requires mediating devices to sustain itself, even if those are as simple as an anecdote or a gesture. Second, the modern reliance on memory "traces" does not mean that more ephemeral and less easily documented means of remembering have been abandoned. The commemoration of the Civil War is a case in point: the proliferation of public monuments, reliquaries, and document collections coincided with equally ubiquitous ritual observances, veterans' reunions, and organizational meetings, as well as less formal activities of remembering in the home, church, or street. These various memory networks were not necessarily mutually exclusive and may in certain ways have been mutually reinforcing.

The modern need to objectify collective memory in tangible traces, which Nora is right to emphasize, does not so much indicate the death of another, more natural memory as it does the presence of a certain hierarchy of memory activities, in which "enduring" (and properly documented) testimonials take on the greatest value and cultural prestige. The great flowering of the public monument in postrevolutionary Western societies is surely linked to the rise of nationalism and the nationalist demand for tangible symbols and traditions that could make the idea of the nation credible; in this age the nation is the ruling collective, and to make collective memory real, physically rooted, is to make the collective real. See Eric Hobsbawm, "Inventing Traditions" and "Mass-Producing Traditions: Europe, 1870–1914," both in *The Invention of Tradition,* ed. Eric Hobsbawm and Terence Ranger (Cambridge: Cambridge University Press, 1983).

7. In the absence of any thorough inventories of monument inscriptions I have relied on the compilations cited above (note 4) and on my own observation.

8. For more on this point see my dissertation, "Race, Memory, and Identity: The National Monuments of the Union and the Confederacy" (University of California at Berkeley, 1990), pp. 13–15.

9. The classic book on racial politics in the postwar period is Leon F. Litwack, *Been in the Storm So Long: The Aftermath of Slavery* (New York: Vintage Books, 1980). The two broadest syntheses of scholarship on the Civil War and its aftermath are James M. McPherson, *Battle Cry of Freedom: The Civil War Era* (New York: Oxford University Press, 1988); and Foner, *Reconstruction.* Also helpful in my thinking have been Kenneth M. Stampp, *The Imperiled Union: Essays on the Background of the Civil War* (New York: Oxford University Press, 1980); and Drew Gilpin Faust, *The Creation of Confederate Nationalism: Ideology and Identity in the Civil War South* (Baton Rouge: Louisiana State University Press, 1988). See also David W. Blight, " 'For Something beyond the Battlefield': Frederick Douglass and the Struggle for the Memory of the Civil War," *Journal of American History* 75 (March 1989): 1156–1178.

10. Landmarks in this process of "reconciliation" include the 1885 funeral of

Ulysses Grant in New York, where Confederate generals marched in the procession, and the 1895 dedication of a Confederate monument in Chicago (see Jno. C. Underwood, *Report of Proceedings Incidental to the Erection and Dedication of the Confederate Monument* [Chicago: Wm. Johnston Printing, 1896]). My argument here will focus instead on the conspicuously national projects to commemorate Lee and Lincoln.

11. For Lee's views on slavery see Douglas Southall Freeman, *R.E. Lee: A Biography* (New York: Scribner's Sons, 1935), 1:371–373. Probably the most sophisticated account of Lee as a commemorative figure is in Foster, *Ghosts of the Confederacy*, esp. pp. 51, 101–103, 120–121. See also Thomas L. Connelly, *The Marble Man: Robert E. Lee and His Image in American Society* (New York: Knopf, 1977); and Alan T. Nolan, *Lee Considered: General Robert E. Lee and Civil War History* (Chapel Hill: University of North Carolina Press, 1991). For more on the reading of Lee's physical appearance see Savage, "Race, Memory, and Identity," pp. 71–74, 82–84.

12. Savage, "Race, Memory, and Identity," pp. 92–94, 190–194.

13. Ibid., pp. 86–90. Mercie's original model, which the sponsors rejected, depicted Lee on a rearing horse surrounded by the scattered bodies of dying soldiers; this Napoleonic conception could not have been further from the canonical image of Lee. For an interesting account of Lee's "true" relationship to his horse, with an explicit racial reading, see "General R.E. Lee's War-Horse," *Southern Historical Society Papers* 35 (1907): 99–101 (originally published in the *Richmond Dispatch*, August 10, 1886).

14. *Richmond Planet*, June 7, 1890, p. 2.

15. Ibid.

16. The *Richmond Dispatch*, June 1, 1890, p. 5, provides a useful sampling of Northern editorials. Note, for example, the rhetoric of the *New York Times*, May 30, 1890, p. 4: "His [Lee's] memory is, therefore, a possession of the American people, and the monument that recalls it is itself a national possession."

17. Charles Francis Adams, *Shall Cromwell Have a Statue?* (Boston: Charles E. Lauriat, 1902), pp. 16, 20, 44. On Frederick Douglass's understanding of this process see Blight, "'For Something beyond the Battlefield,'" p. 1169.

18. One such proposal, initiated by the historian George Washington Williams, was discussed in Congress (John Hope Franklin, *George Washington Williams: A Biography* [Chicago: University of Chicago Press, 1985], pp. 171–174). More obscure proposals appear in the *American Architect and Building News* 20 (August 21, 1886): 81, and 23 (January 7, 1888): 2.

19. Freeman Henry Morris Murray, *Emancipation and the Freed in American Sculpture: A Study in Interpretation* (Washington, D.C.: Murray Brothers, 1916; reprinted Freeport, N.Y.: Books for Libraries Press, 1972), p. 72.

20. Key literature on the memorial includes Homer Saint-Gaudens, ed., *Reminiscences of Augustus Saint-Gaudens* (New York: Century Co., 1913), 1:332–335; Lois Goldreich Marcus, "The *Shaw Memorial* by Augustus Saint-Gaudens: A History Painting in Bronze," *Winterthur Portfolio* 14 (Spring 1979): 1–23; John H. Dryfhout, *The Work of Augustus Saint-Gaudens* (Hanover, N.H.: University Press of New England, 1982), pp. 222–229; Stephen J. Whitfield, "'Sacred in History and in Art': The *Shaw Memorial*," *New England Quarterly* 60 (March 1987): 3–

27; and most recently Albert Boime, *The Art of Exclusion: Representing Blacks in the Nineteenth Century* (Washington, D.C.: Smithsonian Institution Press, 1990), pp. 199–219.

21. The evolution of Saint-Gaudens's design is discussed in Marcus, "The *Shaw Memorial*," pp. 16–19, and can be charted in the preparatory drawings published in Dryfhout, *Work of Augustus Saint-Gaudens*, pp. 224–225. Marcus's analysis, while thorough, still underestimates the critical shift involved in Saint-Gaudens's eventual decision to change from a three-quarter view to a profile view, with Shaw therefore placed beside rather than ahead of his troops.

22. Murray, *Emancipation and the Freed in American Sculpture*, pp. 168–174; quote on p. 172.

23. Charles Caffin, *American Masters of Sculpture* (Garden City, N.Y.: Doubleday, 1913), p. 11; *Reminiscences of Augustus Saint-Gaudens*, 1:335.

Albert Boime, while rejecting Caffin's racism, finds Caffin's reading more correct than Murray's (*Art of Exclusion*, pp. 209–211). Boime's argument hinges chiefly on the visual conflation of the soldiers' legs and the horse's legs; this compositional strategy he thinks belongs to a long racist tradition of identifying blacks with animals. I see the same strategy as a conflation of foreground and background rather than animal and black, a view I think is justified by other visual details, such as Shaw's sword, which extends and echoes the diagonals of the rifles behind. In my view there is a significant disparity between Saint-Gaudens's written representations of his black models and the more ambivalent representations of the sculpture itself.

24. Savage, "Race, Memory, and Identity," pp. 47–53.

25. National Archives, Microfilm M371 (Records of the Commissioner of Public Buildings and Grounds), reel 27, frame 331. See also *Celebration by the colored people's Educational Monument Association in memory of Abraham Lincoln on the Fourth of July, 1865 in the Presidential grounds* (Washington, D.C.: McGill & Witherow, Printers, 1865).

26. The National Lincoln Monument Association, *Organization and Design, Proceedings of the Board of Managers . . .* (Washington, D.C.: Office of the New National Era, 1870), p. 6.

27. Since the papers of the organization appear to be lost, the sponsor's actions can be pieced together only through scattered publications and archival fragments; for a more complete account see Savage, "Race, Memory, and Identity," pp. 53–65.

28. *Inaugural Ceremonies of the Freedmen's Memorial Monument to Abraham Lincoln, Washington City, April 14, 1876* (St. Louis: Levison and Blythe, 1876).

29. Douglass's impromptu remarks were reported by an eyewitness observer, John W. Cromwell, whose account is published in part in Murray, *Emancipation and the Freed in American Sculpture*, p. 199. For more on the speech see Blight, "'For Something beyond the Battlefield,'" pp. 1164–1165.

30. The McMillan Plan was published as *The Improvement of the Park System of the District of Columbia*, ed. Charles Moore (Washington, D.C.: Government Printing Office, 1902).

31. For all my remarks on the Lincoln Memorial I am indebted to Christopher Thomas for sharing his knowledge and the manuscript of his dissertation, "The Lincoln Memorial and Its Architect, Henry Bacon (1866–1924)." The modus

THE POLITICS OF MEMORY

operandi of the two commissions can best be observed in the *Lincoln Memorial Commission Report*, December 5, 1912, Senate Document No. 965, 62d Congress, 3d Session. The criticisms of the process and the design can be traced in the Ideal Scrapbooks of Henry Bacon in the Bacon Papers at Olin Library, Wesleyan University; the critique of Greece as a slaveholding society is from the *New York Independent* 72 (February 8, 1912), pp. 320–322, and 74 (February 6, 1913), pp. 280–281.

32. Taft gave this interpretation during his dedication speech at the memorial, published in Edward F. Concklin, *The Lincoln Memorial* (Washington, D.C.: Government Printing Office, 1927), pp. 83–86; quote on p. 84. His remarks echo the assumptions of the Fine Arts Commission as they are revealed in the reports published in *Lincoln Memorial Commission Report*, December 5, 1912.

33. Royal Cortissoz composed the inscription and wrote to Bacon, "By emphasizing his saving the union you appeal to both sections. By saying nothing about slavery you avoid the rubbing of old sores" (letter, April 6 [1919], Lincoln Memorial correspondence, Bacon Papers, Olin Library, Wesleyan University).

34. *New York Sun*, undated clipping in Ideal Scrapbook no. 2, Bacon Papers, Olin Library, Wesleyan University: "In choosing his models for negro types he [Jules Guerin] did not attempt to typify the central African negro races we know most familiarly in America. Anthropologically, the models who posed for his figures of 'The Black Peoples,' especially in the central group of one of the panels [emancipation mural], are a mixed lot. Decoration, rather than realism, was what the painter sought."

35. Concklin, *Lincoln Memorial*, pp. 75, 79. *Washington Tribune*, June 3, 1922, pp. 1, 8. Constance McGlaughlin Green writes that Moton himself was forced to sit in the segregated section, but this was not reported in the black press coverage; moreover, a photograph published on the front page of the *Washington Tribune*, June 3, 1922, shows Moton delivering his speech from the top step of the memorial. See Green, *The Secret City: A History of Race Relations in the Nation's Capital* (Princeton, N.J.: Princeton University Press, 1967), p. 199.

36. In Richmond proposals have recently been aired to expand (and alter) Monument Avenue's commemorative function by adding statues of black Civil Rights leaders from Virginia and a statue of Governor Wilder, the nation's first elected black governor since Reconstruction; proponents seem to be framing these counter-heritages as compatible, while opponents decry the discontinuity and disjunction with the Confederate past. See John F. Harris, "Monumental Issue Divides Old Dominion: New Statues Proposed for Richmond Boulevard," *Washington Post*, September 29, 1991, p. B3–1.

Chapter VIII

MEMORY AND NAMING IN THE GREAT WAR

Thomas W. Laqueur

At the end of Shakespeare's *Henry V* the king asks his herald about the casualties of what would become known as the Battle of Agincourt: "Where is the number of our English dead?" He is handed a piece of paper and reads:

> Edward the Duke of York, the Earl of Suffolk,
> Sir Richard Ketly, Davy Gam, esquire:
> None else of name; and of all other men
> But five and twenty . . .
> (IV, viii, 107–111)

Similarly, at the beginning of *Much Ado About Nothing*, the messenger replies to Leonato's question "How many gentlemen have you lost in this action?" with the news: "But few of any sort, and none of name" (I, i, 5–7). "None else of name" in fact largely sufficed to efface the overwhelming majority of dead soldiers from public memory from ancient times, when battlefield stelae stood watch over their collective ashes, until the fall and early winter of 1914, when all of this changed.

We know, for example, the *name*, rank, and regiment of the first British soldier killed in the Great War: Private J. Paul of the Middlesex Regiment, Rifles, who fought with the British Expeditionary Force (B.E.F.) near Mons and died on August 23, 1914. He is buried in the military cemetery of Saint Symphorien, a few yards across the grass from the grave of the last Commonwealth soldier to die in World War I: Private George L. Price, Twenty-eighth North West Battalion, Second Canadian Brigade, killed at a canal crossing, also near Mons, at 10:58 in the morning, two minutes before the armistice that was to end the carnage at the eleventh hour of the eleventh day of the eleventh month of 1918. (Their proximity in dust and the fact that they share a burial ground with four years' worth of German dead bespeak the military futility of their actions.)

Both of these men and their named comrades lie within twelve miles of the site of the Battle of Malplaquet, where in 1709 the duke of Marlborough lost twenty thousand men. We do not know, or at least there is not commemorated at the battlefield, the name of a single one of them. Likewise, we can search up and down the Iberian peninsula at the sites of the great battles and sieges of Wellington's famous campaign—Vimiera (eight hundred allied casualties), Corunna (a thousand British losses), Albuera (seven thousand dead, including one-half of the entire British force), Badajoz and Burgos (five thousand and seven thousand dead, respectively, at their sieges), the site of the Battle of the Pyrenees (seven thousand losses), to name only the largest—without encountering the name of so much as one common soldier or even a memorial to their having lived, fought, and died here.[1]

At Waterloo on June 18 Wellington lost fifteen thousand men, arrayed in some cases with geometrical precision: "the 27th [Inniskilling] were lying literally dead in a square." Although there is a monument on the battlefield to Victor Hugo, commemorating his stay at the Hotel des Colonees for the purpose of writing the Waterloo chapter of *Les Misérables*, there is none to any of these. Back in the village church of Waterloo itself there are names: twelve private soldiers, all listed on one plaque dedicated to the memory of the fallen of the Twelfth Light Dragoons.

In sharp contrast to the treatment of the dead of Europe's next great war, a century later, the image one is left with at Waterloo is one not only of anonymity but of complete individual dissolution. Almost like one of John Donne's reveries in which the atoms of his body are scattered through the seas and into the bodies of fish to be gathered together and resurrected by an all-powerful God on the day of judgment, the poetry of Waterloo speaks of ground that erases the differences not only between men but between all creatures, all creation: Earth, Robert Southey writes,

> had received into her silent womb
> Her slaughtered creatures; horse and man they lay,
> And friend and foe, within the general tomb.
> Equal had been their lot; one fatal day
> For all, . . . one labour, . . . and one place of rest
> They found within their common parents breast.

Aspects of this democracy of death reappear as a major theme in World War I memorials, but in a very different guise. In 1815 only "the breeze upon its breath" bore "a taint of death." The "shoe, and belt, and broken bandoleer / And hat which bore the mark of mortal wound," were all that marked the thousands who did not return from the last great battle of the revolutionary wars.[2] (Debris of this sort would be cleared before a modern battlefield could become a memorial ground.)

One could of course go on. Forty-five thousand died in the Crimean War from battles and disease; "shoveled into the ground and so forgotten," as Thackeray put it. A few more graves were individually marked than in previous wars: 51 out of 324 in one of the burial grounds of the Second Brigade, Light Division; 22 out of 1,334 in the cemeteries of the Third

Division. In fact the former of these cemeteries was said to resemble a "humble imitation of Kensal Green, and contain some handsome monuments, in design and execution far from inferior to many in England."[3] But as in Kensal Green Cemetery back home the poor were packed into common and often unmarked graves; and as in commercial cemeteries generally all commemoration was private. The state did nothing and indeed let Crimean graves vanish into the landscape: "Over the graves of our dead heroes, and their no less heroic hospital nurses and attendants, browsed three donkeys belonging to some wandering Yuruks," reports a letter to the London *Times*. "The grass, nourished into life by the autumn rains, was greening upon the nameless and undistinguished graves of our countrymen."

Oblivion reached ludicrous heights during the nineteenth century. At the Battle of Maiwand (July 27, 1880) in the Second Afghan War 962 officers and men died. A burial party returned in September, reinterred the hastily covered dead, and erected a single marker: to Major Blackwood of the Royal Horse Artillery. But a pet dog survived and, after all his friends had been killed, managed to catch up with the bedraggled retreating British forces. He returned to England and was invited to Osborne House, where he was awarded a medal by Queen Victoria. His stuffed body as well as his *name* is preserved in the regimental museum: "Bobbie" of the Royal Berkshires.[4]

By the Boer War, in which some five thousand British soldiers died, the government was willing to provide small iron crosses to mark the graves of those not privately commemorated, but even this was done almost as a second thought. The secretary of state for war opposed the consolidation of the more than 170 burial places, and thus the creation of substantial commemorative sites, despite the fact that the status quo, at least by 1914 standards, was intolerable. "Scattered graves," wrote an officer of the Loyal Woman's Guild, which had taken upon itself the task of maintenance, are "impossible to preserve." The graves at Magersfontern, she reports, had been "disturbed by jackals and other animals burrowing" and were "causing great grief to those concerned."[5] Nothing was done, and the remains of the dead remain scattered and haphazardly named.

In January 1915—one can date this remarkable change with a precision not usual in cultural history—a new era of remembrance began: the era of the common soldier's name or its self-conscious and sacralized oblivion. Common soldiers ceased to be "buried where they fell—in the fields, in the roadsides, sometimes singly, sometimes together"; it became his and his colleagues' job, writes a member of a British Red Cross unit in his war diary, "to search for graves, identify soldiers, mark them with a cross, register their position." This was essentially a mopping-up operation at first, taking care of the fallen from Mons and the first battle of Ypres in

1914 and early 1915, since before then "no unit of the army existed to do such registration work."[6]

By March 1915, however, these hastily assembled Red Cross units had been reorganized as the Graves Registration Commission. By September, in the course of British negotiations with France for a treaty providing for permanent cemeteries, it had become clear that, as Field Marshal Sir John French put it, the "care, registration, etc, of graves now assumes a national character" and should therefore become the responsibility of the state.[7] These responsibilities were subsumed under the office of the adjutant general. By March 1916, two hundred cemetery sites had already been chosen, and plans for an additional three hundred to three thousand, depending "on the extent of future fighting," were in the works. For the first time in British military history scattered bodies were to be gathered together, reinterred, and individually marked. And by March too the policy of complete state control over the bodies of the dead and their final resting place had been laid down. Sir Lionel Earle, permanent secretary of the Ministry of Works and member of the new National Committee for the Care of Soldier's Cemeteries, "laid great stress," the committee's minutes say, "on the necessity for taking strong action to prevent the public from putting up unsuitable effigies in cemeteries and thought that the monuments on all graves should be uniform."[8]

From these administrative decisions there followed a historically unprecedented planting of names on the landscapes of battle. A thousand cemeteries in Belgium and France trace the contours of combat or mark the sites of base hospitals on the western front. These are, and were so regarded at the time, "a memorial of those lost in the war such as never had been dreamt of before," in the words of Sir Reginald Blomfield, who was one of the three senior architects in charge of their design.[9] Each of those cemeteries with more than four hundred dead is presided over by an austerely classical Stone of Remembrance, with "Their *name* liveth for evermore" engraved on it. In August 1918 these words still had a strange ring. They come from the Apocryphal Book of *Ecclesiasticus* (44:14) and had never before been used for commemorative purposes. "Their name liveth evermore," muses Sir Edwin Lutyens, the designer of the stone: "But what are names?"[10]

Rudyard Kipling, who proposed the epitaph, knew; his only son had disappeared. Or should one say that his body had become separated from his name, which remains as a trace on the Irish Guards panel, one of 20,589 names on the panels of the Loos Memorial to the Missing? By 1938, when the Imperial War Graves Commission had completed its World War I work, it had overseen the construction of 1,850 cemeteries, the great majority of which (a thousand), and the largest, being in Belgium and France. By 1930 557,520 soldiers of the Empire (454,574 from the

United Kingdom) had been buried in identified, that is, named, graves. Another 180,861 unidentified bodies were put each in a separate grave; even at cemeteries like Cabaret Rouge in the Somme, where five thousand of the seventy-five hundred dead are "unknown," there were almost no Commonwealth mass graves. The names of these men, and of a further 336,912 whose bodies had simply disappeared, blown into the air or ground into the mud, are inscribed in stone on a monument near the place where they were thought to have died.

These are the imposing, major monuments of the western front. The central problem of their design was to find room for the plethora of names. "I had to find space for a vast number of names, estimated at first at some 40,000, but increased as we went on to about 58,600," says Blomfield in his account of building Menin Gate. And, in fact, despite cramming twelve hundred panels on all the major columns, along stairs, and on the walls of the terraces that abut the ramparts of Ypres, the structure would hold only 54,896 names. "So interminably many," as Stephen Zweig put it, "that as on the columns of the Alhambra, the writing becomes decorative." The names that remained from the Ypres salient, men who died after the night of August 15–16, 1917, the night of the Battle of Langemarck, are inscribed on the seemingly endless walls of Tyne Cot, in the midst of the site of the Battle of Passchendaele, where 34,888 names surround 11,908 individual gravestones on a site that has no other distinctive memorial structure. It is a place for the pure display of names. (Names of the New Zealand missing were also transferred to sites nearer to where they fell, which took some additional pressure off Menin Gate.)[11]

And the string of names continues down the front. The names of 11,447 men—the dead of battles from Armentières and Aubers Ridge in 1914 to Hazebrouck and Scherpenberg in 1918—line the colonnades of the Ploegstreet Memorial. Fifteen kilometers south, near Neuve Chapelle, 4,843 names of missing Indian soldiers fill the walls of Sir Herbert Baker's Indo-Saracenic courtyard, guarded by the Asoka lions, incongruously set in the northern French countryside. Another fifteen or so kilometers away is the Duds Corner Memorial, where one enters a courtyard formed by panels with 20,589 names from the battles around Loos. Then ten kilometers on, more than eleven thousand names of Canadians with no known graves stretch out from two of Walter Allard's monumental figures on Vimy Ridge. Thirty kilometers to the southwest the curiously broken bodies of Jaeger's reliefs flank the entrance to a yard where thirteen bays with twelve tablets each record 7,048 names from the Battle of Cambrai. About the same distance due south is Lutyens's reworking of the motifs of Albert Cathedral, the great monument of Thiepval, where the sixteen weight-bearing columns that hold up the structure are faced on three or four sides with panels holding the names of 73,367 men with no known resting place who died in the Battle of the Somme.

There are, of course, also the cemeteries, which contain as few as a score or so to more than ten thousand grave markers, some with names, others with the notation that here lies a soldier whose name is known but to God. The pyramids pale by comparison with the sheer scale of British—let alone German, French, Belgian, Portuguese—commemorative imposition on the landscape. More than four hundred kilometers of concrete beams were used to undergird the 678,000 absolutely identical plain Portland lime-stone headstones—2 feet, six inches, by 1 foot, three inches—over the graves; ninety kilometers of wall were built to surround the cemeteries; innumerable plants and trees were set in the ground; and almost ten million pounds were expended.[12] (The precision of these numbers testifies to their bureaucratic origins, not necessarily to their accuracy, but that is another story.) In other words, both during the war and after, the state poured enormous human, financial, administrative, artistic, and diplo-matic resources into preserving and remembering the names of individual common soldiers.

This represents a radical departure not only from earlier military practice—the B.E.F. had no more elaborate plans for dealing with the dead in the first Battle of Mons than the army had in the Napoleonic Wars—but also from nineteenth-century British domestic custom. Although a decent funeral was considered immensely important by the working classes, from which the great majority of soldiers came, individual burial was not. Most people—not only paupers—were buried in collective, that is, shaft, graves, with the tombstone listing occupants in the order of interment, or in ground that could be reused for further burial after some number of years. The great ribbons of war cemeteries across Europe and the other theaters of war, with their neat individual grave markers, were thus genuinely new and were, in fact, regarded by their proponents as explicit rejections of the Victorian aesthetic of death. "We must make every effort," writes the permanent secretary of the Ministry of Works to Sir Sidney Greville, "to make these cemeteries as attractive as possible, and prevent them from becoming eyesores on the countryside of France through the hideous effi-gies relatives often have a tendency to erect."[13]

The sheer magnitude of the commitment to remembrance is evident as well in the day-to-day records of those who performed the ghastly work of finding, identifying, and burying bodies. It was dangerous: continuing battle and sniper fire put burial parties at risk of being killed.[14] Reginald Bryson's commander was killed watching the bombardment on the Ypres-Menin Road, but only after surviving the "many occasions [on which] he would go into the front line trenches in order to put a cross on a grave or to see a chaplain." It was extremely hard work, physically and emotionally. On July 3 a chaplain went with fifty men to collect the dead: "163 Devons covered up in a copse"; "crew dead beat—task of filling trench was awfully slow." A photographer attached to the Red Cross was constantly pressed to hurry, to utilize every minute of daylight he could, to record as many graves as possible.[15] Another chaplain writes of the desperately sad task of going through the papers taken from the bodies of the dead: "A child's first letter to 'Daddy', printed crooked, ill-spelt . . . a paper of peppermints . . . the pictured face of an old woman."[16]

And cleaning up the battlefield after a major campaign and once the war had stopped was not only gruesome but was bedeviled by the sorts of snafus common in large-scale military operations: Captain W.E. Southgate is sitting with his men in the Cambrai subsector in the fall of 1919. He knows of two hundred bodies to be exhumed and reburied and is worried about being unfavorably compared to other groups, but he has no canvas, only thirty picks and not enough shovels, and no crosses. Even if he had them he couldn't get them to the burial site because promised transport has not appeared.[17] In fact, the problem of insufficient army support for gathering together the estimated 180,000 scattered graves generated considerable worries in the highest circles. "I need scarcely point out," writes Sir Robert Borden to Lloyd George, "that if there were any carelessness or avoidable failure in this work it would be most unfortunate." Clearly here was an issue the public in Britain and in the Empire generally cared about deeply. "Nothing," Borden says in one report to the prime minister, "could be more calculated to produce a public outcry." "Any reasonable suspicion that there has been negligence or inattention with respect to the graves of our soldiers in France would arouse a feeling of stern resentment in Canada and I believe in every one of the dominions." The Army Council apologized for any avoidable delays.[18]

"The vastness of the work of exhumation and concentration of scattered graves" slowed progress, announced the War Graves Commission in 1920, although it had already overseen the reburial of 128,577 men, of whom 6,273 had been identified for the first time and 66,796 were still, and thus probably would forever remain, unknown.[19] A year later, when systematic efforts to find bodies ceased, the remains of 204,650 dead had been reburied; subsequently, up to 1938, 38,000 more bodies, 80 percent unknown, had been found by farmers, metal searchers, and others.

These unknowns—517,000 or so by the time the counting stopped—provided the other new focus of memory in World War I: on Armistice Day, 1920, the king unveiled the Cenotaph—the empty tomb—on Whitehall and was chief mourner at the burial of an unknown warrior in Westminster Abbey. Thus was created perhaps the first national holy site, at a time when not only national grief but acute political tensions that would culminate in the General Strike seemed to cry out for one. Again, the histories of both the empty tomb and the occupied grave need to be written. Briefly, the idea of the former seems to have grown out of a suggestion of Lloyd George's that for the victory parade on July 19 a catafalque be set up past which troops could march and salute the dead. Sir Edwin Lutyens designed the austere temporary monument—he actually dashed off his first sketch of it while having dinner with his mistress, Lady Sackville—and suggested that it be called a cenotaph. But neither Lloyd George nor Lutyens, nor anyone else, anticipated the spontaneous response of the people to the infinite meanings of emptiness.[20] Thousands of the bereaved left wreaths at the makeshift altar, projecting their grief onto the void within or the un-adorned classical facade of the makeshift structure. Public opinion de-manded that what had been intended as a temporary prop made of wood and plaster be rebuilt as a monument in permanent stone.

The origins of the idea for the burial of an unknown soldier are more obscure. It is attributed by some to Dean Ryle of Westminster Abbey, by others to the Reverend D. Railton, who says that the idea came to him in his billet near Armentières in 1916.[21] But of course most European countries as well as the United States have their shrine to an unknown soldier, created after World War I, so that the notion of having a cipher in bones as *the* site of national memory is obviously of transnational origin and significance. (National variations, however, are potentially revealing of how a particular political community's collective consciousness is formed; Britain, for ex-ample, self-consciously excluded foreign dignitaries, including those of its former allies, from the funeral of the unknown warrior and the unveiling of the Cenotaph. A body representing all bodies resting in Westminster Abbey has different resonances than one buried under the Arc de Triomphe.) In any case, whatever controversy or reluctance among ceremonial planners may have surrounded this new addition to the Armistice ceremony, it was an instant success. More than a million and a quarter people filed slowly by the open grave on the days after November 11. "Enough to say that the great symbolical act of allowing an unidentified body to represent all the mighty inarticulate sacrifice of the nation is justified, because all people heartily understand it and approve of it." But what makes "every heart, in however simple or poor a body it beats," intimately engaged in "the great symbolic act" is that "every bereaved man or woman can say, 'That body may belong to me.'"[22] Obviously questions remain as to how profoundly the burial of the unknown warrior elided class and political divisions and how cynical the government was in regarding the ceremony as an occasion for mending the social fabric. The fact that "a duchess would sit down with the char woman" during the abbey ceremony was certainly regarded by the planners as contributing "in its small way" to interclass tranquillity, even if this was not the purpose foremost in their minds.[23]

But the dominant public interpretation of the event, judging from a wide range of newspapers and periodicals, was that here, in Westminster Abbey, the social body was made whole and manifest: "Never before has there been such a proclamation, gladly made, that we are all equal, all members of one body, or rather one soul." "All of us were members of one orchestra . . . [there was] one forgetfulness of self in that quiet ritual, one desire that prophecy be fulfilled . . . that we may, indeed, all become members of one body politic and of one immortal soul."[24]

The unknown warrior became the opposite pole in the formation of memory to the graves I discussed earlier, although the two are part of what I take to be a distinctively modern way of creating meaning. While the names and markers that gird the battlefields of France and Belgium cry out in their specificity, their one-to-one correspondence with a body at, or near, the place of the sign, the unknown warrior becomes in his universality the cipher that can mean anything, the bones that represent any and all bones equally well or badly. He was, as a nurse said in her memoirs about a soldier who died without anyone knowing who he was, among those "poor fellows" who had "given even their names."[25] As the semioticians tell us, it is, at the same time, itself, the sign of itself, and the sign also of a half million other selves.

How are we to account for these new forms of memorialization? One way, of course, is to say that they are not so new. The Gettysburg National Cemetery, for example, begun in 1863, stands as a precedent. But Gettysburg, with its individual graves, was itself a major innovation; of the three thousand or so soldiers who died at Valley Forge during the winter of 1777–78 as members of the world's most democratically recruited army, the grave of only one—a lieutenant from Rhode Island—is marked. And Gettysburg was something of an exception. Even by the Civil War neither the Union nor the Confederate army had any great interest in marking the graves of dead soldiers; troops of neither side were issued the regular means of identification that would have made this possible. (The identification disc was first issued to British troops in 1901; the two-part discs, one part of which remained with the body while the other was used to register the death, were an invention of Fabian Ware and the Graves Registration Commission.)[26] Moreover, similar cemeteries were not built on other and even bloodier battle sites; there are no rows of individual graves at Antietam, for example.[27] Finally, those who planned Gettysburg were still only groping toward the creation of national burial grounds or cemeteries that primarily marked individuals. Between 1864 and 1895 the landscape, as one historian noted, became "a vast outdoor gallery of state and regimental monuments," not singular or national ones.[28]

There are, in contrast, few collective memorials along the World War I fronts—the national memorials to the missing of Canada, Australia, New

Zealand, India, and the Empire generally; some regimental memorials, although these are rarely set among graves; and a few memorials to troops of an area or province, such as the Newfoundland Stag and the Norman tower erected to commemorate the northern Irish who fought, both located near Albert—and again these are distinct from cemeteries. Altogether there are throughout the world only about two hundred memorials to the Commonwealth soldiers of both world wars. At the heart of World War I cemeteries is the specific name or grave.

Of course, one must also put the developments I have been discussing in the context of the democratization of memory, the history of which Reinhard Koselleck has outlined, beginning in the French Revolution. The first monument to dead soldiers is in Lucerne and is dedicated to the memory of the Swiss Guard killed in the attack on the Tuileries, August 10, 1792. (It is itself something of an irony that soldiers who died defending a king against the Demos were the first to be memorialized.)[29] There are 509 names of citizens who died in the Revolution of 1830 on the Colonne de Juillet.[30] The eleven who died in the Peterloo Massacre in 1819 are memorialized in Manchester. But within this history the First World War represents such a leap in sheer numbers—not only of those being remembered but of those remembering, that is, mass society—as to represent a qualitative rupture as well.

Finally, there are functionalist explanations for new burial arrangements in World War I. Earlier battles, even very deadly ones and even ones that followed a siege, were over quickly and the army moved on. The heroic march is the stuff of military legends, and bodies were simply left behind. By June 19, 1815, everything was over at Waterloo. But not so in the Great War. The fact that the first and last man killed on the British side are buried so close together bears testimony to the immobility of this war, to the fact that soldiers died year after year over and among the decomposed bodies of their former comrades. Edmund Blunden illustrates "what once seemed to be the insoluble problem of burying the dead in modern war conditions" by recounting the fate of an area east of Festubert. In May 1915 British forces launched an attack on the Germans over swampy ground. There was little movement; as soldiers built or rebuilt trenches, they could hardly dig without discovering the remains of their countrymen or enemies. "Hamlet and Horatio might have meditated there many a dark hour." Then came the next summer and the Battle of the Somme, so fierce and so mired in miles of mud that thousands of bodies were irrecoverable. Relief battalions in the "fire-splashed night" stumbled over corpse after corpse. No wonder that Red Cross workers spoke of the desperate military and sanitary urgency of burial. But this explains only the problem, not the particular constellation of memory this war wrought.

The gravestones and the names, on the one hand, and the unknown warrior, on the other, are specific solutions to two new cultural facts of the early twentieth century. The former reflects both the domestic sensibilities of the nineteenth-century novel and the vast network of domestic ties that bound home front to battlefront. Soldiers never really left that aura of feelings that surround a father, a brother, a friend. So, while British working men may not have been given a marked individual grave in their prewar homeland and while the care of the bodies of the poor was something of a scandal, the state would have to do better by them if it sent them by the hundreds of thousands to die abroad. "Very hard to believe," writes Vera Brittain early in the war, "that far away men were being slain ruthlessly, and their poor disfigured bodies heaped together and crowded in ghastly indiscrimination into quickly provided common graves as if they were *nameless* vermin." "Nothing in life or death, amidst all the varied scenes of pain and sorrow in wartime," writes a future member of Parliament who worked at grave registration for the Red Cross from the very beginnings of the project in October 1914, "impresses the mind with so dark a picture of utter loneliness and desertion as does the sight of a soldier's grave standing alone . . . with nothing to mark it but the remains of a tiny flag or a forage cap or a dilapidated cross." The question is why someone like Catherine Stevens, sister of the poet Wallace Stevens, whose journal was returned with her body from the western front, would feel, on seeing still another cross during her almost phantasmagoric ride across one of Flanders' fields, that she "just had to go to it and see if I could read the name."[31] Under these circumstances a continuation of the previous two millennia's practices of military burial was impossible.

The second "fact" is that, as Pierre Nora points out, history and culture no longer define what is meaningful. Specific places of memory do not simply arise out of lived experience in the way that features of the landscape or churchyards do for a people more rooted in their geography; instead, they have to be created. And there is a further difficulty: heretofore resonant symbols, at least to an elite, become what the postwar generation came to call the "lies of the old men." In this semiotically arid world, a solution is to eschew representation and the production of meaning as far as possible and to resort to a sort of commemorative hyper-nominalism.

The case for the graves and the tens of thousands of names on tablets is most obvious. How does one grasp and remember death on the scale and with the apparent lack of generally accepted significance as the slaughters of this war? Blunden and others try to help by geographical analogues: a column of the dead four abreast would stretch from Durham to Westminster Abbey, from Quebec to Ottawa, and take four days and nights to pass a reviewing spot. But on the ground another scene unfolds in all its particularity: a thousand cemeteries that follow the contours of battle from the North Sea to the south (Passchendaele, Ploegstreet, Sens, Ypres, Armentières, Bethune, Lens, Vimy, the ridge on which is the Canadian sacred site) and on down through the battlefield of the Somme (Thiepval, Delville Woods, High Wood) and then east along the Marne Valley to Verdun (there are relatively few British bodies here). In other words, cemeteries and their graves are as close as one can come to having the men lie where they fell, a sign of their own multitude, their incomprehensively vast numbers.

What is being represented, in the absence of some commonly accepted idea, some notion of glory, patriotism, or elation in victory—the purpose of the war had been and in memory remained hotly contested—is thus the thing itself and the democracy of death that this collection of things makes so manifest. Bodies, of course, being in the ground, are hidden and cannot be their own memorials, but markers of their skeletal uniformity serve the purpose. Numbers. The human imagination is forced to see, as concretely as possible, what a million dead men look like. On all but the closest inspection, the stones, like the dust they mark, are indistinguishable from one another. (Crosses were rejected as leaving too little room for inscriptions, although that could only have been part of the reason, since the French used a cross, a Star of David, or a dome-shaped stone to mark respectively Christian, Jewish, and Muslim dead.)[32]

Indeed the War Graves Commission resisted any sort of diversity or even the possibility of some individual eccentricity that would spoil the leveling of death. The Dowager Lady Minto proposed, for example, that the age of the deceased be routinely inscribed on the gravestone. This seemingly innocent request, supported by a number of prominent figures, including Lord Haig, was rejected by the commission on the grounds that it would open the way to all manner of other requests to include information and that, if relatives insisted, they could include this information in the sixty-six character text that next of kin could, with commission approval of its contents and payment of a per-letter fee, have inscribed on a tombstone.[33]

More significant is the commission's long-standing and successful resistance, against an array of powerful men and interests, including Balfour, Churchill, the Cecils, and the king himself, to any deviation from absolute uniformity of memorialization. "What is done for one should be done for all," argued Burdett-Coutts in his parliamentary defense of the War Graves Commission's conformity with a policy articulated at the very first meeting of the National Committee for the Care of Graves that "the monuments on all graves should be uniform."[34] Churchill was simply wrong when in 1919 he wrote that the Commission could not adhere to its position that "no individual memorials are to be allowed." His opposition to this restriction—on the grounds that "in this matter, more perhaps than any other, people have the right to have their feelings studied," and that "large areas filled with uniform stones like those that mark kilometers by the roadside" would look horrible—came to naught.[35]

Appeals for exceptions by individual families, however well placed, were equally unsuccessful. When Vice Admiral Sir Lionel Halsey wrote a memorandum on behalf of two parents who had asked the help of the king in gaining permission to replace the wooden crosses that marked the probable resting place of their missing sons with more permanent stone memorials, he was firmly if politely rebuffed. Why should these parents be treated any differently from those of the two hundred thousand or so other missing, General Ware asked on behalf of the War Graves Commission. Finally, relatives were prohibited not only from choosing their own memorials for graves along the front but also from bringing bodies home. No soldier who had died overseas, with the exception of the unknown warrior, was allowed to return home.

The United States government, by contrast, had promised the mothers of America upon entering the war that the bodies of their sons would, if they so requested, be repatriated. For all sorts of reasons—not wanting to leave memories as hostages to a subsequent defense of Europe, the sentiment that "I sent you my son, now send him back," the absence of public cultivation of U.S. forces as a national collectivity—70 percent of the American dead were repatriated.[36] The French government tried to maintain control of that country's dead, but opposition from the Catholic church, which felt that this was but another ploy by the government of the Third Republic to accrue secular charisma, and from relatives, who simply took to stealing bodies from military cemeteries, meant that, in fact, French battlefield memorialization varies considerably.[37]

There lie the British and other imperial dead, all of them, in as much specificity as the passage of time will allow, different from all others.

Their memorials at each cemetery site are also remarkably devoid of general meaning. True, there is a flaming bronze sword on a cross—the Cross of Sacrifice—but the authorities were quick to point out that this was not in violation of or in accordance with any particular religion. It was, at least officially, not a sign of Christian sacrifice. The other common feature, "an altar-like Stone of Remembrance," designed by Lutyens with "Their *name* liveth for evermore" inscribed on it, was the result of a prolonged battle by the architect, who argued against a Christian cross, a five-pointed star, or any other iconographical symbol.[38]

In the 337,000 cases *all* that remained of those who fell was the name through which they had represented themselves and the carnage of war near where they had fallen. Names are the traces of bones or of the last place on earth where a soldier had been seen. Extraordinary efforts were made, for example, to trace the serial numbers of fuselages, engine cylinders, and even rubber tire rims in order to find the base from which a downed, and lost, aviator came so that his name could be preserved near his flight's point of origin. If his body was found, it was of course buried near the place where he had died.[39] Lost soldiers were commemorated near the camp where they were last seen; the 25,563 naval ranks and rating lost or buried at sea (out of 48,000 killed) are recorded on one of three memorials in each of the manning ports of the Royal Navy: Chatham, Plymouth, Portsmouth.[40]

The major monuments themselves, however grand, are little more than venues for names. Certainly, Menin Arch is meant to mark the gateway onto the battlefields: the road that passes through it and proceeds from Ypres to Menin to the east more or less bisects the front of the site of the first battle of Ypres. But its architectural meaning is obscure. It is decidedly not a triumphal arch; its specific historical allusion to the military fortifications of seventeenth-century Nancy cannot have had much resonance. The stone lions that guarded it were soon sent off to Australia, and the arch itself evokes nothing so much as a ghostly army beyond. (Will Longstaff's "Menin Gate at Midnight," 1927, painted to commemorate the unveiling ceremony, makes this case.)[41] And at Thiepval what might seem a Roman triumphal arch or a reference to the nearby much-damaged cathedral at Albert turns out to be a complex intersection of arches designed to provide not a venue for victory but extra wall space for names. Meaning, in other words, is squeezed out of the forms so that tablets and names—signs of the army of the dead—are all that remain.

The Cenotaph and the Tomb of the Unknown Warrior—forms reproduced at the same time in Europe and America—concentrate the hypernominalism of the headstones and inscriptions. A common-denominator body, in other words, is the opposite end of the same discursive strategy that is evident in the enumeration of names. The Cenotaph, of course, contained nothing; in the tomb, marked only by a slab set into the ground, rested bones that were construed, quite literally, as *the* generic body. It represented not the collectivity of the dead but rather one, and each and every one, of the names recorded, though not carved on a specific headstone, somewhere in France. In short, by being so intensely *a* body, it was *all* bodies.

Lord Curzon "strongly emphasized" prior to the burial service that "the unknown warrior will remain unknown."[42] The body was chosen from among those who had died with the B.E.F. in 1914 so that it would be as decayed, as much unlike a specific body and as much like the dust to which we all return, as possible. (In fact, four bodies were chosen at first, and one of them—the only one of more than a million bodies to be returned home, since such shipment of remains was forbidden—was then picked by lot and transported across the Channel by Royal Navy destroyer. Presumably the others were returned to ordinary graves.)[43] The concreteness of this process and thus of making memory is stunning: receipts dated November 10, 1920, written on Office of Works, Supply Division, forms, acknowledge that "16 barrels stated to contain 50 bags of French soil were delivered into my hands" and were signed by Lieutenant Swift, who had received the barrels from H.P. Allum, who, in turn, had accompanied the consigned "16 barrels, numbered 1–16" on the Dover ferry. And so, as Rupert Brooke would have it, the English body rested still in French soil.

Of course names were not the only memorials of the war—far from it. But they were an enormous and historically unprecedented part of it. In the absence of the physical remains of fallen soldiers save those of the one in Westminster Abbey, the names recorded at sites on the front and in village squares were the primary sites of mourning. Thus in Oldham a roll of honor was buried in the "sacred chamber" beneath the town memorial. In Blayton, the committee that organized the town memorial with its list of names suggested that since few could visit the graves of their loved ones abroad, "it will be of some slight consolation to them to come to the beautiful monument and lay their tributes of affection at its base." In Saddleworth, the names are even placed as one would a body, head to the east, in a churchyard. Its monument's "first function is to record the names of the fallen," 259 of them, positioned around the obelisk "as near as possible on that side which looks over toward the men's old homes."[44]

Together, the names and headstones are like shadows of the dead, standing in one-to-one correspondence with the fallen, representing them to the living in their ungraspable quantitative specificity. They are like the army of the living, both democratic and individual in their singularity, mere numbers in their aggregate. But their precise meaning was neither defined nor definable. Each of the living was free to remember as he or she chose. As with the Vietnam Memorial in Washington, the sources of modern memory in World War I derive their meaning from their intrinsic lack of it and bear testimony to their own artifice.

NOTES

1. These figures are from the *Encyclopaedia Britannica*, 11th ed., 1913, *s.v.* "peninsular campaign." The article points out that one cannot disaggregate deaths from wounded or missing—itself a telling fact in light of later efforts to enumerate these precisely.

2. Robert Southey.

3. Thackeray is quoted in Edmund Blunden, "Introduction," in Philip Longworth, *The Unending Vigil* (London: Leo Cooper, 1985), p. xx; Capts. the Hons. John Colborne and Frederic Brine, *The Last of the Brave; or the Resting Places of Our Fallen Heroes* (London, 1857), p. iv and statistics throughout.

4. *Chowkidar* (Journal of the British Association for Cemeteries in South Asia), vol. 2 (March 1980–March 1982), no. 1, pp. 1–2. On the other hand, when the Northumberland Fusiliers were transferred from India to Singapore, a group of officers organized an extraordinary effort to locate and mark the graves of 232 men

who had died at the various stopping places during the course of the regiment's service there (*Chowkidar,* vol. 3 [Oct. 1982–Oct. 1984], no. 2, p. 13).

5. "Care of Cemeteries in the Colonies," Public Record Office, WO 32/6023, Feb. 14, 1903, and June 2, 1903.

6. Reginald Harold Bryson, clerk, "My War Diary," p. 10, Imperial War Museum MS. 72/88/1.

7. PRO, WO 32/5847.

8. Minutes of the War Graves Commission, Windsor Archives, Box 244, folio 27, March 6, 1917.

9. Sir Reginald Blomfield, *Memoirs of an Architect* (London: Macmillan, 1932), p. 176.

10. Letter of August 10, 1918, in *The Letters of Edwin Lutyens to His Wife Lady Emily,* ed. Glayre Percy and Jane Ridley (London: Collins, 1985), p. 365.

11. Blomfield, *Memoirs,* pp. 186–187; Zweig is quoted from *Berliner Tageblatt,* Sept. 16, 1928, p. 190. See also Richard Fellows, *Sir Reginald Blomfield: An Edwardian Architect* (London: Zwemmer, 1985), pp. 112–113.

12. Figures from Fabian Ware, *The Immortal Heritage* (Cambridge: Cambridge University Press, 1937), pp. 47, 30.

13. Earle to Greville, March 30, 1916, Windsor Archives, Papers of Prince of Wales, National Committee on the Care of War Graves, Box 244.

14. MS. Diary of the Rev. Ernest Couteny Crosse, Chaplain, Eighth and Ninth Battalions, Devonshire Regiment, Somme, 1916, Imperial War Museum.

15. Memo in folder, Imperial War Museum 75/89/1, I.L. Bawtree, photographer assigned to Major Ware's unit.

16. Major A.H. Mure, *With the Incomparable 29th* (London: Chambers, 1919), pp. 87–88.

17. Imperial War Museum, Misc. 2118. Papers relating to the Eighty-Third Labour Group.

18. Lloyd George Papers, House of Lords Record Office, April 30, 1919, F/5/3/46; May 15, 1919, F/5/3/65. A copy of the Army Council's reply, April 15, 1919, is in F/5/3/46.

19. Annual Report, 1919–1920 [Cmd. 1076], p. 9.

20. Susan Mary Alsop, *Lady Sackville: A Biography* (London: Weidenfeld and Nicolson, 1978), p. 221. See the *London Times,* July 20, 1919, for an account of these spontaneous gestures.

21. See his obituary in the *London Times,* July 1, 1955.

22. *Spectator,* Nov. 13, 1920 (no. 4820), p. 621.

23. Lloyd George Papers, House of Lords Record Office.

24. *London Times Armistice Day Supplement I,* Nov. 12, 1920, p. 1.

25. S. MacNaughtan, *My War Experiences in Two Continents* (London: John Murray, 1919), p. 70.

26. For this information on Civil War identification, I am indebted to the privately circulated mimeographed information sheet "Identification Tags: 'Dog Tags'" produced by military researcher and collector C.C. Sweeting. I am grateful to him for sending it to me. There is nothing written on the history of identification discs in the British army, but the National Army Museum, Chelsea, has a disc from 1901 that it identifies as the earliest one extant.

27. John S. Patterson, "A Patriotic Landscape: Gettysburg 1863–1913," *Prospects* 7 (1982), pp. 317–321 and 315–333 passim.

28. Reuben M. Rainey, "Hallowed Grounds and Rituals of Remembrance: Union Regimental Monuments at Gettysburg," unpublished typescript presented at the J.B. Jackson Memorial Conference at Berkeley, 1989.

29. Reinhard Koselleck, "Kriegerdenkmale als Indentitatsstiftungen der Uberlebenen," in Otto Marquand and Karlheinz Stierle, eds., *Identitat* (Munich: Wilhelm Fink, 1979), pp. 255–276. See also Philippe Aries, *The Hour of Our Death* (New York: Vintage, 1982).

30. Michel Ragon, *The Space of Death* (Charlottesville: University of Virginia Press, 1983), pp. 111–112. Of course, naming is not necessarily democratic. As Ragon points out, a commission in the early nineteenth century came up with names of the generals for a triumphal arch at the Place de l'Étoile, where the French tomb of the unknown soldier is now located.

31. Vera Brittain, *Testament of Youth* (Harmondsworth: Penguin, 1989), p. 97, emphasis mine; Ian Malcolm, *War Pictures behind the Lines* (London: Smith Elder, 1915), pp. 50–51, quoted in James Langebach, "The Fellowship of Men That Perish: Wallace Stevens and the First World War," *Wallace Stevens Journal*, 13, 2 (Fall 1989), p. 96.

32. On the design of the gravestone, see Imperial War Graves Commission, *The Graves of the Fallen* (London: His Majesty's Stationery Office, 1919), p. 6.

33. Mary Minto to War Graves Commission, July 28, 1921, and WGC to Sir Godfrey Thomas, Private Secretary to H.R.H. Prince of Wales, Sept. 27, 1921, Windsor Archives, Box 244.

34. William Lehman Burdett-Coutts, "War Graves: A Statement of Reasons in Support of the Proposal of the Imperial War Graves Commission" (London, 1920), p. 7, written in opposition to the position of Sir James Remnant in the House of Commons, Hansard's, 22, March 22, 1920, col. 79; Windsor Archives, Meeting of March 27, 1915, Box 244.

35. W. Churchill to Lord Peel, PRO, WO 32/5853, March 3, 1919.

36. I am grateful to Kurt Piehler for this information.

37. This point is developed by Dr. Jay Winter in his *Persistence of Tradition: The Cultural History of Bereavement in the Period of the Great War,* forthcoming.

38. Between July and October 1917 Lutyens, in his letters to Lady Sackville, is clearly obsessed with fighting for a classical, pagan "stone" in opposition to all comers. On August 17, for example, he reports lobbying the archbishop of Canterbury and other bishops "for my big stone idea" at the Athenaeum, and he is "shocked and grieved" on September 14 that the archbishop had not at least remained neutral. (Lutyens Correspondence Box, Royal Institute of British Architects Archives, London).

39. MS. Notebooks of Miss C.M. Marx, Imperial War Museum 86/75/1.

40. *Introduction to the Registers of the Naval Memorials Erected at Chatham, Plymouth, and Portsmouth* (London: Imperial War Graves Commission, 1924), pp. 5–7.

41. See Anne Gray, "Menin Gate," *Journal of the Australian War Memorial,* April 12, 1988. Purple poppies in shimmering light suggest a harvest of men.

42. *London Times,* Nov. 6, 1920, p. 10.

43. I have not yet found the archives on this process, but photographs of the four bodies are in the photographic collection of the Imperial War Museum.

44. "Unveiling the War Memorial, 28 April 1923 [in Oldham]," Imperial War Museum 26 (=427.2) 36; entombing a roll of honor was in fact a common practice. "Blaydon War Memorial Unveiling Ceremony," Imperial War Museum 26 (=428) 36; "Saddleworth War Memorial Unveiling Ceremony," October 6, 1927, Imperial War Museum 26 (=427.4) 36.

Chapter IX

THE WAR DEAD AND THE GOLD STAR:
AMERICAN COMMEMORATION OF
THE FIRST WORLD WAR

G. KURT PIEHLER

THE FIRST WORLD WAR shattered the established order in Europe and offered an unprecedented challenge to the legitimacy of the nation-state. Military theorists and political leaders expected war in 1914 to produce a quick and decisive victory. Instead, this conflict turned into a long and protracted war that required the total mobilization of the entire society by combatant nations. Modern technology heightened the alienation and dehumanization inherent in combat. Life for soldiers who served in the trenches was dirty, brutal, and often short, particularly if one served in an active sector. On both sides, soldiers expressed increasing cynicism and disillusionment over being used as cannon fodder by incompetent leaders safely ensconced behind the lines.[1]

To counter the alienation and cynicism caused by the First World War national leaders not only turned to propaganda but also nationalized the memorialization of war. Until the First World War, the common soldier who died in battle was usually placed in a hastily dug grave near the battlefield and forgotten by his monarchist nation. Paradoxically, the average soldier who died in the First World War received far better "care" than his counterpart of earlier generations. In 1914 the armies of Great Britain, France, and Germany went to great lengths to mark, register, and preserve war graves. When the war ended, the British government created an Imperial War Graves Commission to build permanent cemeteries and memorials to those who died on behalf of the Empire in the 1914 conflict.[2]

Efforts to grant the average soldier a "decent" burial during and after the First World War reflected the need to sustain morale among combatants and on the home front. In another, more macabre sense, the war dead were still being pressed into service by their governments. In the postwar era, as revolution swept across Europe, the fallen were portrayed as bulwarks of stability who transcended class divisions. Since they were silent, the war dead could offer their complete allegiance to the nation. For instance, the British government decided that those who had fallen in France would remain in official national cemeteries, irrespective of the wishes of family members. In the case of Germany, officially sponsored cemeteries often obliterated individual grave markers and commemorated the fallen through collective memorials.[3]

This essay will examine how political and military leaders in the United States joined their European counterparts in seeking to nationalize the war dead and in creating an official memory of this conflict. As in Europe, American leaders looked to make the war dead a central symbol of a national identity divorced from the often divisive ties of class, ethnicity, religion, and region. Moreover, they wanted the commemoration of the fallen to exemplify the willingness of males to serve and die for their country. At the same time, American national leaders envisioned creating a series of cemeteries and memorials in Europe that would reflect the power and prestige of the United States, which had been greatly enhanced during the conflict. Since it delayed entering the war until 1917, the United States was spared the enormous casualty rolls that had afflicted the other combatants. American economic and military power had proven decisive in defeating Germany. In the postwar era, a bankrupt Europe owed billions to the American government and private bankers.

Efforts to press the war dead into further national service required the consent or at least the compliance of their parents and widows. As this essay will show, many parents and widows in the United States refused to make an additional sacrifice to the nation and demanded the return of their loved ones for burial in their local communities. In effect, many Americans rejected a vision of nationalism that saw individuals as servants of the state. Moreover, the opposition to maintaining American cemeteries in Europe mirrored the ambivalence of the United States toward Europe. Although President Woodrow Wilson authored the League of Nations, the United States never joined this international organization. During the interwar years, it refused to enter into any formal political or military alliance with Europe.

Historians have long examined how the First World War exacerbated the divisions of class, ethnicity, religion, and region in the United States, but only recently have they begun to explore fully the war's impact on women. The First World War expanded, at least temporarily, the roles and opportunities available to women. It also divided the women of America. Some women's organizations, most notably the Women's Section of the Navy League, supported American involvement in the conflict. The longtime suffragette leader Alice Howard Shaw organized a women's division within the federal government's Committee of National Defense under which women in local chapters provided a range of volunteer services in support of the war effort. Other women had campaigned for American neutrality and sought to counter preparedness sentiment. The Woman's Peace Party, founded in 1915, attracted a large number of suffragettes who insisted that Americans must not enter the war. Even after the United States declared war in 1917, some women, such as Emma Goldman, continued to voice their opposition to the conflict.[4]

The First World War, combined with the momentum of the women's suffrage movement, impelled American society, and women themselves, to define an identity for women as citizens. This essay will focus on the federal government's efforts to foster an official memory of war that stressed the role of the good citizen as mother. Through the symbol of the Gold Star Mother and the ritual of the Gold Star Mother's Pilgrimage, the federal government created a civic role for women that presented them as heroic mothers who bravely gave up their sons to the nation. The emphasis placed on motherhood can only partly be explained simply as an effort to use ritual and symbol to "turn back the clock" by reestablishing separate spheres for men and women. In short, a number of war mothers in the 1920s and 1930s defined themselves as citizens and expected and were allowed to play a far more active civic role than their counterparts of the nineteenth century.[5]

I

Since the founding of the republic, women were expected and were often eager to play a major role in mourning the fallen and preserving the memory of past wars for future generations. During the antebellum period, numerous women's organizations provided the funds to complete war memorials and preserve historic sites. When Congress refused to purchase Mount Vernon in the 1850s, the Mount Vernon Ladies Association came forward to purchase and maintain it. After the Civil War, both Union and Confederate veteran organizations acquired women's auxiliaries. Women were given the task of decorating the graves of the fallen from the Civil War on each region's Decoration (Memorial) Day. In the South, women played a central role in preserving an alternative memory of the Civil War that emphasized regional autonomy. Through ladies' memorial associations, they ensured that the Confederate dead received a proper burial and served as honored "symbols" of the Lost Cause, by providing them with separate cemeteries and memorials. Many of the Confederate soldiers who had fallen in northern battles were disinterred and returned to the South.[6]

The role granted and carved out by women in commemorating past wars rested on the premise that combat remained a masculine endeavor. In their separate sphere, most women during the conflict had encouraged men to fight while they kept the home fires burning. When the war ended, women ensured that their sons, husbands, and ancestors would be mourned and remembered. Of course, even in the nineteenth century, the separate spheres of men and women were never that neat and precise. For instance, men also remembered their fallen comrades and sons. Often when men marched off to battle, women out of sheer necessity were required to take on tasks traditionally reserved to men. Despite an ideology that celebrated white feminine leisure and helplessness, white women in the South during the Civil War frequently took over the management of plantations or entered factories.[7]

The First World War further eroded the fiction that war remained largely the domain of men. Since total war required the full mobilization of all resources, the labor of women took on added importance. Women took the place of men in scores of factories and offices. The military not only enlisted women as nurses, but it also employed them in other support functions. The domestic sphere itself took on an added political and military significance in this war. Federal agencies exhorted housewives to conserve food, clothing, and fuel as well as to serve as volunteers in a host of service organizations.[8]

When the United States entered the First World War in 1917, the federal government expected mothers to mourn their fallen sons, but it wanted to ensure that grief did not disrupt the war effort. In order to sustain morale on the home front, the Women's Section of the Committee of National Defense urged women not to wear black when mourning the loss of a son killed in the nation's service. Instead, the Women's Section convinced many families to display a distinctive Gold Star emblem to express their sacrifice of a son to the nation as they waited for the return of their loved one's body.[9]

II

The decision by national leaders in 1919 to maintain permanent overseas cemeteries represented a reversal of earlier policy made by the federal government. When the First World War began, the War Department had decided to repatriate the war dead and follow precedents established in earlier overseas conflicts. After the Spanish-American War and the Philippines Insurrection, the federal government had repatriated the bodies of the several thousand who had died in these conflicts. Most families assumed that if a relative died in France his body eventually would be returned to them.

Some volunteers stepped forward to aid the army in discharging its responsibilities to the war dead. A newly created funeral industry organization, the self-styled Purple Cross, offered to send a legion of embalmers to France to ensure that the bodies of those who died in battle received professional attention. According to the embalmers' organization, "each

American Hero" who died in battle could be returned to the states "in a sanitary and recognizable condition a number of years after death" if he benefited from the latest advances in "mortuary sciences."[10]

A skeptical War Department rejected the services of the Purple Cross; instead, it initially planned to entrust the burial of the dead to the newly created Graves Registration Service of the United States Army. But by 1917 the slow pace of mobilization and the lack of adequate shipping had forced the American Expeditionary Force commander in France, General John J. Pershing, to limit the role of the Graves Registration Service. Pershing ruled that individual units must assume prime responsibility for the disposition of the battle dead, as in earlier conflicts. The Graves Registration Service would be responsible for registering all graves and concentrating hasty or scattered burials into centralized cemeteries in France. Scarce cargo space could not be used for burial supplies or equipment; moreover, repatriation of the dead would have to wait until hostilities ended.[11]

When the war ended, many within the army, Congress, and other positions of leadership argued that the war dead should remain buried overseas as a symbol of the United States' commitment to Europe. Former President William H. Taft, American Federation of Labor President Samuel Gompers, American Expeditionary Force Chief Chaplain Charles H. Brent, and other supporters of overseas burial formed the American Field of Honor organization in January 1920 to work for the establishment of overseas cemeteries. This distinguished group explained to the public that the "sacred dust" of American soldiers had made the soil of cemeteries in France forever American and a place where the Stars and Stripes would always fly proudly.[12]

The War Department, under pressure from the army's Quartermaster Corps, objected to the repatriation of the war dead for more practical reasons, particularly emphasizing the logistical problems raised in removing thousands of decomposing bodies from France. Despite these misgivings, Secretary of War Newton D. Baker insisted in 1919 that his department would honor its commitment to bring fallen soldiers home. Baker allowed family members to make the final decision on whether they wanted their loved ones to remain in France, to be brought home for interment in a national cemetery, or to be returned to them for burial in a family plot.

Supporters of overseas cemeteries waged a vigorous campaign in 1919 and 1920 to convince widows and parents of the fallen not to bring them home. They pointed out many of the obvious problems in disinterring so many bodies that had been in the ground from one to three years. In addition, war-devastated France had raised serious objections to using scarce railroad stock for the evacuation of the war dead. Although never fully comfortable with publicly bringing up the subject, opponents of repatriation did from time to time note the tremendous financial cost of the undertaking. Many privately hoped that the French government would forbid the removal of the war dead from France, thus taking the decision out of the hands of the U.S. government.[13]

Instead of dwelling upon the financial and logistical problems of repatriation, however, American supporters of military cemeteries in France emphasized the continued service the war dead could perform for their country and Western civilization. Each individual soldier's grave would serve as an enduring monument to the cause of freedom for which he had bled and died. By not scattering the war dead across the United States but leaving them massed together in France, their survivors could ensure that their valiant role in history would not be forgotten or obscured. Moreover, the presence of fallen American soldiers in France would serve to heighten the bonds of friendship between the two countries. Already, it was claimed, the French people treated American graves with reverence and considered them "sacred."[14]

Widows and relatives, especially "Gold Star" mothers, were asked to make one more sacrifice to the nation—the sacrifice of leaving their loved ones' bodies in France. Opponents of repatriation urged parents to follow the example of former president Theodore Roosevelt. After Roosevelt learned about the death of his son Quentin at the western front, he insisted that he be buried on the spot where he fell, declaring that the proper resting place for a fallen warrior was on the battlefield.[15]

Most families, however, refused to join Roosevelt in making an additional offering to the nation; almost 70 percent opted for repatriation. Many of these families feared that the federal government would use French objections to the removal of the American war dead as a pretext for maintaining American cemeteries. In 1919 some of those urging repatriation formed the "Bring Back the Dead League" to ensure "an American tomb in America for every American hero who died on foreign soil."[16]

Men dominated the leadership of the Bring Back the Dead League. Under War Department regulations widows and fathers ranked ahead of mothers in determining whether an American soldier remained buried in France or would be returned to the United States. Nevertheless, the league made the wishes of the mothers central to the debate over whether the war dead should be returned. In one letter to Secretary of State Robert Lansing, the president of the league insisted that countless mothers would be heartbroken unless they were reunited with their sons.[17]

Many mothers demanded that their sons be returned to them. Often inspired by the league's campaign, letters poured into Washington, reminding the Wilson administration and Congress of their previous commitments to the relatives of the fallen. One mother from Pittsburgh asked Lansing to "understand and appreciate [a] mother's feelings" and implored him to do everything in his power "to lessen her grief by having her boys [sic] remains brought home and entombed where she can honor his memory." One mother from Brooklyn bluntly declared to Lansing, "You took my son from me and sent him to war . . . my son sacrificed his life to America's call, and now you *must* as a duty of yours bring my son back to me."[18]

The fight over what to do with the war dead became bitter. Supporters of repatriation insisted that France crassly wanted to benefit by the maintenance of overseas cemeteries. One member of Congress suggested that France hoped to gouge the thousands of sorrowing Americans who would have to journey across the ocean in order to see their loved ones' graves. Another, an apparent isolationist, feared that France planned to keep American soldiers buried in France as "hostages" in order to compel the United States to defend their graves if German aggression should reappear.[19]

In turn, those who wanted American cemeteries in Europe attempted to portray unscrupulous funeral directors as the driving force behind the movement for repatriation. In fact, some funeral-industry trade publications and organizations had talked bluntly about the financial gain to be made from bringing home for burial fifty thousand bodies. Although this connection remains nebulous, the funeral industry had played a major role in organizing the campaign for repatriation. Nevertheless, the movement would not have succeeded without the strong desire of most parents and widows to see their sons and husbands brought back to the United States.[20]

In the end, the War Department heeded the wishes of the majority of parents and widows. After France dropped its objections to removal in March 1920, more than 70 percent of those Americans killed in the First World War were returned to the United States. At the same time, for the remainder of the American war dead, the U.S. government established several permanent cemeteries in France as well as in Belgium and England. A sizable minority of mothers allowed and wanted their sons to be used as symbols of the nation or did not want to experience the grief of reburying their sons at home.

III

The overseas cemeteries were not the only effort by the federal government to nationalize the dead. In 1921 the United States, following the example of Great Britain, France, and several other European nations, honored an Unknown Soldier killed during the conflict. With great ceremony, the United States selected an unidentified American soldier who had fallen in France and accorded him a hero's funeral and burial in a special tomb in Arlington National Cemetery. On behalf of all the fallen, the Unknown Soldier received the gratitude of the nation in the form of medals, wreaths, poems, and eulogies.[21]

The anonymity of the Unknown Soldier allowed national leaders to commemorate the "average" soldier as a uniquely "American" figure that remained above the ties of race, religion, class, and region. President Warren G. Harding, General John J. Pershing, and other prominent political and military figures hailed the Unknown for his bravery, loyalty, selfless service, and devotion to the nation. The more humble joined Harding and others in mourning the Unknown Soldier and offering their tributes. Dozens sent unsolicited poems to the War Department hailing the noble qualities of this anonymous hero. Thousands paid their respect to the Unknown Soldier as he lay in state in the Capitol rotunda. Hundreds of thousands lined the funeral route from the Capitol to Arlington National Cemetery. To this day, millions of Americans, often as part of family vacations to Washington, D.C., continue to visit the Tomb of the Unknown Soldier.

Why did Americans venerate the Unknown Soldier? In one sense, his very lack of an individual identity permitted almost everyone to claim the Unknown Soldier as his or her own. In 1921 parents, especially those whose sons were missing in action, could identify with him. Native-born Americans, but also the new immigrants from eastern and southern Europe, could embrace him. Few white Americans envisioned the Unknown Soldier as being black, but a delegation of African-American leaders disagreed and went to the Capitol to lay flowers by his casket. During the interwar years, veterans claimed him as a former comrade and the American Legion took a proprietary interest in his tomb, but one peace activist in these years created a play that made the Unknown Soldier an activist for peace.[22]

IV

Many war mothers joined veterans and others in identifying with the Unknown Soldier. In the aftermath of the First World War, the American War Mothers, founded in 1919, asserted a special claim over the tomb and the memory of this conflict. The American War Mothers insisted that a good mother willingly, albeit reluctantly, sacrificed her son to the interests of the state. This organization, open to all mothers who had a son or daughter who had served in the First World War, insisted that America had not been mistaken in entering the conflict and challenged those women who equated motherhood with pacifism, arguing that the great lesson of the First World War remained the ongoing need for military preparedness. During the 1920s and 1930s, the American War Mothers supported increased expenditures on defense and favored universal military service.[23]

The War Mothers claimed to represent and promote an American identity, but tensions existed over how to define it. War remained central to the American past, and the War Mothers joined other "patriotic" organizations in a campaign to make the "Star-Spangled Banner" the official national anthem. In their view, military service remained the highest calling of male citizens. A predominantly white Anglo-Saxon Protestant organization, the War Mothers supported legislation in the 1920s that restricted immigration to the United States. It remained fervently anti-Communist and feared the threat of subversion from foreign radicals.[24]

Although wary of the new immigrants, the organization could not completely exclude or ignore them, especially if their sons had served in the war. In the 1920s leaders of the War Mothers believed that the ties of motherhood and the mutual sacrifice of their sons to the war effort would unite native-born Americans and the new immigrants from southern and eastern Europe. On occasion, the organization's official magazine, the *American War Mother,* published articles that argued for a pluralistic vision of nationhood that affirmed a multiplicity of religions and ethnic origins. Moreover, the society did have within its ranks a small number of Jewish and African-American women.[25]

The War Mothers gained substantial recognition from the federal government over the course of the interwar years. In 1925 the organization received a congressional charter. The War Department that same year allowed the War Mothers to hold an annual memorial service at the Tomb of the Unknown Soldier. In 1926 the War Mothers received permission to fly a "national service flag" they had themselves made over the Capitol on Armistice Day.[26]

Congress and the White House supported the aims of the War Mothers during the 1920s and early 1930s because the organization affirmed a national identity that buttressed the status quo. The War Mothers declared that women as citizens recognized the need to enter the First World War and continued to support a strong defense establishment. At the same time, the War Mothers affirmed a traditional vision of women in American society as mothers and nurturers.[27]

Although the War Mothers supported the need for a strong military defense and believed America had wisely entered the First World War, their attitudes were somewhat ambiguous. For example, they continued to see war as a male domain and did not want to break down the prohibitions placed on women in the military. In addition, the desire for peace, albeit an armed one, pervades much of their literature. Like many of their male counterparts, they believed that military preparedness represented a way to avoid future European wars, and they expressed little desire to fight another one.

Mothers who had lost their sons in the First World War could join a separate organization, the American Gold Star Mothers Association. This smaller organization, founded in 1928, remained similar to the American War Mothers in outlook and purpose. Like the American War Mothers, it supported preparedness and wanted the First World War remembered as a noble crusade. In contrast to the American War Mothers, it offered a less pluralistic definition of nationhood and granted membership only to qualified members of the "Caucasian" race.[28]

In the 1920s the American Gold Star Mothers, the American War Mothers, and the American Legion vigorously lobbied Congress to fund a pilgrimage to Europe for mothers who had allowed their sons to be interred in overseas cemeteries. They insisted that the federal government owed every mother who had sacrificed her son to the nation at least one visit to his grave. Gold Star Mothers and their supporters in Congress dwelt on the inseparable bond existing between mother and child. As one Gold Star Mother declared, they had given their sons freely to the nation, and their hearts were "just breaking for the sight of the grave of their boy."[29]

A Gold Star pilgrimage to France proved impossible to resist politically, and throughout the 1920s scores of congressmen sponsored legislation to authorize it. Although few publicly questioned the wisdom of the idea, some in Congress grumbled about the cost of such a pilgrimage. When the subject of cost emerged, however, authors of pilgrimage bills noted that the mothers who had not brought their sons back to the United States had saved the federal government more than $23 million. Given these figures, they insisted that the cost entailed in such a pilgrimage was irrelevant. In 1929 Congress passed legislation authorizing the secretary of war to allow mothers and widows to travel to Europe as guests of the nation. The notoriously frugal Calvin Coolidge signed this legislation shortly before he left office in March 1929. The administrations of Herbert Hoover and later Franklin D. Roosevelt authorized these pilgrimages from 1931 to 1933, even as the depression raged and the federal government reduced expenditures in the face of deficits.[30]

Why, in an era when the federal government refused to fund maternity clinics, did it spend such a lavish sum on a pilgrimage? Gold Star Mothers maintained that their service to the nation as mothers of the war dead entitled them to a special claim on the nation. Although war mothers believed that a good mother freely sacrificed her son to the nation, they argued that this service still remained extraordinary and should be recognized as such. This argument was not unique to the Gold Star Mothers but was also frequently used by veterans to gain a wide range of social welfare benefits.

The Gold Star pilgrimage declared that a woman's greatest role as citizen remained that of mother and nurturer. Widows received invitations almost as an afterthought; the sponsor of one unsuccessful pilgrimage bill in 1924 excluded them because he believed that their relationships with their husbands paled in comparison with the one mothers had with their sons.

Although there had been some talk of including fathers, in the end Congress decided that only women could take part in the pilgrimage. No doubt congressional leaders believed that inclusion of men would have blurred the sharp distinction they wanted to make between the bonds uniting mother and son and other bonds. In the rituals of remembrance, a son could be a nineteen-year-old lad or a thirty-five-year-old father with several sons of his own. Men fought and were honored for their participation in the First World War; those who survived the conflict received recognition through victory parades, participation in veterans' organizations, and the erection of memorials. The Gold Star pilgrimage continued a long tradition that held that women should mourn the war dead and place flowers at their graves. It tried to forge a link between the individual memories of mothers and a broader national purpose.[31]

The Gold Star pilgrimage affirmed for its participants and the larger society that those who had died for their country in Europe had fought for a noble cause. The lavish care extended to the mothers and widows during the journey highlighted how exceptional their contribution had been in giving up their sons and husbands to the nation. From the moment a mother or widow stepped aboard a train to leave her hometown, the federal government paid all reasonable expenses. Before their departure for Europe, Gold Star pilgrims assembled in New York, where they attended a reception in City Hall and were greeted by local civic officials. As specified by Congress, women taking part in the pilgrimage traveled cabin class, stayed at first-class hotels, and had army officers, physicians, and nurses accompany them abroad. Not only were the pilgrims taken to the graves of their sons and husbands, but each party spent a week either in Paris or London and was honored by the French and British governments with receptions.[32]

The War Department and press accounts of the pilgrimage stressed how each woman who participated received equal treatment. War had united women from all walks of life and regions of the country by creating a common bond among them. Socialites and farm women, Catholics, Protestants, and Jews, native-born and foreign-born had all sacrificed their sons to the nation and now shared the same feelings of loss.[33] In a speech released to the press by the War Department, one army officer described how the First World War had given sons and mothers a common national identity: "Like the draft, they are a cross-section of American life. Some are well-to-do, some are very poor, some have traveled extensively, some have never been outside the state in which they were born; some are educated, some are illiterate—but all receive the same treatment."[34]

But in reality not all women received the same treatment, for the Gold Star pilgrimage offered a vision of nationhood that placed African-Americans in a subordinate position. The War Department segregated black pilgrims from their white counterparts, even placing them on separate ships. Whereas the white pilgrims traveled aboard luxury liners, black women went over in commercial steamers. Neither the protest of African-American organizations nor the refusal of some black Gold Star Mothers to take part in the pilgrimage convinced the War Department to alter its policy.[35]

The War Department responded to the barrage of criticism from African-American leaders and the unfavorable press coverage of the policy of segregation by lavishing attention on the black mothers. Except for the choice of hotel in Paris, the African-American press applauded the care given to the black mothers in France. The *New York Age* observed that for most of these mothers the pilgrimage had given them "their first real taste of luxury, and perhaps their last." Although the Baltimore *Afro-American* lambasted the Hoover administration for allowing the policy of segregation, it urged mothers to join the pilgrimage. It noted that the first wave of black mothers who returned from France indicated "a peace and satisfaction that made the pilgrimage for them the crowning event of their lives."[36]

Noble Sissle, an African-American expatriate musician who performed for the black mothers in Paris, observed that the policy of segregation accurately reflected what their sons had experienced. He recounted: "We came over on segregated ships during the war. Many came over only because they had to. The others had the power to force them. These people still have the power and they are going to use it." Nonetheless, Sissle applauded the mothers for making the pilgrimage and declared that if he had been killed he "would have liked to [have] known that my mother had a chance to see my grave, and to be as well-treated as these women have been."[37]

Sissle's ambivalent response offers important insights into why efforts by national leaders to create and foster national rituals and symbols succeed or fail. Plans to create overseas cemeteries met resistance because they failed to incorporate individual and local acts of mourning into the national ritual. In short, many mothers and fathers in 1919 refused to allow the federal government to nationalize their sons or daughters because they wanted them close to home. Even those patriotic mothers who gave up their sons to the nation wanted a chance to visit their graves and place flowers on them. Likewise, the desire of many African-American mothers to visit the graves of their sons overrode their objections to segregation.

National leaders wanted the war and the Gold Star pilgrimage to consecrate military service as a symbol uniting all citizens behind a common purpose and American identity. The segregation practiced by the War Department exposed the hypocrisy in the application of this ideal, but many African-American leaders did not reject the predicated vision of equality. They declared that if black soldiers and their mothers could sacrifice for their country, they should be accorded the same equality of rights. After the Second World War, the equation between military service and citizenship made it impossible to continue the policy of segregation in the armed forces. Even before 1945, Jim Crow frayed under the ideological assault made by African-American leaders and the manpower needs of the war.

The link made between motherhood and citizenship struck a responsive chord among many Americans. Culturally, the 1910s and 1920s witnessed the growing acceptance and celebration by women and men of Mother's Day. This holiday, created in 1908, originated in the efforts of Anna Jarvis to honor the memory of her own mother. Originally, observances of this holiday centered in the Protestant churches, but Mother's Day quickly received the blessing of scores of mayors and governors who issued proclamations urging public observance of the day. In 1914 Woodrow Wilson issued a presidential proclamation calling upon all Americans to honor the nation's mothers on the second Sunday in May. During the interwar period, the business community, particularly florists, found a receptive audience for commercialized observances of this day, with many daughters and sons honoring their mothers with flowers, cards, and other gifts.[38]

Although most women accepted the association between motherhood and citizenship, many refused to accept the willing sacrifice of their sons to the nation. Women's involvement in the peace movement increased during the 1920s and 1930s. Not only did they play a key role in a host of male-dominated peace organizations, but they also formed a series of separate women's groups designed to promote this cause. They argued that women by virtue of their gender had a special role to play in ensuring an end to mass bloodshed. The women's peace movement declared that the hatred, destruction, and senselessness of armed conflict were antithetical to all the qualities represented by womanhood: love, nurturance, and cooperation.[39]

V

The peace movement failed to prevent the outbreak of the Second World War. As a result, a new generation of sons marched off to war, and new life was breathed into the American War Mothers. During the 1950s and early 1960s, the American War Mothers attracted more members than it had during the interwar years. The organization continued to campaign for a strong national defense and also stressed the need for adequate civil-defense measures to meet the threat of atomic warfare. The revitalization of the Gold Star Mothers mirrored the increasing emphasis placed on domesticity in the postwar period. "Rosie the Riveter," symbol of the participation of women in heavy industry in the Second World War, abruptly gave way to the image of women as suburban housewives and mothers.[40]

The continued vitality of the Gold Star Mothers was only one example of how rituals designed to commemorate the First World War shaped the commemoration of the Second World War. Armistice Day, originally created during the interwar years to keep alive the memory of the First World War, was recast in 1954 as Veterans Day. The American Legion, a World War I veterans' organization, opened its ranks to servicemen and servicewomen from the Second World War. Few communities built new memorials to the Second World War; instead most merely added plaques to their existing monuments from the First World War.[41]

In 1945 army and national leaders again wanted to create and maintain overseas cemeteries for the dead from the Second World War. Once again, a debate developed over whether the overseas dead should be returned to the United States. To a large degree, the precedents established by the First World War again limited efforts to nationalize fully all the war dead. After some misgivings, the military allowed the next of kin to make the final decision on whether a relative killed during the war would be placed in an overseas cemetery or returned to the United States. Even after what many viewed as the "good war," the majority of families and widows elected to bring the war dead home for final burial.[42]

But there would be no Gold Star pilgrimage after 1945. In part, this reflected the nature of the Second World War and the events of the postwar period. In contrast to the First World War, the Second World War engendered widespread support from across the ideological spectrum. The Japanese attack on Pearl Harbor and later the discovery of the German death camps removed any doubt in the eyes of most Americans about the need to go to war. Moreover, the federal government tried to create fewer illusions about the Second World War, and it offered no promise that this would be a war to "end all wars."[43]

Finally, the Second World War and the subsequent Cold War committed the United States to Europe and ended the fiction that Americans were pilgrims to this continent. Both conflicts narrowed the distinction that existed between combatant and noncombatant. Although the United States had won a great victory in 1945, the Cold War ensured that the lines between peace and war would be blurred. The power of nuclear weapons meant that both sons and mothers would suffer the same fate in the event of an all-out war with the Soviet Union; consequently, civilians and soldiers alike considered themselves participants battling for the future of the nation and the world.

NOTES

1. Paul Fussell, *The Great War and Modern Memory* (New York: Oxford University Press, 1975); Eric J. Leed, *No Man's Land: Combat and Identity in World War I* (Cambridge: Cambridge University Press, 1979); J. M. Winter, *The Great War and the British People* (Cambridge: Harvard University Press, 1986).

2. George L. Mosse, *Fallen Soldiers: Reshaping the Memory of the World Wars* (New York: Oxford University Press, 1990).

3. Ibid., passim; Philip Longworth, *The Unending Vigil: A History of the Commonwealth War Graves Commission, 1917–1967* (London: Constable and Co., 1967).

4. For an overview of the First World War and the interwar period in the United States see: John Whiteclay Chambers II, *The Tyranny of Change: America in the Progressive Era, 1890–1920*, 2d ed. (New York: St. Martin's Press, 1992); David M. Kennedy, *Over Here: The First World War and American Society* (New York: Oxford University Press, 1980); and Ellis Hawley, *The Great War and the Search for Modern Order: A History of the American People and Their Institutions, 1917–1933* (New York: St. Martin's Press, 1979). For the role of women in the First World War see: Blanche Wiesen Cook, "The Woman's Peace Party: Collaboration and Non-Cooperation," *Peace and Change: A Journal of Peace Research* 1 (March 1972): 36–42; Candace Falk, *Love, Anarchy, and Emma Goldman* (New York: Holt, Rinehart and Winston, 1984); and Barbara J. Steinson, *American Women's Activism in World War I* (New York: Garland Publishing Co., 1982).

5. Although two recent studies make an important contribution to understanding the role of the federal government in fostering an official memory of the past, neither offers a sustained analysis of the question of gender and the commemoration of the First World War: John Bodnar, *Remaking America: Public Memory, Commemoration, and Patriotism in the Twentieth Century* (Princeton: Princeton University Press, 1992); Michael Kammen, *Mystic Chords of Memory: The Transformation of Tradition in American Culture* (New York: Alfred A. Knopf, 1991). For an overview of the impact of the First World War on gender relations in the United States and Europe see: Margaret Randolph Higonnet et al., eds., *Behind the Lines: Gender and the Two World Wars* (New Haven: Yale University Press, 1987). For the relationship between women and war see: Cynthia H. Enloe, *Does Khaki Become You? The Militarization of Women's Lives* (Boston: South End Press, 1983); Jean Bethke Elshtain, *Women and War* (New York: Basic Books, 1987).

6. Mary P. Ryan, *Women in Public: Between Banner and Ballots, 1825–1880* (Baltimore: Johns Hopkins Press, 1990); Wallace Evan Davies, *Patriotism on Parade: The Story of Veterans' and Hereditary Organizations in America, 1783–1900* (Cambridge: Harvard University Press, 1955). Gaines M. Foster, *Ghosts of the Confederacy: Defeat, the Lost Cause, and the Emergence of the New South, 1865–1913* (New York: Oxford University Press, 1987), 36–46.

7. Drew Gilpin Faust, "Altars of Sacrifice: Confederate Women and the Narratives of War," *Journal of American History* 76 (March 1990): 1200–1228.

8. Steinson, *American Women's Activism*, passim.

9. "Minutes of the Meeting of the Council of National Defense," February 14, 1918, 456, Records of the Council of National Defense, 1916–1921, RG 62, Microfilm Publication M-1069, National Archives, Washington, D.C.; Arthur S. Link et al., eds., *The Papers of Woodrow Wilson*, 65 vols. (Princeton: Princeton University Press, 1966–), 48:24–27, 111, 117.

10. U.S. Congress, House, Committee on Military Affairs, *American Purple Cross Association: Hearings*, 65th Cong., 1st sess., September 5, 1917, 14, 27; "American Purple Cross Society," *The Casket* 42 (August 1, 1917): 13–15; "Bids Rejected by War Department," *The Casket* 42 (October 1, 1917): 17–18.

11. Erna Risch, *Quartermaster Support of the Army: A History of the Corps, 1775–1939* (Washington, D.C.: GPO, 1962), 690–91.

12. "Brent Wants Dead to Stay in France," *New York Times,* January 16, 1920, 8; "Objection to Bringing Home Soldier Dead," *New York Times,* January 18, 1920, 8:9.

13. Major H. R. Lemly to the Quartermaster General, August 11, 1919, Memorandum, File No. 293.7 Cemeterial, Copy, Minutes, November 21, 1919, Exhibit B, Commission of Fine Arts; Charles Moore to Henry White, Commissioner Plenipotentiary, Paris, June 5, 1919, White to Moore, July 22, 1919, File: American Cemeteries in Europe—World War I Graves, Box 5, Project Files, Records of the Commission of Fine Arts (RG 66); Adjutant General P. L. Harris to the Chief of Staff, June 4, 1919, Untitled Press Release, July 19, 1919, File 293.8, Box 566, Central Decimal File, 1917–1925, Records of the Adjutant General's Office (RG 407), National Archives, Washington, D.C.

14. V. J. Oldshue, "France Remembers," *The American Legion Weekly,* July 9, 1920, 5; Elizabeth Hamm, "American Graves in France," *The New Republic,* June 2, 1920, 14–15; "French Pleas to Let Our Dead Rest," *The Literary Digest,* April 17, 1920, 45; Horace W. Scandlin, "How Mother France Honors the Gold Star American," *World Outlook,* September–October 1920, 32.

15. "A Solution Perhaps Acceptable," *New York Times,* January 1, 1919, 16.

16. "Plan to Bring Back Hero Dead Abroad," *Washington Times,* November 26, 1919, article in File: Headstones, W.W. I Graves, Box 73, Project Files (RG 66).

17. D. B. Maxwell, Chairman and others to Robert E. Lansing, Secretary of State, November 3, 1919, File 351.116, Box 4201, Central Decimal File, 1920–1929, Records of the Department of State (RG 59), National Archives, Washington, D.C.

18. "Plan to Bring Back Hero Dead Abroad"; Elizabeth Debrey? to Secretary of State Robert Lansing, January 11, 1920, File 351.116, Box 4201; Margaret Vascimini to Secretary of State Robert Lansing, January 11, 1920, File 351.116, Box 4202, Central Decimal File, 1910–1929 (RG 59).

19. U.S. Congress, House, Representative Edward J. King of Illinois, Extension of Remarks, 66th Cong., 2d sess., *Congressional Record* (February 11, 1920), vol. 59, pt. 9, 8790; Representative Clement C. Dikinson of Missouri, *Congressional Record* (January 27, 1920), vol. 59, pt. 2, 2132–33.

20. U.S. Congress, House, Representative John W. Rainey of Illinois, 66th Cong., 2d sess., *Congressional Record* (February 6, 1920), vol. 59, pt. 3, 2562–64; "Paris Director in League with Purple Cross (?)," *The Embalmers' Monthly* 33 (January 1920): 10–11; "Rid the Profession of Odium That Has Come to It," *The Embalmers' Monthly* 33 (February 1920): 1.

21. Allan Greenberg, "Lutyens's Cenotaph," *Journal of the Society of Architectural Historians* 48 (1989): 5–23.

22. For a full discussion of the Tomb of the Unknown Soldier see: Guenter Kurt Piehler, "Remembering War the American Way, 1783 to the Present" (Ph.D. diss., Rutgers University, 1990), 154–65.

23. American War Mothers, *American War Mothers: Fifty Year History, 1917–1967* (Washington, D.C.?: American War Mothers, 1981); "Resolutions: Report of the Resolution Committee," *American War Mother* 2 (November 1925): 6–8.

24. "National Patriotic Conference," *American War Mother* 5 (March 1928): 7–12.

25. "Copy of Minutes of the First Meeting of 'The Executive Board' of the National American War Mothers Convened at Louisville, Kentucky, Begun Wednesday, September 29, 1920"; "Proceedings of the Sixth National Convention of the American War Mothers, September 26–October 1, 1927," p. 23; "National Convention of War Mothers Held at Louisville, Ky., Sept. 19–28, 1929," American War Mothers Headquarters, Washington, D.C.; "Heroes All," *American War Mother* 5 (January 1929): 9.

26. "Mother's Day at the Tomb of the Unknown Soldier in Arlington Cemetery," *American War Mother* 2 (June 1925): 7–9; *American War Mothers: Fifty Year History*, passim.

27. "The Children We Keep," *American War Mother* 6 (September 1929): 11; "Indiana Mothers Interested in Child Welfare," *American War Mother* 6 (February 1930): 7; "New York's Mayor Calls War Mother 'Greatest' Woman in History," *American War Mother* 5 (May 1928): 21.

28. "American Gold Star Mothers, Statement in Regard to Bill S. 459 and H.R. 9," Scrapbook 9, Box 9; American Gold Star Mothers, Inc., "History of the Gold Star Insignia, 1940," File: History of Insignia; "Report of the Fourth Biennial Convention of the American Gold Star Mothers, Inc. May 11–13, 1938," File: Conventions, Reports, etc., Box 6, Papers of the American Gold Star Mothers, Library of Congress, Washington, D.C.

29. U.S. Congress, House, Committee on Military Affairs, *To Authorize Mothers of Deceased World War Veterans Buried in Europe to Visit the Graves: Hearings Before the House Committee on Military Affairs*, 68th Cong., 1st sess., February 19, 1924, 20–21.

30. U.S. Congress, House, Committee on Military Affairs, *To Authorize Mothers and Unmarried Widows of Deceased World War Veterans Buried in Europe to Visit the Graves: Hearing Before the House Committee on Military Affairs*, 70th Cong., 1st sess., January 27, 1928, 25–26.

31. U.S. Congress, House, February 19, 1924, 10.

32. A. D. Hughes, "Pilgrims," *Quartermaster Review* (May–June 1931): 29–39.

33. Morris Fradin, "Gold Star Mothers and Widows End Pilgrimages," *Sunday Star* (Washington, D.C.) [November 5, 1933], 10; "Gold Star Mother," *Mobile Register* (Alabama), August 16, 1933; "War Department Studies Minutest Needs of Gold Star Mothers' Pilgrimage," *New York World*, March 23, 1930, in File: Press Clippings, Mothers and Widows Pilgrimages to the Cemeteries of Europe, Box 348, Correspondence Relating to the Gold Star Pilgrimage, 1922–1933, Central Records, 1917–1954, General Records (RG 92); John J. Noll, "Crosses," *American Legion Monthly* (September 1930): 14–17, 52–54.

34. "Address of Captain Robert E. Shannon, QMC, at luncheon meeting of the Washington (D.C.) Transportation Club held at the Raleigh Hotel, Washington, D.C., Thursday afternoon, September 15, 1932," File: Press Releases, 1930–1933, Box 348, Correspondence Relating to the Gold Star Pilgrimage (RG 92).

35. Secretary of War to Walter White, Secretary, National Association for the Advancement of Colored People [June 5, 1933], copy; Perry C. Thompson to

Secretary of War George H. Dern, May 9, 1933, copy; Secretary of War to Perry C. Thompson, Editor, *The Chicago Review* [May 1933?], copy, File: Colored M & W, Correspondence Relative to Segregation, Box 345; "Negro Gold Star Mothers Refuse Trip to Sons' Graves," *Washington Post,* May 30, 1930; "55 Negro War Mothers Cancel Trip, Write Hoover of 'Insult,'" *New York World,* July 10, 1930, in File: Press Clippings, Mothers and Widows Pilgrimages to the Cemeteries of Europe, Box 348, Correspondence Relating to the Gold Star Pilgrimage, 1922–1933 (RG 92). See also: Donald J. Lisio, *Hoover, Blacks, Lily Whites: A Study of Southern Strategies* (Chapel Hill: University of North Carolina Press, 1985), 234–36.

36. "To Visit or Not to Visit," *Afro-American* (Baltimore), 1930; "Gold Star Mothers Are Recipients of Splendid Treatment at Hands of Government Officials and Ship Crew," *New York Age,* August 23, 1930, in File: Press Clippings, Mothers and Widows Pilgrimages to the Cemeteries of Europe, Box 348, Correspondence Relating to the Gold Star Pilgrimage (RG 92).

37. "Noble Sissle Would Have Wanted His Mother to See His Grave," *Afro-American* (Baltimore), August 23, 1930, in File: Press Clippings, Mothers and Widows Pilgrimages to Cemeteries of Europe, Box 348, Correspondence Relating to the Gold Star Pilgrimage (RG 92).

38. Kathleen W. Jones, "Mother's Day: The Creation, Promotion and Meaning of a New Holiday in the Progressive Era," *Texas Studies in Literature and Language* 22 (Summer 1980): 175–96; Leigh Eric Schmidt, "The Commercialization of the Calendar: American Holidays and the Culture of Consumption, 1870–1930," *Journal of American History* 78 (December 1991): 887–916.

39. Harriet Hyman Alonso, *The Women's Peace Union and the Outlawry of War, 1921–1942* (Knoxville: University of Tennessee Press, 1990); Charles De-Benedetti, *The Peace Reform in American History* (Bloomington: Indiana University Press, 1980), 108–37.

40. "The American War Mothers, General Session," September 21, 1961, American War Mothers Headquarters, Washington, D.C. For the role of women in the Second World War and postwar period see: Sonya Michel, "American Women and the Discourse of the Democratic Family in World War II," and Ruth Milkman, "American Women and Industrial Unionism during World War II," in *Behind the Lines,* 154–81; William H. Chafe, *The American Woman: Her Changing Social, Economic, and Political Roles, 1920–1970* (New York: Oxford University Press, 1972), passim.

41. For a discussion of the commemoration of the Second World War see: Piehler, "Remembering War the American Way," 174–210.

42. Record of the Proceedings: Forty-Ninth Meeting, February 13, 1947, American Battle Monuments Commission (RG 117), Records of the American Battle Monuments Commission, National Archives, Washington, D.C.

43. John Morton Blum, *V Was for Victory: Politics and American Culture During World War II* (New York: Harcourt Brace Jovanovich, 1976); Paul Fussell, *Wartime: Understanding and Behavior in the Second World War* (New York: Oxford University Press, 1989).

Chapter X

ART, COMMERCE, AND THE PRODUCTION
OF MEMORY IN FRANCE AFTER
WORLD WAR I

Daniel J. Sherman

RECENT SCHOLARLY INTEREST in collective memory, spurred by such ambitious publishing projects as Pierre Nora's *Les lieux de mémoire,* has
brought new attention to those proverbially overlooked artifacts of public
art, local war memorials.[1] Owing perhaps to their profusion and their
striking conjunction of variety and sameness, French monuments to the
World War I dead have garnered a considerable share of this attention. Yet
in the absence of a coherent theoretical framework, studies of such monuments too often present anecdotes, taxonomies, or metaphysical speculations as ends in themselves rather than as starting points for sustained
historical analysis. Such a theoretical framework must, it seems to me,
begin with a conception of collective memory not as something inherent to
a group or groups, reflected unproblematically in objects like monuments,
but as a socially constructed discourse. In this view, as culturally specific
beliefs about a historical event merge with individual memories and take
on visible and legible form, collective memory emerges as a construct of the
political, social, and economic structures that condition, if they do not
determine, the production of those forms. Similarly, what we conven-
tionally call "commemoration" I take to be the *practice* of representation
that enacts and gives social substance to the discourse of collective
memory.

The construction of both discourse and practice involves either the production or the reconfiguration, in terms specific to their purpose, of certain
cultural forms: monuments, of course, but also literature, film, and popular visual imagery in such media as postcards, cartoons, and posters. In
most of these productions, formal traditions and received assumptions
enjoy considerable autonomy from larger social structures and processes
such as capitalism, technology, and ideological formulations like the
national-local dichotomy. The role of these larger structures might best be
understood as a kind of mediation: by mapping the terrain in which commemoration operates, molding what Raymond Williams calls the "conditions of a practice," they mediate both the experience and the representa-

tion of memory.[2] In this essay, I seek to illuminate the workings of these mediations both separately and in terms of their interaction. For the construction of monuments takes place at the conjunction of a variety of discourses and practices: local and national, commercial and artistic, high and low, and, ultimately perhaps, history and memory.

I

Although societies since antiquity have erected monuments to their military exploits, historians trace the origins of a new, democratic style of commemoration to the period of the Napoleonic wars, when large citizen armies began to replace mercenary troops. Whereas Roman monuments took the form of arches of triumph, with bas-reliefs celebrating the achievements of rulers or generals, the modern nation-state has felt the need to pay tribute to the ordinary soldiers, whether volunteers or conscripts, who sacrifice their lives in its defense.[3] Although various groups and regimes proposed monuments to citizen soldiers from the late eighteenth century on, Maurice Agulhon and June Hargrove have argued that such monuments emerged in France only after the Franco-Prussian War finally removed the sovereign as a potential focus for commemoration. Besides their democratic spirit, monuments to the *mobiles,* the volunteer armies of 1870, broke with past traditions in two other ways that would prove durable: their location in soldiers' hometowns and their frequent recourse to the reproduction of standard models.[4]

No one would deny, of course, that memorials to the World War I dead have an omnipresence in France that distinguishes them even from monuments with which they have much in common: the number of local monuments must approach the total number of French *communes* or townships in the 1920s, thirty-six thousand. The sheer extent of French losses in the war provides the most obvious, and the most common, explanation for the unprecedented scale of postwar commemoration.[5] One estimate puts French military deaths at some 1,327,000, proportionally higher than any other major combatant.[6] Yet it is not self-evident that even widespread grief should so rapidly—within only a few years of the war's end—find monumental expression. The proliferation of monuments to the dead of the Great War did not simply result from a spontaneous outpouring of emotion, however real this was, but involved the fusion of a collective need to mourn with preexisting practices of commemoration. After all, as both Agulhon and William Cohen remind us, the nineteenth century, not the twentieth, gave birth to the expression *statuomanie,* literally a mania for putting up statues.[7]

In the Third Republic the objects of monumental commemoration ranged widely, from signal events to great figures of the past, from Joan of

Arc to Garibaldi. Agulhon's and Cohen's accounts together suggest some of the limits to this commemorative urge. Large-scale figural monuments, on the one hand, most of them original works of art, claimed resources available only to major cities and towns. On the other hand, cheaper images of the Republic, many mass-produced, generally reflected a depth of political commitment unique to certain regions, notably the Mediterranean coast.[8] These limits suggest that monument building in the late nineteenth century took place chiefly in areas (in both the discursive and the geographical senses) of political contestation, as virtually all major cities were and as most of the areas Agulhon discusses had been as recently as 1851. The 1870–71 war became an object of commemoration particularly in areas that had suffered directly from the Prussian invasion, but elsewhere it was quickly eclipsed by the more contentious issues of the nature of the polity and its relation to the church. Significantly, a new wave of commemoration of 1870 coincided with the emergence of an aggressive (the French called it *revanchist*) nationalism in the late 1880s and 1890s. Many of these new monuments and plaques, still located predominantly in eastern France, were the work of an organization called the Souvenir français, founded shortly after the war and dedicated to the preservation of French war graves and memorials—particularly in the "lost" province of Alsace.[9]

To observe that World War I gave rise to a vast number of monuments suggests, then, that it created a new discursive field, a new space of contestation that insistently called out for monumental resolution. This assertion may at first seem to fly in the face of the register in which monuments operate. What Americans call war memorials the French call *monuments aux morts,* monuments to the dead, and with inscriptions dedicating them *to* the dead of a particular town, they evoke a community unified in mourning and in tribute.[10] Yet besides the vigorous controversies that occasionally developed over the site, design, and financing of monuments, debates that went to their very purpose,[11] the decision to construct a monument implicated a community in several kinds of latent contestation. One might be characterized as a secular/religious question: in the face of precocious moves to place memorial plaques inside parish churches, the building of a monument stakes a claim for a specifically civic commemoration, one that may or may not be in conflict with the claims of the church.[12]

A second kind of tension inherent in the construction of monuments involved the negotiation of local and national claims to the memory of the dead. The scope of this conflict, of course, far exceeded the field of commemoration proper; perhaps its most visceral embodiment came in the prolonged debate over where the war dead should be buried, at the front or in their hometowns. Ultimately, in the face of persistent entreaties from the families of victims, the government reluctantly agreed to pay for the return of soldiers' remains to their place of birth or their prewar residence; it also offered a free annual trip to the former front to those relatives who agreed to leave their dead in a battlefield cemetery.[13] Yet neither the transfer of remains nor battlefield visits offered any consolation to the many relatives whose loved ones' bodies had never been found. A 1922 article on the Verdun theater estimated that, despite continuing efforts to recover and identify remains, no more than a quarter of the four hundred thousand Frenchmen killed there would ever be given individual graves.[14]

The plight of families who lacked the demarcated site of mourning that a tombstone offered, as well as the consolation of proximity to physical remains, had much to do with the rapid spread of monuments in the immediate postwar period. Many speeches at monument dedications referred to them as substitute tombs, and enjoined members of the community, especially children, to show them the same respect they would a cemetery.[15] This discourse of substitution gives much of its significance to the designation *monument aux morts,* and helps to explain the one feature common to virtually all monuments, even the rare ones that feature allegories of victory: the prominent inscription of the names of the dead (fig. 1).

Fig. 1. Names on the war memorial in Euville (Meuse).
(Photo: author)

These names were invariably read out at monument dedications and at subsequent Armistice Day ceremonies; in some towns they find an echo in faded enamel plaques with photographs of the dead and, occasionally, a brief encapsulation of their life histories (fig. 2). The purpose of this discourse was largely consolatory, but it was not simply a discourse of mourning. Although the proportions vary, fewer than a third of the communes in three very different departments—the conservative Morbihan, in Brittany, the leftist Vaucluse, in Provence, and the centrist Loir-et-Cher—decided to build their monuments in the cemetery, the space most suited to mourning. The rest chose to place them in more or less open spaces: in front of the church or town hall, in a public square or park, or at the entrance to the village.[16] Such a public position served clearly to identify the community with its monument, and to claim for the locality a privileged place in the hierarchy of postwar commemorations.

Commemoration does not simply involve urges, however: it also requires means, and what made universal commemoration possible in France after

Fig. 2. Mourning plaque near the war memorial in
Thésée (Morbihan). (Photo: author)

the war was the existence of a commercial monument industry. Agulhon's study of Republican imagery from 1880 to 1914 makes clear the prior importance of the mass production of standard monumental forms, but after World War I it was to reach unparalleled heights.[17] For if major towns had the resources to sponsor competitions for their monuments and to hire reasonably well-known architects and sculptors to execute them, the vast majority of France's communes did not. To meet their needs a number of major suppliers, from well-known foundries to commercial quarries, offered for sale both low-cost monuments and standard designs that local stonecutters could copy or finish. Their sales pitches ranged from brochures and fliers to newspapers and sales catalogs, and they pursued prospective clients aggressively. The state, its local representatives, and art critics disparaged both the producers and the product, calling it dated, unoriginal, pretentious, and quite simply not art. For localities, however, these mass-produced or standardized memorials represented not only all they could afford, but also a way of situating a sense of loss they shared with the whole nation in the particular context of their own community.

II

As soon as the war ended, the Fine Arts Ministry in Paris found itself flooded with requests from members of Parliament, prefects, and mayors for models of monuments or for competitions to create them. Some local officials also sought the names of artists who specialized in commemorative art. Their letters suggested that the state provide inexpensive but aesthetically acceptable designs that could be built by communes of varying resources: "bon marché, sans vulgarité" (cheap, but not vulgar) as the mayor of Chançay, in the Indre-et-Loire, put it. Provincials with ties to the capital seem to have had a real fear that purely local initiative would lead to considerable aesthetic embarrassment: a deputy from the Ain wrote, "we must not let our land become covered with horrors. Between a work of art and an abomination there is room for something suitable [*convenable*]."[18] But the state consistently refused to provide any such models, saying that to do so would both interfere with localities' right to make their own artistic choices and impede artists' exercise of their creative freedom.[19] From July of 1919 the Fine Arts Ministry replied to all such requests with the same formulaic statement: "the ministry has abstained from intervening in the choice of artists in order to leave towns and [monument] committees the greatest scope for initiative."[20] In addition, the ministry refused to consider subventions for monuments in towns with populations of fewer than five thousand, on the assumption that these could not be considered works of art.[21]

This cutoff point referred to a law of October 1919 that offered subsidies for monuments in towns of fewer than five thousand inhabitants. The law provided a formula for calculating the subsidy based on two scales, the percentage of the town's 1914 population killed in the war, and the value of local tax revenues. The total ranged from a minimum of 4 to a maximum of 25 percent of the cost of the monument borne by the commune; the product of subscriptions and other private contributions was not taken into account. The proffered grants, administered not by the Fine Arts Ministry but by the Public Commemoration Division of the Ministry of the Interior, amounted to too little to give the state an effective role in monument design. In theory all monuments required approval from the state, but in practice only communes wanting a subsidy had to submit documentation to Paris. Since the stakes were so small, many did not bother, or did so only late in the process.[22]

But the Interior Ministry did want to assure some quality control, to avoid what it considered the worst excesses of mass-produced monuments. In 1920, accordingly, it called on prefects to create review commissions, including as members the departmental architect and others with competence in design matters, to evaluate local proposals for monuments.[23] The commissions paid little attention to the Fine Arts Ministry's rhetoric about local initiative. The Breton town of La Trinité-sur-Mer, in the Morbihan, wanted to erect a monument in the shape of a menhir, the neolithic stone formation typical of the region, but the departmental commission considered this "lacking in harmony." Furthermore, it declared, "it does not seem a good idea to put a megalith on a masonry base." (After the monument's designer, a Paris sculptor and longtime summer resident of La Trinité, vigorously defended the regional particularity of his design, pointing out that the base was to be in native blue granite, the commission reversed itself and approved the project.)[24] Commissioners were far more concerned with issues of originality, which they contrasted absolutely with serial or mass production. The rapporteur for the Var commission criticized the proposed monuments in Artignosc and Les Salles, two stelae with pyramidal tops, saying their designer should have taken inspiration from classical models. Yet the appearance of the monuments concerned him less than the fact that the same workshop had produced both of the monuments, and that, at least in basic form, they were identical.[25]

Commissioners were also concerned with maladroit designs by amateurs, and they continually urged communes to have recourse to trained architects and sculptors like themselves. Commission members did in fact design monuments, generally for larger towns, and naturally they responded to their colleagues' designs with great enthusiasm.[26] When the project of the departmental architect Barla for a relatively simple monument in Callas came before the Var panel, the curator of the Draguignan museum wrote in his report, "Of all the commemorative projects sent to us up to now, this is certainly the one that, through the simplicity of its lines, the sobriety of its ornamentation, and the harmony of the whole responds the best and the most artistically to the desired end."[27] The commissioners did, however, realize that most smaller communities could not afford their services. Discussing the proposed monument in Bargemon, in the Var (fig. 3), which he called "a post-war horror," Barla declared that "certain towns seem unaware of the prefect's considered warning . . . to avoid the pretension of statues that can only be beautiful if their execution is entrusted to artists worthy of the name, whose inspiration, drawn from the faith of their art, realizes moving works, which are generally too costly to be within reach of our smaller villages."[28]

But their reliance on models and sketches, as well as the primacy attached to originality, could blind commissioners to the way monuments work within specific locales. Arguably, the site of the Bargemon monument, in the hills of Haute Provence, lends it a dignity and power that go beyond its formal qualities. On the other hand, the Var commission lavished praise on the design for a monument in Cotignac, finding in it "the

Fig. 3. War memorial, Bargemon (Var). (Photo: author)

rare merit of being original, simple, and imposing at the same time. The poilu, the principal element of the work, becomes the soul of the stone, becomes an integral part of it as he became an integral part of the earth of the trenches."[29] But in the actual monument (fig. 4), the soldier looks as though he is peeping over the top of the stone out of which he is carved, and the effect, particularly from the back, is more comical than imposing.

In contrast to their praise for professionally produced unique memorials, commissions objected with particular vehemence to monuments ordered from catalogs, which they criticized for "a false luxury of details scattered without any ordering principle, and for the pretentious mannerism of statues that pretend to be allegorical."[30] Their comments reproduce a discourse widespread among critics working in the "high art" arena, one that attributed the generally perceived low aesthetic quality of small-town monuments to the intervention of commerce and entrepreneurship. Wrote one critic in the spring of 1922, "the weather has already dilapidated the cheap enamel, the flashy gilding, the patinas of fake bronze that clever manufacturers used to disguise [maquiller] their commercial junk." Another critic, referring to "factories where commemorative war memorials

Fig. 4. War memorial, Cotignac (Var). (Photo: author)

are fabricated serially according to the principles of Taylorism," asked rhetorically, "is it not sad to think that so many pretty French villages have thus been disfigured by the manufacturers of patriotic sculpture?"[31]

But the manufacturers, whatever their aesthetic deficiencies, proved skillful at appropriating this discourse for their own purposes. Like the commissioner who reported on the Bargemon memorial, they realized that small towns lacked the resources to commission original art; indeed, this was the commercial producers' whole raison d'être. Yet rather than emphasizing the economy they offered, the firms' sales pitches to prospective clients sought to associate them and their product with the prestige of high art. They thus adopted a similar distinction between what they offered and a construct they labeled "serial" or "commercial." The Paris architectural firm of Clermont put out a flier that began, "Your commune wants to build a monument that is not serially produced"; the accompanying letter said that "to avoid, following the wishes of the Minister of Fine Arts, marring our sites and public squares with monuments without cachet and in dubious taste . . . it is indispensable to provide oneself with all desirable guarantees." Specifically, the firm trumpeted the qualifications of its lead architect, "graduate of the state art school [diplômé du gouvernement] and a prize winner at the Paris Salon and in various competitions."[32]

A much larger firm, the Rombaux-Roland company in the Nord, claimed that "our designs are always approved without difficulty" by prefectural review boards. Yet the price list and the numbered designs that accompany this flier, which could be recombined in a kind of mix-and-match fashion (figs. 5 and 6), leave no doubt of the commercial nature of the Rombaux-Roland enterprise.[33] You could, for example, have the monument in plate 357E with or without a "victorious poilu" on it, in marble, bronze, or bronzed cast iron (the marble costing no more than the cast iron but executed, following the "same interpretation," by a different artist). The monuments in plate 363[ter], all based on the same stele form, came in a variety of sizes; on some the decorations could be either sculpted in relief or cast in "patinated bronze"; the Gallic cock in no. 1029G could be ordered in either marble or granite; and prices ranged from 1,450 francs to 4,450.

The printed circular of a Paris company, "La Pensée" (its letterhead shows the flower of that name, in English the pansy, which because of its association with memory was often planted around war memorials), assured the generic mayor to whom it was addressed that its "monuments are not produced serially, which is to say that when one is executed it is not reproduced a second time." Yet the enclosed questionnaire, beginning, "Do you desire a commemorative monument?" and including such questions as "What approximate sum do you wish to spend on it?" and "Do you want the letters painted, a) in black, b) in red, c) or gilded?" together with the promise of a free sketch and estimate within two to three weeks,

Fig. 5. Plates 357E and 357H from the Rombaux-Roland monument catalog, ca. 1920. Archives Départementales du Var, deposited Archives Communales de Montferrat. (Photo: author). The monument in plate 357E cost 21,100 francs alone and between 31,250 and 37,550 with the poilu, depending on the material.

suggests a file of standard designs with only minor modifications for each client.[34] Other companies, such as the Marbreries Générales in Paris, or a smaller Nice firm, insisted that they were specialists, that they could modify standard designs to suit particular sites and programs, and that their designs had "great artistic cachet."[35]

The appropriation of artistic discourse to commercial ends reached something of an apex in a monthly (occasionally semimonthly) newspaper called *L'art funéraire et commémoratif*. In four tabloid-size pages, each issue of *L'art funéraire* juxtaposed critical articles such as those quoted above, historical pieces on past masters of French commemorative sculpture like Mercié and Dalou, and articles, photographs, and advertisements promoting the monuments of the sculptor Charles-Henri Pourquet, a serious artist of modest talent whom the newspaper vaunted as the master of Great War commemoration.[36] Praise in these terms reinforced *L'art funéraire*'s constant insistence, in editorials and in brief slogans interspersed throughout the text, that only trained artists and architects could produce monuments of a suitable aesthetic character.[37] But the newspaper did not limit itself to urgings of a purely artistic kind. Another of its slogans ran,

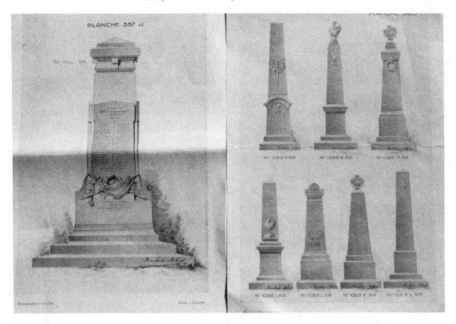

Fig. 6. Plates 357J and 363ᵗᵉʳ from the Rombaux-Roland monument catalog, ca. 1920. Archives Départementales du Var, deposited Archives Communales de Montferrat. (Photo: author)

"There is a truth that those who undertake commemorative monuments too often do not know: in art, the beautiful is no more costly than the ugly."[38] On the last page of almost every issue, *L'art funéraire* advertised its availability to towns "proposing to build commemorative monuments of the Great War that will leave behind the current banality," and offered, at no charge, "artistic designs, models, sketches, reasonable estimates, even cost prices." These were undoubtedly the works of Pourquet; under the photograph of perhaps his best-known, *La Résistance,* the newspaper wrote that it could provide information "on the reproduction of this beautiful work in any material at all."[39]

In the absence of entrepreneurial archives, it is difficult to know how successful this rhetorical strategy proved in attracting clients. A price list issued by Rombaux-Roland a few months after the one discussed earlier offered new variations on certain models and price reductions of up to 15 percent on some of the more expensive ones. But this may simply indicate a routine market adjustment, as most prices, and all of the cheapest ones, remained the same.[40] More significantly, the monument business could tap a set of local attitudes that lent itself to precisely the kind of product, both discursive and physical, it was offering. The responses of local officials to the criticisms of prefectural review boards show a surprising confidence in their own ability to determine the type of monument appropriate to their community. The mayor of Les Salles, in the Var, considered the similarity of its monument to others, which the commission criticized as a sign it lacked originality, proof of the contractor's ability. "The entrepreneur is not very good at drawing," the mayor noted, as though this explained the commissioner's reservations, "but he handles a chisel very skillfully; that's well known."[41]

Recognizing the photography on the Pourcieux plan as a commercial product, the rapporteur on the Var commission wrote that the statue "cannot be considered an original work. It will doubtless be seen in several communes and will create more of a commercial than an artistic impression."[42] The "original" realistic paint job applied by the town, in fact a fairly common practice, would hardly have changed his mind, but like most of his colleagues in similar cases he acquiesced, reasoning that small towns could hardly be expected either to produce or to appreciate original works of art.[43] In some cases review boards were able to secure minor changes in the dimensions of a monument, in order say to harmonize a statue with a pedestal, but when presented with what the prefect called a *fait accompli,* a monument completed prior to their examination, they could not even do that.[44]

Yet though the dichotomy between art and commerce, or between high and popular art, clearly constituted one of the basic divisions between the state and localities, it was not the only one. The town of Nans-les-Pins, also in the Var, prompted criticism from the commission because of its plan to use an old fountain as the base for its monument; the commissioner also suggested, not very helpfully, that the monument should be "more artistic."[45] In a polite but obviously deeply felt reply, the mayor observed that "the value of an object does not depend on its cost, but on the memory attached to it; our modest monument will perpetuate the memory of our dear departed just as well as one costing ten times as much." The town, the mayor wrote later, already had a monument in the cemetery, but the "population insists on having its poilu in a public square."[46] This apparently simple assertion actually contains two references that need to be considered separately: to the poilu and to the public square with its fountain.

For its poilu Nans chose a variation on the hugely popular product of the Jacomet company in the Vaucluse. Jacomet boasted in its literature, usually accompanied by a photograph (figs. 7 and 8), that "LE POILU is the only subject that fully represents the idea that has been developed [*qu'on se fait*] of a Monument to the Dead of the Great War."[47] Of course, many sculptors and companies produced versions of the poilu, and although the Jacomet monument (fig. 9) can be found all over the country, other types

Fig. 7. Jacomet publicity flier, ca. 1920. Archives
Municipales de Vannes. (Photo: author)

were popular as well. In addition, statistical surveys in a number of departments make clear that the most common monument, undoubtedly because
it was the cheapest, had no figural representation at all: the simple stele
(fig. 10).[48] Yet Jacomet's carefully worded advertisement makes a conceptual claim, not a statistical one, and certainly the poilu, who could be
represented in busts, plaques, or full-length figures in a variety of poses,
constitutes one of the most common motifs of a national order on French
World War I memorials. In the Morbihan, out of 154 monuments surveyed,
79, or just over half, lack any figural motif; in the Loir-et-Cher the percentage is greater, 74 out of 113.[49] But in both cases, of the monuments with
figures, the overwhelming majority—25 out of 30 in the Loir-et-Cher; 54
out of 62 in the Morbihan—include the poilu, either alone or grouped with
other figures.

    That the common soldier should emerge as the most pervasive image of
the war memorial in France may not seem surprising, but its significance

Fig. 8. Photograph of the Jacomet poilu
model. Archives Départementales de la
Meuse, deposited Archives Communales de
Neuville. (Photo: author)

deserves closer examination. The poilu, to be sure, comes out of a stylistic
tradition particular to war memorials, one extant in France since the
Franco-Prussian War and with examples from the United States (in Civil
War memorials of both the Union and the Confederacy) to New Zealand.[50]
But this form itself represents a radical break with the prevailing tradition
of monumental representation, the female allegory. This tradition had
hardly seemed moribund in France, for in the three decades prior to the
war it had found an embodiment in Marianne, the personification of the
newly reestablished Republic. Nor can this new preference for the male
body be attributed simply to commercial availability; the letter from the
mayor of Nans-les-Pins suggests that in this case suppliers were largely
responding to demand. Lower-end monument concerns such as Rombaux-
Roland did not show female allegories in their publicity materials, and
probably did not sell them. But suppliers aiming for the middle and upper
ranges of the market like the Marbreries Générales and the well-known Val
d'Osne foundry did offer such designs, usually winged victories, and a few

Fig. 9. War memorial, Beignon (Morbihan). The classic
Jacomet poilu. (Photo: author)

towns did select them, either with or without a poilu (figs. 11 and 12 show
two Morbihan monuments purchased from the Marbreries Générales, in
Plumelin and St. Dolay).[51]

Why, then, did so few towns choose female allegories; why did so many,
like Nans-les-Pins, want an unadorned poilu in the public square? Simple
explanations largely unrelated to the nature of monuments are not lacking:
the higher cost of elaborate sculptures, the pressure of veterans' groups for
realistic representations of their dead comrades, or more generally the
inappropriateness of a heroic idiom to the mood of postwar France.[52] All of
these explanations have some merit, but we also need to consider factors
proper to the order of representation itself. Marina Warner has observed
that monuments in the form of the female body have historically represented abstractions, signified by particular devices: Marianne's cap, Victory's wings, Justice's blindfold and scales. Logically, then, "female figures

Fig. 10. War memorial, Chailles (Loir-et-Cher).
The classic stele. (Photo: author)

representing an ideal or an abstraction hardly ever intersect with real
individual women."[53] Though a specially commissioned monument could
transcend this abstraction, for example by clothing women in regional
costume or widow's weeds, a mass-produced standard figure could do so
only with great difficulty.[54]

The soldier in uniform, in contrast, was, even in the exaggeratedly heroic
pose favored by Pourquet and others, immediately recognizable as a realistic type, an important attribute for grieving relatives. This is true in a
general as well as a particular sense: Warner notes that male representations of the nation, such as John Bull or Uncle Sam, have particular characters in ways that Britannia or the Statue of Liberty does not.[55] France
before the war lacked such a common male representation; the poilu supplied one. Yet the special appeal of the poilu lay in his ability to conjoin
national with local resonances. Not only a standard figure, he was also a
local one; given local roots by the names at his feet, he stood not only for

Fig. 11. War memorial, Plumelin (Morbihan). A
Marbreries Générales design: Victory hovering over
a poilu. (Photo: author)

the nation but for the individuals a particular community had given up in
its name.

Returning to Nans-les-Pins, we remember that the community did not
only want a poilu, it wanted a poilu on an existing fountain base (fig. 13).
Such a combination did not lack precedents: Agulhon has found a number
of Third Republic Mariannes with what he calls "hydraulic supports." A
Marianne so placed clearly associated social progress—the easy availability of water in the center of the village, rather than in some distant well—
with a particular political commitment.[56] In one of his letters to the prefect
the mayor gave a capsule history of the fountain, built in 1887 "for a great
deal of money" and clearly the pride of the town.[57] The fusion of the
fountain, a symbol of the community's civic identity, with the poilu, which

204   DANIEL J. SHERMAN

Fig. 12. War memorial, St. Dolay (Morbihan). A
Marbreries Générales design: Victory alone.
(Photo: author)

embodied the link between the community and the nation that the monument itself sought to enact, thus signified not a solution of convenience but
a profoundly meaningful commemorative act.

Towns wanted poilus, or stelae with standard decorations, or defused
shells to form balustrades, because these forms signified commemoration.
Their resemblance to other forms, far from disqualifying them as art,
provided a link to an order of signification that towns lacking experience
with high cultural discourse construed as artistic, and thus the worthiest
signifier of their own highest emotions. Nor could the repetition of forms
compromise the distinctiveness of individual monuments. Having inscribed monuments with the names of their own dead, having placed them
in churchyards or in town squares newly renamed Place du Maréchal Foch,
or Place Verdun, or, as in St. Maurice-sous-les Côtes, Place du Poilu, towns
saw in them more than mass-produced compendiums of artistic clichés.[58]

Fig. 13. War memorial, Nans-les-Pins (Var). The monument on its fountain base. (Photo: author)

For these monuments, recognizable as such by their association with standard types, yet distinctive in their locations and in the names they inscribed, presented towns with an image of their community in terms both
of what they shared with others and of what remained distinctly their own.
   This is not to say that the meaning monuments conveyed was either clear
or fixed. As objects, monuments from the moment of their conception
offered themselves up to a variety of interpretations. Indeed, even at their
dedication or on subsequent Armistice Days, ceremonial occasions when
monuments most ostentatiously signified unity, practiced rhetoricians
could appropriate them to their own political purposes. Where a leftist
deputy might find in a monument, whatever its form, an exhortation to
avoid senseless slaughter in the future, one of his conservative colleagues
could, at the same ceremony, extract from it an endorsement of a strong
defense and an uncompromising foreign policy.[59] Whatever the views of

the commentator, the monument could be interpreted to suit them. As Warner has written, "it is in the intrinsic nature of public art that it seems to adapt, to collaborate. It could be said that it has no coat to turn."[60]

It seems clear, however, on the basis of some suggestive empirical evidence, that for most communities their monument embodied, more than anything else, a sense of loss. The stele alone, a form derived from funerary architecture, accounts for at least half the monuments in most departments, and often adjoins the figure of the poilu. Another 5 or 10 percent of monuments in surveyed regions take the form of tombs, either with or without mourning figures, altars, or in Brittany even calvaries. Among figural monuments, few convey an attitude of triumph, either allegorically or in the pose or expression of the poilu. One finds as many dying soldiers as victorious ones, and most frequently the soldier stands at rest, solemn, pensive. A poilu in Normandy, not from a standard model, even seems to be mourning a German helmet at his feet, a sign of the international reconciliation that many veterans' groups advocated in the postwar period.[61]

But meaning is not a matter of proportions, frequencies, statistics; like memory it is profoundly unstable. The monument, in its tendency to blend into the landscape, embodies this instability in a particularly ironic way. Warner cites Robert Musil on this phenomenon: "The most striking feature of monuments is that you do not notice them. There is nothing in the world as invisible as monuments. Doubtless they have been erected to be seen—even to attract attention; yet at the same time something has impregnated them against attention. Like a drop of water on an oilskin, attention runs down them without stopping for a moment."[62] The builders of World War I monuments in France were conscious of the tendency of memory to fade, and their inaugural speeches often testify to a certain pessimism about the efficacy of the means, monuments, they had chosen to combat it: "In these parts," the mayor of a small Breton town declared bluntly, "forgetting comes quickly."[63]

This inevitable dialectic between memory and forgetting affords a context at once poignant and revealing for the single most consistent feature of these monuments, their inscription of names. However odd or simply ugly we may find the ensemble of which they form a vital part, even today those long, heartbreaking lists, strangely echoed by the silence that usually surrounds them, cannot fail to move us. The names more than anything else constitute the monument as a place of mourning, inscribing it with the particularity of a place that the denomination of its inhabitants embodies. More than this, by virtue of their inscription the names constitute themselves as part of a signifying process that seeks to transcend memory and its limitations by assigning it, in its constructed "collective" form, a historical role. In a manner both poignant and troubling, names as the irreducible synecdoche for monuments stake a community's claim to a place in history, representing its loss as its most essential link to the nation.

NOTES

1. *Les lieux de mémoire* currently numbers four volumes, with three more in the offing. For the scope of the project and its theoretical presuppositions, see Pierre Nora, "Présentation," pp. vii–xiii, and "Entre mémoire et histoire: La problématique des lieux," pp. xvii–xlii, in Nora, ed., *Les lieux de mémoire*, 3 vols., 1: *La République* (Paris: Gallimard, 1984); the latter essay is translated (by Marc Roudebush) as "Between Memory and History: *Les Lieux de Mémoire*," *Representations*, no. 26 (Spring 1989), pp. 7–25. On attitudes toward the study of war memorials see Jean-Pierre Marby, "Les monuments ardennais aux morts de la grande guerre," *Revue historique ardennaise* 22 (1987), pp. 137–153, who begins by observing, "Il s'avère que l'étude d'un tel sujet n'allait pas sans déclencher l'étonnement, voir le rire."

2. R. Williams, "Base and Superstructure in Marxist Cultural Theory," in his *Problems in Materialism and Culture: Selected Essays* (London: Verso, 1980), p. 48. On the conception of relative autonomy in cultural theory, see Janet Wolff, *The Social Production of Art* (Houndmills: Macmillan Education, 1981), pp. 71–94. Her remarks on Bourdieu and cultural production, pp. 137–139, are also helpful.

3. George Mosse, *Fallen Soldiers: Reshaping the Memory of the World Wars* (New York: Oxford University Press, 1990), pp. 9–10.

4. M. Agulhon, *Marianne au pouvoir: L'imagerie et la symbolique républicaines de 1880 à 1914* (Paris: Flammarion, 1989), pp. 128–136; J. Hargrove, "Souviens-toi," *Monuments historiques*, no. 124 (December 1982–January 1983), pp. 59–60.

5. See, among others, Mosse, *Fallen Soldiers*, pp. 3–4; Antoine Prost, "Les monuments aux morts: Culte républicain? Culte civique? Culte patriotique?" in Nora, ed., *Les lieux de mémoire*, 1: *La République*, p. 196; Monique Luirard, *La France et ses morts: Les monuments commémoratifs dans la Loire* (St. Etienne: Université de St. Etienne, Centre Interdisciplinaire d'Etudes et de Recherches sur les Structures Régionales, 1977), pp. 15–17.

6. For every thousand inhabitants of France in 1914, 168 were mobilized and 34 killed, as opposed to 154 and 30 in Germany. See Jean-Jacques Becker, *Les français dans la grande guerre*, Les hommes et l'histoire (Paris: Robert Laffont, 1980), pp. 11–12.

7. M. Agulhon, "La 'statuomanie' et l'histoire," *Ethnologie française*, n.s. 8 (1978), pp. 145–172; W. Cohen, "Symbols of Power: Statues in Nineteenth-Century Provincial France," *Comparative Studies in Society and History* 31 (1989), pp. 491–513.

8. Cohen, "Symbols of Power," passim; Agulhon, *Marianne au pouvoir*, pp. 210–220.

9. Prost, "Les monuments aux morts," p. 196; Agulhon, *Marianne au pouvoir*, p. 132; on the rarity of monuments outside the invaded area, Luirard, *La France et ses morts*, p. 14 (she cites a handful built under the aegis of the Souvenir français);

and Remi Roques, "Monuments aux morts du sud-est de la France," *Provence historique* 31 (1981), pp. 247–248.

10. On the significance of inscriptions, see Yves Hélias, "Pour une sémiologie politique des monuments aux morts," *Revue française de science politique* 29 (1979), pp. 742–744.

11. I have discussed some of these controversies in "The Nation: In What Community?: The Politics of Commemoration in Interwar France," in Linda Miller and Michael B. Smith, eds., *Ideas and Ideals: Essays on Politics in Honor of Stanley Hoffmann* (Boulder: Westview Press, forthcoming).

12. On this issue see Luirard, *La France et ses morts*, pp. 17–22.

13. Articles on this issue can be found in newspapers published by veterans' associations throughout the early 1920s; see especially *La voix du combattant*, 1 August 1920 and 11 December 1921. Some of the state's deliberations on war grave policy are in Archives Nationales (AN), F² 2125.

14. *Echo de l'Ossuaire de Douaumont*, no. 3 (January–February 1922), pp. 93–94. The traumatic effects of this search for bodies have recently received widespread attention in France thanks to Bertrand Tavernier's 1989 film *La vie et rien d'autre* and Jean Rouaud's novel *Les champs d'honneur* (Paris: Minuit, 1990), winner of the 1990 Prix Goncourt.

15. See, for example, remarks about respect and observance at the inaugurations of two war memorials in the Loir-et-Cher: Coulanges, 11 November 1921 (*La République de Loir-et-Cher*, 12 December 1921), and Theillay, 28 May 1922 (*Echo de la Sologne*, 4 June 1922).

16. On the Vaucluse, see Jean Giroud, Raymond Michel, and Maryse Michel, *Les monuments aux morts de la guerre 1914–1918 dans le Vaucluse* (L'Isle sur la Sorgue: Scriba, 1991), p. 104. In the Vaucluse 38.2 percent of monuments are in cemeteries; figures for the Morbihan and the Loir-et-Cher, based on my own preliminary research and subject to revision, are 28.4 and 29.6 percent respectively. If one adds to the Loir-et-Cher figure monuments located *outside* cemetery gates, the percentage rises to 38.4, but there are good reasons to put such sites in the category of open rather than of enclosed spaces.

17. Agulhon, *Marianne au pouvoir*, pp. 229–239.

18. AN, F²¹ 4770, Dossier 2i: Mayor Chançay to Ministre de l'Instruction Publique et des Beaux-Arts; A. Laguerre, Deputy to Ministre des Pensions, 22 July 1919.

19. See AN, F²¹ 4770: one suggestion for a competition came in the form of a parliamentary question from the deputy Simonet (*Journal Officiel*, hereafter *JO*, 19 April 1919); the reply said that the Conseil Supérieur des Beaux-Arts "s'est prononcé à l'unanimité contre l'organisation d'un concours de cette nature, qui serait une attente à la liberté des communes et ne pourrait que nuire aux intérêts de l'art et des artistes."

20. AN, F²¹ 4770, Dossier 2i, copy of Ministre to Maire Périers (Manche), 31 July 1919.

21. This assumption can be found in AN, F²¹ 4770, Dossier 2i, the draft of a letter from the Ministre de l'Instruction Publique et des Beaux-Arts to the Ministre de l'Intérieur, 16 July 1919.

22. On the basic provision for state subsidies, contained in a law of 25 October

1919, see AN, F²¹ 4770, Dossier 2i; the actual scales delineating state support as a percentage of the monument's cost are in *JO*, 1 August 1920, p. 10940. Prefects then transmitted these scales to mayors, along with a list of the supporting material the state required to be submitted with a subsidy request; see, for example, Archives Départementales de la Meuse (hereafter ADMe), E Dépôt 353/1 M 7, a circular of the Préfet de la Meuse, dated 4 September 1920. The subsidy program expired at the end of 1924; see, for example, Archives Départementales du Morbihan (hereafter ADM), O 93, circular dated 25 October 1924.

23. AN, F²¹ 4770, Dossier 2i, Ministre de l'Intérieur to Ministre de l'Instruction Publique et des Beaux-Arts, 18 May 1920, enclosing a copy of the circular to prefects of 5 May 1920.

24. ADM, O 94, minutes of meeting of 9 June 1921 and 16 December 1921; for the defense of the artist, André Rivaud, see ADM, O 2125, his letters to the mayor of 30 August 1921 and to the prefect of 5 November 1921.

25. Archives Départementales du Var (hereafter ADV), 9T4-4, report of Roustan for the commission meeting of 25 October 1920.

26. In one instance, an architect on the Var review board had to excuse himself from evaluating a monument he himself had designed: ADV, 9T4-4, Roustan to Préfet, 19 June 1922, regarding the monument in Brignoles.

27. ADV, 9T4-4, report of 13 May 1921 (Callas).

28. ADV, 9T4-4, report of Barla, 23 July 1921.

29. ADV, 9T4-4 report of Jules Roustan, 19 January 1921.

30. ADV, 9T4-4, report of Roustan for the commission meeting of 25 October 1920; the comments concern the proposed monument in Carcès.

31. Lucien Marie, "Une Renaissance monumentale," *L'art funéraire et commémoratif* (hereafter *AFC*), no. 36, April 1922, p. 1; "Un article sensationnel de M. Clément Vautel," *AFC*, no. 53, November 1924, p. 2 (quoting from *Le Journal*).

32. ADV, deposited Archives Communales de Montferrat, Series M (hereafter ACM), undated circular.

33. All materials from ADV/ACM.

34. ADM, 79 Es 41 (deposited Archives Communales de Guillac), brochure dated 1920.

35. ADM, O 93, circular of Marbreries Générales, undated but with attachments from fall 1920; ADV/ACM, letter from Lesage, Biagetti, et Bottala, dated 21 July 1919.

36. In one two-page feature about his recent work, the newspaper's lead critic wrote, "No one more than this excellent artist has struggled more successfully against the vulgarity and banality of certain funeral monuments, and no one will have honored the memory of the war with more feeling, of a sound instinct, of sincerity and constancy." See L. Marie, "Les oeuvres commémoratives du sculpteur Pourquet," *AFC*, June 1922. On Pourquet, see Annette Becker, *Les monuments aux morts: Patrimoine et mémoire de la Grande Guerre* (Paris: Errance, [1988]), pp. 29–32.

37. "You want, do you not," one of these slogans read, "to erect a commemorative monument that is a work of art? The first condition is to apply to an artist." *AFC*, February–March 1922, July 1922, and other issues.

38. *AFC*, January 1924 and other issues.

39. *AFC*, May 1922.

40. ADV/ACM, price list dated February 1921. For an indication of the sales of a rival concern, see note 47 below.

41. ADV, 9T4-4, Maire to Préfet, 1 December 1920. The mayor actually used the word *aiguille,* or needle; since *aiguille* can refer to an engraving needle, he may have been confusing it with another term, *burin,* which can mean either an engraving needle or a chisel.

42. ADV, 9T4-4, report of 28 July 1921.

43. ADV, 9T4-4: such attitudes are expressed in reports on Sillans-la-Cascade (report of 8 November 1921) and Tanneron (report of 17 July 1921).

44. ADV, 9T4-4: cases involving changes in proportions include Figanières (report of 15 November 1921) and Mazauges (report of 25 November 1921); cases of *faits accomplis* include Comps-sur-Artuby (Préfet to Ministre de l'Intérieur, 3 January 1921) and Ginasservis (Préfet to Ministre de l'Intérieur, 3 January 1921) and Ginasservis (Préfet to Ministre, 22 December 1920).

45. ADV, 9T4-4, report of Barla, 15 September 1924.

46. ADV, 9T4-4, Maire to Préfet, 10 October and 14 November 1924.

47. ADV/ACM, undated photograph and flier. The photograph was quite common: I have also found it in Archives Départementales de la Meuse, E Dépôt 289/1 M 2, the communal archives of Neuville-sur-Ornain (which in the end did not incorporate a poilu in its monument); and in Archives Municipales de Vannes (hereafter AM Vannes), 1 M 199, which also contain a brochure published by Jacomet entitled *Livre d'Or du "Poilu."* Unfortunately undated (it does not include all the communes in which I have located Jacomet designs), it lists 274 communes in metropolitan France and 6 in Algeria that had adopted the Jacomet poilu, as well as the names of the firm's local agents.

48. On the stele as the typical war memorial, see Antoine Prost; *Les anciens combattants et la société française, 1914–1939,* 3 vols., 3: *Mentalités et idéologies* (Paris: Presses de la Fondation Nationale des Sciences Politiques, 1977), p. 42; Giroud, Michel, and Michel, *Les monuments,* p. 98. In the Morbihan, stelae amount to nearly half of the monuments I surveyed, 73 out of 154; in the Loir-et-Cher they are a clear majority, 76 out of 113.

49. Based on both archival research in ADM and the Archives Départementales du Loir-et-Cher and on research in the field; the figures are not identical to the ones in note 48 above because they include, among monuments with figural motifs, stelae decorated with small medallions depicting poilus in bust or in profile. The Morbihan group is a representative sample of the 263 communes in the department; the Loir-et-Cher sample (out of 285 communes) is skewed in favor of monuments costing more than 5,000 francs, and so if anything probably overrepresents sculptural monuments.

50. On the United States, see Kirk Savage, "The Politics of Memory: Black Emancipation and the Civil War Monument," in this volume; on New Zealand, see Chris Maclean and Jock Phillips, *The Sorrow and the Pride: New Zealand War Memorials* (Wellington: Historical Branch/GP Books, 1990), especially chapters 3 and 4.

51. Brochures and photographs in AM Vannes, 1 M 199. The Val d'Osne "Winged Victory" was one of its more expensive monuments, costing from 8,800

to 18,000 francs depending on the material, but it also offered a Richefeu poilu costing somewhat more (10,750 to 22,000 francs for the equivalent size) and a Pourquet poilu for rather less (5,300 to 11,000). The Marbreries Générales offered a wide range of prices, and for similar kinds of monuments poilus and female allegories went for similar prices.

52. On veterans' group pressure, see my "The Nation? In What Community."

53. M. Warner, *Monuments and Maidens: The Allegory of the Female Form* (London: Weidenfeld and Nicolson, 1985), pp. xix–xxi, 28.

54. On some female allegories in World War I memorials, see A. Becker, *Les monuments aux morts,* pp. 59–64, 73–75; Christiane Massonnet, "Patrimoine méconnu: La figure féminine dans les monuments aux morts de la guerre de 1914–18 dans les Bouches-du-Rhône," *Provence historique* 31 (1981), pp. 263–270.

55. Warner, *Monuments and Maidens,* p. 12.

56. Agulhon, *Marianne au pouvoir,* pp. 260–263.

57. ADV, 9T4-4, Maire to Préfet, 14 November 1924.

58. The name Place du Poilu is from a postcard, dated 1927, in the author's collection.

59. I have considered this issue in "Les inaugurations et la politique," in Philippe Rivé, Annette Becker, Olivier Pelletier, et al., eds., *Monuments de Mémoire: Les monuments aux morts de la Première Guerre Mondiale* (Paris: Mission Permanente aux Commémorations et à l'Information Historique, Secrétariat d'Etat aux Anciens Combattants, 1991)), pp. 277–281; see also Luirard, *La France et ses morts,* pp. 21–22, 39–74.

60. Warner, *Monuments and Maidens,* p. 32.

61. The monument is in Bacqueville (Seine-Maritime).

62. Robert Musil, "Denkmale," in *Nachlass su Lebzeiten* (Zurich, 1936), pp. 87–93, translated and cited in Warner, *Monuments and Maidens,* p. 21.

63. *Ouest-Républicain,* 8 June 1922 (on the inauguration of the monument in Cléguer).

PART FOUR

Politics of Memory and Identity

Chapter XI

BUILDING PASTS: HISTORIC PRESERVATION AND IDENTITY IN TWENTIETH-CENTURY GERMANY

Rudy J. Koshar

I

Gertrude Stein once wrote that "everything destroys itself in the twentieth century and nothing continues."[1] Stein was enthusiastic about the creative destructiveness of modern artists such as Picasso, but I think this statement could also serve as a fitting aphorism in discussing why modern public life so often consists of an anxious call for memory. One result of this anxiety is historic preservation, the maintenance, restoration, and recycling of buildings, districts, and townscapes that have commemorative value. A recurrent feature of European and North American cultural politics in the past two centuries, historic preservation, as both state practice and social movement, has been so influential in German-speaking lands that observers refer to a "cult of monuments." The twentieth-century genealogy of this term takes us back at least to 1905, when the Austrian art historian Alois Riegl used it, and well into the 1970s, when the Hessian conservator Reinhard Bentmann deployed it to criticize West German nostalgia.[2] The notion of a cult of monuments reveals a belief, held by observers and observed, that in Germany there has been an unusually strong interest in history and architectural heritage, a kind of special way (*Sonderweg*) for memory and the preoccupation with continuity.

The well-discussed controversy over whether Germany has a peculiar path through time that diverges in significant ways from Western history is undecidable.[3] Individuals, families, voluntary groups, and nations construct pasts that are by definition peculiar and unique, after all. Such pasts are also by definition inaccessible to the "other," even though, paradoxically, all individuals and collectivities are said to have pasts. Regardless of the position one takes on the issue, it is worth noting that asserting the existence of an indigenous and peculiar cult of monuments, as many Germans do, makes the absence of comprehensive historical discussions of the relation between the "micropolitics" of historic preservation—its daily discourse and practice—and modern German political culture in the twentieth century surprising if not perplexing.[4] But then there is no comprehensive scholarly work that discusses this connection for other Western or non-Western political cultures either.[5] Exploring such relationships is the goal of the larger project on which this speculative essay is based. The following brief remarks isolate a single strand from my research by discussing not what images of the past were created through preservation (although this is part of the research), but rather what contradictions the building of pasts generated.

The main title of this paper has a double meaning. Buildings "have" pasts because human beings create narratives that tell readers when a building was erected, what historical events it endured, who lived in it, and how it has been used. A large part of historic preservation consists of producing building-pasts. Yet it goes well beyond this. The already built environment, considered broadly as a changing ensemble of extant paths, edges, districts, nodes, and landmarks, has been a central referent in efforts to construct collective memories of neighborhood, voluntary association, generation, class, gender, or nation.[6] The point of using the built environment in this way has been to invent such identities, to stress the sameness of individuals who, because they are engaged in multiple social relations, are in fact marked by difference. This process consists of discursively using building-pasts to "build" those collective pasts that give continuity, stability, and familiarity to particular social configurations in particular historical contexts. And it consists of containing building-pasts that preservationists, states, and others find threatening or unsavory. It is, in other words, a process of creation *and* containment in which traces of the tensions and clashes of the larger political culture are indelibly present.

The argument of the following pages is that in Germany—and no doubt elsewhere—the process of building pasts has always been limited by what makes it possible, and that preservationists and their political allies have developed historically specific rhetorics to deal with what might be called the self-betrayal of this important form of cultural politics.

The notion of self-betrayal will become clearer when the historical examples are discussed. But it is worth emphasizing that it refers to the inherent instability of collective identity formation, to which preservation is inextricably tied and from which preservation inherits its own peculiar tensions. Richard Handler argues that social scientists as well as historical actors think of collective identity in terms of the same metaphors of boundedness and continuity that characterize personal identity.[7] But this proves to be unworkable as social practice as well as epistemology, in Handler's argument, because collective identity, like personal identity, falls victim to the logic of possessive individualism. In the West nations (or classes, or other social groups) are seen as collective individuals whose "essence" depends on the things they appropriate and "objectify" through display, performance, and preservation. These objects can of course include historic buildings and monuments. Yet there is no end to the process of appropriating things that demonstrate the identity of the possessor. Perpetual motion is needed to assert the unique and inviolable core of identity, to escape the nightmare of finding that the bounded individuals of native ideology and social scientific narrative are embedded in fragmented discursive relations rather than in irreducible and autonomous units. Nationalist discourse, or any cognate collective discourse, is constantly insecure, having a vision of "the integrity of the collectivity" as well as "a dark vision of national disintegration."[8] A desire for totality and continuity in nationalist rhetoric is bedeviled by "the negative vision that will not go away";[9] the bounded entity is unbounded by the very processes and artifacts that were to secure a stable identity. For Handler, nationalist insecurity is not a result of historical contingency, but rather a "function of the logic of possessive individualism" that inheres in all nationalist rhetorics of the modern West.[10]

In contrast to this last point, I would assert that the *form* of nationalist insecurity *is* dependent on historical contingency above all else, as the conclusion will reiterate. As useful as it has been to my conceptualization, Handler's view nonetheless potentially elides the specific metaphors and arguments used to express such insecurities. It overlooks why some insecurities are voiced at one moment and others are left unsaid or expressed only indirectly. Implicitly it leaves little room for discussing how different discourses of the same national political culture may "process" such anxieties in contrasting or even irreconcilable ways. I hope that my discussion of the self-betrayal of identity through the activity of architectural preservation in a single country will put back some of the historical specificity that Handler's argument potentially discounts. At the same time, I want to avoid making the assumption that so many scholars of the German *Sonderweg* make, namely that Germany was *essentially* different from France, Britain, or the United States.

II

I will construct three moments in the history of building pasts in twentieth-century Germany. The first of these deals in some detail with the two decades before World War I, whereas the other two consider the Nazi period (1933 to 1945) and the 1970s in a much more abbreviated format.

The preservation of historic monuments has ancient precedents, but the twenty years or so before the Great War are of particular importance for the present analysis.[11] Focused protection of historic monuments in the nineteenth century was a "child of historicism [and] a grandchild of Romanticism," to use the familial metaphors of the Bonn conservator Paul Clemen, and government inventories of historic landmarks had been published as early as 1870 in Bremen and Hesse-Kassel.[12] Nonetheless, it was from roughly 1890 to 1914 that specialized publications, tougher laws for regulating building and protecting historic sites, and the appearance of new voluntary associations signaled the creation of a wider preservationist public. The appearance in 1899 of *Die Denkmalpflege*, published by the Prussian state as Germany's first journal devoted entirely to historic preservation, and the holding of the first preservationist congress, the Tag für Denkmalpflege, in Dresden in 1900, punctuated and strengthened the new interest.[13]

Turn-of-the-century historic preservation emerged from a chain of impulses: the formation of new social and communications networks, the evolution of a cultural pessimism that criticized capitalist destructiveness, the development of new aesthetic concerns in urban planning, and the rise of a more popular "heritage industry" whose main product was the historic artifact and whose main consumers were the upper and middle classes. But one can sketch out this historical context more broadly. Historic preservation resulted partly from the need of Kaiser Wilhelm II and German elites to promote a political culture worthy of the global ambitions of the Reich, and partly from the need of the mainly Protestant, educated middle classes (*Bildungsbürgertum*) to legitimate themselves in an industrializing, urbanizing society that challenged their social position in the form of a socialist movement on the Left, political catholicism in the Center, and populist movements on the Right. The role of nationalism was crucial here. Nationalism was a "mirror" with which the socially disparate middle classes viewed themselves or, more aptly, framed themselves when there was no real frame. Historic preservation gained much of its legitimacy from a middle-class public that invented its role as collective steward of those "documents of stone," as *Die Denkmalpflege*'s editors put it, that traced a national genealogy.[14] To put it another way, the *Bürgertum* envisioned using history, in the form of disciplined study of the past and preservation of its architectural artifacts, to situate itself at the center of a cultural politics of national memory and the formation of emotional attachments to the idea of Germany. They wanted to create what Nora has called the "memory-nation."[15]

The social makeup of preservation groups reinforces this impression of a close association between the German state (at the Reich, federal [*Land*], and municipal levels) and the educated middle classes. At the 1901 congress of preservationists in Freiburg, for example, there were ninety official participants, twenty-seven of whom were Reich, federal, and municipal officials, and twenty-three of whom were university professors. The others were university students, architects and conservators, directors of archives and museums, artists and writers, and members of the free professions.[16] The most visible preservationists before World War I were academics, professionals, and officials: the Straßburg University art historian Georg

Dehio, the first conservator of the Prussian Rhine province and art historian Paul Clemen of Bonn, the already mentioned Alois Riegl, the building
official from Alsace-Lorraine Paul Tornow, and Bodo Ebhardt of Berlin, an
architect and associate of Wilhelm II who made a name as a restorer and
researcher of castle architecture and founder in 1899 of the well-heeled
Association for the Protection of German Castles.[17]

Significantly, all the official participants at the Freiburg conference were
males, although women, many of them spouses of the participants, often
attended lectures by noted architects or conservators as a part of the social
program of such conferences. This occurred in the first preservation congress in Dresden in 1900 when Bodo Ebhardt gave an evening lecture "for
women" on the conservation of German castles. Unlike the presentations
during the daytime sessions of the conference, this lecture featured no
discussion or question-and-answer period and thus was less "serious."[18]
Males predominated in local and provincial preservation societies too. In
the very active Rhenish Association for the Protection of Historic Sites and
Local Culture (Rheinischer Verein für Denkmalpflege und Heimatschutz,
or RVDH), founded in 1906, there were only 48 women in a membership
of 1,338 in 1916.[19] Of course, the issue of male dominance in historic
preservation societies goes well beyond this. The gender politics of preservation is linked to the problem of the relationship between national identity and bourgeois notions of respectability and sexuality. It is also connected to the more abstract but important issue of the "feminine"
characteristics of certain kinds of historic architecture. For instance, how
does one interpret male preservationists' activity in protecting historic
architecture such as a Gothic cathedral, whose crypt and apse could be
read as signs of a buried "feminine principle"?[20] The history of gender
relations and the protection of cultural heritage has yet to be written, and
any such discussion of the problem here would of course be highly speculative. Nonetheless, it is worth stressing the class and gender politics of
preservation as important bases and cognates of its nationalist rhetoric.

There was much confidence among fin-de-siècle preservationists (and
here the reference is mainly to official, or municipal and state-sponsored,
preservation). They felt they had made Germans finally pay heed, after
years of economic growth and crass materialism, to Bismarck's "golden
words" that it was "of greatest harm to a nation when it allows the living
consciousness of its connection to its heritage and history to fade," as the
lead editorial of the first edition of *Die Denkmalpflege* read in 1899.[21] Yet
instead of bringing about a consensus about how Germans could nurture
this living consciousness, historic preservation became the site of an intense debate among preservationists, city planners, architects, art historians, journalists, mayors, churches, and national and local cultural
officials.

The battle lines in such debates were dependent on the specific groups involved and the types of buildings that were to be protected or restored. The Prussian official von Bremen's address before the Freiburg congress suggested something of the breadth and depth of contention.[22] Surveying the development of preservation in Germany in comparison with other European states, von Bremen noted that "ideal" interests such as those represented by historic preservation were constantly struggling with "the great economic interests" that increasingly determined the tenor of German public being. He complained also that the "needs of practical life" constantly got in the way of heritage conservation. Church officials and congregations were notoriously guilty of overlooking the needs of preservation in their daily use of buildings and artifacts. Municipalities were no better, especially when it came to protecting objects such as medieval city walls. "Every conservator knows what kind of war we must conduct with local communities," said von Bremen of the walls, "in order to get them to save these symbols of ancient military bearing, these memories of true urban autonomy, these elements of picturesque beauty." The inability of conservators to get cities to protect historic landmarks aggressively would remain a leitmotif of preservationist criticism, as was clear in Clemen's address ten years later at the Salzburg congress, where the Bonn art historian referred to the Prussian state's "heroic error" of giving municipalities too much freedom to implement preservation legislation, a freedom that in Clemen's eyes resulted in weakened protection of monuments.[23] Comments such as von Bremen's and Clemen's reflected some of the central conflicts official preservation had with industry, the church, and municipal governments.

No less contentious were debates that originated within the fairly small circle of preservation groups but also engaged governments, newspapers, and the wider public. One of the most well-known debates featured disagreements between what may be called restorationists and conservationists. A function of the larger "crisis of historicism" that occurred in the human sciences and public culture in Europe in the second half of the nineteenth century, the controversy became particularly acute in German historic preservation in the two decades before 1914, when the possibility of restoration (*Wiederherstellung*) of such sites as the Heidelberg castle and the Hohkönigsburg, an Alsatian fortress, was fiercely debated.[24]

To caricature each position, restorationists wanted to return historic buildings to some version of their "original" or historical character, arguing that precise scientific study of the sources would enable them to reconstruct or "complete," as faithfully as possible, the building's authentic style and spirit. Historical authenticity was the goal, positivist methodology the process. Based on a very narrow definition of monuments, this mode of preservation was dominant in most of Europe throughout the nineteenth century. Conservationists also cherished historical authenticity and used positivist methods of research. But for them authenticity did not result from finding the "correct" style of a lost historical epoch or completing a monument according to some ideal notion of historical form, but from accepting the limitations of knowledge about that epoch and the buildings it generated, and thereby renouncing the attempt to restore a building to what they thought was a purely speculative and imagined authenticity. They favored the retention of historical additions because of their documentary value, claiming that this approach allowed a particular site to "speak" of the successive historical periods it had endured. The only reasonable goal was to maintain the building as it had been handed down to the present, to preserve it in this condition without intervening too radically, and then determining whether limited, site-specific restoration or improvement was possible only when it could be shown that this was absolutely necessary.

Of course, the complexities of each position depended on the building in question, the moment in which restoration was proposed or implemented, and the groups involved. There was no cut-and-dried relationship between one mode of preservation and particular occupations or political positions. In the Heidelberg controversy, in which Dehio opposed restoration by the Karlsruhe architect Karl Schäfer in favor of maintaining part of the castle as a ruin, the Straßburg professor argued that the restorationists were mainly architects, whereas the conservationists were art history scholars. But there were architects on both sides of the fence. A somewhat more defensible position is taken by Marion Wohlleben, who wrote that restoration was particularly favored by groups such as the conservative Prussian building officials (including architects) who published Die Denkmalpflege, which theoretically championed conservation (Erhaltung) but featured numerous articles and reports on restorationist practice. Thanks to the efforts of Dehio and the Dresden professor Cornelius Gurlitt, the preservation congresses became a more open forum than Die Denkmalpflege for debates on such issues and for support of conservation.[25]

There were of course other fronts. Dehio argued not only against the restorationists, but also against the (now) influential Viennese art historian Alois Riegl, whose writing implied that passive contemplation of a natural process of decline in historic environments was the only useful basis for preservation. Dehio had especially critical remarks for this approach, which seemed to replace nationalism with hedonism. Dehio believed in the documentary value of historic architecture, which he wanted to use to glorify past achievements of the German people (Volk), which, Dehio said, was his only hero.[26]

On another level, the participants in such debates saw eye to eye. All agreed that the *Bausubstanz,* the building substance of the artifact, was subject to irresistible destructive tendencies—urbanization, industrialization, faulty city planning, apathy, and bad preservation policies (including restoration as such or just inadequate restoration, depending on one's position). Significantly, this sense of threat was often expressed in medical metaphors, as when the engineering professor Landsberg wrote in 1910 of the "illness" (*Krankheit*) of historic buildings, or when a state conservator of the 1930s referred to preservationists as doctors for monuments (*Denkmalarzt*).[27] The "historical school" of restorationists met such illnesses by insisting on "pure" reconstructions in which the old could be not just preserved but rebuilt in the style of the historical age. Dehio and other conservationists placed little faith in the possibility of making past ages come alive again in new or rebuilt stone. Instead, they wanted to keep the patient alive as long as possible not through radical surgery but through preventive medicine that allowed for natural aging. But like the restorationists, they also focused on threats to the life of the artifact. Riegl's notion of "age value" (*Alterswert*), which led the observer to reflect on the natural decay of old buildings, was similarly informed by a sense of pervasive destruction.[28] In short, all preservationists, whether they were engaged in theoretical debates or daily practice, talked more of loss than of salvage, more of death than of life, more of forgetting than of remembering.

One can read the texts generated by such discussions *against* the claims of preservation's positive role in building national memory and identity. If one does, then the notion of *Bausubstanz* acts metaphorically because it may be likened to that national entity that is assumed to exist, but whose identity always eludes its protectors. The medical language of preservation intersects broadly with the notion of the nation as a remembering, living entity, and of cultural property as the objectified image of that entity. If the property, the *Bausubstanz,* can age and eventually pass away, then so too can the nation that derives its identity from remembering and maintaining the cultural heritage. The sickness of aging buildings refers to the sickness, real and potential, of the nation, which if it is not aged and forgetful now, will be so in the course of time.

In the light of such issues, preservationist discourse, couched either in technical language or moral argument, became an extended metaphor, an allegory, of irresolution. And this allegory in turn became the expression of a generalized middle-class and upper-class fear of the transient nature of the German nation, its vulnerability to enemies within and without, its constant exposure to the powers of forgetting, and its inability to compete in the global economic and political struggle of the age of imperialism.[29] The anxieties of the micropolitics of historic preservation thus became

compounded once they engaged the collective anxieties of German political culture.

III

My second example comes from the period of the National Socialist dictatorship, 1933 to 1945. It suggests that the kinds of conflicts and anxieties
I have been talking about were repeated in a quite different context, and
that this repetition led to a dramatic change in the positioning of preservationist discourse itself and the political uses to which it was put. This point
is perhaps a little unsurprising if the extraordinary conflicts of German
political history from 1914 to 1933 are kept in mind. But it is worth
making in light of scholarship's overdrawn continuities between the Imperial period, the Weimar Republic (1918–33), and the "Third Reich."[30]
Preservationists themselves experienced this period as one of unprecedented discontinuity. Sobered by the inability of wartime preservation to
protect historic architecture on the battlefields of France and Belgium,
threatened by the destruction of historic sites by the Bolsheviks after 1917,
and shocked by defeat in World War I, German preservationists entered the
Weimar Republic uncertain of the new democratic regime's support. Although this uncertainty was quickly dispelled as Weimar anchored heritage
protection in the constitution, preservationists labored under the burden of
shortened resources, inflation, economic depression, and political tension.
Nineteen thirty-three was seen as a release from such difficulties.[31]

In terms of government support, historic preservation had seldom seen
better times than in Nazi Germany.[32] Most historical studies have quite
legitimately focused on Hitler's grand schemes to rebuild Berlin and other
German cities.[33] But Nazi propagandists also claimed to love old buildings
and in fact devoted large sums of money to architectural preservation,
urban renewal projects, and related activities. Preservationists reciprocated
by quickly declaring their allegiance to the new regime, going so far as to
say that their language found its culmination in the language of Adolf
Hitler. Paul Clemen was only the most prominent example of a preservationist who spoke admiringly of Hitler's "deep empathy for the mysterious
magic of the world of monuments."[34]

Yet if there was such support, it had a much different political function
than it had before World War I. In Imperial Germany, preservation was the
result of an anxiety-ridden project of saving "documents of stone" whose
vulnerability left many Germans with an uneasy sense of the transiency of
the nation. In the "Third Reich," the regime worked to repress these anxieties, violently discharging them on internal and external "enemies"
through a politics of racism and militarism, and using a language of medi-

cal engineering that reduced human beings to germs that had to be eliminated from the collective body of the nation. The national body that appro-
priates cultural property and has an identity had been hardened by war and
political upheaval, and no enemy would stop it from possessing and "becoming" who its national soul said it was. If the nation was vulnerable, its
response would not be irresolution, but a violent forgetting of the fleeting-
ness of all political relations. And if the *Bausubstanz,* the artifactual referent of collective memory, was prone to decay, then the regime, and specifically Albert Speer, would see to it that monuments would be created with a
"ruin value" that intimidated later generations in ways that hitherto existing buildings had not. Indeed the "theory" of ruin value encapsulates much
about Nazism's violent fear of time. The regime's architecture would be
built so that it would resemble Roman models after centuries had passed, a
goal that meant "a considerable increase in the amount of material used
because the walls would have to be massive if they were to continue to
stand once the supporting effect of roofs and ceilings were removed."[35]
More than a concern for later generations' right to have a memory, which
was a key point of preservationist theory if not always of practice, the
theory of ruin value projected Nazi monumentalism far into the future
in a way that obliterated the sense of history on which preservation was
founded.

If the regime's use of historic environments differed from that of the
Imperial period, then so too did preservation's placement in the new political order. The changing political significance of preservation gave older
conflicts new meanings within professional discourse. Debates over the
objects and practices of preservation persisted, although of course projects
that had the direct stamp of regime approval such as urban rebuilding
schemes were not submitted to the same critical scrutiny as were the standard tasks of restoring cathedrals and castles. But now the debates were
opportunities for a kind of "unintended subversion" that resisted the regime's attempt to control all aspects of professional and daily life.[36] If
historic preservation's disagreements with property owners or city admin-
istrations continued, then this pointed to the immunity of certain areas of
public life to the racial harmony of the new revolution. If certain persistent
issues were technically undecidable (for instance, what was the best way to
save the Cologne cathedral from the deleterious effects of urban pollu-
tion?),[37] then this suggested important limits not only on the public's desire
to have clear-cut answers, but also on the Nazi state's ability to regiment
cultural politics completely. What before 1914 had been an attempt by
preservationists to integrate protection of historic property in the dominant political culture of Imperial Germany became, after 1933, an attempt
to limit the full instrumentalization of historic preservation while still

ensuring its placement in the regime's cultural politics. Elsewhere I have referred to preservation's attempt to establish what might be called a privileged marginality in the "Third Reich."[38] Historic preservation was privileged because it remained an established goal of the regime's cultural policy, but it was marginal because it exercised little real control over how the regime used historic environments for political goals. What preservation's privileged marginality did was to set limits, but not to formulate larger political objectives. This was one of the subtexts of the Breslau professor Dagobert Frey's 1936 remark made on the occasion of the Prussian conservator Robert Hiecke's sixtieth birthday, duly celebrated in the most influential preservationist journal. Frey made the widely accepted argument that historic preservation in Germany had no "catechism." "The ultimate wisdom is that here there is no dogmatism," said Frey. "The way of the conservator is no well-worn byway" but a "small path" along which the conservator moves "searching and testing" and discovering, finally, that historic preservation is "a matter of character."[39] Delivered as an observation on the state conservator's need for a difficult autonomy in the face of competing claims and related to a German bourgeois discourse of "personality," this statement could also be read to suggest that in the practice of protecting historic buildings—an activity without catechism or dogmatism that came down to an instinctive feel for artifacts that only the person of "character" could develop—there was some indefinable element that escaped political totality, that could not be produced by political maneuver.

The implication of such unintended subversion for questions of heritage and identity is clear. In the Nazi regime, the self-subverting aspects of historic preservation persisted, and conservators and their publics insisted on the need to have some autonomy in making difficult choices as to what cultural property should be protected and how it should be protected. Yet in the new context of the "Third Reich," the hesitant practices and fine distinctions of preservation frustrated the regime's goal of total, irreducible identity even more than the Imperial and Weimar periods' less ambitious political-cultural policies had been frustrated. As the regime demanded more of historic preservation, the shortcomings and tensions of heritage became more glaring, even as preservationists declared their loyalty to the national revolution. This was certainly one of the reasons for the chief Nazi propagandist Joseph Goebbels's perverse pleasure in the World War II bombing of Germany's cities. Goebbels said such cultural artifacts were remnants of an "old and used up past" that had to be destroyed if the Nazi revolution was to take place.[40] On the other hand, the inadequacies of cultural property kept its stewards from being completely exploited and represented one effective if unintentional defense against Nazism for his-

toric preservation. The "Third Reich" revealed some of the positive qualities of self-subversion.

IV

The third example is no more than an epilogue. It is taken from West
Germany in the 1970s, a moment when the inherited language of preservation underwent yet another substantial rupture.[41] By the early 1970s, West
Germans had gone through two phases of postwar rebuilding, each with
implications for the fate of historic environments.[42] In the first phase, from
the end of the war until roughly the mid-1950s, restorative and traditional
tendencies prevailed in architecture and planning, though not without
considerable ambivalence, and many badly destroyed German cities and
historic districts reappeared in a form that gave them something of their
pre–World War II character. In the second phase, however, from the
mid-1950s until the early 1970s, extravagant plans for economic growth
and the building of new housing, a modified modernist architecture, and
traffic-oriented urban planning were dominant.

In the third phase—von Beyme and others use 1973 as the starting
date—the energy crisis, growing dissatisfaction with the failures of the
second phase of rebuilding, and a downturn in the building industry starting in 1973–74 redirected attention to historic buildings and town centers
as symbols of bygone ages or as useful fields of investment. In addition, a
growing environmentalist consciousness revived earlier connections between nature conservation and architectural preservation, as half-timber
houses and Gothic cathedrals were thought of (misleadingly, because they
are nonrenewable) as scarce resources in the same fashion that forest lands
and undeveloped swamps were. The rise of postmodern architecture,
which valued playful (and often intentionally superficial) historical citation and the adaptation of new building to surrounding contexts, furthered
the interest in historic architecture, though not always with results that
were satisfying to preservationists or the general public.[43] An additional
factor was the maturation of a postwar generation that felt embittered
about their parents' inability to "come to terms" (if that is possible) with
the history of Nazism, the war, and the extermination camps. This generation equated the second phase of rebuilding with the insensitive forgetfulness of their parents, whose wish to be prosperous and forget the past
found abundant symbolic expression in the modernist high-rises or department stores that punctuated historic city districts throughout the Federal
Republic.

Although the fate of historic architecture differed during each phase and
depended on local constellations of tradition and power, by the third phase
of rebuilding the entire period from 1945 to the mid-1970s was seen by

many West Germans to have been one of unprecedented destruction of historic places. By 1976, 38 percent of West Germans felt too little had been done to protect historic architecture. This figure fell to 32 percent by 1979, but it reflected substantial interest in such matters among population groups that were generally more influential than the "disinterested two-thirds" who were not concerned about the loss of historic places. There was good reason for such dissatisfaction, because during the thirty years after the end of the war the percentage of the building stock dating from before 1840 had in fact fallen from 27 to 15. The result of dissatisfaction was extraordinary: at the end of the 1970s, nearly one in twelve buildings in the Federal Republic was considered to have some historical value, which amounted to about eight hundred thousand structures.[44]

This shift in sensibility had profound effects on historic preservation, which in turn helped to shape such attitudes. The rather elitist character of preservation—it had after all been a matter of "the cultured," the *Gebildeten*—gave way to a more pluralistic public that included upper middle, lower middle, and working classes. The work of established preservation societies and state agencies continued, though not without response to new urbanistic and ecological concerns. In 1970, for example, the RVDH, having operated more or less continuously since 1906, dropped the term *Heimatschutz* from its name after merging with another preservation society the previous year and adopted the more politically anodyne (because it was not associated with Nazi uses) and environmentally correct *Landschaftsschutz,* to become the Rhenish Association for the Protection of Historic and Natural Sites (RVDL).[45] Such established groups were now increasingly challenged by citizens' initiatives, which were small, often temporary networks oriented toward specific projects rather than broader or more continuous agendas. Numbering perhaps fifty thousand and including around two million participants by the end of the 1970s,[46] some initiatives dealt specifically with architecture and planning, aiming to protect local monuments from "development" or trying to resurrect the history of a neglected or forgotten part of the built environment. In Bonn, the *General Anzeiger* noted in April 1980 that citizens' initiatives had grown like "mushrooms" in the capital city in the previous fifteen years.[47] Of those groups concerned with the built environment and conservation, one of the oldest was an association of people working solely to pressure the city council to have a proposed main traffic artery go underground through the city and to have another routed around the city center. Formed in 1969 with the sonorous title of Work Group for the Underground Highway and By-Pass Highway, it claimed to have 350 members but was more or less the one-man operation of a retired engineer, Hermann Disselbeck. Another group, the Association for the Conservation of the Historic Townscape, had just twelve members. Its goal was to uphold the "original character" of the Bonn city center. Working closely with the RVDL and Bonn local history societies, group members, whom the local newspaper described as "professors, architects, lawyers, historians, and geographers," insisted they wanted to be a small group that worked intensively rather than extensively. The small membership could be misleading: the association once collected forty-five hundred signatures in a petition drive to save a historic café.

The approaches to building pasts of such groups varied widely. Because some of the new groups worked closely with established preservation societies and government agencies, they shared a more conservative view of historic places that put emphasis on grand public architecture rather than on vernacular building and urban districts. They thought of historic places in terms of the notion of identity already discussed. For those groups that took a more oppositional stance, however, different objects and different view of the past figured prominently.[48] In the case of the art historian and conservationist Roland Günter, the leading representative of the first citizens' initiative of the 1970s to protect nineteenth-century workers' settlements in the Ruhr, for instance, preservation had definite critical overtones. Writing in 1975 about his efforts to save Eisenheim, a small settlement near Oberhausen begun in 1844 for foundry workers, Günter argued there was "no absolute historicity, but only a relative one—it is the historicity of contingent interests."[49] The Eisenheim workers' initiative was now finally entering a field that hitherto had been reserved for elites. "Nobility, the church, the upper Bürgertum have for a long time made use of their right to history," wrote Günter. "That in a democracy the right to history, that is the right to preservation of one's own historic sites, is still fundamentally withheld from a majority of people, is a scandal." But this could not be a form of preservation based on "status objects" and the representation of prestige—did not Günter mean the historic preservation of Dehio, Clemen, and Ebhardt?—instead it must be based on use and social relations. In a settlement such as Eisenheim, people became "second architects." They went from being objects of the company that built the houses to being subjects who put their own stamp on their dwellings by remodeling them or making gardens and workshops. Günter quoted Walter Benjamin, who said living "means leaving traces behind." These traces, or *Spuren*, as well as the actual living quarters of the inhabitants, were the stakes. Günter's project aimed at giving ordinary people, however they were defined, the right to "see" their past in the built environment, to "image" their social heritage by preserving its traces, and actively to create and re-create the built contexts of their memory.

Such activities were paralleled and shaped by a change in thinking about how monuments were conceptualized within official preservation circles. For much of the twentieth century, preservationists protected a fairly constricted number of monuments on the basis of artistic and national-historical criteria. Although these criteria were by no means irrelevant by the 1970s, social concerns such as those voiced by Günter now broadened the view. At the same time, the differences between historic artifacts and copies diminished, as reconstructions of historic houses were increasingly popular.[50] All of this resulted in the possibility that an unprecedented amount of heritage could be "produced," either by expanding definitions of historic monuments to more and more objects, or by reconstructing artifacts so that copies of historic places took the place of originals. And this in turn led to greater disagreement, as government conservators complained they and their staffs were overtaxed by new demands on their resources, city officials and journalists debated how or whether particular historic sites should be protected or reconstructed, tourists clamored for more and better historic sites to consume, and social groups such as citizens' initiatives formed, dissolved, and formed again to advocate protection of an array of objects. Always an area of lively debate, historic preservation in the 1970s had become more contentious than ever before.

By the late 1960s and early 1970s West German political identity had come to depend on Bonn's integration with the West, the "Eastern politics" of Willy Brandt, and a social-economic dynamism that forsook intense expressions of nationalism in favor of productivity and material comfort.[51] Yet just as this stability was achieved, it began to unravel, as the 1970s saw increasing doubt about West Germany's international alliances and economic standing. National identity is based on the decentering and suppression of other, "non-national" identities, whether those of region, class, neighborhood, or gender.[52] To put it somewhat bluntly, when the earlier consensus unraveled, it unintentionally opened a social and political space in which non-national identities could operate more visibly. Preservationism's close association with the formation of national identity meant it could not escape this development, particularly since its own internal dynamic responded to and shaped the larger fragmentation of national identity. When Georg Dehio said in 1918 that his true hero and audience was the German *Volk*,[53] he had in mind a singular and homogeneous people that recognized, or should recognize, itself in historic monuments. West German preservationists of the 1970s either did not use the term or used it guardedly, as the larger culture did, preferring instead terms such as *Bürger,* which suggested plurality and heterogeneity. In effect, a denationalization of collective memory had occurred. Nonetheless, if preservation had become more contentious and varied, more open to voices other than those of the university-educated, upper-middle-class, nation-thinking males who had dominated activity for so long, its proponents still argued that one could manipulate building-pasts to build the kinds of collective pasts discussed in this piece. Leaders of established societies or government agencies persisted in thinking of German nationhood as something that existed prior to or "underneath" the discursive relations that created such entities and gave them coherence and meaning. Citizens' initiatives continued to operate as if the district, neighborhood, class, or "ordinary people" they were protecting had a bounded and coherent quality independent from the social-linguistic interactions that produced them—Günter's comments on historicity notwithstanding. And because such groups could never produce enough cultural property to stabilize identity on a permanent basis, their ultimate goals were structurally deferred, out of reach. If heritage preservation had become more popular and more "social," it had also inherited the frustrations and intrinsic subversions of such activity. Protecting artifacts was now an allegory not only for the collective irresolutions of national identity, but for those of class, regional, and other identities as well. The conditions that made historic preservation possible served to point to the limitations of a practice whose goal was fixedness, identity, and collective memory. The self-betrayal of building pasts had now been democratized.

V

The argument of this essay has been that the micropolitics of historic preservation in Germany subverted the larger political goal of building pasts, which was the "imaging" of national continuity, stability, and identity in the built environment. The language and practice of preservation pointed to conflict, transitoriness of the built world, and irresolution, making the possibility of this form of cultural politics an insurmountable obstacle to its broader goals. It is useful to explore this relationship in areas such as collecting, museum building, or the staging of folklore, as in Richard Handler's work. But the central point—and this is something that, I think, is often missed in many anthropological studies—is that this is a dynamic, changing relationship; it assumes historically specific forms that depended on numerous layers of political interaction, numerous permutations of the political culture. Therefore, it may be useful to deploy terms such as "constitutive negation," whereby concepts such as identity are subverted by being posited.[54] But one has to explore those concepts by constructing specific historic contexts. Otherwise, we forget that practices such as the formation of collective memory *are* social practices whose outcomes are unpredictable and whose language depends entirely on an endless, broken chain of experience and anticipation.

To say the least, the foregoing suggests a critical perspective on the attempts of any group to create something as elusive as collective identity, and it is skeptical about scholars' deployment of analytical categories that deal with such problems in anything more than a provisional way. But it does not suggest doing away with notions of collective memory, history, and identity, at least not for conducting scholarly research on nineteenth- and twentieth-century Western history, the homeland of such concepts. Instead, the implication of the argument is that historical actors as well as scholars need a more self-consciously reflective language that underscores the subjective nature of their practice, the limits on their understanding, and the nontransferability of such concepts to peoples, times, and places whose central historical experience has included other, less "Western" notions of individual and group identity. Writing of his work in twentieth-century ethnography, James Clifford has said that "ultimately my topic is a pervasive condition of off-centeredness in a world of distinct meaning systems, a state of being in culture while looking at culture, a form of personal and collective self-fashioning."[55] The foregoing suggests that in the West native ideologues as well as scholars would do well to consider the problem of identity formation from "off-center." If they did, their political agitation or scholarly work would *begin* by positing the dynamic and creative futility of saying "we." Perhaps such off-centeredness would save lives if it served to defuse conflict in a situation in which states or ethnic groups defended what seemed to be absolutely irreconcilable collective positions. At the least, it might produce more nuanced and lively scholarly analyses that understand the special privileges of provisionality.

NOTES

1. Quoted in Stephen Kern, *The Culture of Time and Space 1880–1918* (Cambridge: Harvard University Press, 1983), 311.

2. Alois Riegl, "Der moderne Denkmalkultus: Sein Wesen und seine Entstehung," in idem, *Gesammelte Aufsätze* (Augsburg and Vienna: Filser, 1928); Reinhard Bentmann, "Die Kampf um die Erinnerung. Ideologische und methodische Konzepte des modernen Denkmalkultus," in *Denkmalräume-Lebensräume*, ed. Ina-Maria Greverus (Giessen: Schmitz Verlag, 1976).

3. The literature on the subject is voluminous. For a recent concise discussion of it, see Charles S. Maier, *The Unmasterable Past: History, Holocaust, and German National Identity* (Cambridge, MA, and London: Harvard University Press, 1988), esp. chap. 4. But note also the results of the debate, which were quite different on either side of the Atlantic, as discussed in Michael Geyer and Konrad H. Jarausch, "The Future of the German Past: Transatlantic Reflections for the 1990s," *Central European History* 22, 3/4 (September/December, 1989): 229–259, here 239–241.

4. The best sources for fragments of the history of German historic preservation are the journals *Die Alte Stadt* (hereafter DAS; formerly *Zeitschrift für Stadtgeschichte, Stadtsoziologie, und Denkmalpflege*) and *Deutsche Kunst und Denkmalpflege* (hereafter DKD). For more examples and literature, see Klaus von Beyme, *Der Wiederaufbau. Architektur und Städtebaupolitik in beiden deutschen*

Staaten (Munich and Zurich: Piper, 1987), chap. 9; Michael Brix, ed., *Lübeck: Die Altstadt als Denkmal* (Munich: Heinz Moos Verlag, 1975); Werner Durth and Niels Gutschow, eds., *Architektur und Städtebau der Fünfziger Jahre* (Bonn: Deutsches Nationalkomittee für Denkmalschutz, 1990); Peter Findeisen, *Geschichte der Denkmalpflege Sachsen-Anhalt: Von den Anfängen bis zum Neubeginn* (Berlin: Verlag von Bauwesen, 1990); Norbert Huse, ed., *Denkmalpflege. Deutsche Texte aus drei Jahrhunderten* (Munich: Beck, 1984); Rudy J. Koshar, "Altar, Stage, and City: Historic Preservation and Urban Meaning in Nazi Germany," *History & Memory* 3 (Spring 1991): 30–59; Heinrich Magirius, *Geschichte der Denkmalpflege Sachsen: Von den Anfängen bis zum Neubeginn 1945* (Berlin: Verlag von Bauwesen, 1989); Ekkehard Mai and Stephan Wätzoldt, eds., *Kunstverwaltung, Bau- und Denkmal-Politik im Kaiserreich* (Berlin: Mann, 1981); Cord Meckseper and Harald Siebenmorgen, eds., *Die alte Stadt: Denkmal oder Lebensraum?* (Göttingen: Vandenhoeck & Ruprecht, 1985); Uwe K. Paschke, *Die Idee des Stadtdenkmals* (Nuremberg: Hans Carl Verlag, 1972); Rheinischer Verein für Denkmalpflege und Landschaftsschutz, ed., *Erhalten und gestalten: 75 Jahre Rheinischer Verein für Denkmalpflege und Landschaftsschutz* (Neuss: Gesellschaft für Buchdruckerei, 1981); Michael Siegel, *Denkmalpflege als öffentliche Aufgabe: Eine ökonomische, institutionelle, und historische Untersuchung* (Göttingen: Vandenhoeck & Ruprecht, 1985); Winfried Speitkamp, "Denkmalpflege und Heimatschutz in Deutschland zwischen Kulturkritik und Nationalsozialismus," *Archiv für Kulturgeschichte* 70, 1 (1988): 149–193.

5. That there is abundant evidence for doing so is suggested by the detail contained in David Lowenthal, *The Past Is a Foreign Country* (Cambridge: Cambridge University Press, 1985). See also Lowenthal's contribution to this volume. For a more theoretically pointed discussion of issues pertaining to this problem, see Patrick Wright, *On Living in an Old Country: The National Past in Contemporary Britain* (London: Verso, 1985). For recent commentary on such issues from the point of view of cultural sociology, see Wilfried Lipp, "Was ist kulturell bedeutsam? Überlegungen aus der Sicht der Denkmalpflege," 189–214, and Michael Petzet, "Denkmalpflege und Kulturpolitik," 215–235, both in *Kulturpolitik: Standorte, Innensichten, Entwürfe,* ed. Wolfgang Lipp (Berlin: Dietrich Reimer Verlag, 1989). See also Jan Assmann and Tonio Hölscher, eds., *Kultur und Gedächtnis* (Frankfurt am Main: Suhrkamp, 1988).

6. For the definition of the built environment, see Kevin Lynch, *The Image of the City* (Cambridge, MA, and London: MIT Press, 1960), chap. 3. For the built environment, memory, and sense of time, see Lynch, *What Time Is This Place?* (Cambridge, MA, and London: MIT Press, 1972). See also J.B. Jackson, *The Necessity for Ruins* (Amherst: University of Massachusetts Press, 1980).

7. For the following, see Richard Handler, *Nationalism and the Politics of Culture in Quebec* (Madison: University of Wisconsin Press, 1988), chap. 1. See also Handler's contribution to this volume.

8. Handler, *Nationalism and the Politics of Culture in Quebec,* 6.

9. Ibid., 194.

10. Ibid.

11. Note Kern, *The Culture of Time and Space,* 38–40, for brief remarks on turn-of-the-century historic preservation.

12. Clemen made his remarks as one of two discussants on a panel entitled "Entwicklung und Ziele der Denkmalpflege in Deutschland und Österreich" at the 1911 Salzburg congress for historic preservation, as recorded in *Gemeinsame Tagung für Denkmalpflege und Heimatschutz. Salzburg 14. und 15. September 1911. Stenographischer Bericht* (Berlin: Wilhelm Ernst & Sohn, 1911), 61.

13. For a fuller discussion and bibliography, see Koshar, "Altar, Stage, and City." For general background, see also Stefan Muthesius, "The Origins of the German Conservation Movement," in *Planning for Conservation*, ed. Roger Kain (New York: St. Martin's, 1980). *Die Denkmalpflege* (hereafter DP) is the distant predecessor of the DKD (see note 4). For a statement of the DP's mission, see Otto Sarrazin and Oskar Hoßfeld, "Zur Einführung," DP 1 (4 Jan. 1899): 1–2.

14. For the nineteenth-century German *Bürgertum* see David Blackbourn, "The Discreet Charm of the Bourgeoisie: Reappraising German History in the Nineteenth Century," in idem and Geoff Eley, *The Peculiarities of German History: Bourgeois Society and Politics in Nineteenth-Century Germany* (Oxford and New York: Oxford University Press, 1984), as well as *Bürgertum im 19. Jahrhundert. Deutschland im europäischen Vergleich*, 3 vols., ed. Jürgen Kocka (Munich: Deutscher Taschenbuch Verlag, 1988); on the heritage industry, see Robert Hewison, *The Heritage Industry: Britain in a Climate of Decline* (London: Methuen, 1987); on the cultural aspirations of the Imperial German state under Wilhelm II, see Ulrich Scheuner, "Die Kunst als Staatsaufgabe im 19. Jahrhundert," in Mai and Wätzoldt, *Kunstverwaltung*, 13–46; on the middle classes and nationalism, Eric Hobsbawm, "Mass-Producing Traditions: Europe, 1870–1914," in idem and Terence Ranger, *The Invention of Tradition* (Cambridge: Cambridge University Press, 1983); on "documents of stone," see Sarrazin and Hoßfeld, "Zur Einführung," 1.

15. Pierre Nora, "Between Memory and History: *Les Lieux de Mémoire*," *Representations* 26 (Spring 1989): 11. This article is the translation of the introduction to a rather extravagent and nostalgic multivolume project on French national memory edited by Nora. See his *Les lieux de mémoire*, 2 vols. (Paris: Gallimard, 1984, 1986). Additional volumes are being prepared. See also the discussion of Nora's work by Steven Englund, "The Ghost of Nation Past," *Journal of Modern History* 64, 2 (June 1992): 299–320.

16. This information is based on my analysis of "Liste der Teilnehmer," *Zweiter Tag für Denkmalpflege. Freiburg im Breisgau 23. und 24. September 1901. Stenographischer Bericht* (Karlsruhe: Chr. Fr. Müller'sche Hofbuchdruckerei, 1901), 3–5. Conservators and directors of archives and museums were also civil servants.

17. On Dehio and Riegl, see Marion Wohlleben, "Vorwort," in Georg Dehio and Alois Riegl, *Konservieren, nicht restaurieren: Streitschriften zur Denkmalpflege um 1900* (Braunschweig and Wiesbaden: Fried. Vieweg & Sohn, 1988), 7–33; on Clemen, see Hans Peter Hilger, "Paul Clemen und die Denkmäler-Inventarisation in den Rheinlanden," in Mai and Wätzoldt, *Kunstverwaltung*, 383–398; on Ebhardt, see the entry for him in *Neue Deutsche Biographie* 4 (Berlin: Duncker & Humblot, 1957): 260–261. Ebhardt's association, which still exists today, attracted a veritable who's who of the German elite. See the membership listed in Vereinigung zur Erhaltung deutscher Burgen, Einladung zur Teilnahme an der Festversammlung deutscher Burgenfreunde, Marksburg bei

Braubach a. Rhein, 10 Juni 1906, in Nordrhein-Westfälisches Hauptstaatsarchiv Düsseldorf-Kalkum, Regierungs-Präsident-Büro, Aachen, 980.

18. Clemen referred to Ebhardt's talk in *Zweiter Tag für Denkmalpflege 1901,* 112.

19. My data is based on "Verzeichnis der Mitglieder," *Mitteilungen des Rheinischen Verein für Denkmalpflege und Heimatschutz* (hereafter MRVDH) 10, 3 (1916): 387–433. The exclusion of women from the ranks of architectural preservationists was not just a German proclivity but was also typical of the movement in the United States during this period. See Gail Lee Dubrow, "Restoring a Female Presence: New Goals in Historic Preservation," in *Architecture: A Place for Women,* ed. Ellen Perry Berkeley and Matilda McQuaid (Washington and London: Smithsonian Institution Press, 1989), 159–170.

20. On nineteenth-century categorizations of architecture into "masculine" and "feminine," see Miriam Gusevich, "Purity and Transgression: Reflections on the Architectural Avantgarde's Rejection of Kitsch," *Discourse* 10, 1 (Fall-Winter 1987–88): 100–101. On the Gothic cathedral and the feminine principle, see Mimi Lobell, "The Buried Treasure: Women's Ancient Architectural Heritage," in *Architecture: A Place for Women,* 143.

21. Sarrazin and Hoßfeld, "Zur Einführung," 1. The editors paraphrased Bismarck's remarks.

22. Von Bremen's comments appear in *Zweiter Tag für Denkmalpflege 1901,* 16.

23. Clemen, "Entwicklung und Ziele," 56.

24. On the crisis of historicism, see George G. Iggers, *The German Conception of History: The National Tradition of Historical Thought from Herder to the Present,* rev. ed. (Middletown, CT: Wesleyan University Press, 1983), chaps. 6, 7; for a more general perspective taking the issue into the twentieth century, Gunter Scholtz, "Das Historismusproblem und die Geisteswissenschaften im 20. Jahrhundert," *Archiv für Kulturgeschichte* 71, 2 (1989): 463–486; for historicism and the built environment, see Michael Brix and Monika Steinhauser, eds., *'Geschichte allein ist zeitgemäss': Historismus in Deutschland* (Lahn-Giessen: Anabas Verlag, 1978); on Hohkönigsburg, see the debates occasioned by Ebhardt's talk in *Zweiter Tag für Denkmalpflege 1901,* 101–118; on Heidelberg, see Dehio's polemic against restoration in *Was wird aus dem Heidelberger Schloß werden?* (Strassburg: Karl J. Trübner Verlag, 1901, as reprinted in Dehio and Riegl, *Konservieren, nicht restaurieren,* 34–42.

25. For Dehio's remarks on architects, *Was wird aus dem Heidelberger Schloß werden?* 35–36; the point about the DP and preservation congresses is made by Marion Wohlleben in "Vorwort," 9.

26. On Riegl, besides his "Der moderne Denkmalkultus," see Kurt W. Forster, "Monument/Memory and the Mortality of Architecture," *Oppositions* 25 (Fall 1982): 2–19, and Henri Zerner, "Alois Riegl: Art, Value, Historicism," *Daedalus* 105, 1 (Winter 1976): 177–188. On the differences between Dehio and Riegl and Dehio's portrayal of the German *Volk* as hero, see Wohlleben, "Vorwort," 11–14 and 24, respectively.

27. Th. Landsberg, "Aufgaben des Ingenieurs bei der Erhaltung der Baudenkmäler," DP 12, 5 (20 April 1910): 35; on doctors of monuments, see Dagobert

Frey, "Der Denkmalpfleger: Robert Hiecke zum sechzigsten Geburtstage," DKD 38, 10 (1936): 297.

28. Riegl, "Der moderne Denkmalkultus," esp. 160–165.

29. For a general perspective, see Wolfgang Hardtwig, "Bürgertum, Staatssymbolik und Staatsbewußtsein im Deutschen Kaiserreich 1871–1914," *Geschichte und Gesellschaft* 16, 3 (1990): 269–295.

30. A most sophisticated discussion of the continuity issue and the Weimar Republic may be found in Detlev Peukert, *Die Weimarer Republik: Krisenjahre der Klassischen Moderne* (Frankfurt am Main: Suhrkamp, 1987), esp. 13–31, now translated as *The Weimar Republic: The Crisis of Classical Modernity*, trans. Richard Deveson (New York: Hill and Wang, 1992).

31. This is a radically compressed summary of preservationist responses to Weimar and the rise of Nazism based on many sources. However, see Paul Clemen, *Die Deutsche Kunst und die Denkmalpflege: Ein Bekenntnis* (Berlin: Deutscher Kunstverlag, 1933), which features lectures and essays written by the Bonn conservator from 1908 to 1933, and which discusses all of the issues mentioned in this paragraph.

32. Bentmann, "Kampf um die Erinnerung," 215. See also Koshar, "Altar, Stage, and City"; Speitkamp, "Denkmalpflege und Heimatschutz"; for an example of local activity in the period, see Joseph Schlippe, "Die Erhaltung des alten und Gestaltung des neuen Freiburg," in *Der Breisgau*, Jahresband Oberrheinische Heimat, vol. 28, ed. Hermann Eris Busse (Freiburg: Haus Badische Heimat, 1941), 378–400; see also *Tag für Denkmalpflege und Heimatschutz Dresden 1936. Tagungsbericht* (Berlin: Deutscher Kunstverlag, 1938). For a statement of preservation's popularity and regime support, see Hans Hörmann, "Ein Nestor Deutscher Denkmalpflege," DKD 37, 10 (1935): 248, which was a celebration of the preservationist Josef Schmitz's seventy-fifth birthday.

33. Joachim Petsch, *Baukunst und Stadtplanug im Dritten Reich* (Munich and Vienna: Hanser, 1976); Ursula v. Petz, *Stadtsanierung im Dritten Reich* (Dortmund: Informationskreis für Raumplanung, 1987).

34. Nazism's public support of historic preservation is best seen in the articles and photography of *Die Kunst im Deutschen Reich*, edited by Albert Speer from 1937, and appearing in Ausgabe B, *Die Kunst im Deutschen Reich: Die Baukunst*, from 1939. On Clemen's praise of Hitler, see *Die Deutsche Kunst*, viii. For another example portraying Nazism as the culmination of preservation's goals, see Braunschweig Professor F. Hermann Flesche's "Sanierung der Altstadt in Braunschweig," DKD 36, 4 (1934): 78–80.

35. Berthold Hinz, *Art in the Third Reich*, trans. Robert and Rita Kimber (New York: Pantheon, 1979), 197.

36. The concept derives from Michel de Certeau, *The Practice of Everyday Life*, trans. Steven Rendall (Berkeley and Los Angeles: University of California Press, 1984).

37. On conservators' conflicts with the public, see for a very specific example the letter from Provinzialkonservator der Rheinprovinz, Bonn, to Regierungs-Präsident, Aachen, 11 December 1936, in Nordrhein-Westfälisches Hauptstaatsarchiv Düsseldorf, Regierungspräsident Aachen, 16819, which includes the conservator Metternich's criticism of a property owner's planned remodeling of a historic

facade in Aachen. On the Cologne cathedral, note that the 1930 preservation congress was held in Cologne and much of the proceeding revolved around problems of protecting the cathedral's fragile structure. See *Tag für Denkmalpflege und Heimatschutz Köln 1930* (Berlin: Deutscher Kunstverlag, 1931). These debates preceded the 1930 congress by at least two decades, persisted throughout the era of the Nazi dictatorship, and continue today.

38. See Koshar, "Altar, Stage, and City," 45–49.

39. Frey, "Der Denkmalpfleger," 297.

40. See the discussion of Goebbels and quotes in Manfred Bültemann, *Architektur für das Dritte Reich: Die Akademie für Deutsche Jugendführung in Braunschweig* (Berlin: Ernst & Sohn, 1986), 38.

41. The case of East Germany must be left aside in this article, but it is important to point out that despite many differences there were also surprising similarities in the tempo and character of rebuilding in the two German states after World War II, as demonstrated in von Beyme, *Der Wiederaufbau*, esp. chap. 12. For examples of East German preservation, see Institut für Denkmalpflege, ed., *Denkmale der Geschichte und Kultur. Ihre Erhaltung und Pflege in der DDR* (Berlin: Henschel-Verlag, 1976); and Institut für Denkmalpflege, Arbeitstelle Berlin, ed., *Denkmale in Berlin und in der Mark Brandenburg* (Weimar: Hermann Böhlaus, 1988).

42. For the following periodization, von Beyme, *Der Wiederaufbau*, is enormously useful. See also von Beyme et al., eds., *Neue Städte aus Ruinen: Deutscher Städtebau der Nachkriegszeit* (Munich: Prestel, 1992); Jürgen Paul, "Der Wiederaufbau der historischen Städte in Deutschland nach dem Zweiten Weltkrieg," in *Die alte Stadt: Denkmal oder Lebensraum?* 114–156; Jeffry M. Diefendorf, ed., *The Rebuilding of Europe's Bombed Cities* (New York: Macmillan/St. Martin's, 1990); idem, "Konstanty Gutschow and the Reconstruction of Hamburg," *Central European History* 18, 2 (June 1985): 143–169. For the first comprehensive appraisal of World War II destruction of historic buildings for the area of the Federal Republic, see Hartwig Beseler and Niels Gutschow, eds., *Kriegschicksale deutscher Architektur: Verluste-Schäden-Wiederaufbau. Eine Dokumentation für das Gebiet der Bundesrepublik Deutschland*, 2 vols. (Neumünster: Karl Wachholtz Verlag, 1988).

43. See, for example, Dieter Lange, "Altstadt und Warenhaus. Über Denkmalpflege und Postmoderne," in *Die alte Stadt: Denkmal oder Lebensraum?* 157–183.

44. For one of the most evocative examples of the sense of postwar destructiveness, see Erwin Schleich, *Die zweite Zerstörung Münchens* (Stuttgart: J.F. Steinkopf Verlag, 1978); for statistics on the percentage of pre-1840 buildings and attitudes toward historic environments, see von Beyme, *Der Wiederaufbau*, 213 and 232, respectively; for the estimate on the number of monuments, see Hartwig Beseler, "Berufsbild und Berufsausbildung der Denkmalpfleger," in *Denkmalräume-Lebensräume*, 281.

45. For a 1970s example of working-class involvement in preservation, see Janne and Roland Günter, "Architekturelemente und Verhaltensweisen der Bewohner: Denkmalschutz als Sozialschutz," in *Denkmalräume-Lebensräume*, 7–56, which I discuss below; for more recent examples, which go well beyond the more restricted use of the term "preservation" to include the work of oral historians and history

workshops, see Ulla Lachauer, "Geschichte wird gemacht: Beispiele und Hinweise, wie man am eigenen Ort 'Geschichte machen' kann," in *'Die Menschen machen ihre Geschichte nicht aus freien Stücken, aber sie machen sie selbst': Einladung zu einer Geschichte des Volkes in NRW,* ed. Lutz Niethammer et al. (Berlin and Bonn: Dietz, 1985), 250–264. Excellent theoretical perspectives on such developments can be found in Alf Lüdtke, ed., *Alltagsgeschichte: Zur Rekonstruktion historischer Erfahrungen und Lebensweisen* (Frankfurt am Main and New York: Campus Verlag, 1989). For a brief discussion of the RVDH/RVDL's name change, see Josef Ruland, "Kleine Chronik des Rheinischen Vereins für Denkmalpflege und Landschaftsschutz," in *Erhalten und gestalten,* 45–46. There is a good summing-up of what had happened to historic preservation by the mid-1970s from the perspective of European Cultural Heritage Year, which was in 1975, in Manfred Sack, "Brüderschaft mit der Historie," *Die Zeit* 1 (2 January 1976): 9. For the 1970s from a state conservator's view, see Dietrich Ellger, *Konservator und Alltag. Aufsätze und Vorträge* (Bonn: Habelt, 1987). And for preservation theory at mid-decade: Friedrich Mielke, *Die Zukunft der Vergangenheit: Grundlagen, Probleme und Möglichkeiten der Denkmalpflege* (Stuttgart: Deutsche Verlags-Anstalt, 1975).

46. Martin Müller, "Bürgerinitiativen in der politischen Willensbildung," *Aus Politik und Zeitgeschichte* 33, 11 (11 March 1983): 27–39, here 30. See also Peter C. Mayer-Tasch, *Die Bürgerinitiativenbewegung* (Reinbek bei Hamburg: Rowholt, 1977); Otthein Rammstedt, ed., *Bürgerinitiativen in der Gesellschaft* (Villingen: Neckar Verlag, 1980).

47. For the Bonn examples, see "Bonner Bürgerinitiativen: Was sind ihre Ziele— und wer steckt dahinter?" *General Anzeiger* (Bonn), April 12, 1980. For other examples, see Claus-Peter Echter, "Bürgerbeteiligung in Klein- und Mittelstädten im Rahmen von Stadtgestaltung und Denkmalpflege," *DAS* 11, 4 (1984): 339–347. For criticism of the initiatives' role in urban planning and preservation, see Helga Faßbinder, "Bürgerinitiativen und Planungsbeteiligung im Kontext kapitalistischer Regionalpolitik," *Kursbuch* 27 (May 1972): 68–83.

48. Lüdtke, *Alltagsgeschichte,* is useful for discussion of the theoretical fundament of some of this activity.

49. For the following, see Günter, "Architekturelemente und Verhaltensweisen," 7, 19. See also Rolf Düdder, "Wo die Hütte Heimat wird," *Die Zeit* 5 (31 January 1975): 21. For additional analysis, see Wilfried Nelles and Reinhard Oppermann, *Stadtsanierung und Bürgerbeteiligung* (Göttingen: Otto Schwartz, 1979), 49–113.

50. On reconceptualizing the monument, see Willibald Sauerländer, "Erweiterung des Denkmalbegriffs?" *DKD* 33, 1/2 (1975): 117–130; on copies and artifacts, von Beyme, *Der Wiederaufbau,* 230–241.

51. See Harold James, *A German Identity 1770–1990* (New York: Routledge, 1989), 195–209, which carries the narrative into the 1980s.

52. This statement intersects with the problem of the national unit's imposition of what Walter Benjamin called "homogeneous, empty time" on other times, as discussed in Benedict Anderson, *Imagined Communities: Reflections on the Origin and Spread of Nationalism* (London and New York: Verso, 1983), 30. For a brief overview of the interplay of multiple and national identities in German history into

the post–World War II period, see Rudolf Vierhaus, "Historische Entwicklungslinien deutscher Identität," in *Die Frage nach der deutschen Identität*, ed. Bundeszentrale für politische Bildung (Bonn: Bundeszentrale für politische Bildung, 1985), 11–22.

53. Quoted in Wohlleben, "Vorwort," 24.

54. Michael Ryan, *Marxism and Deconstruction: A Critical Articulation* (Baltimore and London: Johns Hopkins University Press, 1982), 76.

55. James Clifford, *The Predicament of Culture: Twentieth-Century Ethnography, Literature, and Art* (Cambridge, MA, and London: Harvard University Press, 1988), 9.

Chapter XII

CREATING THE AUTHENTIC FRANCE: STRUGGLES OVER FRENCH IDENTITY IN THE FIRST HALF OF THE TWENTIETH CENTURY

HERMAN LEBOVICS

THE HISTORY of France is not one of an alliance of peoples with established identities who negotiated the making of a (federal) state, as in the case of the United States or the Dutch Republic. It is rather that of an existing and powerful kingdom/state that, for the sake of its cohesion, survival, and glory, set out to create a people. Because so much power was early concentrated at the center in modern French history, the growth of national identity was complicated by uncertainties—and so power struggles—over who embodied the state. Thus during the Revolution, building on the previous efforts of absolutism, the Jacobins set out to make of a kingdom of many regions and diverse populations a unitary republic. Reacting to an ancien régime that—however much it had lost its nerve in the decades before 1789—dictated the kingdom's religious orthodoxy, rules of language, standards of theater, art, and architecture, how business was to be conducted, and who might practice what profession, the Jacobins seized the revolutionary moment to attempt themselves to create an alternative, but equally all-encompassing, definition of France that would in its totality negate that of the counterrevolution.

Sovereignty was transferred from the king, whose powers were in many respects fictional, to the nation, whose very definition was no less a work of political imagination. We are familiar enough with this mirroring in more modern situations, such as the Stalinist aping of czarist practices, but the alterations of regimes in subsequent French history—and losses of territory (e.g., Alsace-Lorraine in the nineteenth century) and accretions (e.g., Nice and the colonial empire)—kept the question of what was France ever in the forefront of public life. The republic fashioned in the Revolution, and the four other republics created in the next two hundred years, had to address this same problem of how to fashion a national unity in a res publica when the king or emperor, or invader, is removed.

The French solution was to create a melting pot.[1] French political practice interpreted the logic of the nation-state as requiring that political boundaries approximate cultural ones, or, more precisely, that all of the nation that counted, that is, that participated in public life, share a national culture. This equation obliged the leaders of the state to concern themselves with questions of the culture of their citizens both in the sense of aesthetics, an exercise of cultural power inherited from the ancien régime, and, in view of the ever-present menace of clericalism and the need to rule under the constraints of universal male suffrage, with the ways the nation thought and lived. Conversely, cultural concerns such as language, art styles, and ways of living, indeed, even what was credited as common sense, had political weight and meaning.[2] To be sure, various monarchs since at least Louis XIV had attempted to establish cultural hegemony, but only over the high culture. With progress—that is, modernization plus democracy—the culture of all the people became important to manage.

For modern France, the tensions of the state-culture nexus have been— and continue to be—great because until quite recently the French people, embedded in the dominant culture, could imagine but one French identity. That this peculiarity of the French continues to be important in the destiny of the country well into our present century will become evident in what follows. Specifically, this examination of how the discourse of an essential France, a true France, functioned in the anthropology of France and in French politics at key historical moments in this century—in 1900, in the era of the Popular Front, in Vichy France, and at the moment of cultural explosion at the end of the 1960s—will make the politics of culture and identity clearer.

Although in the nineteenth century Left and Right struggled over who would speak for La France, this Franco-French civil war, as Henry Rousso termed its political aspect, took a decisive turn around 1900, just when it appeared that the combatants had concluded a truce in the Ralliement. With the defeat or co-optation of all but the implacable Left and the irreconcilable monarchists in the late nineteenth century, the final consolidation of the Third Republic seemed at hand. Old rulers and new first concluded a narrow alliance around questions of economic self-interest, an alliance of iron and wheat, which with growing trust they extended to other aspects of domestic and foreign policy to cement a long-term, if uneasy, alliance. So was fashioned an enduring conservative republic ruled by an elite held together in a net made from trade-offs and standoffs among growers and industrialists, bankers and state fiscal offices, free traders and protectionists, clericals and republicans, regional elites and national, that is, Parisian, ones. A Socialist party would (eventually) be tolerated and begin to grow, with its great tribune, the southerner Jean Jaurès, accepting the Republic on behalf of the working class and radicalized peasants of the south. Revolutionary syndicalists, by rejecting the politics of the state, implicitly accepted the status quo created by the republican compromise—until the time came to abolish the state once and for all.

But a small contingent of neo-monarchists refused to be reconciled to a secular republic, which in their eyes negated so many of the beliefs, traditions, values, and institutions of historic France. With the spread of the Third Republic's secular school system to every corner of France, military conscription, improved transport and communications, and the consolidation of a national market in the decade before the turn of the century, uprootedness became a major political issue.[3] With the Dreyfus Affair, the far right for the first time was able to dramatize all the issues of an eroding national identity and a disappearing cultural heritage, of the grave danger to the true France, in the simple question—Could an Alsatian Jew be fully loyal to France?—and they seized the opportunity to launch a counterattack against the newly stabilized republican order of France.

In particular Charles Maurras, dominant spirit in the Action Française, rejected the incipient consensus around what France was and would be. Realizing that a world was about to be lost, Maurras refurbished a distinction dating back to the monarchy of 1830, when a very limited suffrage divided the country between voters (*le pays légal*) and the vast body of citizens who could not vote (*le pays réel*), and both in parliamentary life and in the streets advanced the claim that despite universal male suffrage the real France, the true France, was not represented in the regime of that moment. His fellow radical rightist and chief artisan of the reinvention/resuscitation of Joan of Arc in his native Lorraine, Maurice Barrès took a similar line, choosing to describe the French identity in terms of the heritage of "the land and the dead" (*la terre et les morts*). In the social sciences Frédéric Le Play and his followers set out first to find out how French life, in particular family life, was really (statistically) lived and then to suggest proper (Christian) ways to bring the nation back to its true self.

The true France of this new right was rooted in the family. It was rural, rich in regional life, but fiercely loyal to *la mère-patrie*. It was Catholic, of course; neither Protestants nor Jews—and certainly not Muslims—could really be of it. France, although blessed with many climates and ecologies, although rich in regions with varying customs, with different local cultures, this France was finally one. As Caroline Ford has pointed out, the innovation of the new right of the turn of the century was to solve the cultural problem of the one and the many by giving every Frenchman two legitimate homes: his *petite patrie* of village and region and his *grande patrie*, which was the whole of France, or rather the idea of one true France.[4] And this imagined France was unchanging. Regimes might come and go, but the essential *pays* would persist—even under political systems that for the moment falsified the true nature of the historical destiny that was France.

But how does one connect to this authentic France? How could a Frenchman unite *his* destiny with this other, momentarily submerged one, which in the last decades of the century was being effaced by the France of industry and the cities, by rootless workers and cosmopolitan intellectuals, by the disappearance of magic from the social world and the loss of faith? In the late nineteenth century regional academies began actively collecting local artifacts, costumes, and stories. Museums dedicated to the celebration, or perhaps merely monumentalization, of local life began to spring up. Primarily because of his literary and political support in Paris, Frédéric Mistral's museum of Provençal life at Arles was the most famous one. But about the same time the local Learned Society of Finistère in Brittany founded a Musée Breton at Quimper; the Euskalzaleen/Bilzarra founded a museum dedicated to Basque life in Bayonne; and there were others. And often at the cost of suppressing the pluralism of living local dialects, regionalists, who tended to come from the educated petite bourgeoisie, created societies to cultivate *the* reconstructed regional language, the correct usage of which they regulated.[5]

The most famous of these bodies was the Félibrige, the literary society of Provence created in mid-century but reaching its apogee around 1900, which worked for the revival of the culture of the Midi. Although membership included both reactionary Catholics (*blancs*) and more or less progressive republicans (*rouges*), in a great ideological transvaluation around the turn of the century a new generation of young southern conservatives came to the fore. The backward-focused values of contemporary folklore and regionalism melded with the frequently radical-reactionary dispositions of the younger regionalists to imprint the new disciplines with a rightist potential. Maurras and Mistral were great friends, for example: the regionalist subscribed to Maurras's uncompromising nationalism, and the politician championed his friend's cause of regional identity.

Although the regionalists had published local magazines devoted to local cultural themes earlier in the nineteenth century, only in 1877 did Henri Gaidoz and Eugène Roland found *Mélusine*, the first national journal of folklore studies. In 1886 P. Sébillot, who headed the Société des Traditions Populaires, started the *Revue des traditions populaires*. The Musée d'Ethnographie de Trocadéro in Paris, although in existence since 1878, did not take within its purview examples of French popular arts and traditions as such until 1888, when the curator Armand Landrin created a special section devoted to metropolitan specimens.[6] The museum's relative neglect of French artifacts, it is important to note, was part of a larger pattern that placed the study of French ethnology in the shadow of those anthropological disciplines in France concerned with comparative physical anthropology or foreign ethnographic studies.[7]

Moreover, in the years before World War I the study of the ethnography of the regions of France—what in France was called "folklore"—could not gain the university connection that would have both legitimated it and facilitated the systematic yet critical development of its own paradigm. Isac Chiva sees this failure as due to the *political* hostility of the followers of Émile Durkheim.

> Rejecting the role ascribed to tradition and to folklore as manifested in particular in P. Saintyves and P. Sébillot, the school of *L'Année sociologique* displayed a decisive ideological enmity [to the direction they were giving the field]; at the same time these writers were criticized for their ideological opposition to republican consolidation, for their militant Catholicism, for the overblown role they ascribed to the aesthetic and the emblematic.[8]

Emile Nourry, who used the pen name Saintyves, had succeeded Sébillot in the forefront of folklore studies. He and his friends had been discussing founding a new folklore society since before the war, but the project had not yet been launched when the outbreak of hostilities pushed the idea into the background. Only in the late 1920s with the Durkheimians, now, since the founding of their Institut d'Ethnologie at the University of Paris in 1925, more secure about their position in French intellectual life and beginning to practice the kind of academic turf wars that Pierre Bourdieu has helped us understand, do we see the founding of a Société du Folklore Français.[9] But in the mid-1920s most of the great figures of the discipline moved outside the Durkheimian orbit; if the Durkheimians wanted to influence the development of the paradigm(s) of this new field of social science, as they had done in sociology and were beginning to do in ethnography, they would have to engage in academic coalition politics.

In February 1929, under the patronage of Sir James and Lady Frazer, a new society, the Société du Folklore Français, held its founding meeting in—naturally—Paris. The next year the directorate of the organization began the publication of the *Revue de folklore français*, which two years later became the *Revue de folklore français et de folklore colonial*. The professionally coalitional and, in the strategy of the Durkheimians, potentially co-optive nature of the new organization (actually founded in 1928) may be read in the list of names of its principal founders. Saintyves, France's most distinguished folklore scholar, as was fitting, assumed the presidency, which he held until his death in 1935. Arnold Van Gennep, already embarked on writing his massive *Manuel de folklore français contemporain,* an intellectual loner and by conviction an anarchist, who was formally unaffiliated with any scholarly or political circle, supplied additional disciplinary ballast to the society.[10] Another founding member was André Varagnac, nephew of Marcel Sembat, the radical politician and admirer of popular art. Varagnac had been a student of Marcel Mauss, and he shared with the Durkheimians both a great admiration for the works of

Sir James Frazer and a leftist political orientation. He was in fact one of the rare folklorists politically on the left. Finally, in the inner circle we find the triumvirate of the Institut d'Ethnologie: Marcel Mauss, Lucien Lévy-Bruhl, and Paul Rivet.[11] Folklorists of divergent ideological outlooks accepted membership in the new society, but this agreement to provide disciplinary structure to the field would not bring with it agreement on one dominant paradigm.

With Paul Rivet taking over the directorship of the Trocadéro museum in the same year as the founding of the new folklore society, the modern institutional growth of folklore studies may be said to have begun. The chief architect of that development and the personal embodiment of a new cosmopolitan paradigm, different both from the ruralist essentialism of the conservatives and also from the populist essentialism of the Left, was the young man Rivet brought in as associate director in 1928, Georges-Henri Rivière.

Rivière had studied at the Paris Conservatory, served as organist at an elegant church on the Isle St. Louis, played piano at the Folies Bergères, and written songs for Josephine Baker. In 1929 he created a new magazine of modernist culture that he persuaded Georges Wildenstein, the art dealer, to finance. *Documents: doctrines, archéologie, beaux-arts, ethnographie* appeared for two years with Georges Bataille as editor and many surrealists writing for it.[12] The imaginative Rivière managed to unite surrealism with museum administration and fund-raising: to raise money for the ethnographic museum's expedition across Africa, Rivière put on a boxing match in which the Panamanian boxer Al Brown, whom Jean Cocteau called "the black marvel," climbed into the ring and announced that he was fighting for the culture of his African ancestors. Rivière exploited Al Brown's new pride in his roots to persuade the fighter to donate his purse to enhance the museum's African collection.

Rivière was a man of highly refined aesthetic sensibility; he was well connected to the important modernist currents in the world capital of modernism. With his appointment to ever more responsible positions, the avant-garde gained access to the staid world of French museums.[13] Rivet soon made him head of a department dedicated exclusively to the ethnology of France; in 1937 it became an independent museum, the Musée National des Arts et Traditions Populaires (ATP).[14] With him and his patron, Paul Rivet, the unofficial spokesman on cultural matters of the Socialist party, leftist politics entered the museum world. After a total renovation of the museums' building, Rivet renamed his museum the Musée de l'Homme. In 1935 both men threw themselves into the cultural politics of the Popular Front.

At the heart of the struggles in France in the 1930s over power in the parliament and in the streets, the class struggles over the division of the national wealth, the demand of workers for dignity, and the failure of the cultured elite to comprehend this new mood in the population lay the intertwined questions of who made up the nation and what was the French heritage (*patrimoine*). These struggles of the mid-1930s might usefully be understood as major battles in a cultural war fought over French identity.[15] From the time the Popular Front came to power to the triumph of l'Etat Français of Philippe Pétain, France debated, and sometimes fought out in the streets, what was the true essence of French culture, who belonged to it, and, accordingly, who had the right to speak in behalf of the essential country.

We can make two guiding generalizations about the cultural wars of the decades between the mid-1930s and the late 1960s. First, the Left regularly lost *by participating* in struggles framed in this essentialist language and thereby weakened the formulation of resistance against conservative regimes, be they Pétainists championing work, family, fatherland, or Gaullists, with their mystifications about a special French destiny. Second, from at least the end of World War I there was available in France, if not widely embraced, an alternative vision of culture, a richer, more diverse, less deterministic world that was recognized and gained a conditional legitimacy only in the second half of this century. What follows will map these two paths.

When the Popular Front came to office it took its stand on the cultural issues of the Franco-French civil war. But it could offer only the answers to questions of culture its coalition partners—radicals, socialists, and communists—could agree upon and only in the inherited language of the discussion of what truly was Frenchness. The Left accepted the inherited paradigm of a true France, but tried to get added to it, as an afterthought, a kind of Ptolemaic epicycle, workers and industrial life alongside the peasants and the countryside. Jacques Soustelle, in 1936 a young anthropologist on the staff of the Musée de l'Homme, and like Rivet a socialist supporter of the Popular Front, wanted to "open the gates of culture, [to] break down the barriers which, like a beautiful park forbidden to the poor, surround a culture reserved to a privileged elite." The goal of giving access to *the* culture was set largely by the communists, but it was shared by their alliance partners. No one, or no one in office, contemplated fostering new modes of creation or giving popular culture a status approximating that held by high culture. They intended simply to democratize the culture that was. Pascal Ory, in his extraordinary five-volume study of the cultural politics of the period, describes the project as a demand upon the bourgeoisie to give workers back their heritage. Perhaps Jean Jamin has best pinpointed the blind spot of 1930s French left cultural theory when he remarks that, while Rivet and many of his coworkers fought to demonstrate the equality of the races in the face of mounting racism, they never seriously questioned the category "race."

So, too, in matters of literary culture: not only did the inherited canon remain unchallenged, but important cultural spokesmen of the Left, even in statements radically assailing the inheritors of France, continued to think within the Maurrasian paradigm. Louis Aragon, recently broken with his surrealist friends, described his and the French Communist party's literary politics this way in his "Defense of the French Novel": "I deny the quality of *Frenchness* to the prose of Coblentz [the émigré center during the French Revolution], to the prose of the Versaillais [the people who crushed the Paris commune], to the prose of the seditious elements in 1935 [contemporary French fascists]. Our French novel is French because it expresses the profound spirit of the French People. . . . It is the arm of the true French against the 200 families who run the banks, the gambling houses, and the brothels."[16]

Walter Benjamin saw the conservative *political* pull of such a position. In his essay on surrealism he accused "left-wing French intellectuals" and "their Russian counterparts" of feeling an obligation not to the revolution, "but to traditional culture." Moreover, in a brilliant move he turned kinky aestheticism into hardheaded Marxism: the whole function of Satanism—a tendency more associated with Bataille and his friends than with the main (orthodox) movement led by André Breton—once more closely looked at, he argued, was "as a political device, however romantic, to disinfect and isolate against all moralizing dilettantism."[17]

So another position was possible—available—other than fighting over the possession of the heritage of French high culture. Breton stated it clearly in his reply to Aragon, his former cultural revolutionary companion, in a talk written for the Communist-called Congress of Writers for the Defense of Culture held in Paris in 1935, a talk he was not allowed to give because he had slapped Elya Ehrenburg in the face on the street a few days before the congress's opening: "We remain opposed to any claim by a Frenchman that he possesses the cultural patrimony of France alone, and to all extolling of a feeling of Frenchness in France."[18]

Thus the organized Left and Right both agreed that art for the people had once more to root itself in the life of the people, with the difference that the organized Left wished finally to include workers in that idea of a fixed, coherent national cultural heritage.[19] And then there was a small aesthetic Left, the surrealists and some of their friends in the arts—Georges-Henri Rivière, most importantly in the area of folklore and museology—equally keen about popular imagination, but which rejected the project of recovering a lost authenticity as both conservative and dangerous to humanity.

In 1936 Rivière, like the surrealists, neither looked for the essential France nor did he understand culture hierarchically. Like Breton and his circle, Rivière wished by aesthetic means to reveal the social content hidden behind aestheticism, but he also wanted to celebrate the beauty of artifacts of everyday life. And like the surrealists he rejected the idea of the *autonomy* of art.[20] He expected from the triumph of socialism "an improved quality of production in a world which no longer would be split into educated and popular strata and where humankind, finally, would repossess its worth [*dignité*]. Then we could speak of truly collective cultures."[21] Ascribing differences of social power and of the valuation of high and popular culture to class differences, Rivière celebrated the elimination of the barriers between high and popular culture as the predictable consequence of the further democratization of French society. However, unlike the radical Right and the communists, he refused to privilege the inherited high culture or to place past traditions ahead of modern life. In spite of his penchant for dandyism, he did not fall into aestheticism. Nor did he fall for the delusion of cultural purity.

But, rather than moving France toward Rivière's vision of a pluralist French culture, the Popular Front fought to a draw in another engagement of the Franco-French civil war, waged ideologically over the question of who most represented the essential France. Its premier, Léon Blum, who had preferred to stick to literary questions when Breton came to discuss hard political issues with him, had to resign. The nation's defeat at the hands of the Germans brought France back to its fundamentals, or so the followers of Pétain believed. In his proclamation of the renewal of French essentialism at the moment of defeat and transformation, *La Seule France* (France Alone), Maurras celebrated the triumph finally of the *pays réel* in the rule of Marshal Pétain. "The government of the army offers us the shining image of French unity. The government of the parties is the symbol of our divisions," he wrote in 1941. In the new regime he hoped to return to the real France (*pays réel*), so long overshadowed by the legal France (*pays légal*) of republican institutions. This would be a country liberated finally of its étatism and, "*stripped of accumulated artificial [cultural] pastiches, returned to its natural organization.*"[22]

Under the Vichy of Marshal Pétain and with the penchant of the traditional Right for the countryside and the peasant, local ethnographic studies flourished, or, it is more correct to say, continued to flourish, if in a new key. Vichy traditionalists portrayed beliefs, customs, practices as somehow growing from nature; the historical signs of the work of human hands in their creation were obscured by the political mist that covered the *new* eternal order of the fields. The cultural apparatus encouraged local museums and supported the revival of regional theater, music, and arts. Traditional festivals and pilgrimages once more were celebrated. The use of dialect was encouraged along with a sense of pride in one's region. In the government-controlled or censored press, radio, and film, the customs, tales, and ceremonies of the French countryside took on a new prominence.[23]

An image produced by Pétain's personal artists, who were charged with generating works in a new genre officially called "Marshal Art" (l'Art Maréchal), makes the point succinctly. In the beginning of Vichy rule the new state made serious efforts to win over young people to the truths of eternal France. In a Pétainist children's book there is a drawing depicting the marshal shaking the hand of a peasant at his plow, with a tricolor flag waving behind them and the spire of a village church in the distance. Above the picture is the often-used Vichy motto, "La terre, elle, ne ment pas" (The earth does not lie). Underneath, the text directs children to color in appropriate hues the marshal's suit, the horses, and the peasant's clothes. When folded along the dotted lines the drawing made a pretty tableau of eternally patient draft animals, forever respectful farmers, a flag ever waving, a church tower faithfully showing the way to the village, and an old soldier who would always be there when the essential France needed him.[24]

By way of contrast, Rivière was at the same time producing his own visualization of a possible France. In June 1941, under the German occupation of Paris, for an exposition at the Grand Palais with—at that moment—the highly ambiguous title "La France Européenne," Rivière organized a display on the Norman farmhouse, which became the principal attraction at the show. He furnished the main room with a beautiful old cupboard, a chest carved with ancient geometric forms, and a splendid *panetière,* a suspended wooden bread cage. But he also placed a modern desk among the old pieces, and on an antique bureau were a telephone and a radio. Country classics such as the *Almanac des bergers* sat on the shelves alongside modern works on questions of rural management and agricultural engineering.

Nevertheless, always a man of his time who accommodated to circumstances to accomplish his goals, while France was ruled by Pétain, Rivière wrote nothing about workers' folklore; he now played only country tunes and these in the salvage paradigm. But in his heart the enthusiast for peasant life continued to be the urban aesthete who loved American jazz, appreciated beautifully carved hand tools, and enjoyed kitsch.[25] He continued to refuse to privilege older traditions in folklore at the expense of the contemporary practices and beliefs of the countryside. Nor did he wish to isolate the folklore of peasants from other cultural currents in the nation, from urban culture.

Despite his sometime yielding to the Vichy rhetoric of "health," "vitality," and even at times "authenticity," and his willingness to continue to do work welcomed by the Vichy regime, Rivière's folklore was not the French version of *Blut und Boden.* Rather it continued to echo, however cautiously, the hope of a creative, syncretic, cultural community. As he wrote of his Norman farmhouse display, where he mixed old and new, he had wished to exhibit the joining of the peasant heritage with the "forms of a new life."[26] He wished to demonstrate a desirable interpenetration of rural and urban cultures. In June of 1944 he and the anthropologist Marcel Maget, assessing a large-scale study of rural architecture started and carried out under the occupation, rejected economic isolation and quasiautarchical regionalism as a way of keeping rural culture intact. Peasants should not be condemned to live and to eke out poor yields in the quaint peasant towns on mountaintops, for example, to which they had moved centuries before to escape dangers that no longer existed: "*only tradition,*" wrote the folklore specialist, "has kept populations living in utter poverty while clinging to infertile or marginal land."27

At the end of August 1944 Rivière participated in the liberation of the Palais de Chaillot, which housed both the Musée de l'Homme and his own ATP. And when the fighting stopped he began an ambitious series of public exhibitions of the anthropology of the regions of France. With the return to power in 1959 of Charles de Gaulle and his new minister of cultural affairs, André Malraux, a (this time) nonpathological essentialism once more guided French cultural policy. De Gaulle and Malraux budgeted the building of a new Musée National des Arts et Traditions Populaires in the Bois de Boulogne, near where in the years before the war encampments of exotic peoples had been set up for French visitors to look and to wonder at the natives in their natural habitats. But Rivière managed to get a student of Le Corbusier as the architect, and the museum's displays were fashioned very much in the ethos of modernist museums, that is, with as much sensitivity to formalist aesthetic criteria as to ethnological correctness.28 Although Rivière retired from the directorship of the ATP in 1967, once all was in place for its opening, he continued to play an active role in expanding the horizons of the possible in the museum world. He served for many years as head of the UNESCO-sponsored International Council of Museums, thus manifesting his universalist values. And he pioneered France's ecomuseums (*écomusées*).

Rivière was sensitive to the interest in ecology that arose in the 1960s, but he understood ecology in the richest sense of the word: our interaction with both our physical environment and our social one.29 In his vision, the newness of the ecomuseums, which he championed actively as soon as he left the ATP, lay in the way government and local populations, ecology and community life, past and present, intersected.

An ecomuseum is an instrument which public authorities and a population think up, create, and run together. The government supplies the experts, the facilities, and the means. The population makes its contribution of its particular aspirations, its experience, the access it offers to its world.

[An ecomuseum is] a mirror in which this population looks to begin to know itself, in which it seeks explanations of the region [*territoire*] to which it is linked and its connections to the population which came before it, in the discontinuity or continuity of generations. [It is] a mirror which this population puts before its guests so that they might better understand their hosts' work, their behavior, their personal lives.[30]

Rivière was persuasive. Twenty-eight ecomuseums now flourish in France. In the words of Jack Lang, the Socialist minister of culture, Rivière's achievement was to create "a new generation of museums, where the object is kept in its context as expressive evidence [*témoins significatif*] of a culture, a population, and a territory."[31] There is a museum dedicated to industry in the famous and historically conflict-ridden industrial towns of Creusot and Monceau-les-Mines. There are national parks that are organized to highlight the life of a region, as in the Montagne de Reims, France's champagne country, where regional agriculture and industries and a park representing the local ecology are combined. In the park for the region of Monfort in the forest of Brocéliande the theme is forestry and forest industries.

Rivière wished to avoid creating empty green spaces devoid of traces of previous or present inhabitants, as had been the practice of the United States Park Service until recent years. In a country as densely settled as France, with a landscape so deeply modified by centuries of human interaction, a virgin-land ecological ideology made no sense. Nor did such a sterile vision fit the cultural-aesthetic values Rivière had held to for much of his life.[32]

From the very beginning of the campaign for the idea of ecomuseums, Rivière and his collaborators wanted to democratize the practices of the museum as their contribution to the effort to democratize what in many ways was one of the most elitist cultures in the West. To this end the three elements of what was a museum had to be rethought: what should guide what was to be collected, how these objects should be represented, and to whom these objects should be presented. For the first, André Malraux, minister of cultural affairs from 1959 to 1969, had bent his considerable talents to displaying what he considered the greatest treasures of French language and plastic arts (at least those that belonged to the state or were performed in state theaters) as icons of a religion of aesthetics. Even before the cultural explosion of May 1968 Rivière sought to deconsecrate the museum object and once more give it a place in the society from which it came. Second, and more important, here in the new advocacy of ecomuseums, Rivière continued to make the case for the need to redefine the notion of culture. "The new museology was part of a vast increasingly deep movement of affirmation that culture was not One but rather Many. The noble [*généreuse*] idea that the culture was the property of everyone. . . ." Finally, as the metaphor of the mirror employed by Rivière suggests, "the first public [of new museums] was the population" whose culture(s) was displayed. As Hugues de Varine-Bohan, one of the creators of the Burgundian rural-industrial-mining museum at Creusot-Montceau in 1972, described the relation he wanted to create between the museum and the regional population of 180,000, "The museum does not have visitors, it has inhabitants."[33]

The coming of postmodernity as a condition of French life has fulfilled much of the cultural agenda of Rivière and the surrealists. Accordingly, with the specter of pluralism haunting France today, there is inevitably much talk of a national identity crisis.[34] The existence of a late-industrial, late-capitalist society—known in France as threatening Americanization—is changing the ways people live. Moreover, integration in a new Europe promises future peace and prosperity but threatens a hard-won political-cultural autonomy.

Above all, the immigrants living in France pose a double challenge to the historic construction of French culture. Black African and North African immigrants—and, perhaps more disquieting, their French-born children—seem to be resisting the proposition the Republic has historically made to immigrants: that they exchange their first identities for French ones, that they accept being melted down and being reminted as "French" by education in the culture. And today a vocal minority in French society is not eager to extend Frenchness to the new settlers. An eclectic "life-style"—not an easy concept to think in French—may not damage American identity, which, as we saw above, was created pluralist, but if true France were to disappear would not historic France die with it?

If Michel Foucault's central insight—that the powers that be give us *identities* so that they might dominate us—is correct, then we should be wary of continuing to think of ourselves in such terms and, by *metaphoric extension*, of the culture-state as having a substantial identity. Not only is this a case of reification, but that which is being reified is dying; for on both the national and personal scale true France is disappearing.

Association with too many defeats—first that of Vichy; then, in the aftermath of 1968, de Gaulle's; and finally, paradoxically, that of the contemporary French Communist party—has made the idea of an essential France not very enticing to the general public. Although in recent years he has managed to appeal to growing numbers of voters by employing its rhetoric, Jean-Marie Le Pen, the main proponent today of integral Frenchness, remains scorned as a racist demagogue at the margins of politics—at least for the moment.

Moreover, with the increasingly heterogeneous world in which most Westerners live, the old rulers' trick of conferring hegemonic identities on populations as a way of creating political legitimacy and of building popular loyalty no longer makes sense. So, too, ideologies are dying because they can no longer serve as the glues of societies. What can French identity mean if only the rapidly changing *mixture* of external and internal cultural influences, practices, and fads is *uniquely* French, if what is typically French changes at dizzying speeds? What happens to national consciousness when nations become less important in people's lives? For example, from 1993 onward anyone with marketable skills, such as computer know-how, will be able to go anywhere in the twelve countries of the European Community and, if qualified, obtain a job ahead of less skilled nationals of the land in which the firm finds itself. And today, from what external enemies do the French need their state to protect them?[35]

On the personal level, too, True France—or for that matter Real Americanism, the True Brit, and the other essentialisms— seems to be superfluous. Individuals as participants in intimate relationships (of which the family is not always the most important anymore), as perhaps employees of a multinational firm, as clients of banks and insurance companies, live in the power-saturated structures Foucault has described. Culturally, it is possible for the French to be fans of international sporting events, of American sitcoms, of Japanese cartoons, of Chinese or Indian food, to drink French wines from Japanese-owned vineyards, with common-market beef garnished with Kenyan-grown string beans. Where is there a place or utility for identity-language here?

But it is too early to proclaim that cultural essentialism is dead. With the end of ideology and the crisis of the nation from above, more than ever before ethnic and regional groups all over the world are today demanding political recognition. New nations are being created—Germany is one example—while others disintegrate, as in the case of Russia and the nations of eastern Europe. As happened with the end of the Roman Empire in the West, a world is passing and we can think of no replacement for it but ties of *region* and *blood*. However, a new high-tech feudalism is what even the oppressed peoples want least.

The dialectic of unity and of diversity will surely intensify in the years to come, but France's traditions of Enlightenment and cosmopolitanism— however momentarily eclipsed by the apparent liberating charms of Nietzsche—will put it on the side of the angels. More in the Kantian vein of his thinking, Jacques Derrida has posited as a law with no exceptions that assertions of unique cultural identity, whatever form they may take—for example, pluralist or xenophobic—are always ways of claiming inclusion in the universal of humankind by reference to the group's irreplaceable uniqueness, that "*key piece of evidence* of the human essence and of the uniqueness of humankind." Decoded: that affirmations of unique cultural identity are claims, finally, of the desire to participate in the life of humanity with a special contribution to the whole—not to pull away from it.[36]

Writing in 1939 just before Hitler could mobilize wounded German identities in a furious war against the Others, Paul Valéry tried to define

French uniqueness, and at the same time, because of it, he suggested a role France could play in creating a better world. "Our particularity (and sometimes our silliness [*ridicule*]), but often our most beautiful quality [*titre*] is to believe ourselves, to feel ourselves, to be universal—I mean: *a universalist people*. . . . Note the paradox: to have as your specialness the sense of the universal."[37] Perhaps after a bloody history of struggle over national and cultural identity, a new Western European Community, created as a solution to the problem of combining universal and particular, might become a teacher of the nations. For Walter Benjamin, Paris was the capital of the nineteenth century. Perhaps a new Paris in a new world might serve admirably as the capital of the twenty-first.

NOTES

1. Gérard Noiriel, *Le Creuset française. Histoire de l'immigration XIXe–XXe siècles* (Paris, 1988), 50–67. Eugen Weber, *Peasants into Frenchmen: The Modernization of Rural France* (Stanford, 1976).

2. French regimes have always—and still do—put great efforts into managing, or at least determining, production in the cultural realm. See Patricia Mainardi's innovative study if the role of the state in the struggles over the salon system in art, *An Aesthetic Return to Order: The End of the Salon in the Early Third Republic* (Cambridge, Engl., 1993).

3. Maurice Agulhon, *The Republic in the Village: The People of the Var from the French Revolution to the Second Republic,* trans. J. Lloyd (Cambridge, Engl., 1982). Weber, *Peasants into Frenchmen.* Peter Sahlins, "The Nation in the Village: State-Building and Communal Struggles in the Catalan Borderland during the Eighteenth and Nineteenth Centuries," *Journal of Modern History* 60 (1988), 234–63. See also Sahlins's *Boundaries: The Making of France and Spain in the Pyrenees* (Berkeley, 1989). André Varagnac, *Civilisation traditionnelle et genre de vie* (Paris, 1948), 16–38, 64. Varagnac explains the change by reference to the spread of industrial civilization. In contradiction to both Varagnac and Weber, Caroline Ford has persuasively argued that in one French countryside at least, Lower Brittany, regional culture was by no means dying off at the turn of the century, but rather was creatively renewing its institutions and values in the face of heavy political obstacles created by Paris ("Religion and the Politics of Cultural Change in Provincial France: The Resistance of 1902 in Lower Brittany," *Journal of Modern History* 62 [1990], 1–33).

4. Caroline Ford, *Creating the Nation in Provincial France: Religion and Political Identity in Brittany* (Princeton, 1993). Perhaps that is why Paris was not viewed as such a terrible *alien* place in French letters, as Berlin was in German literature or New York was in American. Paris, for French culture, was the meeting place of the provincials of France, the place where the *grande patrie* was most in evidence. Provincials could experience disaster and defeat there, as did the hero of Balzac's *Lost Illusions,* but there French culture could also attain its greatest heights— including the advocacy of regionalism and regional cultures on the part of Maurras, the southerner, and Barrès, the Lorraine patriot.

5. See Anne-Marie Thiesse's seven-hundred page thesis on regionalist literary movements: "Ecrire la France, Le Mouvement littéraire régionaliste de la langue française entre la belle époque et la libération," 2 vols. (continuous pagination) (thèse pour le doctorat d'Etat, University of Lyon II, 1989), 33. Thiesse describes the typical biography of the regionalist writer: it reports the writer's interest in literature (including local literature) as a youth, his "going up" to Paris, where the smart literary set mocked him as a bumpkin for his literary tastes and his return home, not with lost illusions but instead determined to wear his literary regionalism as a badge of identity and of honor.

6. Christian Faure, "Folklore et révolution nationale: doctrine et action sous Vichy (1940–44)," 2 vols. (thèse doctorat l'université de Lyon II, Histoire, Soutenu le 21 mars 1986), photocopied edition, 19–20.

7. Isac Chiva, "Entre livre et musée. Emergence d'une ethnologie de la France," in Isac Chiva and Utz Jeggle, eds., Ethnologies en miroir. La France et les pays de langue allemande (Paris, 1987), 20.

8. Ibid. Raymonde Courtas and François-A. Isambert, "Ethnologues et sociologues aux prises avec la notion de 'populaire,'" La Maison-Dieu 122 (1975), 20–32.

9. Pierre Bourdieu, "Le Champ scientifique," Actes de la recherche en science sociales 2/3 (1976), 88–104, esp. 89–94. Idem, "Les Conditions sociales de la production sociologique. Sociologie coloniale et decolonisation de la sociologie," in Pierre Bourdieu, ed., Cahiers Jussieu N° 2. Université de Paris VII: Le Mal de voir: ethnologie et orientalisme. Politique et épistémologie, critique et autocritique (Paris, 1975), 416–27; in the same volume see Fanny Colonna, "Production scientifique et position dans le champ intellectuel et politique, deux cas: Augustin Berque et Joseph Desparmet," 398–414. See further my article following Bourdieu's approach, "Le Conservatisme en anthropologie et la fin de la Troisième République," Gradhiva: Revue d'histoire et de l'archives de l'anthropologie publiée par le Musée de l'Homme (Paris) 4 (May 1988), 3–17.

10. Although he acknowledged affinities with Durkheimian theory, and the members of the school tolerated his personal crankiness. Arnold van Gennep, "La Décadence et la persistence des patois," Revue des Idées 8 (1911), 412–24. Here, for example, he writes about the role of the state and of capitalism in wiping out the patois of peasants and workers.

11. Chiva, "Entre livre et musée," 21; Faure, "Folklore et révolution nationale," 19–20. Before the Great War Sembat himself had discussed with James Frazer the possibility of creating a society dedicated to French folklore, but he soon thereafter died. Georges-Henri Rivière, "Les Musées de folklore à l'étranger et le futur 'Musée français des arts et traditions populaires,'" Revue de folklore français et de folklore colonial 3 (1936), 66. Varagnac, Civilisation traditionnelle et genre de vie, 12.

12. Bernard-Henri Lévy singles out Bataille, Michel Leiris, and Rogers Caillois, along with André Breton and Artaud, as profoundly farsighted for having early understood and taken stands against the "forces of regression of the age." "Perhaps a key to understanding the century: the truly political, that is literally anti-fascist, consequences of an ethic of literature" (L'Idéologie française [Paris, 1981], 123).

13. Jean Jamin, in his preface to his edition of the Bulletin du musée d'ethnogra-

phie du trocadéro, highlights very well the importance for both the discipline and for the society of the modernist direction that the new ethnographic museum took under the influence of Rivière with Rivet's close support, xvi, xviii–xix. See Jamin's "De l'humaine condition de 'Minotaure,'" in Charles Georg, ed., *Regards sur Minotaure* (Geneva, 1987), 79–87, esp. 81. Further, there is James Clifford, "On Ethnographic Surrealism," *Comparative Studies in Society and History* 23 (1981), 539–64. Rivière's desire to live like his friends of Tout Paris caused him to miscalculate in 1929 when he agreed to marry Nina Spalding Stevens, a wealthy American who wanted entrée to his world in exchange for funding a better life-style than he could himself afford. Apparently she was the only person in his circle not to know that he was gay. They married in Paris on 26 January 1929. The marriage—which Rivière had understood to be a *marriage blanc*—broke up immediately, and she returned to New York. His nephew, Jean-François Leroux-Dhuys, tells this intimate story as a comic episode in a biographical sketch, but paradoxically he has little to say about the years 1941 to 1944 ("Georges Henri Rivière: un homme dans le siècle," in the posthumously edited volume, Georges Henri Rivière, *La Muséologie selon Georges Henri Rivière* [Paris, 1989], 22).

14. At Rivière's request the director of the ATP reported to the director of museums of the beaux-arts administration, rather than to the science section of the Ministry of Education.

15. See, for example, the papers gathered in the conference volume of the Institut d'Histoire du Temps Présent: Jean-Pierre Rioux, ed., *Politiques et pratiques culturelles dans la France de Vichy* (Paris, 1988), especially the essay by Henry Rousso, "Vichy: Politique, idéologie et culture," 13–25; see further the special section of *Le Mouvement social* 153 (1990), 3–61, on changes in the political culture of the Left at the same time as changes were taking place in the politics of culture.

16. Pascal Ory, "La Politique culturelle du Front Populaire française (1935–1938)' (thèse pour le doctorat d'Etat, Histoire, University of Paris X [Nanterre], 1990), 177, 191–219. Julian Jackson, *The Popular Front in France* (Cambridge, Engl., 1988), 113, 120, 126.

17. Walter Benjamin, "Surrealism: The Last Snapshot of the European Intelligentsia," in *Reflections,* trans. Edmund Jephcott (New York, 1978), 177–92, esp. 186–87.

18. André Breton, "Speech to the Congress of Writers (1935)," in *Manifestoes of Surrealism,* trans. Richard Seaver and Helen R. Lane (Ann Arbor, 1969), 237.

19. Pascal Ory and Jean-François Sirinelli, *Les Intellectuels en France de L'affaire Dreyfus à nos jours* (Paris, 1986), 96–102. Michèle Cointet, *Histoire culturelle de la France, 1918–1958* (Paris, 1958), 107.

20. See Jack Spector, "The Avant-garde Object: Form and Fetish between World War I and World War II," *Res* 12 (1986), 125–43, on the politics of surrealists and their enterprise of unmasking the social content and role of aestheticism, and especially the idea of the *autonomy* of art. See also Peter Berger, *Theory of the Avant-Garde* (Minneapolis, 1984). On an exhibition and a publication coming from it that attempted to appropriate surrealist ideas for the fashion industry, we have an inclusive review by Spector, "Fashion and Surrealism," *Art Journal* 47 (1988), 372–75.

21. Rivière, "Les Musées de folklore," 59–71.

22. Charles Maurras, *La Seule France. chronique des jours d'épreuve* (Lyon, 1941), 19, 171. Emphasis mine. Isac Chiva has argued that in times of crisis throughout the last centuries French society has tended to react by looking to nature, returning to the past, and embracing the local. On the level of ideology the generalization is descriptive, but it does not help us understand the aspects of Vichy that were technocratic, modernizing, and centralizing. Most curious is the conjunction of both reactions, as is the most typical case of national crisis under Vichy. Isac Chiva, "Le Patrimoine ethnologique de la France," unpublished manuscript, 17.

23. Christian Faure, "Le Film documentaire sous Vichy: une promotion du terroir," *Ethnologie française* 18 (1988), 284–90.

24. Laurent Gervereau, "Y a-t-il un 'style Vichy,'" in Laurent Gervereau and Denis Peschanski, eds., *La Propagande sous Vichy, 1940–1944*, (Paris, 1990), 147. Laurence Bertrand-Dorléac, "La Question artistique et le régime de Vichy," in Jean-Pierre Rioux, ed., *La Vie culturelle sous Vichy* (Paris, 1990), 137–60; see further by the same author, *L'Histoire de l'art: Paris, 1940–1944. Ordre national, traditions et modernité* (Paris, 1986), 25–48, 115.

25. In his last years he kept on a table in his modest apartment, which was furnished with simple, functional furniture, a kind of absurd museum containing among other things a beautifully lathed children's top given him by a Provençal craftsman, a sculpted ashtray in the shape of a cat, and—perhaps added after the de Gaulle–Malraux government insisted on his retirement in 1967—a glass ball full of blue-tinted water, which, when turned upside down, dropped snow upon a miniature statue of General de Gaulle.

26. Georges-Henri Rivière, "Logis de la ferme normande," *La France européene: revue mensuelle de l'exposition du grand palais*, no. 1 (June 1941), 23. As usual for him in this period, the words "new life" are ambiguous to a fault. However, his modernizing instincts here revealed themselves before the Vichy technocrats changed the direction of the state from that Pétain had given it.

27. Marcel Maget and Georges-Henri Rivière, "Habitat rural et tradition paysanne," *Journées d'études de l'habitat rural, 13 au 17 juin 1944* (Paris, n.d. [1944?]), 1–9. Emphasis mine.

28. The display cases remain largely as Rivière had planned them. Their quasi-modernist organization of the display space has aged well.

29. François Hubert, Hervé Joubeaux, and Jean-Yves Veillard, *Découvrir les écomusées* (Rennes, 1984), 14.

30. Georges-Henri Rivière, *Dossier écomusée: avant-propos, aperçu historique, définition évolutive, fonctionnement statistique* (n.p., 1980). See further the publication of the Ecomusées en France, *En avant la mémoire* (Paris, 1990), 3.

31. *En avant la mémoire*, 1.

32. Isac Chiva, "Georges Henri Rivière," *Terrain* (1985), 79. For variations of such sentiments, which have now become tropes in French museology, see the addresses by Jacques Vallerant, ethnologist and curator, and Louis Mermez, president of the Assemblée Nationale and local notable at the inauguration of an ecomuseum in the north of France, the Musée Nord-Dauphiné, in *Bilans et perspectives* (St. Julien-Molin-Molette [Loire], 1983 [dept. of l'Isère]), 11, 14–15.

33. Jean-Michel Barbe, "Presence et avenir du passé," *Les Cahiers de l'anima-*

tion 3 (1985), 55–63. Hugues de Varine-Bohan, "Un Musée 'eclaté'—le Musée de l'Homme et de l'Industrie," *Museum* 25 (1973), 242.

34. So pervasive is this sense of an identity crisis that *Time International* (15 July 1991) began its special issue on "The New France" with a discussion of "How can a people so certain of their birthright be disoriented? Yet they are."

35. This is not to say that governments will not go to war, as France did in the Middle East in 1991. However, whatever the reasons of state, the French population treated the combat much as they treat their hometown soccer teams: with pride, hopes, disappointments, and boos; and when the match ended, they went back to more serious things.

36. Jacques Derrida, *L'Autre cap* (Paris, 1991), 71–72. Italics in original. The uniqueness of Europe, Derrida argues, is that it does not close itself off in a narrow identity, but is always open to others, always unfinished. For a parallel analysis focusing on the idea of Central Europe today, see the interesting article by Michael Geyer, "Historical Fictions of Autonomy and the Europeanization of National History," *Central European History* 22 (1989), 316–42.

37. Paul Valéry, *Pensée et art français*, cited in Derrida, *L'Autre cap*, 73.

Chapter XIII

BETWEEN MEMORY AND OBLIVION: CONCENTRATION CAMPS IN GERMAN MEMORY

Claudia Koonz

Václav Havel, in an open letter to Czech President Gustav Husák in 1975, described the psychological effects of an imposed official history that bears little resemblance to what people remember. Events and individuals blur into a gray mass of proclamations. Individual identity fades, Havel wrote, and "one has the impression that for some time there has been no history. Slowly but surely, we are losing the sense of time. We begin to forget what happened when, what came earlier and what later, and the feeling that it really doesn't matter overwhelms us."[1] "Organized oblivion" in totalitarian states imposes a single narrative that vindicates the leaders and villifies their enemies, but it leaves average citizens cynical and alienated. A kind of historical weightlessness renders words, values, actions, and ideas meaningless. As national leaders in the former Soviet bloc face the task of restoring civil society in the 1990s, the reconstruction of an authentic history takes on special urgency. Nowhere is the difficulty of this challenge clearer than in the controversy surrounding the physical and symbolic territory of former concentration camps.

Past events seem fixed in the landscape where they occurred. Written texts can be edited or even created, films can recast key narratives, and photos can be airbrushed.[2] Landscapes, by contrast, feel immutable. For centuries, this impression of fixity has drawn pilgrims to geographical locations that have "contained" the memory of sacred events. Secular shrines, like the Invalides, the Liberty Bell, and the Brandenburg Gate, rekindle memories of the awesome events they commemorate. Although the link between landscape and history is an ancient one, the semiotics of place remained largely unnoticed until Maurice Halbwachs, French sociologist and student of Émile Durkheim, examined its role in the formation of "collective memory."[3] Halbwachs felt drawn by the timeless, stable quality of geographical sites. Because, he wrote, "space is a reality that endures," it exerts a unique power to "pull" individuals together. In Halbwachs's almost Jungian conception, "The collective thought of the group of believers has the best chance of immobilizing itself and enduring when it concentrates on places, sealing itself within their confines and molding its character to theirs."[4] Memory, he believed, can exist only within "social frames" (*les Cadres sociaux de la Mémoire*), produced by collectivities and reified in particular settings. "Since our impressions rush by . . . we can . . . recapture the past only by understanding how it is, in effect, preserved by our physical surroundings."[5]

Writing amidst the strife of interwar France, Halbwachs was attracted to spiritual, celebratory, and commemorative landmarks that inspired their visitors with idealism and pride. In the modern world, however, topographies of evil have begun to attract visitors. Auschwitz, Buchenwald, Dachau, and dozens of smaller camps have become powerful landmarks that draw millions not to marvel but to mourn.

The silent landscapes embody a reality beyond words.[6] In *Nuit et Brouillard*, the first major film to grapple with the reality of the extermination camps, Alain Renais anchored his narrative in the geography of extermination. Technicolor shots of railway tracks and former camp sites framed black-and-white original footage. Claude Lanzmann set *Shoah* in the green fields and railways on which extermination occurred. Survivors of the camps often locate their experiences in a geographical setting, perhaps because the human environment defied description. Guiliana Tedeschi, for example, opens her account of Birkenau with, "There is a place on earth, a desolate heath, where the shadows of the dead are multitudes, where the living are dead, where there is only death, hate, and pain."[7] Walking among the overgrown ditches of Majdanek, across the heath of Bergen-Belsen, or through the hay fields of Birkenau, one may still find fragments of bones or shards. Standing as monuments to unspeakable crimes, these camps command their visitors to ponder the depths of evil. "Pause. Stop and think," they seem to say. Indeed, the German word for monument, *Denkmal*, conveys that meaning. For concentration camp sites, a new noun, *Mahnmal*, commands us to take warning. At these places of remembering (*Gedenkstätte*), memory feels monolithic, unambiguous, and terrible. A violent past haunts the present there.

Written texts, by contrast, seem infinitely malleable. "Genocide," first coined in 1942, has broadened in popular usage to include the AIDS epidemic and starvation in Somalia. Even "Holocaust," used after the 1960s to refer specifically to the mass murder of Jews, now refers to many crimes and victims.[8] Such polysemy, it might appear, could not possibly affect the meaning of, for example, the concrete fence posts capped by arches with fittings for electrified barbed wire. Halbwachs, however, anticipated this paradox when he observed that the intrinsic instability of supposedly fixed and immortal landscapes gives them their power.[9] In his *Legendary Topography of the Evangelists in the Holy Land* (1941), Halbwachs analyzed the fluctuating meanings of putatively unambiguous holy sites. Landmarks, he noted, exude a sense of timelessness, even as they shift to meet new cultural and political demands on memory. Throughout Europe, the meanings and memories indexed by camp sites have been in constant flux for half a century.

As in all communication, historical memorialization depends upon the interpretation of a signifier, a word or symbol that stands between the viewer and the event commemorated; once a powerful icon enters into circulation, its connotations are set in motion. Thus, historical revision inheres in the process of memorialization.[10] And nowhere have the parameters of who remembers what about World War II shifted as dramatically as at the concentration camp memorial museums in Germany. The emotional force of the stark terrain exerts what seems like a universal pull, but each memorial museum shapes that force in specific narratives about the perpetrators, the victims, the guilty, and even the crime itself.

In this essay I will compare the alternations between memorialization and amnesia in East and West Germany since 1945 and conclude with an account of how these distinct historical understandings have clashed in the period after reunification. Before examining the multiple revisions of public memory embodied in East and West German camps, it is worth noting some crucial distinctions that separate German camps from other camp memorials in nations formerly occupied by the Nazis. Outside Germany, concentration camps and memorials recall an unproblematic narrative of national martyrs killed by a foreign enemy. German atrocities can be remembered and collaborators forgotten. National resisters can be enshrined, while other victims (including Jews) are easily forgotten. A wall-size photomontage at Auschwitz proclaims, for example, "6,000,000 Poles slaughtered by German Fascists!" At Mauthausen, the exhibits depict Austrians as Hitler's first victims and, until recently, overlooked Austrian complicity in Nazi racial crimes. In 1991 Lithuanians condemned as war criminals were rehabilitated and given financial compensation because they were declared victims of Soviet crimes. In April 1992 a French high court pronounced Paul Touvier, who facilitated the murder of hundreds, innocent. Outside Germany, even in Austria, perpetrators are cast as German.

In Germany this scenario does not work. When Germans erect monuments and establish concentration camp museums, they commemorate victims of their grandparents' and parents' government. To appreciate the significance of this, we have only to think about the controversy that erupted over how to memorialize the 57,939 Americans who died in Vietnam. Imagine the debates that might have ensued if Congress had commissioned a memorial to the Vietnamese who died because of United States "pacification" of their nation.[11] Only in the late 1980s did the U.S. government begin to acknowledge part of its debt to the more than sixty thousand

Japanese-Americans interned in camps during World War II.[12] A monument to their memory was dedicated in 1992. In Germany, by contrast, thousands of commemorative plaques, dozens of memorials, and eight major concentration camp museums testify to German shame, admonishing visitors with "Never Forget," "Never Again." But what must be remembered? What must never happen? East and West memories diverge.

The debates that have raged around Holocaust commemoration and amnesia in East and West Germany follow similar chronological patterns: the shock of discovery in 1945, a retreat into oblivion, followed by a flood of memory beginning in the 1960s, and the quest for a new German past in the post–Cold War world. However, the chronological continuities fade against sharp contrasts regarding representations of victims, perpetrators, and heritage. In West Germany, historical representation in the camp museums has developed in tandem with public opinion, film and television specials, books, and legislation. Memory in the former GDR, by contrast, closely resembles the official memory promulgated by the Communist party (SED) leadership. Nevertheless, in both Germanies, it makes sense to distinguish popular memory (as reflected for example, in the media, newspapers, oral histories, memoirs, and opinion polls) from official memory (as expressed in ceremonies and leaders' speeches). Public memory is the battlefield on which these two compete for hegemony.

I

As Paul Connerton has argued in the context of the French Revolution, after destroying the old regime, postrevolutionary leaders must sever all ties with past politics so that citizens who have suffered under the previous government will feel secure. "A barrier is to be erected against future transgression. The present is to be separated from what preceded it by an act of unequivocal demarcation."[13] However, in drawing a parallel between the trial of Louis XVI and the Nuremberg Trials, Connerton overlooked a crucial difference between the two. While revolutionary *citoyens* may have hated the monarchy, Germans generally had not suffered under Nazi rule until the tides of war turned. Indeed, historians in the early 1990s have discovered how pleasant life seemed even to the men who committed mass murder.[14] Certainly, the bombing raids, military devastation, and humiliating surrender brought Germans grief, but this did not preclude their remembering the "old days" of the Third Reich before Stalingrad with great fondness. Thus, when the victorious Allies put Nazi leaders on trial, the impact was bound to be ambiguous.

As each concentration camp was liberated, Allied troops and reporters registered their horror at what they saw. After attending to the immediate needs of the starving and sick, soldiers spontaneously summoned residents

from hundreds of towns and cities near each camp and marched them past
the reality they had ignored for years. Camp guards and Wehrmacht soldiers, as well as local mayors, teachers, and ordinary citizens, were required
to bury the dead and clean the warehouses after hundreds of decomposing
corpses had been removed.[15] In Dachau, citizens were forced to walk past
more than six thousand corpses decomposing in the sun. Men were ordered to bury the bodies, and women to clean the thirty-nine cars of the
"death train" in which nearly all passengers perished because SS guards
had not unlocked the doors. Two thousand citizens of Weimar, men and
women, were paraded through the human wasteland at nearby Buchenwald.[16]

Painful as this encounter was for average Germans, survivors' committees demanded more. At Buchenwald former prisoners pledged, "We swear
in front of the whole world . . . We will only give up the fight when the last
guilty parties stand before the people's judges!"[17] In the town of Dachau,
forty local administrators stood trial, and occupation authorities endorsed
proposals to commemorate their victims with new street names, a monument, and three holidays.[18] From 1946 through 1947 the major war criminals faced their accusers at Nuremberg. Newsreels and photos shot by
foreign photographers imposed memory on defeated Germans. But most
Germans built what Connerton called a "memory wall" against the recent
past. Jolted by the double trauma of devastating defeat and the realization
of their government's wartime crimes, they forgot. Unlike revolutionaries,
they could not kill their defeated leaders or even put them on trial. The
victorious Allies did that.

Germans constructed a new identity based on a fresh start or a clean
break with the past. Calling it "Zero Hour" (*Stunde Null*), they forged a
new vision of their identity based on a rejection of Nazism. Further, each
occupation zone assumed a second negation as a foundational identity. In
the East new leaders told citizens to be proud they were not West Germans.
West Germans heard the opposite message: their civil society was anchored
in its opposition to Communism in the East. As a result of this complex
process of negative identification, remembering took different forms in the
East and the West. However, in East and West, for nearly two decades, the
concentration camps were virtually ignored as places of memory.

II

Denial about the camps before May 1945, followed by the brief shock of
confrontation, gave way to "forgetting" after 1946. Besides the urge to
repress, desperate scarcities occupied everyone's immediate attention.
Sixty-six million Germans faced an influx of ten million German refugees
(*Flüchtlinge*) from territories formerly under German control. Eight million occupation soldiers and displaced persons had to be fed and housed.

Severe shortages of food, fuel, and housing made living conditions worse in the first year of peace than during the last year of the war. Against that background, few Germans cared much about commemorating the dead or exposing Nazi crimes.

With the exception of Eugen Kogon's *Der SS Staat,* no indictment of Nazism attracted much attention in the West. In East and West, more than fifty memoirs by survivors of concentration camps appeared, but they occasioned little comment. Even the *Diary of Anne Frank* was rejected by more than a dozen publishers. Aside from Karl Jaspers's book *The Question of German Guilt* and Friedrich Meinecke's *German Catastrophe,* West German intellectuals virtually ignored Nazism. In the East, politicians railed against Nazi terror and analyzed it within a Marxist-Leninist scheme that had no place for genocide. Two brilliant accounts of Nazi power written in 1946 remained completely unnoticed until the 1980s: Viktor Klemperer's *LTI* and Max Picard's *Hitler in uns selbst.*[19] One reason for German writers' reluctance to examine Hitler's extermination camps was suggested in an essay by Hannah Arendt just after the war. "The production of corpses . . . cannot be grasped in political categories," she wrote.[20]

Silence about genocide, terror, and racism settled in. In the West a few memoirs salvaged the image of average Germans with reports of everyday and unsung bravery against Nazi power. In 1946 and 1947, Ruth Andreas-Friedrichs's *Shadowman,* Allen Dulles's *Germany's Underground,* Karl Paetel's *German Inner Immigration,* and Fabian von Schlabrendorff's *Officers Against Hitler* all celebrated opposition to Hitler and ignored both Nazi crimes and civilian compliance.[21]

In the Soviet zone, survivors toured the schools to inform students about Nazi brutality. Memoirs described conditions in the camps and extolled the courageous resistance among Marxists. A series of "rubble films" (*Trümmerfilmen*) featured life in the aftermath of defeat, but only one, *Die Mörder sind unter uns,* obliquely referred to Nazi crimes, in this case the shooting of partisans.[22] A few years later, in 1949, one Czech film, *Distant Journey,* depicted genocide against the Jews, but it was banned after one showing.

By the late 1940s the "Iron Curtain" bifurcated German memory. East Germans forgot the Jews.[23] West Germans forgot the Nazis and for a time also submerged the memory of genocide. The Western Allies, eager to rebuild the country quickly, dropped the ban against former Nazis. Sentences were commuted and Nazi affiliations overlooked.

In the East, as in the West, genocide was forgotten, but unlike the West, the East remembered Nazi crimes. Soviet occupation officials rigorously carried out de-Nazification, imprisoning thousands of suspected war criminals and Nazi sympathizers in jails and former concentration camps.

Brutal Nazi crimes and heroic Communist opposition became part of the founding myth of the Socialist state. Postwar leaders rallied their new subjects with the bombastic anti-Fascist discourse so reminiscent of Communist rhetoric from the 1930s.[24] The new leaders enshrined their Communist victory as the glorious outcome of a historical struggle between workers and capitalists. To this end, thousands of plaques, small monuments, gravestones, and historical markers were erected throughout the GDR. Streets, previously named for Prussian generals or Nazi heroes, became Lenin or Stalin boulevards, Luxemburg, Demitroff, Bebel, or Liebknecht streets. Karl Marx squares dotted cityscapes.

Survivors, as they left the camps, swore to preserve their dead comrades' memory, to defy the wretched anonymity of Nazi mass atrocities. Out of the numbing statistics and mass graves, survivors and local citizens retrieved information about individual deaths. Villages, towns, and neighborhoods through the GDR erected thousands of small markers telling passersby of the tragedies that had occurred at those sites. In the tiny village of Trebbus, for example, a simple sign notes, "Here rests the Soviet slave laborer, Wanda Schipula, born on June 14, 1916." In Daasdorf am Berge, visitors learn about "the two Italian forced laborers Virgino Guissanne and Pietro Cerruli. On April 3, 1945 they were shot by village Fascists when villagers discovered them taking a few potatoes . . . to still their hunger." On a street corner in a village near Salzwedel, a small monument explains, "Here after July 1944 was located a satellite camp of Neuengamme. Over 400 women, mainly Hungarian Jews, were forced to work in the wire factory that stood here. Many of them died as the result of poor treatment and deprivation."[25] While hundreds of Soviet soldiers and German Communist resisters received mention, some inscriptions honor "victims of the fascist racial craze" and of the "political terror against non-Communists." In the first years after 1945, no one thought of preserving the camps. Disavowing any connection with the Nazi past, GDR leaders refused to pay reparations to Germans who had suffered under Nazism.

Chancellor Konrad Adenauer, who included former Nazis among his close advisers, in 1952–53 did persuade the Bundestag to grant reparations (*Widergutmachung*) to victims. Diplomatic expediency, not moral considerations, prompted the decision. After Germany was excluded from the newly founded North Atlantic Treaty Organization, Adenauer took a bold and domestically unpopular step. He asked the Bundestag to agree to pay reparations (*Shilumim*) to the state of Israel and its designated representatives of Jewish victims. Despite the lack of public support (polls showed that only 11 percent of all Germans approved the act), the legislature ratified the agreement. The action transformed Germany from a "moral leper" into a responsible member of the Western military alliance. As historian Anson Rabinbach observed, "Adenauer's genius was to find the Jewish Question useful, where his political colleagues saw only a permanent source of embarrassment."[26] Tolerating former Nazis in high office, while simultaneously compensating victims of Nazi racial policies, the Adenauer government put the past to rest.

At Dachau, where the camp barracks were used to house refugees from the East, citizen opposition blocked Allied-sponsored plans for commemoration. On April 16, 1950, when more than a thousand former prisoners of the Dachau camp met to celebrate the fifth anniversary of their liberation, they demanded that the site be declared a memorial. Although the Tavern at the Crematorium (*Gaststätte zum Crematorium*) did change its name, town leaders opposed preserving the site. One afternoon in the fall of 1960, I visited Dachau with a fellow student, who, having grown up in Bavaria, could talk freely with local men around their *Stammtisch*. He suggested that if I remained silent my accent would not betray me and I would hear a conversation I would never forget. He was right. The men laughed boisterously about the "good old days" when the "riffraff" got what was coming to them and the village prospered. With private memories like these, it was not surprising that Dachau residents objected to public commemoration. Nevertheless, a small memorial was erected, and during 1960–61 more than forty-five thousand visitors from abroad came to Dachau. Complaining of too much tourism, the town officials then closed the crematorium area. In 1964, when the last of the German refugees had been resettled, the barracks and administrative buildings were razed. Only the ruins near the crematoriums remained.

In the West, memory was sealed off in post-traumatic oblivion behind the "Zero Hour" of 1945. In the East the government enshrined courageous Communist anti-Fascists and omitted other victims from its memorials. In both sectors, the camps were put to pragmatic use or razed. Not until the 1960s did war and Nazism return to public consciousness in East and West Germany. When the Third Reich emerged in memory, the political and cultural histories of who remembered what differed significantly.

III

Censorship in the former GDR makes public opinion almost impossible to gauge, although fiction, memoirs, and oral histories provide some useful hints.[27] While in the FRG survivor committees, student protesters, and civic initiatives gradually won support for preserving concentration camp memorials, in the GDR it was the Politburo that issued an edict in 1955 to preserve the camps at Buchenwald, Ravensbrück, and Sachsenhausen. In the FRG construction proceeded unevenly, often hampered by bitter opposition from local residents. Centralized planning in the GDR, however, assured uniformity. All GDR camp memorials taught three lessons: that

Fascism and monopoly capitalism bore the responsibility for war crimes; that the German working class, led by the German Communist party and aided by Soviet troops, had bravely resisted Nazi rule; and that this heroic heritage set the stage for the GDR's unflagging battle against international capitalism in the future.[28] A single message inspired the final exhibit in each camp museum. Communism ultimately would triumph over Fascism, that is, Western capitalism.

The camp museums dramatized Marxist historical principles with powerful visual material. In Ravensbrück, a photomontage depicted the militaristic, neo-Fascist, and capitalist West, while the counterimage held out the promise of peace, happiness, and equality in the Communist future. In Sachsenhausen, the guidebook praised "the sacrificial battle of courageous people who gave their lives in the fight against Fascism and War."[29] Museum literature featured photos of industrialists Flick, Krupp, Thyssen, and Klöckner: "German monopoly capital—they gave the orders for murder." Below them, in a style reminiscent of John Heartfield's 1930s collages, appeared Himmler and his deputies Baranowski, Sorge, and Essarius: "The SS—executioners and hangmen."[30] The Buchenwald film concluded with a mushroom-shaped nuclear cloud and a call for vigilance against the war-mongering forces of international Fascism. "They" dropped atomic bombs before, the message implied, and might well drop them again.

Even though the museums omitted references to Jews, Gypsies, and non-Marxist victims, a visit to the camps could nonetheless evoke long-suppressed memories about events not officially "remembered" in the museums. Bernhard Hardt, a Protestant pastor in the GDR, told an interviewer that although he had witnessed the pogrom of November 10, 1938, he had not really thought much about Jews until he saw the "terrifying" film in Buchenwald. Since then, he said, he just could not shake himself free of the problem of Jewish-Christian relations.[31] However, the film he saw included no mention of Jewish victims. The experience of visiting the camp must have brought together in Hardt's mind scattered and opposing fragments of memory that reconstituted images of forgotten Jews. Herr Topfer, a former schoolteacher and in 1991 a guide in Buchenwald, told how a visit to the museum triggered his boyhood memories of the starving, disoriented-looking prisoners who were herded daily through the Weimar streets. Now that the Berlin Wall has crumbled, he feels free to talk about this repressed past.[32]

Of all the monuments to anti-Fascism, Buchenwald stood preeminent. Before 1989 eleven million tourists, students, and party leaders relived the founding myth of the GDR at Buchenwald. A guest house (formerly the SS quarters), youth hostel, conference facilities, and clean air made it an ideal site for conventions. At Buchenwald, the most terrible of the camps on GDR soil, the government constructed a veritable shrine commemorating the dead and celebrating the liberation. Paradoxically, its massive scale, dogmatic commemorative verse, and austere representational aesthetic bear an eerie resemblance to National Socialist monuments. Tourists are guided along spacious aisles of mourning. The majestic "Freedom Street" is flanked by commemorative stelae. In the massive 150-foot-high tower, the bell tolls solemnly. "In honor of all those who made the supreme sacrifice, who gave their lives, we have built this everlasting Memorial on this blood-soaked earth in the heart of Germany. The Memorial is no inanimate stone. It will tell the coming generations of the immortal glory of the courageous struggle against the tyrants and for peace. . . . We must never again allow the world to be drowned in a pool of blood and suffering."[33] After walking along the Street of the Nations, adorned by eighteen pylons, one arrives at the vast Ceremonial Square, with rows of graves. Visitors may choose to meditate in quiet spaces: the stone quarry, shrines to Ernst Thälmann and Ernst Breitschied, or at the tablet marking the spot where Goethe and his companions once rested under a giant oak tree during their walks atop this hill. Where the barracks once stood in the main camp, granite tombstones commemorate victims by national identity. A collection of prisoners' drawings and paintings reminds visitors that the creative spirit persevered even in this brutal setting.

Personal identification with the martyred heroes is enhanced by the sculpture in all three camps. Unlike West German memorials, which are nonrepresentational, East German sculpture is strongly Socialist Realist in style. In Sachsenhausen and Buchenwald, statues depict defiant male prisoners—often with raised fists—and staunch Soviet liberators. The predominance of men does not reflect the historical reality. In the Buchenwald archives, hundreds of documents testify to the existence of thousands of women prisoners who labored in the satellite camps around Weimar.[34] Official memory has forgotten them and immortalized, instead, the men who led the anti-Fascist struggle and founded the GDR. Ravensbrück, a women's camp, of course contains exhibits, photos, and memorials that testify amply to women's political opposition.[35] While exhibits in the men's camps feature resistance artifacts (like an illegal radio transmitter and handmade grenades), Ravensbrück displays needlework, dolls, and other objects fashioned secretly by women prisoners. In the commemorative statues at Ravensbrück, women appear as enduring and noble victims, usually with arms at their sides, level gaze, and proud tilt of the head. In the historical iconography of GDR sculpture, heroic males resist and women (if depicted at all) persevere.[36] Jews are absent.

The process of memory recovery in the FRG could not have been more different than the centrally planned monuments and museums in the GDR. Museums, monuments, and ceremonies emerged from often hostile interactions among the Bonn government, local councils, survivors' commit-

tees, citizens' initiatives, and political parties. Whereas in East Germany a
national commission laid out a single pedagogical mission, in the West
public consciousness was jolted by periodicals, books, radio, and film.
Alain Renais's *Nuit et Brouillard* (1955) and *The Diary of Anne Frank*
(1962), Rolf Hochhuth's *Der Stellvertreter* (1963), and Peter Weiss's *Die
Ermittlung* (1964) confronted Germans with the question of responsibility
for Nazi crimes. The Eichmann trial in 1961, together with trials of concentration camp commandants, *Einsatzkommando*, administrators, and
employees, generated heated debates throughout the 1960s.[37] Raul
Hilberg's *Destruction of the European Jews* and Hannah Arendt's
Eichmann in Jerusalem aroused wide public comment. After two decades
of amnesia, the student movement of the late 1960s broke through the
silence about genocide. At the time, it almost seemed that Alexander and
Margarete Mitscherlich's *Inability to Mourn* in 1967 inspired Germans to
prove them wrong.[38]

In the ensuing years, a veritable flood of commemoration swept over
West Germany. In 1968 the Dachau concentration camp memorial re-
opened, and the memorials at Bergen-Belsen and Neuengamme were begun. Genocide entered official memory. Then, in 1979, the Hollywood
television series " Holocaust" aroused a national furor.[39] While critics
assailed it as kitsch, German audiences were riveted. Call-in shows, public
debates, and newspaper specials mobilized an unprecedented airing of
memories about genocide. A generation born since 1945 used this opening
to interrogate their elders about their actions in the Third Reich.[40] Local
and regional archives, churches, and schools sponsored exhibits, lectures,
and debates about the Third Reich. In 1980 high-school students all over
the FRG wrote essays on their own towns or neighborhoods under Nazism
for a national competition sponsored by the government. The film *Nasty
Girl (Das schrechlichte Mädchen)* records one teenager's investigation.
Oral history projects and local archives, often conducted by interested
citizens (dubbed "barefoot historians"), captured average people's experiences during the Third Reich.

The commemoration culture that developed in the 1980s inspired hun-
dreds of cities and towns to commission memorials to Jews, to restore
Jewish cemeteries, and to revive synagogues as museums. Inscriptions like
"To the memory of our Jewish fellow citizens" replaced vague phrases like
"No more war" or "To all victims." Dozens of cities and towns invited
former Jewish residents and their children to return for civic memorials.[41]
The German Tourist Office published a brochure titled "Germany for the
Jewish Traveller." During the 1980s, the fortieth anniversaries began. West
German politicians followed the example of Willy Brandt, who in 1970
had knelt at the Warsaw monument to the ghetto uprising. In May 1985
von Weizsäcker commemorated the German surrender in 1945 by admon-

ishing Germans to accept the responsibilities of their past.[42] An American president could speak of Wehrmacht soldiers as "victims" at Bitburg, but when in 1988 Bundestag President Philip Jeninger made a clumsy attempt to confront anti-Semitism, a storm of protest forced his resignation.[43] In 1985–86 historians, philosophers, and intellectuals attracted national media attention to an acrimonious debate about the appropriate historical interpretation of genocide.[44]

East and West official histories of Nazism could hardly have been more different when unification occurred. The official anti-Fascist memory remained in full force even as Mikhail Gorbachev was urging Honecker to relent in his hard-line policies. Only weeks before the wall disappeared, Communist party historians still extolled "the historical mission of the working class" and taught that "the history of the antifascist Resistance belongs to the best traditions of our state; it is . . . a kind of prehistory of the GDR."[45]

While GDR historians emphasized the continuity of Fascism under Hitler and Kohl, FRG historians likened the GDR to Hitler's totalitarian state. From the late 1940s until 1989, Jews and other non-Marxist victims were forgotten in the East, but after the early 1970s the Holocaust came to assume center stage in the West.

IV

Even before national independence seemed possible, citizens of the Soviet bloc had demanded (in the words of protesters at Gdansk in 1981) "a true history." Like a common currency and culture, the public memory of historical events structures a sense of civil society across generations, classes, and regions. Without a shared memory, as Havel had predicted, identity fades and unity dissolves.[46] Public cynicism about the fabricated past in the Soviet Union was captured in a joke that gained universal currency in the post-*glasnost* era. A television host asks his sociologist guest about the uncertain future. The expert retorts, "Ah, the future. We can foresee that with total accuracy. It's the past that we have trouble predicting." Small wonder that Soviet history examinations were suspended in 1988 because no authoritative textbook existed. In Germany, however, a historical canon already existed in the West.

As in so many other aspects of unification, the forging of shared civil society did not proceed according to plan. Although GDR citizens voted in March 1990 to merge with the FRG, it quickly became obvious that the creation of a shared identity could take decades. While tensions and outright hostility repolarized East and West Germans, the public memory of their shared Nazi past also became a site of dispute.

Without awaiting new written histories, citizens in the East have re-created public memory by attacking geographical icons: one wall and many landmarks, monuments, museums, and Stasi headquarters. Foreign Marxists, like Lenin and Dimitroff, disappeared quickly as street names, as did East German Communists, like Albert Norden and Otto Grotewohl. Although the international agreements prior to unification guaranteed the maintenance of all monuments, the giant statue of Lenin in Berlin-Friedrichshain was destroyed, and the world's most massive monument to Stalin, in Treptow, became a skateboarder's paradise.[47]

As East and West began to stitch together a common future from divergent cloths, a new kind of debate about the past erupted. Citizens of the ex-GDR refused to reshape their version of World War II on the West German model. The three major concentration camps became objects of anger, resentment, and even scorn, a fate they share with other sites in the former Soviet bloc.[48] Because these sites have been suffused with Communist doctrine, they symbolize not only National Socialist crimes but Soviet domination as well. By "forgetting" them, people in Central Europe are constructing a memory wall against both Nazism and Communism.

Immediately after the collapse of the Honecker regime, signs of transformation appeared. Curators at all three East German camps posted signs promising that the exhibits would be overhauled. In Ravensbrück, nearly half of the exhibit rooms stood empty, and the guide said their reconstruction awaited documents from Moscow. The historical film about the camp was rarely shown. At Sachsenhausen, a new photomontage about genocide was added and a wall-sized chart revised older views. Where once victims were classed by their nationality and a red triangle that identified them as "political" criminals, a new display includes the full range of color-coded triangles used by the Nazis to denote the reasons for each prisoner's deportation. One of the first official acts of the newly elected East German *Volkskammer* in the spring of 1990 was to promise reparations to Jewish victims of Nazi policies.[49]

These kinds of revisions, however, did not satisfy all Germans in the East. Many townspeople who lived near the three East German camps hated the museum memorials. Much like Germans living near Dachau, Neuengamme, and Bergen-Belsen in the 1960s, they hated the camps that blemished the reputation of their communities. In 1990 the government of Brandenburg, which financed Ravensbrück and Sachsenhausen, declared that it had no funds to maintain either camp. Local officials in Oranienburg attempted to convert the Sachsenhausen museum building into a financial office. After that effort failed, an educational exhibit designed to combat racism was installed. In the fall of 1992, that exhibit was firebombed.[50]

At Ravensbrück, located on a peaceful lake with a brisk tourist business, town officials granted construction permits for a shopping center at the edge of the memorial park. The cobblestone pavement built by women slave laborers was to become part of a pedestrian mall between a Kaiser's supermarket and a Renault showroom. Protest from abroad and from Berlin stopped these plans.

Given Buchenwald's preeminence as a shrine to anti-Fascism, it is not surprising that it also came under attack. Starting in early 1990 the pages of local newspapers were filled with letters, editorials, and articles on the camp. The commemorative signs marking prisoners' death marches out of Buchenwald in 1945 aroused considerable ire. One citizen, Chrisel Holz, complained in a Weimar paper, "I have walked past that death march sign every day on my way to work. That is not my memory! It must go."[51] Other justifications for removing the signs were more subtle. For example, the former Soviet barracks at the edge of the camp were to be rebuilt as housing for the elderly. "The markers must go! We don't want the old people to be reminded of death," said social workers.[52]

Buchenwald had always received subsidies from the Bonn government and the active support of an international committee of former prisoners. Clearly, the camp memorial would remain. But what message would it convey? This question became one focus of a large civic initiative. Immediately after the collapse of Communist power, a Protestant minister led his fellow Weimar citizens on a crusade to excise all vestiges of Communist influence from local government. Citizens vented their wrath at party leaders, local political "hacks," and nests of party privilege. But the most powerful Communist (SED) bosses proved difficult to apprehend. Many had destroyed key records and kept their savings in foreign banks. Often former SED chiefs used their old party connections to establish themselves as post-Communist entrepreneurs. While the party cadres remained elusive, the Buchenwald personnel stood exposed. In early 1991 the initiative accused the staff at Buchenwald of "falsifying history" in their guidebooks, displays, tours, and articles.

To restore "true history," the protesters insisted, would require an entirely new staff. In March, Dr. Ulrich Schneider, a young scholar from Kassel who had specialized in the history of concentration camps, was appointed to replace the former director. Schneider, however, defended staff members' right to retain their positions. Within days, the ministry in charge of the memorial dismissed Schneider on charges that he had once belonged to the West German Communist party.[53] The deputy director, an East German who had begun work at the museum only a year before, Dr. Irmgard Seidel, became acting director. She, however, immediately came under attack from the citizens' initiative for having belonged to the SED and, in her dissertation, for misattributing the blame for the Katyn Forest massacre. She held her ground, asking the new state officials originally from the FRG, "What kind of a democracy [*Rechtsstaat*] is this, in which a qualified person is dismissed because of thought crimes? Finally, we have the freedom to get the history right, and now we face dismissal." At a protest rally against her, Seidel faced her accusers and said, "A Nazi past is being made the equivalent of a Socialist past. Nazi crimes are equated with events after 1945."[54] Besides, Seidel recalled, to her generation, growing up after 1945, the Soviet occupation held out the promise of a humane society.[55]

One longtime staff member, whose father had been imprisoned at Buchenwald by the Soviets, defended his right to remain on the job. While acknowledging that the staff had bowed to SED pressure to glorify the Communist resistance and ignore other victims, he continued, "I still don't understand where I have failed. . . . Just before the Wende, everyone East and West had only the highest praise for our new museum exhibit, which was honored by being installed in the Gropius Museum [West Berlin]. Now they want us out."[56] Herr Topfer, the tour guide who willingly shared his recollections of Nazism, agreed. "Under the Communists, we had to tell visitors only about the victory of anti-Fascism. Now that we are finally free to say more, we will be replaced by young 'Wessies' who know little and remember nothing."

Herr Topfer's remarks in 1991 suggest the contours of a new "Ossie" memory that does not fit the format of either the former FRG or GDR. After discussing capitalism and the origins of National Socialism, Topfer talked also about the persecution of Jews, Gypsies, homosexuals, religious dissenters, and asocials. But to him these remained "marginal" groups (Randfiguren). With considerably more vehemence, he spoke about the German prisoners held by the Soviets after 1945. At other camps, a distinct "Ossie" memory also surfaced after unification. Although it took months to publish new guidebooks, tape-recorded tours reflected the new message instantly. In early 1990 visitors at Sachsenhausen heard, in English, "It is a particularly sad chapter in the history of these camps that they continued to witness human rights violations even after the war between 1945 and 1950. This was the age of Stalinism." Some ten thousand men and eight hundred to a thousand women were detained at any one time. "Although no documentary evidence is available, statements of former internees give reason to believe that a total of between 50,000 and 60,000 prisoners served time at Sachsenhausen. . . . Their relatives were not even informed. How many prisoners died, no one was informed." Many prisoners were held without defense counsel only because neighbors had informed on them. As the tape recording makes clear, this was neither a forced labor nor an extermination camp. Nevertheless, the tape recording devotes about four minutes each to Nazi crimes and Soviet negligence, and it describes both as "civil rights violations." The voice continues, "Until the political upheaval in this country, that is in late 1989, a conspiracy of silence was maintained about these human rights violations and it was forbidden to mention the victims of the internment camps." In 1991 mass graves, supposedly of corpses buried after 1945, were discovered, and a small cemetery of wooden crosses was placed adjacent to monuments for the victims of Nazism.[57]

The men who died in the Soviet camps, who had been arrested because of Nazi sympathies and war crimes, appear today as "victims."[58] Ironically, the Cold War anti-Communist rhetoric of the FRG that equated Nazism and Communism has been taken up by citizens of the former GDR who want their suffering acknowledged. In the former FRG, by contrast, this equation has lost its resonance. Instead, many West Germans tend to fault Germans in the GDR for their complicity in making it a showplace of Communism and in creating a dense surveillance network under the Stasi.

The new GDR historical memory emerged most strongly at Buchenwald under the auspices of Irmgard Seidel and her staff. In 1990 Buchenwald curators added a new room displaying artifacts calculated to inspire empathy for German martyrs under Soviet rule from 1945 to 1949: hand-knit socks and undershirts sent by loving wives to their prisoner husbands; death announcements that sometimes arrived months after the victims' death; and prisoners' letters. Especially after having viewed the immense collection of Nazi torture implements, photos of starving slave laborers, and writings attesting to unspeakable Nazi cruelty, it is difficult to imagine that the new exhibits will arouse deep sympathy.[59] But the symbolic equation of Communist and Nazi oppression may ring true for many residents of the former GDR.

The public responses to two ceremonies at Buchenwald outline the contours of memory about the Holocaust and the Soviet occupation. On April 11, 1990, I attended the first memorial service honoring Jewish victims who had perished at the camp. A sermon-like speech given by a staff member, followed by a reading of poems by Gertrud Kollmar, a Jewish author, and a moment of silence marked the occasion. Aside from a few journalists and photographers, only a handful of people attended. Some of these were former prisoners from abroad, for whom the trip had been very difficult. No one from Weimar, however, bothered to take the six-kilometer city bus trip to the camp. Jews have been added to the list of victims of Buchenwald to bring official discourse into line with West German traditions. In popular memory, however, they still count for little.

Another ceremony, two months later, drew a very different reaction. This event commemorated German victims of Soviet occupation forces. Although there is no way of identifying the bodies in the graves, two mass grave sites have been memorialized as evidence of Soviet crimes. As many as ten thousand Germans may have died. On June 10, 1991, when six wooden crosses were dedicated to the martyrs of Soviet occupation, swarms of politicians, Weimar citizens, journalists, and tourists joined

Chancellor Helmut Kohl as he mourned the victims of "communist terror dictatorship" (*der kommunistischen Schreckherrschaft*).[60] Every major newspaper and television channel carried the story. Subsequently, many families have erected small wooden crosses in memory of relatives thought to have died in the post-1945 Buchenwald camp. At Buchenwald, as elsewhere in Central Europe, these wooden crosses for Christian victims implicitly express a populist resentment against the massive marble and granite monuments erected by Soviet-sponsored governments. The new memory enshrines non- and perhaps anti-Communists who died under Soviet domination.

Meanwhile, since the end of the GDR, West German leaders continue to invoke the official memory of genocide, a process called "mourning work" (*Trauerarbeit*). Reichstag President Rita Süsmuth visited Babi Yar, which she called "a place of horror and shame," on the fiftieth anniversary of the massacre of Soviet Jews there. Political leaders celebrated the first anniversary of unification by paying tribute to the victims of Nazi crimes at Bergen-Belsen, and the first session of the Bundestag was preceded by the laying of a wreath at Neuengamme. When the Holocaust Museum opened on the fiftieth anniversary of the Wannsee Conference, in January 1992, Süsmuth told Germans, "Experience tells us that whatever we repress catches up with us later. No one can flee from their history."[61] After unification President Richard von Weizsüacker continued to remind all Germans of their special commitment to ethnic toleration. Sensitivity on the "Jewish question" remained so high in the former FRG that in 1991 the film *Europa, Europa*, about one young Jewish man's undercover life in Hitler's army, was not submitted for the Oscar competition. Critics believed that the film insulted Jews because the protagonist was portrayed in negative ways.[62] When, in October 1992, the mayor of Rostock bungled his apology to a leader of the Jewish German community, pressure from Bonn forced him to resign.[63]

But while these official exhortations win widespread respect abroad and among liberals in Germany, public opinion in Germany has not kept pace. Even before unification, the depiction of Nazism in West German television specials, best-sellers, and films contradicted political leaders' rhetoric of mourning. Six years after "Holocaust" shocked the nation, a fifteen-hour television special, "Heimat," assuaged the national conscience. This brilliant serialized drama of life in a backwater village depicted a nostalgic memory of Nazism without slave labor camps, Jews, anti-Semitism, evil Nazis, racial laws, deportations, or militarism. The strong characters were apolitical women, especially the mother, Maria. Other popular films, like the Fassbinder trio (*Lili Marlene*, *Veronika Voss*, and *The Marriage of Maria Braun*), Joachim Fest's *Hitler: A Career*, Hans Jürgen Syberberg's *Hitler: A Film from Germany*, and Helma Sanders-Brahms's *Deutschland*

Bleiche Mutter, depict a Third Reich sanitized of racial hatred, political terror, and war crimes.

In 1990 a supposedly antiwar documentary film, *Our Battle (Unser Kampf)*, made from footage shot by German soldiers on the eastern front, overlooked German atrocities and centered on average soldiers' tribulations. *Prisoners of Conscience* (1992) enshrined noble resisters against Hitler as if they typified all Germans. In September 1992 the Bonn government prepared a celebration of the fiftieth anniversary of the launching of the V-2 rocket, hailing it as a major step in the conquest of outer space and forgetting about the twenty-six thousand slave laborers who died in its construction. Only vehement protest halted the celebration at the last minute.[64] In post-Bitburg recollections, Germans began to feel entitled to describe their own victimhood under Hitler.[65] Public opinion polls taken when the Wannsee Museum opened in 1992 suggested that Germans' anti-Semitism, while muted in public, remained strong in private.[66] More than half of all Germans polled in 1990 believed the war ought to be forgotten. The memory of the "racial outcasts" who died in the camps is being forgotten even as attacks against the new "outsiders" escalate.

The concentration camps continue to haunt the German landscape, but the categories of victimhood have expanded beyond the anti-Fascists memorialized in the East and the victims of the Holocaust mourned in the West. Average citizens remember their own wartime tragedies along with the devastation of Allied bombing raids and the desperate conditions after 1945. Racially charged incidents, together with electoral victories for right-wing parties, bring a new urgency to the memorialization of the Jews, Gypsies, homosexuals, and religious dissidents who died in the concentration camps. As "ethnic cleansing" forces tens of thousands of refugees into exile, many Germans want to retract their nation's fundamental commitment to provide a haven for victims of persecution.[67]

The landscapes of Nazi brutality retain their power to horrify. Nazi atrocities must remain at the core of a shared public memory, even as we confront the complex heritage that shapes our post-postwar world. To accomplish this, the camp memorials must both commemorate the Soviet role in the Allied liberation of the camps and recognize that some Germans died unjustly in the "special camps." The enduring legacy of the camps, however, must be to serve as warnings (*Mahnmäler*) against all forms of political terror and racial hatred.

NOTES

1. Václav Havel, "Dear Dr. Husák," in *Open Letters: Selected Writings, 1964–1990* (New York: Knopf, 1991), 73–74. On the parallels between Czech official memory deprivation after 1618 and 1968, see Paul Connerton, *How Societies Remember* (Cambridge: Cambridge University Press, 1989), 13–15.

2. Pierre Nora, however, argues that modern people's need for identity has created a "demand for history that has largely overflowed the circle of professional historians." See "Between Memory and History: *Les lieux de mémoire*," *Representations* 26 (Spring 1989): 7–25.

3. History began when memory ended, when an event or individual began to recede from group consciousness, according to Halbwachs. See *The Collective Memory*, trans. Francis J. Ditter, Jr., and Vida Y. Ditter (New York: Harper Colophon, 1980), 80ff. First published as *La mémoire collective*, 1950.

4. Halbwachs, *The Collective Memory*, 156.

5. Ibid., 140. Unlike recent analysts, Halbwachs was not interested in the imaginary, constructed nature of communities themselves. Cf. Benedict O. Anderson, *Imagined Communities* (New York and London: Verso, 1991), and Eric Hobsbawm and Terence Ranger, eds., *Invented Traditions* (Cambridge: Cambridge University Press, 1983). Theresa Wobbe, "Das Dilemma der Überlieferung," in Theresa Wobbe, ed., *Nach Osten. Verdeckte Spuren nationalsozialistischer Verbrechen* (Berlin: Verlag neue Kritik, 1992).

6. Perhaps the Holocaust was not totally inconceivable. Jonathan Swift imagined such a world, but he wrote it as satire. See *A Modest Proposal*, illustrated by Leonard Baskin (New York: Grossman, 1969).

7. Guiliana Tedeschi, *There Is a Place on Earth: A Woman in Birkenau*, trans. Tim Parks (New York: Pantheon, 1992), 1.

8. In Milwaukee, there is a memorial to the "black holocaust." See Scott Sherman, "Preserving Black History," *The Progressive* 55 (December 1991): 12, 15. Tammy Bakker tells talk-show host Sally Jessy Raphaël, "Jim and I have lived through our own private holocaust" (transcript, November 22, 1988). The term is also applied to the "ethnic cleansing" in Bosnia and Herzegovina (Aryeh Neier, "Fight Abuses," *New York Times*, November 20, 1992, A15).

9. Pierre Nora writes that places of memory "have no referent in reality; or, rather, they are their own referent: pure, exclusively self-referential signs"; he also observes that their power to "escape from history" opens them up to "the full range of [their] possible significations" (Nora, " Between Memory and History," 23–24).

10. James Young, *Writing and Rewriting the Holocaust: Narrative and the Consequences of Interpretation* (Bloomington: Indiana University Press, 1990), 174–75.

11. In 1991 American artist Chris Burden constructed *The Other Vietnam Memorial*, on which he inscribed the names of "the three million [Vietnamese] . . . the displaced persons of the American conscience." Quoted in *Dislocations*, text accompanying the exhibit of that name, Museum of Modern Art, October 20, 1991, to January 7, 1992. In California the Manzanar Japanese-American internment camp commemorates the internment of Japanese-Americans ("California Internment Camp," *New York Times*, April 27, 1992, 13).

12. Warren Weaver, Jr., "U.S. Hunts Its Once-Captive Americans," *New York Times*, December 18, 1988. In 1992 a monument in the desert was dedicated ("California Internment Camp Commemorated," *New York Times*, April 26, 1992). Finally, too, reparations are being paid.

13. Connerton, *How Societies Remember*, 7.

14. Christopher Browning, *Ordinary Men: Reserve Police Battalion 101 and the*

Final Solution in Poland (New York: Harper Collins, 1991). Ernst Klee, Willi Dressen, and Volker Riess, eds., *"The Good Old Days": The Holocaust as Seen by Its Perpetrators and Bystanders*, trans. Deborah Burnstons (New York: Free Press, 1991).

15. Robert Abzug, *Inside the Vicious Heart: Americans and the Liberation of Nazi Concentration Camps* (New York: Oxford, 1985), 73, 77–78, 82, and 89–103. The film at the Buchenwald museum includes footage of local residents forced to "inspect" the camp.

16. Peter Sonnet, "Gedenkstätten für Opfer des Nationalsozialismus in der DDR," in Ulrike Puvogel, ed., *Gedenkstätten für die Opfer des Nationalsozialismus. Eine Dokumentation* (Bonn: Schriftenreihe der Bundeszentrale für politische Bildung, n.d.), 245, 769–801.

17. Oath of April 19, 1945, quoted in *Buchenwald: Guide to the National Memorial* (Dietz, n.d.).

18. Harold Marcuse, "Das ehemalige Konzentrationslager Dachau," *Erinnern oder Verewigen. Dachauer Hefte* 6, 184–86. Cf. also Timothy W. Rybeck, "Report from Dachau," *New Yorker*, August 3, 1992, 43–61.

19. Viktor Klemperer, *LTI: Notizbuch eines. Philologen* (Frankfurt: Röderberg, 1987). First published by VEB Max Niemeyer in Halle (Saale), DDR. Max Picard, *Hitler in uns selbst* (Erlenbach-Zurich, 1946).

20. Hannah Arendt, *Sechs Essays,* with an introduction by Karl Jaspers (Heidelberg, 1948), 9. In one of these essays, "Organized Guilt" (written in November 1944), Arendt warns that prosecution of war criminals will prove fruitless.

21. Ruth Andreas-Friedrichs, *Der Schattenmann* (Berlin: Suhrkampf, 1947); Allen W. Dulles, *Germany's Underground* (New York: Macmillan, 1947); Karl Otto Paetel, *Die Deutsche Innere Immigration. Anti-national sozialistische Zeugnisse aus Deutschland*, introduction by Dorothy Thompson and Carl Zuckmeyer (New York: Krause, 1946); and Fabian von Schlabrendorff, *Offiziere gegen Hitler* (Zurich: Europa, 1946).

22. The film obliquely referred to the persecution of the Jews through one character, Dr. Mondschein, whose son has escaped to the United States. Dr. Mondschein, perhaps a Jew, survived the war.

23. Austria provides a fascinating test case that combines elements of both East and West Germany. Cf. Judith Miller, *One by One by One* (New York: Touchstone, 1990), 61–92. Austrians, considering themselves the first victims of Nazism, believed they had nothing to remember.

24. For an excellent account of how wartime solidarity persisted in the USSR, cf. Judith Miller, *One by One by One,* 158–219.

25. Anna Dora Miethe, ed., *Gedenkstätten. Arbeiterbewegung Antifaschister Widerstand Aufbau des Sozialismus* (Leipzig: Jena and Berlin: Urania, 1972), quotations are from pages 209 and 251.

26. Anson Rabinbach, "The Jewish Question in the German Question," *New German Critique* 44 (Spring/Summer 1988): 165–66. Lilly Gardner-Feldman, *The Special Relationship between West Germany and Israel* (Boston: Allen and Unwin, 1984).

27. Lutz Niethammer, Alexander von Plato, and Dorothee Wierling, *Die volk-*

seigene Erfahrung. Eine Archäologie des Lebens in der Industrieprovinz der DDR (Berlin: Rowohlt, 1991). Each contributor to the collection of GDR autobiographies recalled having heard about mass murder of Jewish victims. Wolfgang Herzberg, Ich bin doch wer. Arbeiter und Arbeiterinnen des VEB Berliner Glühlampenwerk erzählen ihr Leben 1900–1980. Protokolle aus der DDR (Darmstadt: Luchterhand, 1987), 29, 78–80, 114, 198.

28. Sonnet, "Gedenkstätten," 770–75.

29. Karl Stenzel, director of the Camp Committee Sachsenhausen, Sachsenhausen. "Besonders jetzt tu Deine Pflicht!" no. 6 (Oranienburg: NMG Sachsenhausen, 1989), 4–5.

30. Sachsenhausen (a guidebook) (N.p., n.d.).

31. Niethammer, von Plato, and Wierling, Die volkseigene Erfahrung, 226. For a discussion of memory in GDR fiction, cf. Sonia Combe, "Mémoire collective et histoire officielle. Le passé nazi en RDA," Esprit: Changer la culture et la politique (October 1987): 36–49.

32. Conversation with the author, April 1991.

33. Last page of Buchenwald: Guide to the National Memorial.

34. Bruno Eisert, Buchenwald Häftl. Nr. 1585, December 21, 1961, Buchenwaldarchiv 63 26-3; Aussprache mit Herrn Paul Schulze, March 25, 1957, Buchenwaldarchiv 63 26-7; Aussprache mit Frau Janek, n.d., Buchenwaldarchiv 63 26-2.

35. A dramatic illustration of the stylistic contrast can be seen at Mauthausen, where the government of each nation whose citizens died there dedicated a monument. In these works, women are absent, except for the GDR statue of a stolid, larger-than-life woman seated on a bench wrapped in barbed wire. On the wall behind her Brecht's poem "Deutschland bleiche Mutter" is engraved, followed by this postscript to Mother Germany, "Your sons, who fought and died here, embodied the faith in the true [wahr] Germany and in the future."

36. Terrence des Pres, The Survivor: An Anatomy of Life in the Death Camps (New York: Oxford University Press, 1976), 3–26. Here men are classical heroes, while women represent a wholly modern character, the survivor. Des Pres did not draw this conclusion, although he noted the typologies.

37. For example, the investigation and trial of 210 men in reserve Police Battalion 101 from Hamburg. See Christopher Browning, Ordinary Men, and Gitta Sereny, Into That Darkness: An Examination of Conscience (New York: Vintage, 1983), 233, 251–66.

38. Mitscherlich and Mitscherlich, The Inability to Mourn: Principles of Collective Behavior, trans. Beverley R. Placzek (New York: Grove Press, 1975). First published as Die Unfähigkeit zu Trauern (Munich: Piper, 1967).

39. Eric Santner, Stranded Objects: Mourning, Memory and Film in Postwar Germany (Ithaca and London: Cornell University Press, 1990), 73–75.

40. Anton Kaes, "History and Film: Public Memory in the Age of Electronic Dissemination," History and Memory: Studies in Representation of the Past (1990): 111–28.

41. Miller, One by One by One, 13–33. For reflections on these encounters, cf. Judith Isaacson, Seed of Sarah (Champaign-Urbana: University of Illinois Press, 1988).

42. Richard von Weizsäcker, "Speeches for Our Time," edited with an introduction by David Clay Large, *German Issues* 10 (1992): 17–30.

43. Elisabeth Domansky, "'Kristallnacht,' the Holocaust and German Unity: The Meaning of November 9 as an Anniversary in Germany," *History and Memory: Studies in Representation of the Past* 4:1 (Spring/Summer 1992): 60–87. Of course, conservatives like Franz Schönhuber frequently remind Germans of their victimhood.

44. Charles S. Maier, *The Unmasterable Past: History, Holocaust, and German National Identity* (Cambridge: Harvard University Press, 1988), and *"Historikerstreit"* Die Dokumentation der Kontroverse um die Einzigartigkeit der nationalsozialistischen Judenvernichtung (Munich: Piper, 1987).

45. Kurt Finker, "Zum Widerstandskampf kleinbürgerlicher und bürgerlicher Nazigegner in Deutschland," in Helmut Meier and Walter Schmnidt, eds., *Erbe und Tradition in der DDR. Die Diskussion der Historiker* (Berlin: Pahl-Rugenstein, 1989), 103. The author bases the Communists' superiority not on matters of personal bravery, but on their "scientific" analysis (*Erkenntnis*). The anti-Fascist Resistance was for them the "continuation of their fight against Imperialism and Militarism" (110). The exception to this persistent amnesia was Kurt Pätzold, "Wo der Weg nach Auschwitz begann. Der deutsche Antisemitismus und der Massenmord an den europäischen Juden," *Blätter für deutsche und internationale Politik* 32 (1987): 160–72.

46. Milan Kundera commented, "The future is an apathetic void of no interest to anyone. The past is full of life, eager to irritate us, provoke and insult us, tempt us." See *The Book of Laughter and Forgetting,* trans. M. H. Helm (New York: Knopf, 1981).

47. Emmanuel Terray, "L'Allemagne et sa mémoire," *Liber. Revue européene des livres* 10 (June 1992): 14–15. "Berlin Court Ends Troubled Debate by Ordering Removal of 60-foot Statue of Lenin from City Center," *New York Times*, November 2, 1992, 2.

48. Auschwitz and other camp museums already suffer from an acute lack of funding. Maideneck has sold two thousand pairs of shoes to the National Holocaust Museum in Washington, and Auschwitz has placed a boxcar and a barracks on loan. See "Auschwitz verfällt," *Die Zeit*, Nr. 15, April 10, 1992, 13.

49. But popular reaction to that promise often echoed West German responses in the early 1950s (and subsequently). Why should an impoverished GDR treasury give out money to Jews instead of building up the GDR? many asked. When the GDR joined the FRG under Basic Law 23, the question became moot.

50. "Fire Razes Memorial to Jews at Nazi Camp," *New York Times*, September 27, 1992, A10. It's worth noting that shortly thereafter a vandal "wrecked gravestones and painted swastikas" at Überlinden near Lake Constance ("Swastikas Drawn on Death Camp Memorial," *New York Times*, October 25, 1992, A6).

51. "Leserbriefe Ärgernis," *Thüringer Allgemeine*, May 22, 1991. Peter Liebers, "Mahnmal auf dem Ettersberg zwischen den Fronten," *Tribune*, April 12, 1991.

52. "Gedenkstein passt nicht mehr!" *Thüringer Landeszeitung*, May 22, 1991. Frank Schumann, "Ein Dorn im Fleische manchen Bürgers," *Junge Welt* 84 (April 11, 1991). "Pochen auf Rechtsstaat," *Thüringer Tageblatt*, May 29, 1991.

53. Ulrich Schneider, "Noch vieles aufzuarbeiten," *Hessisch-Niedersächische Allgemeine Zeitung,* Nr. 18, May 5, 1991.

54. Conversation with the author, June 1991. Cf. "Nicht leise durch die Hintertuer," *Neues Deutschland,* March 28, 1991, and Gudrun Paetke, "Das Internationale Buchenswaldkommittee bat mich zu bleiben," *Tagespost,* May 30, 1991.

55. Interviews with the author and news clippings from the local press, spring 1989 and summer 1990.

56. Heinz Albertus, Erfurt, letter to the editor of *Thüringer Tageblatt,* March 22, 1991. For a discussion of the exhibit, cf. Christa Piotrowski, "Dem 'Schwur vom Buchenwald' verpflichtet. DDR Ausstellung in Gropius Bau," *Der Tagesspiegel* (Berlin), April 12, 1990, 11.

57. Stephen Kinzer, "Germans Find Mass Graves at Site of a Former Soviet Prison Camp," *New York Times,* September 24, 1992, A15.

58. Sarah Farmer, "A New Sort of Vergangenheitbewältigung," paper read at the German Studies Association convention, Minneapolis, October 3, 1992.

59. This memory of postwar Allied injustice has its counterpart in James Bacque, *Other Losses: An Investigation into the Mass Deaths of German Prisoners in the Hands of French and Americans after World War II* (Toronto: Stoddart, 1989).

60. Kohl laid identical wreaths of yellow and white lilies on the graves of victims of Nazism and at the simple wooden grave markers of thirteen thousand who may have perished in the Soviet "special camp" between 1945 and 1950. See "Die CDU will ihre Leistungen und Erfolge stärker betönen," *Frankfurter Allgemeine Zeitung,* nr. 132, June 11, 1991, 3.

61. "Germany Marks Place Where Horror Began," *New York Times,* January 20, 1992, A1, 7.

62. "Dies ist auch mein Land," session at the German Studies Association convention, Minneapolis, October 3, 1992. On the sensitivity of West Germans toward Jews, cf. Eckhard Jesse, "Philosemitismus, Antisemitismus und Anti-Antisemitismus," in Uwe Backes, Eckhard Jesse, and Rainer Zitelmann, eds., *Die Schatten der Vergangenheit* (Berlin: Propylän, 1990), 543–67.

63. Craig R. Whitney, "A German Local Official Insults Jewish Leader Visiting Riot Site," *New York Times,* November 3, 1992, A5. In March 1992 Kohl offended Israelis and also created a furor. See Clyde Haberman, "Israelis Say Kohl Has Insulted Jews," *New York Times,* March 30, 1992, A6.

64. Stephen Kinzer, "Germans Plan Celebration of Nazi Rocket, Then Cancel It as Protests Grow," *New York Times,* September 29, 1992, A1, A6.

65. "Preface," in Johannes Steinhoff, Peter Pechel, and Dennis Showalter, eds., *Voices from the Third Reich: An Oral History* (Washington, D.C.: Regnery Gateway, 1989), xvi. More troubling are reports that young visitors to concentration camps appear totally unaffected by what they see.

66. Marc Fisher, "Jews in the New German Society," *Washington Post,* January 20, 1992, quotes the Emnid Institute poll. Paul Bendelow, "The Expedient Art of Forgetting," *Times Educational Supplement,* January 25, 1991, 16.

67. Ferdinand Protzman, "German Attacks Rise as Foreigners Become Scapegoat," *New York Times,* November 2, 1992, A1, A6.

INDEX

Harding, Warren G., 175
Hardt, Bernhard, 266
Hargrove, June, 187
Hashimite dynasty, 94–95
Havel, Václav, open letter of, 258
Hebrew national identity, 107–18
Heidelberg castle, restoration of, 220–21
Hellenism, 54
Henry V, on war casualties, 150
Henry VIII, break with Rome, 61
hereditary elites, 47
heritage: archaeological conference on
  management of, 28; categories of, 44;
  identity and, 41–54; ignorance of
  others', 53–54; "industry" of, 42–43,
  218; issues of, 41; of minorities, 46;
  popularization of, 43–44; uniqueness of,
  46–54; universal, 44–46; Western concepts of, 44–46
heritage restitution drive, 51–52
heroes: commitment of to transcendent
  ideal, 120n; cult of, 112–13; legendary,
  106–10
heroism, memory of, 129–31
Hiecke, Robert, 225
Hilberg, Raul, 268
Hindu concepts, 32
Hiroshima, 14
historic preservation, 215–38; Germany's
  first journal of, 218; pre-World War I,
  217–23; in Third Reich, 223–30;
  working-class involvement in, 236–37n
historical authenticity, 220–21
historical legend: concept of, 105; in Israel, 105–23
historicism, crisis of, 220
history: democratization of, 17–18; heritage issues of, 53; vs. legend, 105; as
  modern world's oracle, 19; official, 258
Hitler, Adolf: empathy for monuments of,
  223; opposition to, 263
Hitler in uns selbst, 263
Hobsbawm, Eric, 106
Hochhuth, Rolf, 268
Holland, Thomas, 62
Holocaust: collective memory of, 12, 111;
  commemoration of, 261; expansion of,
  259; German heritage and, 49–50;
  memory of, 268
"Holocaust," 274–75
Honecker, 270

Hoover, Herbert, 177; segregation policy
  of, 179
Hopi thought-world, 31
Horton, Thomas, 68
Howells, William Dean, 127–29
Hugo, Victor, monument to, 151
Husák, Gustav, 258
al-Husari, Sati', 93
Husayn, Saddam, 95; Gulf War and, 100–
  101; Iraq Museum and, 90; power of,
  100

iconoclasm, 18–20
identity: as cross-cultural concept, 27–38;
  definitions of, 3, 28; ethnic, 37–38; of
  groups, 30; growing concern about, 45;
  heritage and, 41–54; intellectual history
  of, 34–37; multiple, 15–16; national,
  4–5; politics of, 4; psychic and social
  implications of, 41–42; self–
  consciousness about, 16–17; in
  twentieth-century Germany, 215–38;
  Western conception of, 31–32
independence, ideology of, 36–37
Independence Day. *See* Bastille Day; July
  Fourth
individualism: identity and, 31; possessive,
  217
International Council of Museums, 249
international heritage disputes, 50–52
Iraq: Arab heritage of, 92; excavation
  movement in, 92; folklore of, 98–101;
  formation of modern state of, 94; Mesopotamian heritage of, 95–97; monarchy
  of, 94; museums in, 18, 90–101; nationalism in, 92–93; politics of social control in, 90–101; popular culture of, 98–
  101; Revolution of, 91–92, 96
Iraq-Iran War, 99
Iraq Museum, 90–101
Iraqi Communist party, 97, 98
Islam, heritage of, 92
Israel: hero cult in, 112–13; invented tradition and memory in, 105–23; as new
  Jewish state, 12; pioneers of, 121n; settler legend of, 9, 106–10; War of Independence of, 111
Israeli-Palestinian conflict, 113

Jacobins, 239
Jacomet monument, 198–99, 200